VOLUME I.
SOCIAL AND POLITICAL THINKERS
OF THE 19TH CENTURY

By the same author.

THE HISTORY OF POLITICAL SCIENCE FROM PLATO TO THE PRESENT

Second Edition.

HEFFER : : CAMBRIDGE

LONDON AGENTS
SIMPKIN MARSHALL LTD

STUDIES IN THE
ENGLISH SOCIAL AND POLITICAL THINKERS

OF THE
NINETEENTH CENTURY

BY THE REV.
ROBERT H. MURRAY, Litt.D.

VOLUME I.
From Malthus to Kingsley.

VOLUME II.
Herbert Spencer to Ramsay MacDonald.

CAMBRIDGE
W. HEFFER & SONS LTD.
1929

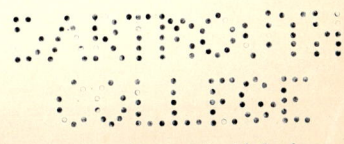

To the Most Rev. Cosmo Gordon Lang,
D.D., D.C.L., LL.D., D.Litt.
Lord Archbishop of Canterbury.

PRINTED IN ENGLAND

Preface

THE historian of political thought has a high enough task to discover what truth he can without assuming finality in his search. He is concerned to enlighten the future, and verdicts are not his affair. He deals with human societies, and knows no more than Burke did how to frame an indictment of a nation. His part is, if he can, to stimulate thought and not to dictate opinion; and the *chose jugée* is to him anathema, a rebuff to research and a bar to the freedom of the truth.

He seeks to explain what conceptions led our fathers to fashion their multifarious laws and institutions. There is no homogeneity among them, and they cannot be resolved into the apparently simple uniformity of a law of nature. The essence of man and of human affairs is their infinite variety and capacity for change; and the complex conceptions of political thought cannot be reduced to simple elements. The experience of mankind has been almost infinite, and the content of history is accordingly inexhaustible. There is no security without a sense of the dependence of the present upon the past; and the just answer to Rousseau's fancy that man is born free is that he is born thousands of years old. The late Ambassador Page used to say of the Southern United States that it is "governed from the grave." In a serious sense the whole world, certainly the English world, is "governed from the grave." We are not ourselves alone but others as well, not merely the living but also the dead without whom we should not have been, and those to come without whom we labour in vain. History bridges time and space: it helps us to answer the question who is our neighbour, to get and to keep in touch, and to acquire that sense of contact and community without which we lose our bearings and drift or are driven about by every turning tide or gust of feeling. History is a church in which the living encounters the memorials, if not the spirits, of the past and it is the baptismal font of the future. The past is not less moving than the future, and it beckons us out of our temporal vision into a wider sphere of sympathy and imagination. The present by itself is an earth without a solar system to give it light and sustenance; and history is the science of the things which have made man what he is and built up the treasures of humanity.

The object of my history is to define the characteristics of English thinkers. It may be done by ignoring difficulties and running to death some generalisation, or, it may be done by taking account of the cumulative effect of a lengthening past and showing how the current of English thought has gathered strength and depth from the gradual working out of the national adventure. The latter is the plan I endeavour to carry out. It demands a wide sympathy which I endeavour to show. The historian must be able to see the worth of the work of Conservatives like Coleridge and Disraeli, of Liberals like Green and Bryce, of Radicals like Bentham and Carlyle, of Individualists like Spencer and Seeley, of old-fashioned Socialists like Owen and Kingsley, and of new-fashioned Socialists like Mr. Sidney Webb (now Lord Passfield) and Mr. Ramsay MacDonald. In order to appreciate Malthus he must not depreciate Dean Inge; he must leave room for Newman and for Chalmers, as well as for Maitland; he must see why Bagehot believed in a deferential nation as well as why Mr. Bertrand Russell would usher in the rule of the Guilds. Much patience and much understanding are required to do justice to competing and completing systems of thought.

My grateful thanks are due to Mr. MacCunn and Lord Phillimore for their readiness to advise me on difficult points, though alas! both have passed beyond the reach of my acknowledgment. My book has had the advantage of the criticisms of three masters of its subject: Mr. E. Barker, Mr. G. P. Gooch, and Mr. H. J. Laski. They most kindly read through the manuscript, and I feel deeply indebted to them. Mr. Gooch furnished me with valuable suggestions. At all times he has been most willing to aid me in my many perplexities.

ROBERT H. MURRAY.

PERSHORE ABBEY,
  WORCS.

Contents

Chap.		Page
	Preface	v
I.	Malthus and the Principle of Population	1
II.	Bentham and his Philosophy of Law Reform	40
III.	James Mill and Middle Class Democracy	96
IV.	Owen: A Practical Socialist	128
V.	Coleridge the Philosophic Conservative	161
VI.	Disraeli the Novelist-Statesman	206
VII.	The Oxford Movement and the Scots Disruption	244
VIII.	Carlyle the Romantic Radical	297
IX.	Cobden and Free Trade	356
X.	J. S. Mill the Optimistic Democrat	370
XI.	Kingsley and Christian Socialism	432
	Index	456

Chapter I.

MALTHUS AND THE PRINCIPLE OF POPULATION

The vision of a golden age has often shimmered far off before the mind of men when they have passed through the crisis of a revolution or a restoration, which not infrequently is but another name for a revolution. Such a vision transported men near the end of the eighteenth century, when it was not unnaturally believed that in redressing the grievances which had given rise to the French Revolution and in proclaiming the principle that government sprang from the consent of all, a long step on the road towards the peace and the happiness of mankind had been taken. The belief in progress is not earlier than the sixteenth century, and with the lapse of the ages men had come to regard it as unbounded. Animated by such a belief, Condorcet wrote his memorable *Esquisse d'un tableau historique des Progrès de l'esprit humain*,[1] and it at once influenced his own generation. To him the problem of the perfectibility of the human race simply consisted in "rendre la justesse d'esprit, une raison indépendante et saine, une conscience éclairée, une soumission habituelle aux règles de l'humanité, à la justice, des qualitès presque universelles." Given compliance with these conditions, the vision of the golden age forthwith became a reality.

Among the ardent believers in the perfectibility of mankind was one Daniel Malthus, whose son, Thomas Robert (1766–1834), by the irony of fate, was to teach a doctrine which cut at the very roots of the doctrine of Condorcet the Frenchman and Godwin the Englishman. A disciple of the teaching of Rousseau's *Émile*, the father sent Robert in 1782 to a school conducted by Gilbert Wakefield at Warrington. To his advantage the lad remained there till he entered Jesus College, Cambridge, in 1784. From Cambridge he writes to his father on November 14, 1784: "I am now

---

[1] It was first published in 1793.

pretty well settled in my rooms. The lectures begin tomorrow; and, as I had time last week to look over my mathematics a little, I was, upon examination yesterday, found prepared to read with the year above me, though I believe I shall attend a few lectures at the same time with those of my own year. We begin with mechanics and Maclaurin, Newton and Neill's *Physics*. We shall also have lectures on Mondays and Fridays in Duncan's *Logick*, and in Tacitus's *Life of Agricola* on Wednesdays and Saturdays. I have subscribed to a bookseller who has supplied me with all the books necessary. We have some clever men at college, and I think it seems rather the fashion to read. The chief study is mathematics, for all honour in taking a degree depends upon that science, and the great aim of most of the men is to take an honours degree. At the same time I believe we have some good classics. I am acquainted with two, one of them of this year, who is indeed an exceedingly clever man and will stand a very good chance for the classical prize if he does not neglect himself. I have read in chapel twice. It seems that it is the custom when the readers are absent that the two juniors should read the lessons, and I believe I am the junior of my year."

On December 29, 1784, he writes that the "bill (for the term) is 44 pounds, 16 of which is the income of my room, and seven tuition and other articles for the two quarters, midsummer and Michaelmas, which I did not reside." His father thought, after the fashion of fathers, £100 a year a reasonable figure for the University expenses of ordinary folk, though £25 covered the cost at Leipzig. His note of warning was scarcely needed, for Robert was on his guard against the peril of running into debt. Though his main study was mathematics, he also read history, poetry, and modern languages, and obtained prizes for Latin and Greek declamations. In spite of an hereditary impediment in his speech, he had long contemplated taking holy orders, and his inclination led him to aspire to a retired country living, where he might have leisure to think and study. He graduated as ninth wrangler in the mathematical tripos in 1788. After his examination he writes on April 9, 1788: "I have laid aside my chemistry for a while and am at present endeavouring to get some knowledge of general history and geography. I have lately been reading Gibbon's *Decline of the Roman Empire*. He gives one useful information concerning the origin and progress of those nations of barbarians which now form the polished states of Europe, and throws some light upon the beginning of that dark period which so long overwhelmed the world, and which cannot, I think, but excite one's curiosity. He is a very entertaining writer, in my opinion; his style is sometimes really sublime, everywhere interesting and agreeable, though perhaps it may in general be call'd rather too florid. I shall like much to see his next volumes." So thought the young wrangler of one-and-twenty, who was able to peruse the concluding Volumes IV, V, and VI of the *Decline and Fall*, published the very next year after his graduation.

On June 10, 1793, Malthus was elected to a fellowship at Jesus, and was one of the fellows who on June 23, 1794, made an order that the name of S. T. Coleridge should be taken off the boards unless he returned and paid his tutor's bill. Malthus held his fellowship until his marriage, but only resided occasionally.

In 1798 he was ordained, holding a curacy at Albury, Surrey. He had been pursuing his studies, thinking about the state of his country then in the throes of that prolonged struggle with France which only terminated with the Battle of Waterloo. In 1796 he had written his first pamphlet, *The Crisis*, and had in vain tried to induce Debrett to print it. In it he attacked Pitt from the Whig angle, though he tendered support of the poor law scheme then under consideration in terms which sufficiently indicate that he had not yet worked out his principle of population. He continued his reading in political economy, meditating on the works of Hume and Adam Smith. Godwin's *Inquirer*, published in 1797, led to discussions between Malthus and his father on some of the questions already handled by Godwin in his *Political Justice*, 1793.

Godwin imagined a society where all were equally comfortable and equal in fact all round. Assuming that it could be established—and Malthus plainly deemed this an unwarrantable assumption—it would inevitably crash through the growth of population. Such was the thesis he advocated in his *Essay on Population*, published anonymously in 1798. Malthus's proof is short and sharp. Population, when unchecked, increases in geometrical ratio, whereas subsistence increases only in arithmetical. The checks to population are vice and misery. This pamphlet instantly attracted attention from Godwin, Mackintosh, Parr, and other writers. Its author was replying to an "obliging" letter from Godwin in August, 1798. Malthus soon discerned that his pamphlet was open to objections, and accordingly in 1799 he travelled abroad in quest of additional information. In the congenial society of college friends, Otter, Clarke the antiquarian and naturalist, and Clarke's pupil, Cripps, he visited Germany, Sweden, Norway, Finland, and part of Russia, these being the only countries at that time open to English travellers. Clarke speaks of Malthus as the best sailor of the four, with plenty of fun in him. If political economy has been called the dismal science, dismalness and Malthus were poles asunder. All who met him felt the charm of his personality. Otter says that during an intimacy of fifty years he never saw Malthus ruffled or angry, and that in success he showed as little vanity as he had shown sensibility in abuse. The doctrines he taught he believed to be essential to the welfare of his fellows, and he taught them at the cost of his preferment in the Church. His devotion to truth was both sincere and disinterested.

The Peace of Amiens gave a short breathing space to Europe, and Malthus took advantage of it to visit France and Switzerland. In 1800 he had published a tract upon the "High Price of Provisions," and promised in the conclusion a new edition of his *Essay*. This, which appeared in June, 1803, was a substantially new book, containing the results of his careful inquiries on the continent and his wide reading in all that bore on his far-reaching subject. It reached its second edition in 1803, its third in 1806, its fourth in 1807, its fifth in 1817, and its sixth in 1826, the last in his lifetime.

At the end of 1806 he became professor of History and Political Economy at the newly founded East India College at Haileybury, holding this chair for the rest of his life. He lectured on Political Economy, and was able to report that the hearers not only understood, but "did not even find dull." Inevitably his lectures led him to consider the question of rent, and the theory he came to formulate is on the lines laid down by Ricardo. Correspondence between the two economists begins in 1810. Malthus was elected F.R.S. in 1819. He helped to found the Political Economy Club in 1821, and the Statistical Society in 1834. Among his colleagues at the former were Ricardo, James Mill, Grote, and Tooke. For nearly thirty years Malthus lectured the future civil servants of India, yet his abiding work was carried out by his pen. His regular handwriting moved men who never came under the influence of his voice—and it moves men to this day. It is at the same time pleasant to read the judgment of Mackintosh: " I have known Adam Smith slightly, Ricardo well, Malthus intimately. Is it not something to say for a science that its three great masters were about the three best men I ever knew?"

The direct importance of Malthus in the history of political science is enormous: his indirect importance is also enormous For he is the grandfather of the evolution theory, which finally disposed of the fixed Utopias dreamed of by the men of the eighteenth and the first half of the nineteenth century. There are coincidences in the reading of great men, but is there anything in its long arm to equal the parallelisms of Darwin and Wallace, the co-discoverers of evolution? It is not altogether surprising that both should have read Chambers' *Vestiges of the Natural History of Creation* (1844), or Lyell's *Principles of Geology* (1830–33). Nor is it surprising that both should have read Humboldt's *Personal Narrative* (1814–18). But surely it is amazing that both should have read Malthus's *Essay on the Principle of Population*. How out of the common it is appears from the following quotations from F. Darwin's *Life of C. Darwin* and A. R. Wallace's *My life*:

DARWIN.	WALLACE.
"In October 1838, that is, fifteen months after I had begun my systematic inquiry, I hap-	"In February 1858, I was suffering from a rather severe attack of intermittent fever at

DARWIN.

pened to read for my amusement *Malthus on Population*, and being well prepared to appreciate the struggle for existence which everywhere goes on from long-continued observations of the habits of animals and plants, it at once struck me that under these circumstances favourable variations would tend to be preserved, and unfavourable ones to be destroyed. The result of this would be the formation of new species. Here, then, I had at last got a theory by which to work; but I was so anxious to avoid prejudice that I determined not for some time to write even the briefest sketch of it. In June, 1842, I first allowed myself the satisfaction of writing a very brief abstract of my theory in pencil, in thirty-five pages, and this was enlarged during the summer of 1844 into one of 230 pages.

WALLACE.

Ternate, in the Moluccas; and one day, while lying on my bed during the cold fit, wrapped in blankets, though the temperature was at 88° Fahr., the problem presented itself to me, and something led me to think of 'the positive checks' described by Malthus in his *Essay on Population*, a work I had read several years before, and which had made a deep and permanent impression on my mind. These checks—wars, disease, famine, and the like—must, it occurred to me, act on animals as well as man. Then I thought of the enormously rapid multiplication of animals, causing these checks to be much more effective in them than in the case of man; and while pondering vaguely on this fact there suddenly flashed upon me the *idea* of the survival of the fittest—that the individuals removed by these checks must be on the whole inferior to those that survived. In the two hours that elapsed before the ague fit was over, I had thought out almost the whole of the theory; and the same evening I sketched the draft of my paper, and in the two succeeding evenings wrote it out in full, and sent it by the next post to Mr. Darwin."

"Where goods are increased, they are increased that eat them." The "struggle for existence"—Malthus uses this very phrase—is a present fact, as it has been a past fact, and will be a future one. In a herd of animals the units are simply the fittest who have survived the struggle for existence. The principle of population is in the foreground; there are no checks to it but famine, disease, and death, the very checks on which Malthus was the first to lay sufficient emphasis. We can therefore understand how the study of the *Essay on Population* led Darwin and Wallace to explain the origin of species by a generalisation which Malthus had known and named, though he did not pursue it beyond man. Indeed, Sir Charles Lyell is so much impressed by these conclusions that he even denied the originality of Darwin and Wallace. Darwinism is Malthusianism on the largest scale: it is the application of the problem of population, animal and vegetable.

Just as Adam Smith had inquired into the nature and causes of wealth in 1776, so Thomas Robert Malthus inquired into the nature and causes of poverty in 1803. An ardent believer in human progress like Condorcet might urge that the golden age was dawning, while a sober inquirer like Malthus saw a serious obstacle standing in the way. Is progress possible when population, being unchecked, increases in geometrical ratio with subsistence increasing only in arithmetical? "A slight acquaintance with numbers," Malthus drily observes, "will show the immensity of the first power in comparison with the second." With remorseless logic he shows that "the race of plants and animals shrinks under this great restrictive law, and the race of men cannot by any efforts of reason escape from it. Among plants and animals its effects are waste of seed, sickness, and premature death; among men, misery and vice." In old countries like Europe, population is constantly checked by want of room and want of food, by vice and misery, and by the fear of vice and misery. In new countries like America there is room and there is food; but the price of the latter is toil, and this toil is at the expense of the women. In old Europe people double their numbers once in a century. In new America they perform the same feat, despite toil and the difficulty of rearing children, once in twenty-five years. Obviously in the happy society of Godwin,

> Where all are proper and well-behaved
> And all are free from sorrow and pain,

the rate of increase will be infinitely faster than doubling the population once in twenty-five years. Godwin, Condorcet and the French school, like some of the Socialists of our own day, are entirely wrong in attributing all inequality to human institutions. The passion of man and woman to reproduce themselves is the root cause of the whole difficulty, and always will be—until, at least, we all become as wise as the eugenists want us to be.

We now turn aside to survey the world of Godwin and Condorcet. When the latter composed his philosophic *Esquisse d'un tableau historique des Progrès l'esprit humain* in 1793, he was hiding from Robespierre. For revolutionary Paris lay in the grip of the Terror. The prospect of violent death and imprisonment has given rise to some of the writings of mankind. There is the pathetic petition which Louis XVI scrawled in the interval between his condemnation on Saturday and his execution on Monday. There is the sombre eloquence of Sir Walter Raleigh's *History of the World*, composed in his weary imprisonment in the Tower. Cervantes wrote the saddest book in the world, and Bunyan wrote one of the gladdest in the seclusion, of a prison. There are the proud verses of Montrose, and the moving letter of Argyle to his wife, both written in Edinburgh after sentence of death, and both breathing as lofty a serenity as that of Condorcet himself.

Condorcet, like a true Frenchman, cares more for equality than liberty. He dreams of a future which is to witness the disappearance of inequality among nations, the appearance of equality among the people of every nation, and the "perfectionnement réel" of man. The disappearance of inequality among nations will be due to the abandonment by Europeans of their commercial monopolies, their treacherous practices, their custom of proselytising, and their attitude of contempt for those of another creed or colour. Nations of course will never be alike, but they will all direct their path towards freedom. The appearance of equality among the people of every nation will be due to the removal of artificial restrictions on the accumulation of property,—he shrinks from the views of Rousseau, Mably, and Babeuf,—the extension of the doctrine of probabilities in general and of annuities and insurance in particular, and increasing facilities for instruction. Condorcet waxes most enthusiastic, as he endeavours to realise what the accomplishment of his dream will mean.

From his point of view he vigorously denounces the subjection of women, and the removal of this subjection will form one of the most important steps in human progress. The laws and institutions of his Utopia will tend to identify the individual with the State. There will be a universal language. Discoveries in science, notably in medicine, will prolong the average duration of life far beyond the short span which it now attains, Man will never become immortal, yet "a period will arrive when death will be nothing more than the effect either of extraordinary accidents or of the increasingly slow destruction of the vital powers; and the duration of the interval between the birth of man and this destruction will itself have no assignable limit." Death will indefinitely recede, and the distance between birth and death will illimitably diminish. For Condorcet abundantly realises that in order to achieve perfectibility man must have time, a very long time indeed. Undoubtedly a new and happier epoch will dawn for the whole human race, women as well as men. For the dower of all will be an ever increasing state of happiness and virtue. The goal, he exultantly proclaims, is nothing short of the endless perfectibility of human nature. Such a picture comforts Condorcet for the errors, the crimes and the wrongs with which the earth is still stained. From the world of the real he withdraws to the world of the ideal, feeling confident that his *Esquisse* will be a bridge between the two. Of it we can write, what has been written of the speech of Demosthenes "On the Crown," that it "breathes the spirit of that high philosophy which, whether learned in the schools or from life, has consoled the noblest of our kind in prisons, and on scaffolds, and under every persecution of adverse fortune."

With all his fervent hopes for the destiny of our species, Condorcet saw clearly some of the rocks that loom ahead of mankind in the nearer or more distant future and threaten to wreck the ship of progress. He anticipated the problem which was raised in an acuter and more insistent form by Malthus. With the progress of science and industry the earth will undoubtedly be forced to yield a greater quantity of food, and hence to support a larger population; but must there not come a time when the increase of the inhabitants of the globe will exceed the increase of the means of subsistence, with the result either of widespread misery or of a reduction of the population, which in turn could not be effected without acute suffering? Thus it might be argued by Malthus that the perfectibility of the human species is strictly limited by the amount of sustenance that can be extracted from the earth, and that though such progress may possibly reach that limit, it can never transcend it. Were the visions of Condorcet to perish before the realities urged by Malthus?

Convincing as the argument afterwards emphasised by Malthus may sound, Condorcet refused to admit it as conclusive. He observed that, should such a time ever come, it must necessarily be at a very distant date, and that in the interval mankind will infallibly have attained a degree of knowledge and enlightenment of which we at present can hardly form any conception. Who, he asked, would venture to predict what may one day be done by art for the conversion of the elements into substances fit for human use? And even though population should ultimately reach such a limit inexorably set by nature on this planet, Condorcet refused to despair; for, as he pointed out, men could meet and evade the difficulty by limiting the production of food to the amount necessary to maintain the inhabitants of the earth in welfare and comfort. Thus there would be no need to reduce the surplus population by the cruel and barbarous expedients of abortion and infanticide to which Malthus was to draw renewed attention.

Condorcet had trusted to the outward development of the arts and sciences while Godwin trusted to the inward development of the mind. By different ways they arrive at the goal of progress, and Malthus meets them on their arrival. He points out to Godwin that there is no sign that the body is becoming subjugated to the mind. Even philosophers, he drily remarked (and he wrote feelingly, as he had the malady at the time of writing) cannot endure the toothache patiently, and he had yet to learn that a merry heart will enable a weak man to walk as fast and as far as a strong man. There is no change in the human body, so he informs Godwin, and little or no change in the relation of the mind to it.

The dreams of Condorcet are, in turn, subjected to the cold analysis of the mathematician. If the arts have made the lengthening of life "indefinite," they have not made it "infinite." Gardeners can grow carnations "indefinitely" large, but can they grow them "infinitely" large? No man can ever say that he has seen the largest carnation that will ever be grown; but this he can say, that a carnation will never be as large as a cabbage. The limit is there, though it is undefined. There is a limit to the lengthening of human life, though no one can fix it to a year. In truth Condorcet has proved earthly immortality simply by a misuse of the word "indefinite." Is there any organic change in man which would prove even the possibility of perfection in this world? Malthus can see no evidence that there is.

Neither Pitt nor Peel made an original contribution to political economy. It was reserved for Adam Smith to make such a contribution, and it was reserved for Pitt and Peel to apply it. As Pascal writes, "*Qu'on ne dit pas que je n'ai rien dit de nouveau: la disposition des matières est nouvelle.*" For originality lies as much in the perception of opportunity or fresh disposition of material as in invention. Such originality belongs to Malthus. In the preface to the second edition he says that the only authors whom he had consulted for the past were Hume, Wallace, Adam Smith, and Dr. Price; he had since found discussions of the topic of population in Plato and Aristotle, in the works of the French economists, especially Montesquieu, and in Franklin, Sir James Stewart, Arthur Young, and Joseph Townshend, the last of whom published in 1786 a *Dissertation on the Poor Laws*, and whose *Travels in Spain* (1786–87) are noticed by Malthus as making a fresh examination of that country unnecessary.

There were such anticipators of the main doctrine of Malthus as Dr. Robert Wallace, Johann Peter Süssmilch, and Dr. John Bruckner. In 1761 Wallace had deemed the community of goods a sovereign cure for the ills of humanity were it not for the excessive population to which it would give rise. His *Various Prospects of Mankind* dissolved, as its author conjured up the vision of the multitudes appearing, under his conditions, at the scanty banquet provided by Nature. The same year Süssmilch produced *The Divine Plan in the Changes through which the Human Race passes in Birth, Death and Marriage*. He is simply a divine who seeks to examine the way in which the earth has been peopled. He indulges in such platitudes as that by which he announces that fertility must be greater than mortality—if population is to grow. In the domain of history we say, Blessed is the man who prints unpublished documents. In the domain of political economy we say, Blessed is the man who prints trustworthy statistics. Süssmilch is entitled to some of the privileges of this beatitude, for he prints statistics. Bruckner had faintly foreshadowed the main thesis of Malthus who is so amply entitled to the credit of putting it upon a basis of accuracy that, in the measured judgment of Alfred Marshall, he claims a place among the founders of historical economists. As astrology is to astronomy, so are Wallace, Süssmilch, and Bruckner to Malthus. He saw the importance of the general principle of population, and he also saw comprehensively its many-sided bearings. Out of the chaos of fact he reduced the cosmos of cause of the fact, and this constitutes his real title to greatness.

A Condorcet or a Godwin might treat of the destiny of the race from the *a priori* point of view. With a faith as firm as that of either of these thinkers in the claims of science and philosophy, Malthus is content to examine: the task of speculation he leaves rather to the one side. Let us see, he exclaims, how nature works, not how she ought to work. We ought not to reason from God to nature, but from nature to God. The difficulties of this world generate talents. "The first awakeners of the mind are the wants of the body." These arouse the intellect of the infant and sharpen the wits of the savage. Necessity, not leisure, is the mother of invention. Locke was more correct than Condorcet or Godwin; the desire to avoid pain is even stronger than the desire to find pleasure. As evil exists not to create despair but activity, so pain, which is a kind of evil, creates effort, and effort creates mind. This is the general rule, and we discern a particular example of it in the fact that want of food, which is one of the gravest of evils, leads to good. By contriving that the earth shall produce food only in small quantities, as the reward of keen labour, God has provided a perpetual spur to human progress. This furnishes the key, according to Malthus, to the puzzle of population. For man is a lotus-eater till hunger turns him into a Ulysses. The people tend to increase more quickly than their food, not in order that men may suffer, but in order that they may be roused to work to save themselves from suffering. As pain indicates to the surgeon the region of the diseased organ, so the tendency of folk to increase indicates the steps to be taken to remedy this evil.

Godwin and Condorcet had laid too little stress on the power of passion and too great on the power of reason: Malthus had laid too great stress on the power of passion and too little on the power of reason. "It is probable," owned Malthus, "that, having found the bow bent too much one way, I was induced to bend it too much the other, in order to make it straight." He had emphasised the co-ordination of the desire of food and the desire of marriage. But are these two desires at bottom co-ordinate? To ask such a question is to answer it. For ascetic reasons some men and more women set marriage aside, but who can set aside the desire of food? Coleridge justly remarks: "The whole case is this: Are they both alike passions of physical necessity; and the one equally with the other independent of the reason and the will? Shame upon our race that there lives the individual who dares even to ask the question!"

The title of Malthus's book in 1798 was: *An Essay on the Principle of Population as it affects the Future Improvement of Society. With remarks on the speculations of Mr. Godwin, M. Condorcet, and other writers.* Its title in 1803 was *An Essay on the Principle of Population; or, A view of its past and present effects on human happiness; with an inquiry into our prospects respecting the future removal or mitigation of the evils which it occasions. A new edition very much enlarged.* In the intervening five years the author had learnt much. The visions of the future, as depicted by either Condorcet or Godwin, no longer attract him. The past and the present are the chief matters that concern him. In the preface to the new edition he informs us that he has "so far differed in principle" from the first edition "as to suppose the action of another check to population which does not come under the head of either vice or misery." This of course is prudential restraint. The comparative pessimism of the first edition is replaced by the comparative optimism of the second. True, the pressure of population remains, but there also remains the pressure of civilisation, which is greater. The disorder, ignorance, and intemperance of ancient times or the Middle Ages are replaced by the order, knowledge, and temperance of modern days. True, the physical checks on population still exist, but they fall into a subordinate position. A check is positive when it cuts down an existing population, and it is preventive when it keeps a new population from growing up. Among animals the only check is misery. Among savage men it is vice as well as misery, and among civilised men it is vice, misery, and moral restraint, and the last forms "the action of another check" which he stresses strongly. Among animals the check takes the positive form: among men it increasingly takes the preventive form. Among men misery may act both positively and preventively. In the shape of war or disease it may cut down hosts. In the shape of the fear of its coming it may prevent marriage, and thus keep down the possibility of a new population. Similarly vice may act positively and preventively. It may act positively as in child murder, and it may act preventively as in the scheme of Condorcet. The first edition of the book left itself open to Godwin's attack that the very purification of society will ruin it, by forbidding vice and misery to check the growth of population. In order to overcome the force of this objection, Malthus in his new edition emphasises the place of moral restraint.

If Malthus was a mathematician, he was a clergyman who well knew the abiding importance of the ascetic element in human nature. Moral restraint does not mean with him impure celibacy, which is simply vice. It means continence, an abstinence from marriage followed by no sexual irregularities. Asceticism in the past found its votaries with solitary anchorites like the hermits of Egypt with pillar-saints like St. Simon Stylites, with flagellants like St. Anthony of Padua, and with the members of the great monastic orders. It is easy to satirise the Puritans, as Butler does, or the Scots Covenanters, as Scott does, yet asceticism forms a permanent feature of human nature. We have to accept what George Meredith calls the lesson of the flesh:—

> The lesson writ in red since first Time ran
> A hunter hunting down the beast in man;
> That till the chasing out of its last vice,
> The flesh was formed for sacrifice.

Malthus invoked this sentiment when he called moral restraint to the rescue. The sage or the savage, as well as the saint, stands in need of religion. "The fear of the Lord," according to Malthus, "is the beginning of wisdom; but the end of wisdom is the love of the Lord and the admiration of moral good."

Malthus, like Godwin, taught that a political reform was worthless unless achieved by reason. Argument and instruction constitute the cure for the social evils to which the human flesh is heir. Malthus, like Adam Smith, recommended schools before the days of Bell and Lancaster. *Laissez-faire* might be the rule, but it was a rule to which there were not a few exceptions. The Industrial Revolution had been a generation-and-a-half in progress, yet Malthus expressed his keen sympathy with the workmen displaced by the advent of the new machinery, and he was neither afraid nor ashamed to put forward the view, despite the opposition of Say and Ricardo, that there ought to be an embargo on inventions.

The first edition of Malthus's pamphlet had, in some measure, demolished the ideals set up by Condorcet and Godwin. Still, the author had sense enough to perceive that the particular problem of population was one more fitted for his genius than the general social question. Accordingly, in 1803 he confined his attention to the tendency of living beings to increase beyond the means of their sustenance. His subject, then, is "the constant tendency in all animated life to increase beyond the nourishment prepared for it." He harks back to the two outstanding desires, the desire of food and the desire of marriage. Obviously, the greater the supply of food, the greater the increase of population. The most rapid increase in numbers would take place if the supply of food exceeded the demand. "In no state that we have yet known has the power of population been left to exert itself with perfect freedom." Malthus quoted Benjamin Franklin who supposed that if the earth were bared of other plants it might be replenished in a few years with fennel alone. From such a fancy we come to fact in the instance quoted by Townshend, who points out that Juan Fernando, the first discoverer of the island on which he was shipwrecked, had covered it with goats from a single pair.

From animals we rise to human beings. Here the strength of Malthus lies in the abundant facts he adduces in support of his thesis. "In the northern states of America, where the means of subsistence have been more ample, the manners of the people more pure, and the checks to early marriages fewer than in any of the modern states of Europe, the population was found to double itself for some successive periods every twenty-five years." This approaches the ideal of an unchecked increase of the people, and it also approaches the ideal of an unchecked increase of food as well. Population is increased by itself: food is not increased by itself, but by the human beings who require it. Compare the increase due to an instinctive desire with an increase due to labour, and "a slight comparison will show the immensity of the first power over the second." The ninth wrangler informs us that the one is to the other as an arithmetical ratio is to a geometrical ratio. Assume the population and the food at the beginning of, say, the eighteenth century to be represented each by 100, and assume that both double themselves every twenty-five years. The arithmetical figures for food are:—

	1700–25	1725–50	1750–75	1775–1800.
100	200	300	400	500

The geometrical figures for population are:—

	1700–25	1725–50	1750–75	1775–1800
100	200	400	800	1600.

In 1700 the unit of food is 100 and the unit of population is 100. In 1800 the unit of food is 500 and the unit of population is 1600. How can this population possibly live? It is the plain truth, so Malthus insists, that nature is niggardly in her gifts to man, and by no means keeps pace with his desires. If men would satisfy their desire for food at the old rate of speed, they must exert their mind or their body more than at first, for the amount they harvest diminishes more proportionately than what is due to their efforts. The first edition of his book barely recognised the existence of this law of diminishing returns, though the later ones paid due attention to it. J. S. Mill so emphasised it that to Utilitarians the *magnum opus* of Malthus proved a veritable Bible. "Little improvement can be expected in morality," confessed J. S. Mill in his *Principles of Political Economy*, "until the producing large families is regarded with the same feelings as drunkenness or any other physical excess. But while the aristocracy and clergy are foremost to set the example of this kind of incontinence, what can be expected from the poor?"

Impressive as the figures of the philosopher are, a parable Malthus narrates is even more impressive: "A man who is born into a world already possessed, if he cannot get subsistence from his parents, on whom he has a just demand, and if the society do not want his labour, has no claim of *right* to the smallest portion of food, and, in fact, has no business to be where he is. At nature's mighty feast there is no vacant cover for him. She tells him to be gone, and will quickly execute her own orders, if he do not work upon the compassion of some of her guests. If these guests get up and make room for him, other intruders immediately appear demanding the same favour. The report of a provision for all that come fills the hall with numerous claimants. The order and harmony of the feast is disturbed, the plenty that before reigned is changed into scarcity; and the happiness of the guests is destroyed by the spectacle of misery and dependence in every part of the hall, and by the clamorous importunity of those who are justly enraged at not finding the provision which they had been taught to expect. The guests learn too late their error in counteracting those strict orders to all intruders, issued by the great mistress of the feast, who, wishing that all her guests should have plenty, and knowing that she could not provide for unlimited numbers, humanely refused to admit fresh comers when her table was already full."

The figures and the parable proved sufficiently startling to those who read them for the first time. Nor did Malthus confine his statement of the geometrical increase to population, for he extended it to all life whatever. The arithmetical increase was confined simply to food. The main matter to grasp is that the increase of population is greater than the increase of food. The one is to the other as the hare is to the tortoise in the fable. To ensure the slow tortoise winning the race, Malthus thinks we must send the hare to sleep. Geometrical ratios were then the fashion. Dr. Price had appealed to them in his arguments about the sinking fund; and had pointed out that a penny put out to 5 per cent. compound interest at the birth of Christ would, in the days of Pitt, have been worth some millions of globes of solid gold, each as big as the earth. In turn, Malthus also pointed out that if population doubles in twenty-five years, the numbers in two centuries would be to the present number as 256 to 1, and in three as 4096 to 1. The difference between the two cases lay in the circumstances that the penny had not been put out to 5 per cent. compound interest, whereas in North America the facts were proving that Malthus's figures were really correct.

The first book of the *Essay on Population* is concerned with the past, the second with the present, and the third and fourth with the future, and, in the opinion of their author, the past and the present count for much more than the future. The first book deals with the less uncivilised parts of the world as it now is, and the uncivilised past times; the second with the different states of modern Europe; the third criticises popular schemes of future improvement; while the fourth gives the philosopher's own views of the possible progress of humanity.

The survey begins in barbarism and ends in civilisation. The inhabitants of Tierra del Fuego, the Andaman Islands, Van Diemen's Land, the New Hollanders, who are the aborigines of north-west Australia, and the North American Indians all receive attention. On the last set of people we may spend some space, for Malthus assuredly does. The question he asks is, How is this population of Indians cut down to the level of its food? In his answer he remarks that, first, what limits the numbers of a people is not the possible but the actual food. Second, what destroys a population comes less often directly by starvation than indirectly through the medium of manners and customs. Third, the mere pressure of impending starvation does not lead to progress.

It is needful to bear in mind that what our author lays stress on is not the possible but the actual food at any given time. It is perfectly possible that the valley of the Mississippi, when highly cultivated, may support a hundred millions; but the all-important matter is not what it may support at some future date, but what it actually supports now. The ultimate check to numbers is starvation. The hard lot of the Indians destroys their fondness for their women; the latter are less likely to become mothers, and, if they do, their own hardships and heavy tasks prove a grave hindrance to nursing. The wars they wage, the pestilences they endure, the famines they suffer, and the miseries they encounter by their failure to provide for the future all help to curtail their numbers. Given the barest necessaries of life, competition does not make for progress. Given the animal necessaries of life, competition does make for progress.

Malthus turns from North America to the South Sea Islanders, and there too he finds the familiar cycle of war, disease, and famine coupled with infanticide. The position of the Polynesian savages suggests to him the state of ancient Europe when it was peopled by nomadic pastoral folk. All countries bear traces of incessant movement—growth, expansion, short-lived conquest, followed by shrinkage, defeat, expulsion or absorption by another set of nomads. One is tempted to write the history of the past, from this standpoint, as an account of the struggle for boundaries. The written history of mankind is to be read largely in the shiftings of peoples, now going forward, now thrusting backward. Society in olden time was essentially dynamic, though of course it is never static. There is a stationary state in books, e.g. J. S. Mill's *Principles of Political Economy*, but it is never realised in life. Herder is right in thinking that "history is geography in motion." The dispersive elements are favoured by the physical adaptation of the human race to all climates and external conditions, food question, the pressure of foes, and the resultant restlessness of an unstable primitive society. Motion there is in the worlds above, and incessant motion there is in the world beneath. Much of this motion is due to the quest for food. The increase of population, with the consequent increasing pressure on the means of subsistence, lies behind the war spirit. Now there may be a lust of conquest: in nomadic days the lust was for food.

Before the appearance of Sir Charles Lyell's *Principles of Geology* in 1830 science contemplated changes as catastrophic. Earthquakes, volcanoes, eruptions, and floods were phenomena ordinarily shaping the world. For these Lyell substituted glacial action, the slow denudation of rivers, subsidence and elevation, and the like. In the history of mankind the point of view is still similar. The attention of the observer is arrested by such a dramatic scene as the Völkerwanderung. As in geology the outstanding forces are not the seemingly vast ones, but the steady almost imperceptible action of the small powers. Nature, we have long learnt, never makes a leap. Migrations of nomads are not rare phenomena, historical storms as it were in the monotonous quiet of the life of man.

There has always been a great human current, now swift, now slow, which through the centuries flows from place to place, and the history of the nomadic peoples, which Malthus investigates, reveals its restlessness. On the whole it is without great haste, and unmistakably without any great rest. There are countless small eddies which nevertheless do not impede the steady flow of the great stream. The current is sluggish now, compared with its former strength. In early times mankind was of all forms of luggage the most easily transported, for he was alive. In a border foray, in the course of which he had plundered much cattle, Scott of Harden came across a pike of hay. Surveying it, he exclaimed, "Had you but four legs, you would not long remain there." Man had two legs, and consequently did not long remain anywhere. He was continually mixing with other men. Purity of race has at all times been a sheer delusion which no competent anthropologist shares. The failure of a crop, the dryness of a summer, the disappearance of fish or game, the pressure of numbers—any one of these is sufficient to set a tribe in motion. The difficulty is to conceive it ever at rest. The attachment to land was so weak as to be almost negligible. The wanderlust was in the blood of early man. Had it not been for the existence of natural obstacles, nomadic man would have been as eagerly in constant motion as the globe he inhabited. "What renders nations of shepherds so formidable," in the judgment of Malthus, "is the power which they possess of moving altogether, and the necessity they feel of frequently exerting their power in search of fresh pasture for their herds."

We all know that the issue between the claims of literature in antiquity and in the modern age had been debated independently in England and France during the seventeenth century. Sir William Temple's *Essay*, Wotton's *Reflections*, and Swift's satire on the *Battle of the Books* form three of the outstanding works in that famous quarrel. Malthus takes it up in the eighteenth century in the shape of the populousness of ancient nations, and he pronounces decisively in favour of the great number of people in modern nations. His reasons are conclusive. First, without the extension of agriculture or the better distribution of its fruits there can be no increase in population. Second, whatever is unfavourable to industry is also unfavourable to the growth of population. The truth is that the broad difference between a savage and a civilised population is that while the positive checks prevail in the one, the preventive prevail in the other. That is to say, vice and misery prevail in the former, moral restraint in the latter. Malthus's own travels in 1799 in Germany, Sweden, Norway, Finland, and part of Russia confirm him in the truth of these conclusions.

In 1803 France had been ten years at war with England, and, in spite of her losses on the battlefield, the number of Frenchmen had increased during these ten years. During these years the increase had been 2,000,000, or 200,000 a year. By employing statistics Malthus solved this puzzle, for he showed that the numbers of the unmarried survivors at home were more than enough to have kept up in case of necessity the old rate of marriages and the old rate of increase. On general principles he also deduced a presumption in favour of a rapid increase in time of war, and he pointed out that the social and industrial conditions of the country since 1789 were favourable to an increase. With an almost uncanny prescience, Sir Francis Ivernois, from whom Malthus took some of his figures, lamented that the losses due to war were not so much to be looked for in the actual deaths in battle or in hospital as in the number of children whom the existence of war prevented from coming into the world. We ought, according to Sir Francis, to mourn not only for the two-and-a-half millions killed, but for the twelve millions whom their death prevented from being born. It is a line of argument that has been pursued by Mr. Vedel-Petersen in *Losses of Life caused by War*, when he reckons that in France from 1915 to 1918 there were 913,900 fewer births than the normal average. To the figures of Sir Francis Ivernois, Malthus makes the reply that the slain, being full-grown men, reared at no little cost to themselves and their country, may fitly be mourned, but not the unborn twelve millions, whose appearance in the world would only have sent or kept a corresponding number out of it, and "if in the best-governed country in Europe we were to mourn the posterity which is prevented from coming into being, we should always wear a habit of grief."

Malthus was afraid that the law of inheritance and compulsory division of property would lead to an excessive and impoverished country population, but this fear has not been realised. On the other hand, there is little doubt that these causes have been at work in maintaining the stationary nature of the French population. Its birth-rate is among the lowest in Europe, though its death-rate is higher than ours. The prospects of France were once upon a time far brighter than those of England. The sailors of Britanny and Normandy were every whit as skilful and venturesome as our own. The French too found it easy to adapt themselves to their life in the New World. They were ready to live with the Indians, to hunt with them, and to marry among them. The Spaniards on the one hand looked on the Indians as beasts, and the English on the other looked on them as devils. Fortunate as the French were in their national character, they were less fortunate in their selection of the places for their colonising energies. For the icebound valley of the St. Lawrence in the north and the malarial swamps of Florida in the south were not so desirable as the rich east coast on which the Puritans pitched their tents. Besides, a sovereign like Louis XIV was so immersed in home affairs that he had no time for colonial. A governor of the stature of Frontenac did not receive that support to which he was entitled, and court favour meant everything—if given—and equally meant the loss of everything—if withdrawn. To her own permanent loss and to the world's gain, France too elected to expel the Huguenots who possessed the very elements needed for the expansion of her social structure. Coligny had seen the vision of a Huguenot State arising in South America, but St. Bartholomew's Day had prevented promise maturing into performance.

France, as Malthus duly notes, has set her foot in many regions, under many constellations; she has never been backward to advance, but nowhere has she held her offspring. Since Francis I asked "What clause it was in Adam's will that bequeathed the whole earth to Spaniards and Portuguese?", France has given ample reason for the cry of one of her sons, "What country in the world have we not conquered—and lost?" Not only once, but three times France has built up a colonial empire. The first, begun under Francis I and Henry IV, spread perhaps up to its widest when Madagascar was merely to be the keystone of a great Eastern France. That Empire fell in consequence of the grasping policy of Louis XIV. *Qui trop embrase mal étreint* has always been the sentence pronounced upon French ambition. Yet the edifice of Colbert, shattered in the war of the Spanish Succession, was rapidly renewed. In America the English colonies were isolated settlements on the Atlantic seaboard, with Canada to the north and New France to the south of them, and a line of outposts pushed down the Ohio to connect the two vast tracts in the rear of the British. The English only assumed a militant attitude under compulsion, but, when they assumed it, soon it was apparent that their petty settlements contained ten white men for every Frenchman in the huge domains that surrounded and enclosed them. Long before the conflict between Wolfe and Montcalm on the heights of Abraham, the contrast in the numbers of the English and the French had settled the destiny of North America. In the East the empire of Dupleix swelled like a bubble and burst as quickly. The fall of Napoleon in 1814 left France at the nadir of her colonial power, yet since then a third empire of foreign dependencies is far advanced in building. The Legitimist monarchy gave the people Algiers: Louis Philippe added Algeria and the occupation of parts of Oceania; since then has come the enormous increase in West Africa and the revived dreams of Indo-Chinese ascendency. But with each of these three successive attempts the impulse from the people itself has been fainter. There is no apparent reason why France should not again succeed, as before she succeeded, for the ultimate benefit of others.

The French, during the sixteenth and the early part of the seventeenth centuries, used to rely on individual character. Among the alterations effected in the national character by Louis XIV, none was more far-reaching than that by which he taught them to rely on the State, on himself, for *l'Etat, c'est moi*. True, the two cardinals, Richelieu and Mazarin, had begun the change, but it was he who carried it to its high stage of development. In his letters on the French and English two hundred years ago,

Béat de Muralt noted the likeness of one Frenchman to another: they had all been obliged to conform to the type the Government liked. Ask a Frenchman, Béat de Muralt says, the reason of his conduct, and you will get nothing from him in the last resort but *Cela se fait,* or *Cela ne se fait pas;* whereas the English will "go boldly against a custom, however well established, when their reason or their inclination estranges them from it." That shrewd old lady, Madame du Deffand, uttered the same sentiment when she wrote to Horace Walpole: "The English are an odd people; each individual is an original; there are no two of the same type. We are just the opposite; with us all people of the same profession resemble one another. To have seen one courtier is to have seen all." The old individuality, the old enterprise, must return to France if she is to regain her old proud position. Her third empire has grown greatly, but it requires citizens, colonists. Of the people who will go out and work in her colonies and establish interests of their own, she has too few. Until French character changes there is little probability that French history will change, and the radical interests of the Frenchman are caution in private life, temerity in public employment. The population is stationary because Frenchmen and women desire that it should be so. At the same time be it noted that Malthus laid down the postponement of marriage: he did not lay down what is taking place in France.

The maintenance of the standard of living forms a conspicuous feature in French history, and according to Malthus, it forms a no less conspicuous feature in English history. Anything attempting to weaken this standard meets with his liveliest abhorrence. With us, in his opinion, the middle and upper classes increase at a slow rate because they are anxious to preserve their station in life. Men, thus influenced, when they fall in love do not marry at once. When their passion is too strong or their judgment too weak for the exercise of this restraint, doubtless they have blessings that counterbalance the obvious evils, "but I fear it must be owned that the mere general consequence of such marriages are rather calculated to justify than to repress the forebodings of the prudent."

Malthus was not at all anxious to witness the introduction of the cheapest forms of food, and this attitude was due to his desire to maintain the standard of living for the poorest. If in good times the majority of the people enjoy fresh meat and wheat, then in bad times they can fall back on such cheaper forms of food as rice and potatoes. There is a margin, and the value of this margin is enormous. As Malthus divined not a little of the future of France, so he divined the potato famine in Ireland in 1846, the direst famine that country ever endured. Arthur Young, who knew Ireland well, published in 1800 his pamphlet on "Scarcity and its Remedies." In it he thought that "If each country labourer with three children and upwards has his ample potato ground and a cow, the price of wheat would be of little more consequence to him than it is to their brethren in Ireland. Every one admits the system to be good, but the question is how to enforce it." With his customary prescience Malthus rejoins that "I was by no means aware that the excellence of the system had been so generally admitted. For myself, I strongly protest against being included in the general term of *every one*, as I should consider the adoption of this system as the most cruel and fatal blow to the happiness of the lower classes in this country that they had ever received."

There was no census in England till 1801, and there were reasons for this. One was the feeling attaching to the story of the attempted numbering of the Israelites by David. Some thoughtful men considered that such a numbering was quite wrong in principle. Others felt that as an Englishman's house was his castle, it was an infraction of his liberty to inquire into the size of his family. Besides, in the days when the population of France was treble that of our own land, it laid our weakness bare. There was also the feeling that the census-collector was simply the forerunner of the tax-collector. Motives like these deferred the taking of the first census till 1801. The first census settled the actual numbers of the people in 1801, but it settled no more than this. For the population at the Revolution of 1688, Malthus depended on the old calculations from the number of houses. He thinks that the rapid increase of the people since 1780 was due to the decrease of deaths rather than to the increase of births. In undeveloped countries, like America and Russia, a large proportion of births may be a good sign, "but in the average state of well-peopled territory there cannot well be a worse sign than a large proportion of births, nor can there be a better sign than a small proportion." Malthus also emphasises the circumstance that "we should need to attend less to the column giving the number of children born, than to the one giving the number which reached manhood, and this number will almost invariably be the greatest where the proportion of births to the whole population is the least." On this test he lays much stress, and tried by it our own country stood—and stands—high.

Malthus suggested in 1803 that the experiment of 1801 should be repeated every ten years, and that registrar's reports should be made every year. On the 1811 census he remarks in a new edition of his book: "This is a rate of increase which in the nature of things cannot be permanent. It has been occasioned by the stimulus of a greatly increased demand for labour, combined with a greatly increased power of production, both in agriculture and manufactures. These are the two elements which form the most effective encouragement to a rapid increase of population. What has taken place is a striking illustration of the principle of population, and a proof that, in spite of great towns, manufacturing occupations, and the gradually acquired habits of an opulent and luxuriant people, if the resources of a country will admit of a rapid increase, and if these resources are so advantageously distributed as to occasion a constantly increasing demand for labour, the population will not fail to keep pace with them."

Malthus is well aware that if we change from agriculture to manufactures, we alter the character of our people. Manufacturing industry conduces to mental activity, to an expansion of comforts, to the growth of the middle classes, and to the growth with them of political moderation; but it is more subject than agriculture to the fluctuations of fashion, which lead to chronic destitution, and discontent, and the conditions of artisan life are "even in their best state unfavourable to health and virtue." Wealth, population, and power are but the means to an end, and that end—virtue and happiness. Our philosopher leans to the view that there is something like a golden mean, a balance of the two employments, which legislation may preserve.

In his analysis of rent, Malthus holds that fertile soils yield a produce that more than feeds the farmer. The next cause of rent is the peculiarity belonging to agricultural land by which the demand increases with the supply. Where there is food there will be mouths to devour it. His third cause is the scarceness of good land, which is due to the law of diminishing returns. The connection between the law of rent in its second cause and the law of population is obvious. Of course Malthus does not foresee the revolution to be wrought in the means of transport by which the land of distant America was to play its part in the reduction of rent in England. He lives in the pre-railway and pre-steamboat age. Nor does he foresee the time when we were to derive the bulk of our food from overseas, a prospect that Adam Smith thought too good to be likely, and that Malthus thought too dangerous to be desirable. The old agriculture is worth more to us than the new industries. He takes occasion to point out that "in the history of the world the nations whose wealth has been derived from manufactures and commerce have been perfectly ephemeral beings compared with those the basis of whose wealth has been agriculture. It is in the nature of things that a state which subsists upon a revenue furnished by other countries must be infinitely more exposed to all the accidents of time and chance than one which produces its own."

The Napoleonic Wars were making their slow progress, and Malthus was writing in the middle of them. Defence, in his opinion, as in Adam Smith's, was more than opulence. The growing population of England stood face to face with a shortage in food, a shortage which we who have lived through the World War can better appreciate than our fathers. By a curious working of the Mercantile Theory we escaped in the days of Malthus some of the effects of the shortage. For the French sent corn here in the hope that the sooner they exhausted our store of gold the sooner the war would come to an end. Did not Louis XIV say that, after all, the owner of the last louis d'or must win? The evils of scarcity had made themselves felt in the first decade of the nineteenth century, and we can readily understand why Malthus advocated that special encouragement was due to agriculture, for otherwise "we shall be laid so bare to the shafts of fortune that nothing but a miracle can save us from being struck." Indeed "if England continues yearly her importations of corn, she cannot ultimately escape the decline which seems to be the natural and necessary consequence of excessive commercial wealth; and the growing prosperity of those countries which supply her with corn must in the end diminish her population, her riches, and her power"—not this year or the year following, but " in the next two hundred or three hundred."

The dream our philosopher sets before him is a state which combines agriculture and commerce in equal proportions. As the people of the South Sea Islands lived by taking in one another's washing, so agriculture and commerce can each live by the other. As each provides a market for the other, wealth will constantly and steadily— this is an important matter—grow. Foreign trade is nothing like so steady as home, for it is subject to manifold influences. The prosperity of such a country, he thinks, may last practically for ever. Under his ideal we come close to the ideal Berkeley laid down in his *Querist*: "Whether if there was a wall of brass a thousand cubits high round this kingdom, our natives might not nevertheless live cleanly and comfortably, till the land, and reap the fruits of it?" Malthus agrees, for he proceeds to remark: "The countries which unite great landed resources with a prosperous state of commerce and manufactures, and in which the commercial part of the population never essentially exceeds the agricultural part, are eminently secure from sudden reverses. Their increasing wealth seems to be out of the reach of all common accidents, and there is no reason to say that they might not go on increasing in riches and population for hundreds, nay almost thousands of years." They would in truth progress till they had reached the extreme limit of population.

In his consideration of the agricultural labourer, Malthus thinks that his wages consist not merely of such necessaries as corn, but also of many conveniences which have become necessaries, as soap, shoes, and candle-light. Once more he falls back on the standard of living, and insists that the way to raise wages is the diffusion of the desire of conveniences. The luxuries of the few rich, he deems, harass the industry of the poor by varying with the fashion; but the luxuries of the poor, when embodied in their standard of living, are not only the best kind of check to population, but the steadiest encouragement to general trade. "When our wages of labour in wheat were high in the early part of the last century it did not appear that they were employed merely in the maintenance of more families, but in improving the condition of the people in their general mode of living." Plainly, Malthus is among the first to advocate the theory of the Wage Fund, according to which wages depend on the ratio of population to circulating capital. Equally plainly he holds that the awaking of man's wants for luxuries creates a high standard of living, and thereby prevents over-population. His attitude to wages is clear in such a statement as, "If a country can only be rich, by running a successful race for low wages, I should be disposed to say at once: 'Perish such riches!'" Consider such a view as that "it is most desirable that the labouring classes should be well paid, for a much more important reason than any that can relate to wealth, namely, the happiness of the great mass of society." When asked the question whether, from a national point of view, if low wages turned out to the advantage of the capitalist, it were not desirable that labour should be kept permanently in a state bordering on distress, his answer was: "I should say, by no means fitting; I consider the labouring classes as forming the largest part of the nation, and therefore that their general condition is the most important of all."

Malthus was of opinion that, if called for, general wealth must give way to general welfare. His ideal was shorter hours of labour than the appallingly long hours of his generation, for "I have always thought and felt that many among the labouring classes in this country work too hard for their health, happiness, and intellectual improvement." Naturally as a Whig he approved of popular education and of the Factory Acts for the prevention of children from labouring too long or too young, and naturally he disapproved of popular ignorance and of Factory Acts for adults on the ground that they inflicted an injustice on the workers and that they uselessly interfered with "the principles of competition, one of the most general principles by which the business of society is carried on." At the same time we note that he allows medical assistance to the poor, assists emigration, and restricts foreign trade when it inflicts more loss on the public than it confers gain on the traders.

Malthus is not among the founders of political economy as a dismal science. True, he had narrated his famous parable on the mighty feast of nature, but in later editions of his book he had withdrawn it. He never, however, withdrew his views that the poor cannot claim relief as a right, but only as a favour, and he never withdrew his view that poor relief simply elevates one man at the expense of another. If everyone exercised the right, the supposed right, of demanding relief, the community could not grant it. "Upon the whole, the sum of good to be expected from a compulsory maintenance of the poor will be far outbalanced by the sum of evil which it will inevitably create." You relieve one, and at the same time you inflict general suffering. In fact, you create the poor you maintain, for you lead men to marry with the certainty of parish assistance lying before them. You increase the population without increasing the food of the country, and you sap the ancient spirit of independence. "Hard as it may appear in individual instances, dependent poverty ought to be held disgraceful." The justices supplement wages when the price of corn is high, with the result that prices rise still higher. The ideal is high wages, independence, and moral restraint rather than low wages, dependence, a parish supplement, and a pauper family. "I feel persuaded that if the Poor Laws had never existed in this country, though there might have been a few more instances of very severe distress, the aggregate mass of happiness among the common people would have been much greater than it is at present."

Malthus holds no *a priori* views about the Poor Law, or indeed about anything else. He simply judges the Poor Law by its effects, and these he finds to be injurious. Still, "the desire of bettering our condition, and the fear of making it worse, like the *vis medicatrix naturae* in physics, is the *vis medicatrix reipublicae* in politics, and is continually counteracting the disorders arising from narrow human institutions." Bad as the Elizabethan Poor Law was, Malthus admits that it was largely inoperative, as the magistrates refused to enforce the fixed rate of wages of the labourer. Room had been left for some feelings of independence and of moral restraint. He notes that pauper children, like foundlings, do not live long, and he entertains as hearty a hatred of Foundling Hospitals as he does of the Poor Law. His ground of dislike of the latter lies in the circumstance that it impaired the sense of personal responsibility of the worker. A child ought to be supported by his parents, not by the public.

Malthus advocated the gradual abolition of the Poor Law. Let a law be passed, he held, declaring that no legitimate child born of a marriage taking place a year after the law's enactment, and no illegitimate child born two years after, shall ever be entitled to parish relief. "And to give a more general knowledge of this law, and to enforce it more strongly on the minds of the lower classes of the people, the clergyman of each parish should, previously to the solemnisation of a marriage, read a short address to the parties, stating the strong obligation on every man to support his own children; the impropriety, and even immorality, of marrying without a fair prospect of being able to do this; the evils which had resulted to the poor themselves, from the attempt which had been made to assist, by public institutions, in a duty which ought to be exclusively appropriated to parents, and the absolute necessity which had at length appeared, of abandoning all such institutions, on account of their producing effects totally opposite to those which were intended. This would operate as a fair, distinct, and precise notice which no man could well mistake, and without pressing hard upon any particular individuals, would at once throw off the rising generation from their miserable and helpless dependence upon the Government and the rich." In the judgment of our thinker the poor are victimised by "the wretched system of governing too much. When the poor were once taught, by the abolition of the Poor Laws, and a proper knowledge of their real situation, to depend more upon themselves, we might rest secure that they would be so fruitful enough in their resources, and that the evils which were absolutely irremediable they would bear with fortitude of men and the resignation of Christians."

Thus spake an apostle of *laissez-faire*, and it is not too much to say that the new Poor Law of 1834 breathed his very spirit. In justice to the independent worker, the relief of the dependent worker should be made rigorous. The sense of personal responsibility was to be brought home, and there can be little doubt that the legislation of 1834 served this purpose. Nor does this feeling of responsibility take away from our happiness. "When we contemplate the constant and severe toil of the greatest part of mankind, it is impossible not to be forcibly impressed with the reflection that the sources of human happiness would be most cruelly diminished if the prospect of a good meal, and a warm house, and a comfortable fireside in the evening were not incitements sufficiently vivid to give interest and cheerfulness to the labours and privations of the day." To serve as Jacob served for Rachel means strength of character. Nor did Malthus fail to practise what he preached, for he did not marry till he had been appointed Professor at the East India College. He confessed that "Perhaps there is scarcely a man who has once experienced the genuine delights of virtuous love, however great his intellectual pleasures may have been, that does not look back to the period as the sunny spot in his whole life, where his imagination loves to bask, which he recollects and contemplates with the fondest regrets, and which he would most wish to live over again." The enlightened lover, during his engagement, will put away some of his earnings, and Savings Banks and

Friendly Societies, properly regarded, form a sure aid to the permanence of romance; and truly "in a natural state of society such institutions, with the aid of private charity well directed, would probably be all the means necessary to produce the best practicable effects."

The principle of self-help, long before the days of Samuel Smiles, met with a warm reception from our philosopher. Nor does a lover of freedom like him overlook "the effects of the knowledge of the principal cause of poverty on civil liberty." Where there are distress and destitution, there follow in their train discontent and sedition. Where there are discontent and sedition, there follow in their train coercion and despotism. If men realised that the chief cause of poverty was an excessive population, and if they put their knowledge into practice, they would afford no excuse for tyranny. "The pressure of distress on the lower classes of people, together with the habit of attributing this distress to their rulers, appears to me to be the rock of defence, the castle, the guardian spirit of despotism. It affords to the tyrant the fatal and unanswerable plea of necessity. It is the reason why every free Government tends constantly to destruction, and that its appointed guardian becomes less jealous of the encroachments of power."

With the French Revolution still in progress, it was not easy for Malthus to resist the reflection that the number of Frenchmen was in part responsible for the outbreak of 1789. Was not the unhappiness of the French due to their rulers? So they had been told, and they overthrew their rulers. This unhappiness persisted, and they overthrew their new rulers; and they continued this process till they met a despot like Napoleon. As Malthus thought of the growth of the population of his own country, he discerned the circumstance that "the Government of the last twenty years has shown no great love of peace or liberty."

Malthus regarded Pitt and Paley as his most brilliant converts, and no one can doubt his influence on the statesman as well as on the utilitarian philosopher. Among other converts were Copleston, Hallam, James Mill, Senior, and Ricardo, though Malthus was never a pure Ricardian. On the other hand, he had to meet the attacks of such members of the revolutionary school as Godwin, Hazlitt, and Cobbett, and he also had to meet the attacks of such members of the "sentimental" conservative school as Coleridge and Southey. Sydney Smith asserted that "Malthus took the trouble of refuting him, and we hear no more of Mr. Godwin." The *Edinburgh Review* supported Malthus, and, in spite of hostility at first, so did the *Quarterly Review*. Sadler's onslaught is simply remembered because Macaulay replied to it in the *Edinburgh Review* of January, 1831. The influence of Malthus has been far-reaching, especially on the course of legislation, and his teaching and Ricardo's, independently of Bentham's, exercised a profound influence. Much that is traced to the great exponent of Utilitarianism might be traced to Malthus, not to mention Adam Smith and Priestley.

The attack of Godwin has been considered, and his argument is fundamentally that of Condorcet who believed in the perfectibility of man. On his steps towards perfectibility man is interrupted by the births of babies, and this of itself will stop him in the most effectual manner. Godwin may urge that he retains his faith in the future discovery of some contrary principle, and Malthus replied in effect to Condorcet:

> What can we reason but from what we know?

Godwin criticises the arithmetical and geometrical ratios, as Sadler, Carey and Henry George did. He thinks with Sadler that checks to population are not necessary. He holds with Southey and Henry George, that the inclusion of moral restraint stultifies the original doctrine. He points out that some checks have been omitted. Among these checks he counts misgovernment and bad laws, Doubleday counts high feeding, and Herbert Spencer counts intellectual development. Sadler holds with Carey and Henry George that the increase of food is at a more rapid rate than a mere arithmetical one. Sadler more sensibly believes that vice and misery sometimes add to population and do not tend to diminish it. Cobbett urges that moral restraint may involve as grave an evil as excessive numbers. As Karl Marx seeks to demonstrate the hopelessness of the labourer's position, and as Malthus seeks to demonstrate its hopefulness—provided the sense of personal responsibility is not lost—the bitterness with which the German economist assaults him is intelligible. The redundant class, whose existence Malthus explores, is in the opinion of Marx essential to the continuance of the capitalist *régime*. As a matter of fact, Malthus did not recognise that the existence of an industrial reserve was necessary. It took place, but his belief was that, if the workers did as he advised them, it would disappear. For he was invariably anxious to insist that over-population was relative, relative to the actual amount of food.

One line of approach to the *Essay on Population* to-day assumes the form of eugenics. If evolution were the true doctrine of the development of living forms, then our generation, following in the steps of Sir Francis Galton, thinks it desirable to take stock of the varieties of man, mental and physical, to measure their evolutionary value, and to shape the future of mankind by deliberate purpose, in the fashion that nature made possible. As a probable effect of deliberately running counter to nature Galton adduced the law of celibacy in the Roman Catholic Church by which the most gentle, sincere and humane of both sexes were forbidden to leave progeny, and attributed to it the brutality of the Middle Ages. So he also set down the decay of Spain to the annual removal by the Inquisition of those with the greatest tendency to independence of thought. In the same spirit, although he did not anticipate the modern popularity of the neo-Malthusian doctrines grouped under the phrase "birth-control," he denounced in advance all tendencies to a reduction in the fertility rate affecting chiefly the classes of society with the greatest intelligence and self-discipline. It is to be noted that he advanced more quickly than Darwin in the application of natural law to the mental and moral qualities as well as to the physical qualities of mankind; and that he differed absolutely from the thesis advanced by Huxley in his Romanes lecture as to the independence of the moral law from the cosmic process.

Galton's theory of eugenics could not be excluded from

a Utopia in which the units on which it had to play were abstractions. But does it apply to the real world of men and women? The question raises many difficulties on which scientific opinion is not so certain as Galton assumed. First, there is the interplay of inheritance and environment. Galton admitted that the best seed would fail, or at least not surpass seed of a baser stock, unless it were sown on a good soil. He admitted, for example, that a child brought up in an atmosphere of reverence for truth and devotion to free inquiry would be far more likely to succeed as a man of science than one nurtured in dogmatic respect for conventional beliefs. But he ascribed preponderating weight to natural inheritance. He laid much stress on an investigation he made into the character of twins. He distinguished between those twins which might be of different sexes and were no more alike than any two of a family, and what he called "identical twins," always of the same sex, and presumably the product of the abnormal division of a single egg-cell. He thought, from evidence he had collected, that identical twins brought up and living their lives in different environment continued to show an identity of physical, mental, and emotional constitution. Naturally he did not believe in the transmission of acquired characters, and therefore for the improvement of the race relied entirely on the selection of favourable and the rejection of unfavourable inherited constitutions. Apart from the controversial scientific side of the case, there remains the practical side; the control of human breeding offers a maximum of difficulties; the amelioration of the human environment commands universal sympathy, and instead of being a Utopian principle is a plank on every political platform. Yet take an instance. John Napier was born before his father completed his sixteenth year. On eugenic principles, who can defend the father of the inventor of logarithms?

If each generation has its capacities limited by its constitutional inheritance, the more reason for supplying the physical, mental, and moral environments which will make the most of a possibly indifferent seed. We may suggest a final difficulty in eugenics. Were the scientific problems solved, did it become possible to act on Galton's scheme of developing a "gifted race" by selecting men and women for rare and eminent talent, and mating them together generation after generation, how are we to choose and who is to choose the physical, mental, and moral qualities? Is it to be Pascal or a pugilist, a St. Francis or Bismarck? Are we to breed for reverence or for freedom of thought, for the artist or for the mechanic, for endurance or for beauty? Galton entertained the happy belief that on the average, great men were of great physical constitutions; an equally good case might be made out for the correlation of poor health and unusual ability. Darwin and Seeley are cases in point. Hobbes, Newton, Bentham, Burke, Constable, Keats, and Dickens, were all weakly children. Hume, Byron, Scott, Chatterton, Goldsmith, Fanny Burney, and Landor, were all backward children. Possibly there might be general agreement in selecting a fraction of one per cent. of the population from whose progeny only disaster might be expected, and a half of one per cent. as worthy of encouragement. But even in the thoughtless conditions of the modern world the absolute dregs of the population are discouraged almost to elimination, and reward somehow reaches the supreme.

References

BAGEHOT, W. *Economic Studies*. (London, 1898.)
BONAR, J. *Parson Malthus*. (Glasgow, 1881.)
BONAR, J. *Ricardo's Letters to Malthus*. (Oxford, 1889.)
BONAR, J. *Malthus and his Work*. (London, 1924.)
BRENTANO, L. *Die Malthussche Lehre u. d. Bevölkerungsbewegung d. Letzten Dezennien*. (Berlin, 1909.)
CANNAN, E. *A History of the Theories of Production and Distribution in English Political Economy*. (London, 1903.)
COMTE, C. *Transactions of the Acad. des Sciences Morales et Politiques*. He has a *Notice Historique sur la vie et les travaux of Malthus*. (December 28th, 1836.)
COSSA, E. *Il principio di Popolazione di T. R. Malthus*. (Bologna, 1895.)
DRYSDALE, C. R. *Life and Writings of Malthus*. (London, 1892.)
DRYSDALE, C. R. *The Population question according to Mill and Malthus*. (London, 1892.)
DUNCAN, H. G. *Race and Population Problems*. (London, 1929.)
ELLIS, H. H. *Essays in War-time*, 2 vols. (London, 1916–19.)
EMPSON, W. *Edinburgh Review*. (January, 1837.)

References

FERDY, H. *Der Malthusianismus.* (Berlin, 1885.)
GRIFFITH, G. T. *Population Problems of the Age of Malthus.* (Cambridge, 1926.)
HARDY, G. *Malthus et ses Disciples.* (Paris, 1912.)
HELD, A. *Zwei Bücher zur sozialen Geschichte Englands.* (Leipzig, 1881.)
INGE, W. R. *Outspoken Essays,* 2 vols. (London, 1919-22.)
ISAACSON, E. *The Malthusian Limit.* (London, 1912.)
JOIRE, A. *La population. Appreciation des principes de Malthus.* (Paris, 1885.)
LESER, E. *Untersuchungen zur Geschichte der Nationalökonomie.* (Jena, 1881.)
MOLINARI, G. *De Malthus: le principe de population.* (Paris, 1889.)
NICHOLSON, J. S. *Principles of Political Economy,* Vol I. (London, 1902.)
ÖFELE, F. F. v. *Anticoncept. Arzneistoffe.* (Berlin, 1898.)
OTTER, W. Prefixed a memoir of Malthus in Malthus's *Principles of Political Economy.* (London, 1836.)
PARTONAU DU PUYNODE, M. G. *Etudes sur les principaux économistes, Turgot-Adam Smith-Ricardo-Malthus-J. B. Say,-Rossi.* (Paris, 1868.)
SENIOR, N. W. *Two Lectures on Population.* (London, 1831.)
SOETBEER, H. *Die Stellung der Socialisten zur Malthusischen Bevölkerungslehre.* (Berlin, 1886.)
USSHER, R. *Neo-Malthusianism.* (London, 1898.)

Chapter II.

BENTHAM AND HIS PHILOSOPHY OF LAW REFORM

The transition from the principle of population, which with Malthus conduces to public weal, to that of utility is easy, for with Bentham the principle of utility is that which conduces to the greatest happiness of the greatest number. It is naturally a principle with a lengthy pedigree. Though Hobbes had found the obligation of right in contract, Spinoza had changed the issue of right to that of expediency or utility. David Hume made the same attempt as Spinoza, giving us the subtlest form of the Utilitarian philosophy, a philosophy that left its mark in England and in America, though not nearly to the same extent in Europe.

Hume's theory appeared in his three works, but chiefly in his *Essays*. With men of the cast of mind of Burke, morality is as mysterious as it is perplexing to other philosophers. With Hume, mystery and perplexity vanish, and instead of them we have a delightful lucidity. Morality becomes so admirably simple that a doubt steals over the mind. Does this admirable simplicity quite cover all the facts of life? Hume was certain that it did, and his certainty impressed itself on the minds of his many readers. Basing morality on experience, for a time his explanation achieved a wonderful success. We apply our felicific calculus to any matter, and on the balance of pleasures or pains we settle its worth. Nor did he ask us to apply it with those powers of wisdom that Spinoza and Bentham both demand. The champions of reason, he held, had gone wrong because they had rejected pleasure entirely. The difficulty he perceived lay in the adoption of some test of pleasure which should be itself nothing more than a special modification of the primary sense of pleasure. Hume confidently entertained the belief that he had found such a test in the moral sense. In the exercise of this sense there are the two passions of sympathy and, alternatively, either love or pride; love, if the action be contemplated in another; pride, if attributed to ourselves. The need of sympathy is obvious, for it is only by it we can enter into the feelings of another. The need of love or pride is no less obvious. They are the passions naturally and inevitably called forth, according as we either witness the performance of that action by others, or conceive it as performed, or about to be performed, by ourselves. The moral sense is the test of happiness. Hutcheson was the first to lay down the doctrine of the greatest happiness of the greatest number. Whatever may be thought of it in the domain of morals, it is certainly the main guide in the domain of legislation.

Hume maintains that the ultimate motive of obedience to the State is self-interest or utility, though he is too clear-sighted not to admit that with the overwhelming majority of men the motive is the sense of duty. Whatever else the World War demonstrated, it demonstrated that the claim of duty is as insistent as ever it was. Hume assumes that the motive which originally draws men into society is self-interest, which leads the race on to the establishment of a settled government. The theory of contract will not serve; it is a sheer delusion. The weakness of Hume is, however, the absence of that deep feeling which Butler and Burke associate with the word conscience. By his whole train of reasoning Hume is obliged to give duty a secondary place. Is this its place? Life tells us that it is not. Hume himself, in his treatise *On Morals*, makes an admission which destroys the Utilitarian position: "I cannot forbear adding an observation which may perhaps be found of some importance. In every system of morality which I have hitherto met with I have always remarked that the author proceeds for some time in the ordinary way of reasoning, and establishes the being of God, or makes some observation concerning human affairs; when of a sudden I am surprised to find that, instead of the usual copulation of propositions, *is* and *is not*, I meet with no proposition that is not connected with an *ought* or an *ought not*. This change is imperceptible; but is, however, of the last consequence. For as this *ought* or *ought not* expresses some new relation or affirmation, it is necessary that it should be observed and explained, and at the same time that a reason should be given for what seems altogether incomprehensible, how this new relation can be a deduction from others, which are entirely different from it." Newman dots the i's and strokes the t's of Hume's writing when he remarks that while a man will live and die for the sake of a dogma, no man will be a martyr for the sake of a conclusion. Treitschke was right when he discerned "*das unsterbliche Fortwirken der sittlichen Mächte der Geschichte.*"

A double portion of the spirit of Hume did not descend upon Jeremy Bentham (1748–1832), but a double portion of his influence certainly did, for one of the most influential men of the whole nineteenth century among the English-speaking peoples is this distinguished law-reformer. In his painfully vivid *Father and Son,* Sir Edmund Gosse has depicted the clash of the two generations, which Turgenieff has also set forth in his *Father and Sons,* and this clash was present in the Bentham household. The son was to be one of the most successful law-reformers of history, and the father had destined him to be Lord Chancellor. The father believed that "pushing was the one thing needful in life," and his precocious son was one to whom such pushing was absolutely abhorrent. Shy by nature, he lacked that self-confidence indispensable to the man who desires to leave his mark. He was not a son of Adam but destined to be an Adam in a Paradise of his own creation into which, to be sure, he invited all the sons of men. He had of course the defects of his qualities. In his seclusion he avoided personal bitterness, but did he avoid injustice in his outlook to whole classes? In his want of knowledge of the world he imputed evil motives which were at bottom due to ignorance. He forgot that tact implies contact. Erasmus was his ideal rather than Luther. Beaten in the world of action, our philosopher fell back on his study chair from which he was to modify the laws of mankind. He aspired to be the Newton in the field of reform, and let the pages of history attest the astounding success that attended his efforts.

The range of Bentham's reading as a mere child reminds

us of what J. S. Mill records in his *Autobiography*. His parents were as middle class as their son proved to be, sharing the deep prejudices of that class. They objected to light reading, and when three, the lad read Rapin's *History of England*, later to be followed by such substantial volumes as Burnet's *Theory of the Earth*, and Cave's *Lives of the Apostles*. At six or seven he began to learn French. *Télémaque* proved an unending delight to him, and he records "that romance may be regarded as the foundation of my whole character, the starting-point from whence my career of life commenced, the first dawning in my mind of the principles of utility may, I think, be traced to it." It will be remembered that *Télémaque* was also the starting-point of the French Revolution, little as Fénelon would have liked it. Small in stature, sensitive in nature, and delicate in health, the boy left Westminster School with that most dreadful of legacies, the memory of an unhappy youth. Proficient in composing classical verse, he learnt, like Gibbon, to write more easily in French than in English.

On June 28, 1760, he was admitted at Queen's College, Oxford, when only twelve. He has described the reluctance with which he signed the Thirty-nine Articles. Jeremy and some who shared his doubts were induced to sign by one of the Fellows who reproved their presumption in showing hesitation. The impression made upon him never left him even to the very end of his life. From Oxford he carried away neither pleasurable nor profitable recollections, and in after years he noted that "mendacity and insincerity— in these I found the effects—the sure and only sure effects of an English university education," a verdict with which Adam Smith and Gibbon would have concurred. In his last year at Oxford he may have met John Scott, the future Lord Eldon, a man whose legal views were the exact antipodes of his own. Graduating at the age of sixteen with a taste for logic, he began to eat his dinners at Lincoln's Inn in 1783 when he heard "with rebel ears" Blackstone deliver his commentaries on the laws of England. According to the student's own account, he immediately detected the fallacy of Blackstone in expounding natural rights, and deemed the reasoning as to the gravitating downwards of *haereditas* illogical and futile.

The young barrister did not succeed in his profession. His first brief came from a friend of his father. It was a suit in equity on which fifty pounds depended. The advice he gave was that the suit would be better ended, and the money which would be wasted in the contest saved. His father, like the Elder Fairford in *Redgauntlet*, had "a cause or two at nurse" for the son. The son's first thought was to "put them to death." Other experience simply increased his repugnance to his profession. When he should have been studying case-law he was bent on studying the law of cases, for principles ever meant everything to him. Even in 1773–76 he maintained that "it is impossible for a lawyer to wish men out of litigation, as for a physician to wish them out of health." "Barristers," he them observed, "are so called (a man of spleen might say) from à *barrando*, from barring against reformation the entrances of the law."

There have been many Lord Chancellors: there has been only one Jeremy Bentham. What Darwin effected in physical science, Bentham effected in political science. Like Darwin, he owed his leisure for law to the wealth he inherited. Though he lived the larger part of his days in the eighteenth century, Bentham did not attain his name and fame till the nineteenth, and indeed Dicey places the period of his dominance from 1825 to 1870. He lived to a ripe old age, becoming a sort of institution in England. Capable of grasping general principles, he was no less capable of grasping details in all their complexity. Any thoughtful man can throw out ideas. The real question is, Can he work them out in such detail as to convince the average man? Erasmus Darwin threw out an idea of evolution, but it was Charles Darwin who demonstrated the truth of this principle. A Beccaria sketched ideas in outline, but it required a Bentham to perceive the systematic development of their far-reaching consequences.

The details of the law he lit up by the principle of the greatest happiness of the greatest number. When about twenty he found this formula in a pamphlet of Priestley's and accepted it as the guide of his life. "It was by this pamphlet and this phrase in it," confesses Bentham, "that my principles on the subject of morality, public and private, were determined. It was from that pamphlet and that page of it that I drew the phrase, and the words and import of which have been so widely diffused over the civilised world. At the sight of it I cried out as it were in an inward ecstacy, like Archimedes on the discovery of the fundamental principle of hydrostatics, Εὕρηκα! Little did I think of the corrections I found myself under the necessity of applying to it."

There is a base as well as a noble aspect of Utilitarianism, and the very noblest aspect of it appears in the personal life of Bentham. He asks the question: "Would you appear to be actuated by generous passion? be so.—You need then but show yourself as you are. I would have the dearest friend I have to know, that his interests, if they come into competition with those of the public, are as nothing to me. Thus will I serve my friends—thus would I be served by them. Has a man talents? he owes them to his country in every way in which they can be serviceable." He also asks other questions. "Have I a *genius* for anything? What can I produce?" That was the first enquiry he made of himself. Then came another, "What of all earthly pursuits is the most important?" "Legislation," was the answer Helvetius gave. "Have I a genius for legislation?" Again and again was the question put to himself. He turned it over in his thoughts; he sought every symptom he could discover in his natural disposition or acquired habits. "And have I indeed a genius for legislation? I gave myself the answer, fearfully and tremblingly, 'Yes'."

The bent of Bentham's mind was in the direction of the classification and the reclassification of law. He loved to construct a general chart of legislation, with heads and endless sub-heads, neatly and logically arranged. When a particular point came before his mind, it was his delight to relate it to its main principle with its kindred principles duly exhibited. Then came the connections and the ramifications of the heads and sub-heads till one came to believe that what case-law meant to Lord Mansfield his principles and their heads meant to Bentham. According to Dumont, our philosopher would suspend a whole work and begin a new one because a single proposition struck him as a doubtful. A question in procedure would be sufficient to drive him to investigate the whole subject of judicial organisation. A problem in finance would be sufficient to drive him to investigate the whole subject of Political Economy. To reform law was the be-all and end-all of his days. He hated neither the corruptors of the law nor the corrupted, though he hated with his whole heart the abuses to which they gave rise. His general chart of legislation was, however, very dear to him. In fact, it almost seemed as if for the sake of the exercise of his logical faculties he, a true recluse, valued the principles themselves rather than the reforms to which they contributed. This is the weakness of the solitary, but the strength of the man appears on sending an autograph to Lady Hannah Ellice. "The way to be comfortable," he owned, "is to make others comfortable; the way to make others comfortable is to appear to love them; the way to appear to love them is to love them in reality. *Probatur ab experientia* per Jeremy Bentham, Queen's Square Place, Westminster. Born February 15, anno 1748. Written (this copy) 24 October 1831." He was indeed that rare type of disinterested man who professes no belief in his own disinterestedness. Accordingly, among the last lines he penned were these: "I am a selfish man, as selfish as any man can be. But in me somehow or other, so it happens, selfishness has taken the form of benevolence."

In 1776 Bentham was collecting material for a treatise designed to assault the "lawless science of the law," as expounded by men like Blackstone, under the title of *Critical Elements of Jurisprudence*, the book of which a part was afterwards published as *The Introduction to the Principles of Morals and Legislation*. In the light of its after effects from 1825 to 1870, it is not too much to say that this volume, which is not a great book either in plan or performance, takes rank with such labours of this memorable year as the publication of Adam Smith's *Wealth of Nations*, Gibbon's *Decline and Fall*, and the American Declaration of Independence. Bentham meant his book to be a general introduction to a penal code, but this introduction forced him to consider such other problems as the relations of the penal code to the whole body of law. In turn, the consideration of the whole body of law forced him to settle its connexion with the principles underlying legislation.

In 1776 Bentham published anonymously *A Fragment on Government*. This admirably written exposure of Blackstone's views on the origin of government and law was attributed to Lord Mansfield, Lord Camden, and—by Samuel Johnson—to Dunning. In his *Commentaries*, Blackstone had made the customary appeal to the doctrine of the social compact, and Bentham vehemently assailed this Whig view. The test of political conduct, in his judgment, was neither the Whig doctrine of the social compact nor the Tory one of passive obedience, but it indubitably was none other than the principle of utility. The effective employment of this principle would enable men "to break loose from the trammels of authority and ancestor wisdom on the field of law." Nor is Blackstone's constitutional attitude suffered to escape uncensured. In his opinion, the English Constitution forms the best of all possible governments because it is a happy blend of the monarchical, the aristocratical, and the democratical—the several branches being represented by King, Lords, and Commons, three entirely independent powers. Such an ideal scheme of Mixed Government had been acclaimed by Montesquieu and of course admired by Blackstone. Apply the test of utility. Was it not sorely wanting in attaining the greatest happiness of the greatest number?

In his *Fragment*, its author expounds his theory of sovereignty. "When a number of persons whom we may style subjects are supposed to be in the habit of paying obedience to a person or an assemblage of persons, of a known and certain description whom we may call governor or governors, such persons altogether (subjects and governors) are said to be in a state of political society." "Let us avow then . . . that the authority of the supreme body cannot unless where limited by express convention be said to have any assignable, any certain bounds. That to say there is not any act they cannot do, to speak of anything of theirs as being illegal, as being void; to speak of their exceeding their authority (whatever be the phrase), their power, their right,—is, however common, an abuse of language." Such is the position of a country with a sovereign authority, but there is a country with subordinate authority "where one state has upon terms submitted itself to the government of another; or where the governing bodies of a number of states agree to take directions in certain specified cases from some body or other that is distinct from them all; consisting of members for instance appointed out of each."

Bentham agrees with Hobbes that law is the command of the sovereign, whether one or a body, and that the true marks of sovereignty and subjection are the fact of the bulk or majority of the people being in the *habit* of obedience to the commands of the one or the body, such one or body being sovereign, those obeying subjects. Clearly, Bentham and Hobbes think that sovereignty is unlimited by law; but Bentham does not think with Hobbes that sovereignty is morally unlimited. With Hobbes the sovereign may commit iniquity, but not injustice: with Bentham he may commit iniquity which shares deep delinquency, thus making the sovereign morally limited. Express convention and moral convention set limits to the power of the sovereign. Bentham holds with Austin that a sovereign authority cannot be limited by law, although it may be limited by treaty, with a foreign state, at least to the extent of paying obedience to the occasional commands of its sovereign. Bentham differs from Austin in thinking that the obligation of a federal pact is consistent with the character of a sovereign. In spite of his brilliant attack on Blackstone's book, Bentham was fully aware, as a scholar, of the place it occupied in the minds of English-speaking peoples on both sides of the Atlantic. He pays his tribute to its English: "Correct, elegant, unembarrassed, ornamented, the *style* is such as could scarce fail to recommend a work still more vicious in point of *matter* to the multitude of readers. He it is, in short, who first of all institutional writers has taught Jurisprudence to speak the language of the Scholar and the Gentleman; put a polish upon that rugged science; cleansed her from the dust and cobwebs of the office; if he has not enriched her with that precision that is drawn only from the sterling treasury of the sciences, he has decked her out, however, to advantage, from the toilette of classical erudition; enlivened her with metaphors and allusions; and sent her abroad in some measure to instruct, and in still greater measure to entertain, the most miscellaneous and even the most fastidious societies. The merit to which, as much perhaps as to any, the work stands indebted for its reputation, is the enchanting harmony of its numbers; a kind of merit that of itself is sufficient to give a certain degree of celebrity to a work devoid of every other. So much man is governed by the ear." If to Hobbes the papacy is no other than the ghost of the deceased Roman empire, to Blackstone, in Bentham's opinion, Jurisprudence was the Scarlet Woman of the Law who cared but little for the sacred happiness of the greatest number.

Blackstone never took the trouble to answer the attack made upon him; indeed, his position as a Justice of the Common Pleas made a reply almost impossible. Yet the attack was grossly unfair. Bentham accuses Blackstone of trampling on the right of private judgment, with being the professed champion of religious intolerance, with openly setting his face against civil information. None of this is true. Blackstone set forth in his introduction a theory of law with which Bentham the Utilitarian, who had little right as yet to an opinion on the subject, disagreed; but in the body of the work he painted an exact picture of the law as it stood in the mid-eighteenth century. If there was to be a reform at all, a statement of the actual position of the law was essential; and it is amusing to realise that Bentham secured his first real glimpse of the need for reform from Blackstone's lectures and Blackstone's book. The business of the treatise was not the reformation of the law and of the lawyers. The business of the treatise was diagnosis, not treatment. Blackstone saw perfectly well the evils against which Bentham tilted, the frustration of the law by the costs and delays in legislation. But it was not his task to suggest the detailed methods of reform. It is true that he was hopeful. He believed in a rapid evolution of the English Common Law, which would cleanse it from all impurities and bring it into close approximation to an ideal law.

He was temporarily wrong. He had not foreseen that the process of purification was to be forerun by a process of decay. It is to be noted that that decay was most rampant at the time of Bentham's death in 1832, more than fifty years after the death of Blackstone in 1780; that it was from about the date of Bentham's death that the reform movement began which has reached the Property Statutes of 1925. Neither Blackstone nor Bentham was to see the new world. But Blackstone was more of a prophet than Bentham. He saw quite well that the future lay as much with the judges as with the legislature. He boldly adopted the theories of heredity and environment in relation to law. The law at any moment is the resultant of processes of growth and environment. He saw quite clearly that with liberal-minded judges and a wise legislature the system of law which he describes was capable of achieving, without any fundamental changes, superb things for the human race. The position to-day proves that Blackstone was right; to-day when the common law of England shares with the law of Rome the allegiance of civilisation; to-day when the greater part of the human race dwells in freedom and peace under the shadow of the laws that Blackstone was the first to rationalise and perpetuate. Bentham could not have this outlook, could not adjust his principle of utility to the law of Nature and the law of growth. He could not believe that the English Common Law contained great permanent elements of an ideal code and that the business of the jurist was not to destroy but to fulfil that law. Yet, in the august irony of things, it was Bentham who made Blackstone's dream come true.

Whatever result *A Fragment on Government* exercised on the world, it exercised an important one on Bentham himself, for it led to Lord Shelburne calling on him and introducing him to his guests at Bowood. "Lord Shelburne," declared Bentham with unwonted emphasis, "raised me from the bottomless pit of humiliation—he made me feel that I was something." He threw himself into the amusements of the house, playing the violin to the ladies' accompaniment on the harpsichord. He lost his heart to Caroline Fox though she refused it. Nor did he ever forget his only love. To her he made another offer of marriage in 1805 when they had not met for sixteen years. She replied in a friendly letter, regretting the pain which her refusal inflicted on her devoted lover, who associated her with the happiest time in his life. In a letter written in 1827 he says: "I am alive, more than two months advanced in my eightieth year, more lively than when you presented me in ceremony with a flower in Green Lane. Since that day not a single one has passed, not to speak of nights, in which you have not engrossed more of my thoughts than I could have wished. . . . Embrace ——, though it is for me, as it is for you; she will not be severe, nor refuse her lips to me as she did her hand, at a time, perhaps, not yet forgotten by her, any more than by me." At Bowood, Bentham had met Camden and Pitt, Dunning and Barré, but he had also met Caroline Fox, and it is clear that he never could forget her.

From 1775 Bentham had been meditating on what formed his *Rationale of Punishments and Rewards*, though it was first published in 1811 at Paris under the title of *Théorie des Peines et des Recompenses*. His labours began to attract disciples, and among them were that singularly attractive character, Sir Samuel Romilly, who constituted himself our philosopher's practical adviser, and the chief expounder of his schemes in parliament, and Etienne Dumont, the lifelong editor of his master's voluminous works. Dumont had been pastor of the Huguenot Church of St. Petersburg and a friend of Romilly's. "The plan," Bentham confided in the Duc de Liancourt, "was that Dumont should take my half-finished manuscripts as he found them, half English, half English-French, and make what he could of them in Genevan French, without giving me any further trouble about the matter. Instead of that, the lazy rogue comes to me with everything he writes, and teases me to fill up every gap he has observed." Our highest authority on Bentham, M. Halévy, thinks that this correctly represents the literary relationship of the master to his disciple, and that Dumont exaggerates the importance of *ce travail de fusion*. In his essay on Horace Walpole, Macaulay remarks: "The literature of France has been to ours what Aaron was to Moses, the expositor of great truths which would else have perished for want of a voice to utter them with distinctness. The relation which existed between Mr. Bentham and Dumont is an exact illustration of the intellectual relation in which the two countries stand to each other. The great discoveries in physics, in metaphysics, in political science are ours. But scarcely any foreign nation except France has received them from us by direct communication. Isolated by our situation, isolated by our manners, we found truth, but we did not impart it. France has been the interpreter between England and mankind."

It is a regrettable fact that the old relations between English and French society have virtually ceased to exist. The two aristocracies no longer mingle; Mayfair no longer associates with the Faubourg St. Germain or what remains of it. Social relations between the two countries, which lasted almost continuously for two centuries after the Restoration, have been broken up. We go back to the days when there was an English Court at St. Germain and Bolingbroke became half a Frenchman. We all know how they were followed by the vogue of *le grand tour*, when all sorts and conditions of Englishmen, from Chesterfield to his booby son, from Thomas Gray to Peregrine Pickle, "kept terms" at Paris almost as though it were, what Disraeli afterwards called it, the University of the World. We all know Horace Walpole and David Hume and even Laurence Sterne became familiar figures in Paris society, and how Gibbon became a Parisian for sixty pounds a month, with two footmen in handsome liveries behind his coach and his apartment hung with damask. The historian paid a truly Gibbonian compliment to "the first names and characters of France; who distinguished me by such marks of civility and kindness as gratitude will not suffer me to forget, and modesty will not allow me to enumerate." The letters of Horace Walpole show how the continuity of Anglo-French relations was maintained. Then came the Emigration, to turn the flow of intercourse in the reverse direction. Did not the Emigration make Chateaubriand acquainted with a Holborn garret? Did it not marry General D'Arblay to Fanny Burney? Did it not transport the Chevalier de Blois to Blackheath, where that little sentimental episode happened between Mlle. Léonore (afterwards Mme. de Florac) and Master Tom (afterwards Colonel) Newcome? But quite the happiest effect of the Emigration was its conversion of Mme. de Feuillide *en secondes noces* into Mrs. Henry Austen, and the consequent initiation of Henry's cousin Jane into the mysteries of private theatricals. M. de Feuillide, it will be remembered, had perished by the guillotine; and surely that engine almost stands excused when we consider that without it the world would never have possessed *Mansfield Park*!

Perhaps the relations of French and English society were at their zenith a decade or two after Waterloo, when Lord Monmouth, Coningsby's Lord Monmouth, took a splendid hotel in the Faubourg St. Honoré, near the English Embassy. Then Lady Monmouth was "the fashion at Paris; a great lady, greatly admired." Then her lord declared that "Paris and London ought to be the great objects of all travellers; the rest was mere landscape." How distant all this seems! The brilliant circles of Parisian society may be as fascinating as ever, but young English men of fashion are no longer launched into them. It is noteworthy, too, that the author of *Coningsby* pleaded for that commercial treaty with France which was afterwards to do so much for both countries. Disraeli remarked that the French had to dine off cold plates because of their inferior porcelain. "Now," said he, "if we only had that treaty of commerce with France which has been so often on the point of completion, the fabrics of our unrivalled potteries, in exchange for their capital wines, would be found throughout France. The dinners of both nations would be improved; the English would gain a delightful beverage, and the French, for the first time in their lives, would dine off hot plates. An unanswerable instance of the advantages of commercial reciprocity!"

There used to be intercourse through the channel of art in the days when Constable almost revolutionised French painting by exhibiting "The Hay Wain" in the Salon in 1824, or when Delacroix and Bonington came in 1825 to make friends with Lawrence and Wilkie. French and English men of letters no longer mix. The visits of Voltaire and Rousseau to England may be ancient history, but in the fifties Dickens and Thackeray knew Paris, as the French would say, "like their pocket." Did not Taine come among us taking notes? Did not Paul Bourget spend a term, and, what is more, a "vac." at Oxford, and succeed in understanding that peculiarly English place more completely than any Frenchman before or since? Did not Matthew Arnold go and see Georges Sand at Nohant, and Renan come over for a Hibbert lecture, and Alphonse Daudet alight at an Albemarle Street hotel to find London the most noiseless of European capitals? The World War renewed the old tie, and M. Halévy knows the England of to-day as he knows the England of Bentham.

Friends appeared and championed the cause dear to the heart of the reformer, and inevitably enemies also appeared. Among the latter was Wedderburn, Lord Loughborough, who announced *A Fragment on Government* to be "dangerous." When "this appalling word" came to its author's ears, he was puzzled. How can utility be "dangerous"? Is not this self-contradictory? Bentham solved the puzzle. If the principle of utility prevail, with Wedderburn and his like, "it is all over with us. It is our interest, that the mass of power, wealth, and factitious dignity we enjoy at other people's expense, be as great as possible: it is theirs that it be as small as possible. Judge, then, whether it is not dangerous to *us*. And who should *we* think of but ourselves?" Here the author suffers from his lack of association with men. It never seems to strike him that Wedderburn might be a conservative for reasons which appealed to his intellect. Bentham indeed was to find that his *Fragment* was ill received by Mansfield and Camden, by Dunning and Barré, as well as by Wedderburn.

While at Bowood, Bentham was still engaged in elaborating that massive fragment, *An Introduction to the Principles of Morals and Legislation*, the most readable of all his books. In it he defines the principle of utility as "that property in any object whereby it tends to produce benefit, advantage, pleasure, good, or happiness, or to prevent the happening of mischief, pain, evil, or unhappiness to the party whose interest is considered." "Nature has placed mankind," such is his opening phrase, "under the governance of two sovereign masters, pain and pleasure. It is for them alone to point out what we ought to do, as well as to determine what we shall do." "On the one hand, the standard of right and wrong; on the other, the chains of causes and effects are fastened to their throne. They govern us in all we do, in all we say, in all we think, and the principle of utility recognises their subjection."

The authors of the *Federalist* had set up justice as the end of government. "Why not happiness?" demands Bentham. "What happiness is, every man knows; because what pleasure is, every man knows; and what pain is, every man knows. But what justice is—this is what on every occasion is the subject-matter of dispute." Justice is the means, not the end. Is not that just which produces a maximum of happiness? Let Blackstone appeal, if he pleases, to the social contract. Bentham begs us to look closely at this contract. Does not the obligation to obey it rest on utility? As this is the case, why not appeal to utility at once? I am bound to obey, not because my great-grandfather may be regarded as having made a bargain, which he did not really make, with the great-grandfather of George III; but simply because rebellion does more harm than good. "It is the principle of utility," so our philosopher insists, "accurately apprehended and steadily applied, that affords the only clue to guide a man through streights." With point and pungency he proceeds in his examination of such principles as the "ascetic" principle, Adam Smith's doctrine of "sympathy," Francis Hutcheson's "moral sense," James Beattie's "common sense," Richard Price's appeal to the "understanding," and Samuel Clarke's appeal to the "fitness of things."

The "ascetic" principle, we learn, declares pleasure to be evil, and such a principle, consistently carried out, would turn earth into hell. At bottom it really resolves itself into the principle of utility, for it turns out to mean that certain pleasures can only be bought at an excessive cost of pain. The general criticism Bentham passes on the other theories is that they fundamentally make the opinion of the individual thinker an ultimate and sufficient standard. They are all really subjective, and what Bentham demands is an objective test. By his doctrine of "sympathy" Adam Smith makes the sentiment of approval itself the ultimate standard. My feeling echoes yours, and reciprocally. Yet how can each derive authority from the other? Hutcheson invents a thing made on purpose to tell him what is right and wrong. This he calls a "moral sense." Beattie substitutes "common" for "moral" sense, and attracts followers because every man assumes himself to possess that uncommon quality, common sense. Why should he, or Price, or Clarke, invent phrases? Others make their due appeal to the "Law of Nature," or "Right Reason," or "Natural Justice," or anything else you please. In Bentham's judgment, each phrase at bottom means that whatever its author says is infallibly true and self evident. Indeed the "fairest and openest of them all" is the man who simply says, "I am of the number of the Elect"; "God tells the Elect what is right: therefore if you want to know what is right, you have only to come to me."

From asceticism, antipathy, and all the rest of them, Bentham turns to utility, which is unquestionably, in his opinion, objective. The four sanctions or sources of pleasure and pain, analysed in his *Introduction to the Principles of Morals*, physical, political, moral or popular and religious —are defined. It is shown that "the value of a lot of pleasure or pain," our two sovereign masters, is to be measured according to its intensity, its duration, its certainty, its propinquity or remoteness, its fecundity or chance of not being followed by sensations of the opposite sort, and its extent or the number of persons affected by it. Bentham analyses pleasures and pains, and considers the reasons for treating certain actions as crimes. Starting from the principle that the object of all laws is the total happiness of the community, he observes, "All punishment is mischief; all punishment in itself is evil. Upon the principle of utility, if it ought at all to be admitted, it ought only to be admitted so far as it promises to exclude some greater evil." To apply this principle, to distinguish cases unmeet for punishment, to preserve a proportion between punishment and offences, to classify the latter, to determine the fields of ethics and jurisprudence, forms the object of the rest of *An Introduction to the Principles of Morals and Legislation*.

Jeremy Bentham, in August, 1785, set out for Russia in order to pay a visit to his brother Samuel who was then trying to transplant the civilisation of England, ready-made, into the hearts of the men on Prince Potemkin's estate. There he lived for nearly two years in a state of seclusion, attempting to gain the attention of that enlightened despot, Catherine of Russia, on behalf of his plan of the codification of law. A hermit abroad as at home, he shone as an analyst, not as an observer, and indeed his travels affected his mode of thought as little as they affected Macaulay's. Bentham penned his striking *Defence of Usury* at the beginning of 1787, in which he set forth the principle, which was to form the leading principle of *laissez-faire*, that no man of ripe years, of sound mind, acting freely and with his eyes open, ought to be hindered, with a view to his advantage, from making such bargain in the way of obtaining money as he thinks fit. He converted Adam Smith by his denouncement of usury laws, and Smith pronounced this book to be the work of a superior man. " He has given me some hard knocks," Adam Smith admitted, " but in so handsome a manner that I cannot complain." Usury laws had existed for three thousand years, and at last—till our own day—they came to an end.

Samuel Bentham had planned an inspection house or "Panopticon" for the supervision of industry, and Jeremy turned it to the employment of prison discipline. For years his energies were concentrated on this scheme, which he advocated with all the fervour of a prophet. Adopt the "Panopticon" and you will have "morals reformed, health preserved, industry invigorated, instruction diffused, public burdens lightened, economy seated as it were upon a rock, the Gordian knot of the poor laws not cut but untied, all by a simple idea in architecture." This simple idea proved to be the construction of a gaol such that all its parts should be visible from a single point by means of a series of reflectors. By these mirrors the inspector, himself concealed from the observation of the prisoners in order to give rise to "the sentiment of an invisible omniscience," would be able at a glance to see everything that was taking place. Plainly, the author of such a scheme was the contemporary of Arkwright and Watt.

The general principles of the new device of prison reform were laid down: so too were the details. A contractor was to undertake the support of the inmates of the "Panopticon" at a certain sum per head, reserving to himself all profits to be derived from their labour. The manager was bound to insure the lives of all who were entrusted to his care; that is, he was to be obliged to pay a sum for every one beyond a certain average lost to the prison by death or escape. With all the confidence of a prophet he proposed in March, 1792, to the Government to be responsible for a thousand convicts under the Panopticon scheme. He obtained a grant of £2000, an amount he was spending yearly on his plan while his own income was under £600 a year. Though Pitt gave the project favourable consideration, yet in 1795 William Wilberforce described Bentham as "dying of sickness of hope deferred." In 1813 he was awarded £23,000 as compensation for the expenses he had incurred. If he never forgot Caroline Fox, he never forgot a plan on the success of which he had staked as much as Howard or any other prison reformer. Within a few months of his death he owned that his heart sank within him whenever the current of his thought chanced to alight upon the Panopticon and its fate. "I cannot look among Panopticon papers," he used to say, "it is like opening a drawer where devils are locked up—it is breaking into a haunted house."

The individualism of Bentham appears in countless ways, and it comes out in the criticism passed on the Panopticon by the Parliamentary Committee appointed to investigate it. Its members pointed out that the whole system turned upon the profit to be made from the labour of the criminals by Bentham and his brother. With men of their high sense of honour, it would of course work well, but what if their successors manifested a less high sense of honour? The Committee were aware that the adoption of this method of "farming" had in fact led to gross abuses in gaols as well as in workhouses. Such an obvious criticism never seems to have occurred to Bentham, for it was altogether in keeping with his general individualist position. The disappointed devisor had learnt once more how dilatory, how evasive, the average official could be, and henceforth not a little of his reforming zeal was spent in exorcising the demon of officialism.

The astonishing portent of the French Revolution of 1789 attracted the attention—how could it avoid doing so?—of Bentham. Romilly had prepared for the use of the States-General an account of the procedure of the House of Commons. With the aid of Dumont, it was translated into French. When Mirabeau laid it before the deputies at the opening of the States-General they exclaimed with one voice, "*Nous ne sommes pas des Anglais, et nous n'avons pas besoin des Anglais.*" Undeterred by this reception, Bentham prepared his *Political Tactics*, setting forth the principles underlying the conduct and the discipline of political assemblies. Shortly after the meeting of the National Assembly, Dumont wrote that the plan of parliamentary tactics had been shown to Mirabeau and the Duc de la Rochefoucauld, who both expressed their admiration of the "truly philosophic conception." Employing extracts from Bentham's unpublished manuscripts in University College, London, M. Halévy thinks that the reformer was even then working out what may be called a radical essay on representation. Though our reformer was by no means a believer then in democratic government, M. Halévy suggests that Bentham was thinking out his ideas for Mirabeau, and naturally approached the subject from a French angle. Hence Bentham contended that "for France, the constitution that the Father of the People should strive to establish is simply democracy, but under the shelter and protection of a monarchy." The average Utilitarian believed that the constitution of any country would suit any other country, yet Bentham maintained that "the English Constitution is admirable for the English or for the French. The American Constitution is, in itself, still better, but it would not suit either of those nations." This, however, is a height of political wisdom to which Bentham seldom soared. With the desire of acknowledging the assistance proffered, the National Assembly in 1792 bestowed on him the title of Citizen of France, a title they also offered to Washington and Wilberforce.

The attitude of the great Utilitarian to history is quite obvious. He regarded it as little better than an almanac out of date, registering what he and Voltaire looked on as the follies and crimes of mankind. Montesquieu had taught that "laws ought to be so closely adapted to the people for which they are made that it is very improbable that the laws of one nation can ever be suited to the wants of another nation." A constitution must express character, the character of the people who are to work it. Bentham, however, assumed in legislation what J. S. Mill assumed in Political Economy, viz. that all human beings, be their race what it may, are fundamentally the same in their requirements. In 1793 Bentham declared that he could legislate for India as easily as for his own parish, and not a few of our mistakes in that continent have arisen from a declaration like this. He was as ready to devise codes for Spain, Russia, and Morocco as he was for England. Superficially the Spaniard, the Russian, and the Moroccan may differ, but essentially they are all alike. In fact, man is always and everywhere the same in essence, no matter how he differs in accidents. One man is, then, the same as another man. A nation is simply an aggregate of men. The individual wants to be happy: the aggregate of individuals also want to be happy. The happiness Bentham conceives as in store for them is that of a middle-class Englishman like himself.

The study of history reveals how the ideals of men have been constantly changing. In classical antiquity the foremost virtue was the civic. With the rise of Christianity and other religions in the East the contemplative virtues replaced the civic. With the decline of the ascetic virtues the very different ideal of chivalry emerged. So we might survey the pages of history, assuredly not finding the Benthamic standard of happiness in the past. The truth is that there is such a thing as national character, and that the character of each country is different. There are such things as national prepossessions which no process of abstract reasoning can divine. Why should the Englishman prefer liberty? Why should the Frenchman prefer equality? Why should the Irish own such a hunger for land? Why should the American patiently tolerate corruption in government? On the answers to such questions depends the character of the laws each country requires, and these answers are absolutely ignored by Bentham. The verdict of Sir Henry Maine is sound. "No geniuses of an equally high order so completely divorced themselves from history as Hobbes and Bentham."

In the days to come, Bentham was to turn to radicalism, but in the closing decade of the eighteenth century he is a conservative reformer. He then cared for the advance of law reform, not for the advance of liberty. Nor were red ruin and the breaking up of laws at any time to his mind. No doubt M. Halévy has unearthed some unpublished manuscripts, written at this time in French, in which Bentham showed his readiness to criticise "*le galimatias de la répresentation virtuelle*," and his desire to look favourably on secret voting and the lowering of the franchise. It is plain, however, that our philosopher argued that so long as a man has any assured property to lose, there is little fear of his fancying it in his interest to ally himself with those who possess nothing at all, for the purpose of bringing about an equal division of property; since this means nothing less than the destruction of all property. He insisted with Hume that the principle of the security of property was fundamental. If security and equality are in conflict, equality must give way. M. Halévy comes indeed to admit that throughout the French Revolution Bentham displayed "hostile indifference" to the tenets of the Jacobins. His attitude was "Fraternity, if you will; but Equality, no." It would need violence to preserve it—and as to Liberty, subjection, not independence, is the natural state of man.

Bentham had many a *bête noire*, and prominent among them is his deep-seated enmity to natural right. So early as 1789 he had written to Brissot: "I am sorry you have undertaken to publish a Declaration of Rights. It is a metaphysical work, the *ne plus ultra* of metaphysics. It may have been a necessary evil—but it is nevertheless an evil." Nor did the confiscation of Church property by the revolutionists lead him to esteem more highly the view that men had innate rights, for his dear doctrine of security was thereby imperilled. According to the French Declaration of Rights, "*Men (all men) are born free, and equal in respect of rights. Social distinctions cannot be founded, but upon common utility.*" Here is a specimen of Bentham's criticism. "*All men are born free? All men remain free?* No, not a single man; not a single man that ever was, or is, or will be. All men, on the contrary, are born in subjection, and the most absolute subjection—the subjection of a helpless child to the parents on whom he depends every moment of his existence. In this subjection every man is born—in this subjection he continues for years—and the existence of the individual and of the species depends on his so doing. . . ."

"That which has no existence cannot be destroyed—that which cannot be destroyed cannot require anything to preserve it from destruction. *Natural rights* is simple nonsense: natural and imprescriptible rights, rhetorical nonsense,—nonsense upon stilts. But this rhetorical nonsense ends in the old strain of mischievous nonsense: for immediately a list of these pretended natural rights is given, and those are so expressed as to present to view legal rights. And of these rights, whatever they are, there is not, it seems, any one of which any government *can*, upon any occasion whatever, abrogate the smallest particle."

Liberty, in the judgment of Jeremy Bentham, is the simple absence of coercion, though a wider knowledge of the world than he possessed taught others that liberty is anything but simple. Liberty, we learn, is purely negative, merely a branch of security. Personal liberty, so our individualist holds, is security against a certain species of injury which affects the person, while political liberty is security against the injustice of the members of the Government. Liberty, at bottom, rests on the restraints not being imposed on ourselves. Security rests on restraints being imposed on others. In fact, where there is no coercion there is none of that liberty which is produced by law. "Is it by all coercion, then, that liberty is produced? By no means. It is only by restraint. Is it, then, by restraint? Is it by restraining a man from any sort of acts that it may be produced? By no means. But of those acts alone by which, were he to do them, he would restrain the liberty of another man; and then it is plain, it is not in that man whose acts it restrains that it produces liberty, but in the other."

Lord Acton, in elaborating the proposition that slavery itself is a stage on the road to freedom, wrote: "A century ago it was perfectly well known that whoever had an audience of a Master in Chancery was made to pay for three, but no man heeded the enormity until it suggested itself to a young lawyer that it might be well to question and examine with rigorous suspicion every part of the system in which such things were done. The day on which that gleam lighted up the clear hard mind of Jeremy Bentham is memorable in the political calendar beyond the entire administration of many statesmen." But Bentham's zeal for legal reform— and for liberty—would have been useless unless he had linked it on to something that appealed to the popular imagination. Most legal reformers blush unseen and waste their bitterness in the juridical or medical press. Not so Bentham. He attached his besom to the most popular star in the night-sky of mankind—the star of happiness for every one. Lord Acton recalls one of Bentham's cheeriest witticisms: "Jeremy Bentham used to relate how he found the greatest happiness principle in 1768, and gave a shilling for it, at the corner of Queen's Square. He found it in Priestley, and he might have gone on finding it in Beccaria and Hutcheson, all of whom trace their pedigree to the 'Mandragola'." So Lord Acton links Bentham with that supreme realist Machiavelli and his *Il Principe*. Maine sees the star in the Benthamic firmament through another telescope. "The secret of Bentham's immense influence in

England during the past thirty years is his success in placing such an (distinct) object before the country. He gave us a clear rule of reform. . . made the good of the community take precedence of every other object, and thus gave escape to a current which had long been trying to find its way outward."

In 1793 Bentham addressed a characteristically Utilitarian pamphlet to the National Assembly entitled *Emancipate your Colonies*! His argument is that trade is the child of capital. It is, then, the quantity of capital, not the extent of the market, that determines the quantity of trade. Nor does he rely on theoretical reasons, for he appeals to experience. Before the separation of the United States from Britain, the latter owned the monopoly of trade with the thirteen colonies. On the separation she lost this monopoly. How much less is their trade with Britain now than then? So far from being less, it is greater.

The man of thought lives in a world which may not touch his own generation, but which will touch the generations to come. At the same time it is not a little singular how keenly the man of thought envies the man of action his sphere. Sir Walter Scott desired nothing so much as to be a great man of affairs. It was noteworthy how warmly dons in the universities of Cambridge and Oxford embraced the life of action during the war, and found deep contentment in it. Inspired by feelings like these, Bentham ardently desired to take an active part in French affairs. In 1789 he suggested to Wilberforce that as they were English "French citizens," they should set out on a mission to Paris. When this failed, he conceived a strong impulse to enter the House of Commons. It was not enough that he could influence the House through his friend Romilly: he wanted to exercise his influence in person. Accordingly, he addressed himself to Lord Lansdowne, who was his old friend Lord Shelburne, and he failed to provide the necessary pocket-borough. Aristotle, who cared for the State as if it were himself, could find a kindred soul in the great Utilitarian. Our mind instinctively turns to Edmund Burke. What William Burke said of him in 1766 was true of him throughout his life:—"Ned is full of real business, intent upon doing good to his country, as much as if he was to receive twenty per cent. from the Empire." It was every whit as true of Bentham throughout his life. The passion for justice was as intense in Bentham as it was in Burke. The former quotes the Magna Charta that justice shall be denied to no man, and that justice shall be sold to no man. Denied it is, avowed Bentham, to nine-tenths of the people; to the remaining tenth it is sold at an unconscionable price—a sale by the State as pernicious, in point of political effect, as one for the benefit of a king or a judge.

Since Dumont had met the reformer he had been engaged in the task of educing cosmos out of the chaos of his immense mass of manuscripts. In 1802 Dumont published in three volumes the *Traités de Legislation*. In it the main subjects were the principles of the Civil and the Penal Code. "It is very entertaining," confided Romilly in Dumont, "to hear Bentham speak of it. He says that he is very impatient to see the book, because he has a great curiosity to know what his own opinions are upon the subjects you treat of." In an age when the theft of a chicken was a capital offence, when law was saturated with the feeling of an eye for an eye and a tooth for a tooth, it was the mark of a great mind to lay down the true principles of punishment. Montesquieu had adhered to the ancient doctrine of retaliation, and it is not the least of our philosopher's merits that he completely broke away from it. This "reasoning by antipathy," as he phrased it, is but an irrational subjection to the blind impulses of anger and revenge which have in all ages obscured the vision of judges and legislators. The real end to be attained is the protection of society, not the torment of the offender. While the immediate object is the punishment of the culprit, the ultimate one is the benefit of mankind by the repression of crime.

The success of the *Traités* was rapid. As many copies of it had been sold in St. Petersburg as in London, so Dumont reported. The Empress Dowager expressed a wish that Dumont, who was paying a visit to St. Petersburg in 1803, should be presented to her, and orders were given for a careful translation of the *Traités* into Russian. Russian officials wrote glowing letters in which Bentham was placed in a line with Bacon, Newton, and Adam Smith—each the founder of a new science. "You will be pleased," wrote Lord Lansdowne to Lord Holland, "that Dumont and Bentham's book is likely to make its way and lay the foundations of a new science in Legislation." Parr informed Bentham, "I am sure you would not have been sorry to hear what passed between (Fox) and myself about your mighty talents, your profound researches, your important discoveries, your irresistible arguments."

Bentham's circle of friends increased as his reputation increased. As of old, Romilly and Dumont were important members of it. There were such new faces in it as James Mill, perhaps the ablest man in it, David Ricardo, whom Bentham looked on as the disciple rather than the master of Mill, Henry Brougham, intriguing for invitations to dinner at the "Hermitage," Sir James Mackintosh, the philosophic historian, Joseph Hume, the relentless reformer, and Daniel O'Connell, the prince of agitators. Obviously, our thinker exercised through agents the power he could not exercise through himself. Romilly, Dumont, and Mill formed the inner circle. Romilly records his visit to Ford Abbey, near Chard, in 1817: "I was not a little surprised to find in what a palace my friend was lodged. The grandeur and stateliness of the buildings form as strange a contrast to his philosophy as the number and spaciousness of the apartments, the hall, the chapel, the corridors, and the cloisters do to the modesty and scantiness of his domestic establishment. We found him passing his time, as he always has been passing it since I have known him, which is now more than thirty years, closely applying himself, for six or eight hours a day, in writing upon laws and legislation, and in composing his Civil and Criminal Codes; and spending the remaining hours of every day in reading, or taking exercise by way of fitting himself for his labours, or, to use his own strangely invented phraseology, 'taking his ante-jentacular and post-prandial walks,' to prepare himself for his task of codification. There is something burlesque enough in the language; but it is impossible to know Bentham, and to have witnessed his benevolence, his disinterestedness, and the zeal with which he has devoted his whole life to the service of his fellow-creatures, without admiring and revering him." His friends came to see him: the world was kept at a respectful distance. Madame de Stael applied to Dumont for an introduction, saying, "Tell Bentham I will see nobody till I have seen him." "Sorry for it," grumbled the hermit, "for then she will never see anybody."

The seclusion of the reformer led him to form his characteristically harsh judgments. Burke was a madman, an incendiary, a caster of verbal filth, and possessed by the "unqualified thirst for lucre." Johnson was "the miserable and misery-propagating ascetic and instrument of despotism." He wished that Goldsmith had never written *The Deserted Village*. Poetry he defined as "misrepresentation." He discriminated to Lord Holland on the difference between prose and poetry. "But, sir,—oh, yes, my Lord—I know the difference. *Prose* is where all the lines but the last go on the margin—poetry is where some of them fall short of it." We are not surprised to hear that he found Socrates "insipid" and Plato "a philosophy of words." We are more surprised to hear that "before Montesquieu all was unmixed barbarism." Bentham disliked judiciary law, and accordingly judges in making law were guilty of a deliberate usurpation of legislative power. J. S. Mill, who was naturally upset to read such judgments, tenders his explanation. "It is indispensable to a correct estimate of any of Bentham's dealings with the world, to bear in mind that in everything except abstract speculation he was to the last . . . essentially a boy. He had the freshness, the simplicity, the confidingness, the liveliness and activity, all the delightful qualities of boyhood, and the weaknesses which are the reverse side of those qualities—the undue importance attached to trifles, the habitual mismeasurement of the practical bearing and value of things, the readiness to be either delighted or offended on inadequate cause. These were the real sources of what was unreasonable in some of his attacks on individuals . . .; they were no more than the freaks of a pettish child, and are scarcely a fitter subject of censure or criticism."

There is a youthfulness in Bentham's outlook on moral philosophy which has not stood the test of time. His scheme sought to maximise pleasure and minimise pain. He came to see that the greatest happiness of the greatest number was a phrase wanting in clearness and precision. He therefore substituted the expression the greatest happiness, dismissing "the greatest number" as superfluous. His argument implies that there is a felicific calculus, and moral pathometer if you like, weighing the elements of value in the good and evil of the consequence which actions tend to produce. But is there such a calculus? We know of none. On the other hand, Butler maintained that we can determine immediately whether an action is right or wrong without regard to consequences, by a faculty called conscience, a faculty partly moral, partly intellectual. The world recognises the existence of this faculty, though Bentham denies it. Nor can we pass by the theory of natural law with its two thousand years of history lying behind it. This law had inculcated the virtues of mercy and justice, veracity and gratitude. In civil law it had exercised an incomparable sway, and in moral law its sway had been scarcely less potent. Bentham completely disregards conscience and natural law. He had defined the four sanctions of pleasures and pains, and he had analysed the value of each by its measure of intensity, duration, and the like. But are all pleasures reducible to something common? Do they differ simply in intensity? Is there no difference in kind? Croce remarks that the Utilitarians reduce all mental activities to feeling, and, having effected this reduction, they do not see anything except pain or pleasure in any activity. Is the delight of poetry reducible, as Bentham reduced it, to the delight derivable from push-pin? Is it a fact that pleasures and pains are commensurable? Can we compare either of our sovereign masters quantitatively? If we cannot so compare them, the indispensable moral pathometer is unobtainable. Nor can we overlook the consideration that the philosopher who makes morality consist in the calculation of consequences, in calculating for our happiness, loses the main element in it. He forgets that we must have experienced feelings before we begin to calculate about those feelings; that unless we are animated and inspired by a virtuous energy to start with, it is perfectly vain to put forward such an energy, and the happiness attending it, as a goal at which we ought to aim. If the test is the greatest happiness, it is certainly difficult to apply it in the moral sphere. Bentham assumes the business aspect of human affairs as if it covered the whole of them. More comprehensively, Marshall, in his *Principles of Economics*, assumes this aspect, but he also assumes the sphere of religion. Bentham attacks theology, not religion—this is a vital difference—and in his attack on theology he contrives to ignore the existence of the power of sacrifice in human nature. Some possess this power in a pre-eminent degree, but the World War demonstrated how much of it remains within us all. The life of Buddha, with its voluntary renunciation; the life of Francis of Assisi, with its marriage to the Lady Poverty; the life of Voltaire, with its service on behalf of justice; the life of Faraday, with its single-minded devotion to science—all exhibited, in varying degree, the spirit of self-sacrifice. But are not these among the giants of the race? Yes, they are. The heroism manifested on all sides by all ranks from 1914–18 is fresh in the memory of all. We can go back to men like-minded with those of our day. The three hundred Spartans who fell at Thermopylae, the death of Judas Maccabaeus at Eleasa, the Jewish Thermopylae, the Swiss who fell at St. Jacob, the battles of Balaclava and Gravelotte, the soldiers and sailors on board the *Birkenhead*—all exhibit, in varying degree, the spirit of self-sacrifice. Bentham speaks of general happiness, yet it is to the credit of mankind that the power of sacrifice makes a far more effective appeal. Tertullian was wiser far than he dreamt when he boldly said "*Semen est sanguis Christianorum :* the blood of martyrs is indeed a source of life." This saying is as true of the State as of the Church. The past creates the spirit of the present. For the examples of the giant like Faraday and of the average man like the cavalry soldier at Balaclava attests that:

> There shall never be one lost good.

Such men save us from the awful vision of the Roman moralist:

Virtutem videant intabescantque relicta.

A Bentham may retort that his attitude is similar to General Bosquet's. "*C'est magnifique, mais ce n'est pas la guerre.*" But what if it is magnificent and if it is war, the war that the soul wages against the body? No system of moral philosophy is satisfying which excludes the power of sacrifice. In the last public utterance of Mazzini he boldly proclaimed: "Every existence has an aim. Life, human life, has achieved the consciousness of this fact; life is therefore a mission—the mission of reaching the aim: it consists in incessant activity upon the path towards it, and a perennial battle against the obstacles it encounters upon that path. The Ideal is not within, but beyond us, and supreme over us: it is not a *creation*, but the gradual *discovery*, of the human intellect."

If we descend to mundane matters the test of the greatest happiness is assuredly difficult of application. Take the institution of property which Bentham defends because it tends towards the greatest happiness. Is it to the interest of the born burglar and swindler to respect it? How is either, on our philosopher's principles, immoral? Granted he is a bad citizen, yet on the calculation of pains and pleasures either has decided against the institution of property. If he is a born burglar, he feels under no obligation to obey the laws which will leave him to starve. He burgles where he can, weighing the chances of detection against the hopes of escape. In fact, if you remove conscience, as Bentham does, there is no such thing as right or wrong, moral or immoral, acts. There are of course acts generally useful or useless. If the burglar is caught, it is simply a miscalculation on his part. Vice, in truth, is only a miscalculation of chances. Nor is the Benthamic view of punishment in a very much stronger position. Doubtless too much stress had been laid on the instinctive desire for the punishment of the offender, yet such a desire is universal. We all feel that justice must be done. Take away this desire, and is there any moral justification for legal punishment, but the benefit of society? It is open of course to Bentham to argue that when one of two interests is inconsistent with the other, the smaller should yield to the greater, the weal of the burglar to the larger weal of society. It is, however, a position inconsistent with the fundamental utilitarian principle, for it is neither proved nor self-evident that the true test of right action is its tendency to produce the happiness of the majority. If Proudhon holds that property is theft, it is simply necessary for thieves to be in the majority, and in the eyes of Bentham this Frenchman's conclusion is surely proved—provided that there is neither conscience nor natural justice. As our thinker denies conscience and natural justice, it follows that his theory of morals is weak and non-moral. It also follows that his theory of punishment rests in the last resort on the right of the strongest. Butler, so it seems, occupies a far more impregnable position, for his faculty of conscience rests in the last resort on the constitution of human nature.

If everybody is to count for one, nobody for more than one, a man inevitably pursues his own weal. In its pursuit he usually includes his family and his friends, his party, and his church. If he is rather selfish, he may not adopt this course. On utilitarian principles, why should he? Such conduct gains him no pleasure and loses him some. Joan of Arc loves her country and John Howard loves mankind, each rendering that love and service of humanity of which Comte dreamt. The average individual does not soar to this lofty level. Even if he did, and if the test is general happiness, how is he to secure such happiness? It is possible to secure our own happiness: it is impossible to secure the happiness of others. In *The Mill on the Floss*, George Eliot remarks, "We can't choose happiness either for ourselves or for another; we can't tell where that will lie. We can only choose whether we will indulge ourselves in the present moment, or whether we will renounce that for the sake of obeying the Divine voice within us, for the sake of being true to all the motives that sanctify our lives." Even such renunciation has often led to grave infraction on the liberty of others. Indeed the extent to which the interference of other folks has diminished the weal of the individual is quite incalculable. The lines Johnson added to Goldsmith's *Traveller* lay this bare:—

> How small, of all that human hearts endure,
> That part which laws or kings can cause or cure!
> Still to ourselves in every place consigned,
> Our own felicity we make or find.
> With secret course, which no loud storms annoy,
> Glides the smooth current of domestic joy.

We turn from the impracticable—and mischievous, if applicable—dream of Bentham to the sober reality of Butler. The Utilitarian had asked us to work for the greatest happiness: the divine expounds it in his sermon: "Upon the Love of our Neighbour." Butler reminds us that to love our neighbour as ourself must in reason be understood to mean that first a due provision is made for self, for our own happiness, "because we are in a peculiar manner . . . intrusted with ourselves; and therefore care for our own interest as well as of our conduct particularly belongs to us." Thereafter the "more of our care and thought and fortune" is devoted to others, the closer we come to the counsel of perfection—to love our neighbour as ourself. Reason, he explains, points out that our benevolence should not be indiscriminate. Our efforts must be confined to our neighbourhood, that "children and families" come first in our regards; and that "friendship or former obligation" require that we do good to some, preferably to others. There is no precise pathometer here, but there are indications laid down for our guidance which are of more practical use than any reference to the greatest happiness principle. The world of morals is closed to Bentham: the world of legislation is open to him. "Assume," asked Sir Henry Maine, "assume a numerous and tolerably homogeneous community—assume a sovereign whose commands take a legislative shape—assume great energy, actual or potential, in this legislature, the only possible, the only conceivable principle which can guide legislation on a great scale is the greatest happiness of the greatest number." T. H. Green did not bestow his philosophic blessings lightly, and he does not hesitate to call Utilitarianism the moral theory that has been of most public service in modern Europe.

"Whatever the errors arising from its hedonistic psychology, no other theory has been available, for the social and political reformer, containing so much truth with such ready applicability. No other has offered so commanding a point of view from which to criticise the precepts and institutions presented as authoritative."

The mind of the reformer demanded a *tabula rasa* on which was to be written a new utilitarian law by a new lawgiver, by the Moses of the day, by Bentham himself, sent out by the heaven of his own Utilitarian imagination. At the opening of the nineteenth century he sent a message to the American nation, then a quarter of a century old. He begged them "to shut their ports against the Common Law as they would against the Plague." It was a stirring and disquieting message, and it shows exactly the difference between Bentham and Blackstone. Blackstone sent a very different and earlier message, his *Commentaries*; and the shrewd American people accepted the latter. To-day America is the second home of the Common Law; and pilgrims from that home in 1924 visited the original hearth and have given to England a statue of the great man who gave America the law that Bentham regarded as the plague. Yet we must not forget that he had grounds for his denunciation of the Common Law in its then tattered and corrupt garments. He announced this demand for a *tabula rasa*, and he renounced the Common Law because he was a lawyer as well as a philosopher.

In Europe the criminal law was obsolete, resting on custom and tradition, and sustained by forces interested in the survival of both. Bentham attacked it at its base by going back to first principles and examining its functions and operations in the light of its services to mankind. What is the object of law in general, he demanded, and of punishments in particular? What are the conditions best calculated to attain that object? How far does the existence of the law fulfil them, what are its defects, and how should they be amended? This treatment of the problem is radical; it is broad enough to furnish a test for all particular cases and profound enough to be a source of inspiration for advance in an indefinite future. Punishment should suffice for the prevention of similar offences, but it must not be in excess of what is absolutely necessary, a condition which called for the instant repeal of statute after statute in force. The pain of the punishment must preponderate over the pleasure of the crime. Appropriate legal punishments are services imposed on the criminal for the benefit of society, and from this angle punishment is the debt the wrongdoer owes and must needs discharge.

Bentham's ceaseless energy directed itself to the law of evidence, and James Mill prepared an *Introductory View*; but more than one bookseller declined to be responsible for its publication, fearing lest it should be held to constitute a libel on the administration of justice. In 1827, in five volumes, appeared the *Rationale of Evidence*, under the editorship of J. S. Mill. It is a terribly prolix book, and this largely arises from Bentham's habit of applying his doctrine at full length to every case his fertile brain can imagine. What means can be adopted to secure the truth of evidence? What rules can be laid down for estimating the probability of the truth in evidence? Should a witness be cross-examined? Should his evidence be recorded? Should a wife be allowed to tender evidence against her husband? Should the defendant tender evidence? These and innumerable other points are tried by the test of utility. His answers to such questions provide an exhaustive —and exhausting—exposition, lightened by cogent argument. His rule is to take any evidence you can get, though, curiously enough, he admits an exception of confession to a Roman Catholic priest, as he thinks that secrecy in such cases is on the whole useful. The abuses of the time were monstrous. Under Eldon, he holds, "equity has become an instrument of fraud and extortion." Eldon, in his opinion, was worse than Jeffreys. Eldon's victims died a lingering death, and the persecutor had made money out of their sufferings. Jeffreys was openly brutal; while Eldon covered his tyranny under the "most accomplished indifference." In the considered judgment of Romilly the Court of Chancery was "a disgrace to a civilised nation," and Eldon was the cause of many abuses in it, and could have reformed most of the others. Romilly and Erskine were practising barristers, and they were familiar with the legal evils of which they complained. Erskine indeed went so far as to declare that if there was a hell, the Court of Chancery was hell. Bentham gives statistics showing that in the year 1797, five hundred and forty-three out of five hundred and fifty "writs of error" were "shams," or simply vexatious contrivances for delay, and brought a profit to the Chief Justice of over £1400. Romilly narrates a case which came under his notice in 1807, as Solicitor-General, where an innocent young man, charged with mutiny on the *Hermoine* in 1797, thinking to excite the compassion of his judges, in effect admitted his guilt, but pleaded extreme youth and his dread of the mutineers. His relatives procured from the Navy Office a certificate attesting that at the time of the mutiny he was serving as a boy on board the *Marlborough*, far from the scene of the offence alleged against him. In spite of this, he was sentenced to death and executed. In ordinary cases of felony, involving penalties of death or transportation, the counsel for the prisoner was not, until 1836, permitted to address the jury on any of the facts charged against his client. Bentham put all his strength in the securing of publicity, "the soul of justice," for he rightly regarded it as the safeguard of testimony. Justice, he contended, must appear before the bar of opinion as well as exist. "The most tyrannical magistrate," he avowed, "becomes moderate, the most daring circumspect, when exposed to the view of all, he feels that he cannot pronounce a judgment without being judged himself."

Bentham was eager to advance his plan for the codification of law. The distance between himself and his contemporary Savigny can be measured in part by the book of the latter, *On the Mission of our Time in Legislation and Jurisprudence*. Published in 1814, Savigny, taking up the views of Montesquieu, showed that laws are the exact reflection of the life of a people, that they have never been imposed by legislators, but that they have arisen from the nation itself. Saturated with the historic spirit, he decisively pronounced against codification. He condemned in politics all *a priori* notions, all abstract principles in the name of which reforms might be introduced. The change must first come in the mind of the nation, an attitude as familiar to Blackstone as it was unfamiliar to Bentham, and the people themselves will show us their true needs in the light of their past. To Savigny national character and its causes were everything, to Bentham merely nothing.

The widespread fame of the reformer aided his zeal for codification. During his lifetime his influence was probably more felt abroad than at home. This was due to the work of his worshipper Dumont, who absorbed the spirit of his master thoroughly. He translated into French what he believed to be a correct version of Bentham's labours, which our philosopher did not finally accept, and gave them to the Continent. From France Bentham's influence poured forth to practical issues. In Spain he became almost a juristic god. The Constitutional party in Spain and Portugal in 1820 and 1821 consulted him, and he wrote elaborate tracts for their enlightenment. Borrow, when travelling in Spain ten years after Bentham's death, was welcomed by an Alcade on Cape Finisterre, who had upon his shelves all the works of the "grand Baintham," comparing him to Solon, Plato, and even Lope de Vega. The last comparison seemed to Borrow to be overstrained. The Portuguese Cortes voted in December 1821, that he should be invited to prepare an "all-comprehensive code." During the last fourteen years of his life, he was engrossed in the task of the completion of his *Constitutional Code for the Use of all Nations professing Liberal Opinions*. In 1823 he was a member of the Greek Committee, corresponding with Mavrocordato and other leaders. In 1822 and 1823 he tried to bestow sound advice on the government of Tripoli. He renewed his old associations with Russia when he corresponded with Alexander I on his offer to frame a code of laws. The Emperor penned a letter of profuse thanks, and intimated that his commissioners should be commanded to address their inquiries to Bentham. The Emperor also sent the codifier a valuable ring, which was returned sealed up as it was received.

The New World attracted Bentham just as much as the Old. In his lifetime, forty thousand copies of his works in

French were sold in Spanish America alone. The Codes and the Constitutions of the restless South American States were drenched with his ideas. As early as 1810 Bentham believed that he had conquered the earth. There was something to be said for his view. He drafted a law for the freedom of the press of Venezuela, and General Miranda proposed that when his native state was founded, Bentham should be its legislator. Bolivar, the dictator of Columbia, had consulted our philosopher in London. Santander, another South American hero, was an admiring disciple. Six years after Bentham's death, his disciples made his new principle of self-government, the late version of *Emancipate your Colonies*, the basis of the new Canadian polity destined to spread over all the other Dominions. Aaron Burr, who killed that great man, Alexander Hamilton, in a duel, appealed to Bentham to frame schemes for an empire in Mexico. From this adventurer he turned to Madison, then President, in 1811. He offered a "complete body of statute laws, or Pannomion," and Romilly roundly declared it embraced "some of the most important views on the subject of Legislation, and on the nature of common or unwritten law, that have ever been laid before the public." He begged the Governor of Pennsylvania to favour his scheme, feeling confident that if but one State of the Union accepted his offer, all the others would be forced by the evident superiority of his code and the contagion of a good example, to adopt it. Neither the President nor the Governor made any sufficient response. Bentham's aim was the sifting of the mass of the decided cases in the United States and the common law, with the rules and principles involved. By the authority of the Legislature he would turn these rules and principles into statute law, filling up the gaps in them. He implores the people of the United States to receive "These labours of mine, . . . let them be accepted by you; you shall be a people of conquerors. . . . To the conquest to which you are here invited, no ultimate limits can be assigned other than those which bound the habitable globe. To force new laws upon a reluctant and abhorring people is, in addition to unpunishable depredation, the object and effect of vulgar conquest; to behold your laws not only accepted, but sought after—sought after by an admiring people—will be yours." Blackstone had been the protagonist —not the antagonist, because both were necessary to a better world—of Bentham since 1764 in the Old World. They were protagonists in the New. For the acceptance of the *Commentaries* meant the rejection of the codification.

The old man was naturally eager to witness his plans adopted. He was a lawgiver, whose work, like that of Manu or Mohammed, would live for ever. Still, he should like to see a land where it was actually in operation. In 1827 Lord William Bentinck, when he went as Governor-General to India, wrote to Bentham, "I am going to British India, but I shall not be Governor-General. It is you who will be Governor-General." In his *Pannomion* and in his *Theory of Legislation*, had he not founded the science of legislation as it ought to be? Had he not founded universal jurisprudence? True, he had neglected history, despite Savigny's warning, yet if you paid attention to history, could you construct a science? Must the result of your labours not be an art?

In 1825 he paid what M. Halévy calls *son voyage triomphal à Paris*. He travelled there to consult a physician on the treatment of a cutaneous disorder. On entering a Court of Justice the whole Bar rose to welcome him, and the President seated him at his right hand. He saw his old friend Lafayette, and General Foy greeted him with the compliment, "*Vos moeurs et vos écrits sont peints sur notre visage.*" On the Revolution of 1830 he addressed words of advice to the country of which he had been made a citizen nearly forty years before. In 1832 Talleyrand, to whom he talked about the Panopticon in 1792, dined with him alone. Bowring, the editor of Bentham's works, observed to the Prince that they had been plundered. The courteous reply was, "*et pillé de tout le monde, il est toujours riche.*"

Bentham entertained no belief in the equality of St. Just or in that of Robespierre, who affirmed that in a well-constituted Republic no one should possess more than 300 livres a year. He defends property on the ground of utility, not on the ground of natural right or the rights of man. In his *Principles of Legislation* he raises this issue. In what consists the weal of the governed? Chiefly in four things—subsistence, abundance, equality, and, above all, security; under security, liberty, civil and political, being included. The end of the civil law should be these four things, which included the protection of the person and of property, the fruit of the labourer's exertions. The fear of starvation induces men to provide subsistence, if there is not only protection by the government but also against the government. For official agents are sometimes rapacious. Motives similar to subsistence produces abundance, aided by the spirit of saving and accumulation.

Bentham favours equality of property on the ground that increments of happiness to rich men are by no means proportional to increments of wealth. Put, he asks, "a thousand farmers having enough to live upon and a little more. Put on the other side a king, or, not to be encumbered with the cares of government, a prince well-portioned, himself as rich as all the farmers taken together. It is probable, I say, that his happiness is greater than the average happiness of the thousand farmers, but it is by no means probable that it is equal to the sum-total of their happiness, or, what amounts to the same thing, a thousand times greater than the average happiness of one of them. It would be remarkable if his happiness were ten times or even five times greater."

Our thinker had lived through the French Revolution, and he had been deeply impressed by what happened to property then. Security to him was, accordingly, a much better end than equality. By security he means not only security to the person, including reputation, but also and still more to property. Security, "that inestimable good, the distinctive index of civilisation, is entirely the work of the law. Without law there is no security; and consequently no abundance, and not even the certainty of subsistence; and the only equality that can exist in such a state of things is an equality in misery." In any conflict between equality and security, the former must always give way. This security is not merely for to-morrow but all the to-morrows: on this expectation we ground our labour for the future. Laws are indeed to conform to natural expectations, never noticing that all he writes on such expectations is simply a testimony in favour of natural law. He insists on the vital need for security to such an extent that he perhaps atones for his disregard of history. For this need saves him from yielding to the revolutionary spirit of the age. He is in favour of equality of opportunity, not equality of condition. In his later radical days he came to favour political equality, and it is curious to observe that he failed to foresee that political equality might lead to the demand for equality of possessions. Still, if the pursuit of equality come into collision with security, "it will not do to hesitate for a moment. Equality must yield." He favoured the extension of the vote to women. There was no reason why a person of one sex should have less happiness than a person of the other. The weal of a woman constituted as large a part of universal happiness as the weal of a man.

Bentham was not unwilling to admit the Greek notion that a right must answer proportionately to duty done; otherwise, it is sheer injustice. If A and B are two citizens whose virtues differ, the rights a, which are A's ought to differ in amount from the rights b, which are B's, in the manner of $A:B::A+a:B+b$. In fact, equality to the Greek means not equal rights for all, a proposition they would not have understood, but equal rights for equal capacities. To bestow equal rights on citizens with unequal virtues is, in their considered judgment, the essence of inequality. Carlyle raised the same question in his characteristic fashion. Why, if Quashee Nigger be not equal to Socrates or Shakespeare, nor Judas Iscariot to Jesus Christ, nor Bedlam and Gehenna equal to the New Jerusalem, should radicalism give to all alike, not merely equality before the law, nor yet merely equality of political rights, but press on still further to a greater equalisation of worldly means?

The radical reformer tells us that "if property should be overturned with the direct intention of establishing an equality of possessions, the evil would be irreparable. No more security, no more industry, no more abundance, Society would return to the savage state whence it emerged." With the example of France before him he expands his ideas: "If equality ought to prevail to-day it ought to prevail always. Yet it cannot be preserved except by renewing the violence by which it was established. It will need an army of inquisitors and executioners as deaf to favour as to pity; insensible to the seductions of pleasure, inaccessible to personal interest; endowed with all the virtues, though in a service which destroys them all. The levelling apparatus ought to go incessantly backward and forward, cutting off all that rises above the line prescribed. A ceaseless vigilance would be necessary to give to those who had dissipated their portions, and to take from those who by labour had augmented theirs. In such an order of things there would be only one wise course for the governed —that of prodigality; there would be but one foolish course —that of industry. This pretended remedy, seemingly so pleasant, would be a mortal poison, a burning cautery, which would consume till it destroyed the last fibre of life. The hostile sword in its greatest furies is a thousand times less dreadful. It inflicts but partial evils, which time effaces and industry repairs."

Is there no method of reconciling security with greater equality? Yes, he thinks that the State can limit testamentary power, "to prevent too great an accumulation of wealth in the hands of an individual." It may favour equality where the deceased has left no wife or relation in the direct line. If he has made no will, the property should revert to the State, to the exclusion of collaterals who have formed no expectations of succeeding. If there are children in the direct line, the principle of equal division should be followed. He discerns a natural tendency to equality in a nation industrially progressive, if the laws do not set themselves against it by favouring monopolies, shackling trade, or permitting entails. "We see great properties divided little by little without effort, without revolution, without shock, and a much greater number of men coming to participate in the moderate favours of fortune." True as this is of the world of agriculture, it is by no means true of the world of manufactures, where there is to-day a larger proportion of magnates with incomes over £5000 a year then at the beginning of the nineteenth century.

Laissez-faire is to be the order of the day in industry. The individual who promotes his own interest and happiness will best promote the general interest and happiness. We ask, What are the true limits of legislative interference? Bentham's answer is that the aim of "private ethics" and "legislation" is the same, happiness, and the "acts with which they are conversant are *in great measure* the same." Their spheres are different because the acts "are not *perfectly and throughout* the same." What is the differentia? Utility. Apply, such is his counsel, an analysis to determine the cases in which punishment does more harm than good. Obviously the world of the twenties of the nineteenth century was much simpler than the world of the twenties of the twentieth century.

Bentham had hitched his waggon to the star of happiness, and herein lies not a little of the secret of his vast power. The revolutionary creed of Godwin had been confuted by Malthus. True, Godwin had left successors, men like Cartwright who offered childish remedies, Cobbett who was both viewy and inconsistent, Burdett who blustered about radicalism, and Hunt who blustered about himself. Bentham was a man of wealth who belonged to the middle class. In word, the average Englishman thought he knew where to place Bentham. Of course the average Englishman knew nothing of the sort, yet as the philosopher lived in seclusion, who could contradict the views generally formed of him? The conservatism of the middle class predisposed its members to receive the views of one of themselves. Nor can we overlook the fact that Johnson in his day and Paley in his day—he was the accepted moralist in the twenties—had prepared the way for the prophet of Utilitarianism. There was much in common between the individualism of the Utilitarian and the individualism of the Evangelical. Both cared for the salvation of the body, though of course the Evangelical spent his strength on the salvation of the soul. Paley's *Principles of Moral and Political Philosophy* appeared in 1785 and Bentham's *Principles of Morals and Legislation* in 1789, and both expounded the greatest happiness principle. As he lay dying Wesley wrote to encourage Wilberforce in his "glorious enterprise, in opposing that execrable villany (the slave trade) which is the scandal of religion, of England, and of human nature." Bentham also expressed his sympathy with the long-continued efforts of Wilberforce "in behalf of the race of innocents, whose lot it has hitherto been to be made the subject-matter of depredation, for the purpose of being treated worse than the authors of such crimes are treated for those crimes in other places." There is little in common between Wesley and Bentham, though there is much in common between Wesley and Wilberforce, but what is common to all three is the splendid humanitarianism that characterised them.

The current of humanitarianism joined the current of Evangelicalism, and their union provided them with a swiftly increasing river. A lover of cats, Bentham does not forget animals. "The question is not," he maintains, "Can they reason? nor, Can they talk? but, Can they suffer?" No one who knows the annals of bull-baiting or cock-fighting can deny that they did suffer. He insisted that acts of cruelty to animals should be crimes cognisable by law. Men, he thought, may be allowed to kill, or inflict pain on animals with a determinable object, if that object be beneficial to mankind; but no man should be suffered to torment them. In 1809 there was a debate in the House of Commons on a measure with this aim in view. During the course of the debate Romilly remarked that nothing could be more just than the observation of Hogarth, who, beyond all others in his profession, had devoted his talents to the cause of morality. This artist, in tracing cruelty through its different stages, had represented it as beginning with delight in the sufferings of animals and ending in the most savage manner in men.

Cruelty either to man or to animal was not more widespread in Bentham's time than in Beccaria's. The conditions over Europe remained pretty much the same, yet mankind suddenly became conscious of conditions that they had not noticed before, and found them intolerable. Evangelicalism can in England claim credit for this changed attitude, yet religion was not the only cause, for in France it was accompanied by a great wave of scepticism, advancing to atheism. Nor can it be ascribed to intellectual advance, for many of the objects had nothing to do with knowledge or reason, and the humanitarians of the eighteenth and nineteenth centuries were conspicuously inferior to the intellectual giants of the seventeenth century. It is true that the latter part of the eighteenth century was called the Age of Reason, and the men of that day prided themselves on their intellectual superiority; but at that very time knowledge, once pursued for its own sake, was becoming the handmaid of utility, and the claims of the body were taking the precedence that has been allowed them in increasing measure ever since. The humanitarian movement was a matter of feeling, not of intellectual or spiritual activity. Lecky ascribes the change to the progress of civilisation. What does this mean? For it is a phrase as chameleon-like as national character.

The question is, Why did the sympathies of men become more expansive, their perceptions of the sufferings of others more acute? There had been predecessors, of course. The great ethical teachers of the Middle Ages denounced cruelty, inculcated pity, sympathy and benevolence, and laid down the principles of punishment for crime. Nor was the practical application of these sentiments lacking. The establishment of hospitals, the practice of almsgiving, the benevolence exercised by monasteries surely displayed sympathy with suffering, and even the rigour of the penal law was mitigated by leniency. There is, however, a marked difference between medieval humanity and the humanitarian movement of the late eighteenth and early nineteenth century. In the earlier period kindness and sympathy might be enjoined as a moral duty, but the spectacle of bodily suffering evoked none of the instinctive repugnance that characterises the later period. The voluntary mortification of the flesh was indeed deemed praiseworthy, torture was allowed by common consent, and burning at the stake was regarded not merely with equanimity but with satisfaction. It is clear that when humane and enlightened men could endure and approve such sights, the valuation of pain was quite different from our own.

We get nearer to modern conceptions in the sixteenth

century. Sir Thomas More denounced severe punishments for trivial offences, but even he argued rather as a lawyer than as a man revolted by the infliction of needless pain. Montaigne, however, fairly anticipated the humane spirit not only of the Benthamic period, but of more recent times. He detested cruelty of every kind with all his heart. "Among all other vices," he writes, "there is none I hate more than cruelty, both by nature and judgment, as the extremest of all vices." He anticipated by two hundred years Beccaria's argument against torture as an instrument of justice, and was altogether far in advance of his age. His premature and modern sensitiveness to suffering is revealed more clearly by the extension to other animals of his "very feeling and tender compassion of other men's afflictions."

How are we to account for the great change which takes place during the end of the eighteenth century? In 1764 Beccaria suggests that "in proportion as the minds of men become softened by their intercourse in society, the severity of punishments should be diminished." But do they become softened by their intercourse in society? Is it not rather by the rising standard of comfort, as Malthus says, and the gradual removal of hardships once accepted as inevitable in the natural order of things that increases sensitiveness to bodily conditions in general? As Herbert Spencer pointed out, the more things improve the greater the outcry about them. And we know from common experience that this is so. No one is so acutely conscious of the least speck of dirt as the cleanest housewife: the slattern is unconscious. The higher the mountaineer climbs the more eagerly he looks on the next peak and the more determined he is to scale it.

Is there not something more than this psychological process? May there not be a physiological change, due to easier conditions of life, which heightens sensibility to pain and causes men to shrink from the thought and the spectacle of the suffering to which they were formerly indifferent because pain was then really less felt? It is possible, and no one can say that such a change has not taken place. We know but little about the nervous mechanism of pain. Its development may, for all we know, keep pace with the progressive increase of comfort and diminution of pain-exciting stimuli in the ordinary course of life. Individuals differ enormously in their sensibility to pain, and there is nothing inherently improbable in the hypothesis of a general increase of sensitiveness. People certainly used to make little of bodily suffering which they could not stand at all to-day, such as operations without anaesthetics or floggings of five hundred lashes. Think of the hardships and perils they used to undergo and calmly accept as a matter of course in the way of ordinary travel, and contrast that indifference with the fuss made to-day over the most trifling inconveniences. Torture of old surely meant far less in actual physical effects than it would mean to-day. On the other hand, it may be argued that if the humanitarian movement which began in the eighteenth century and developed in the nineteenth was due to physiological change and a consequent revaluation of pain and suffering, then it must have been more than skin deep and would not have given place again to outbursts of savagery so readily as appears to have done under the stress of conflict between nations and within them in these latter days.

Whatever may be the solution of this riddle, the fact is clear that we count this humanitarian movement among the forces urging Bentham to take a more radical attitude to reform in the politics of the State. He feels increasingly that we can note more folly than wisdom in our ancestors. Experience in the present, not history in the past, is the very mother of wisdom. In his analysis of anarchical fallacies, he yet holds that "the things that people stand most in need of being reminded of are, one would think, their duties—for their rights—whatever they may be, they are apt enough to attend to themselves." A *Catechism of Parliamentary Reform* appeared in 1817, urging the necessity of radical, and the inadequacy of moderate, reform. He practically advocates universal suffrage, excluding minors, persons of unsound mind, persons unable to read, perhaps sailors and soldiers, and perhaps women. To guard against bribery and intimidation, vote is to be by ballot and parliaments are to be annual, because the "impermanence" of their seat would form the greatest check on members' abuse of their trust. In his *Radicalism (or Democracy) not Dangerous*, 1819, he thinks confiscation of property in their favour would be ruinous for the people, and would not be attempted by the members chosen by them. In the twenties he was the oracle of the Radicals, yet, according to M. Halévy, *par le fait même que Bentham devient radical, le parti radical va changer de caractère.* In 1839 he declared his preference for the English Constitution: "such as it is"—to non-government, and indeed to every other but that of the United States. In 1822 he had described the English Government as the least bad of all bad governments, that of the United States as the first of all governments to which the epithet *good*, in the positive sense of the word, could with propriety be applied. In 1830 he wrote of our constitution: "I do not prefer it, such as it is, teeming with abuses and other imperfections, to what it would be if cleared, in the whole or part, of all or any of these same imperfections."

Bentham stood for the reform of the representative system in Parliament; he demanded municipal reform; he prayed for the mitigation of the terrible criminal law, for the abolition of transportation, and for the improvement of prisons. He clamoured for the removal of defects in the jury system, pleaded for the abolition of grand juries, but indicated his belief that the proper Court of Appeal is a jury. He demanded the abolition of imprisonment for debt, the sweeping away of the usury laws, the reform of the law of evidence, the repeal of religious tests. He clamoured for the reform of the Poor Law, for the training of pauper children, for the establishment of a national system of education. He demanded an extension of the idea of savings bank and friendly societies, cheap postage without the object of national profit coupled with post office money orders. He insisted on a complete and uniform registration of births, deaths, and marriages, a code for merchant shipping, full census returns, the circulation of parliamentary papers, the protection of inventors. He demanded local courts, uniform and scientific methods of drafting acts of parliament, a general register of real property, of deeds and all transactions, and last, but certainly not least, the passing of public health legislation. All these things he asked for, in addition to definite legal reforms in procedure. He attacked the division of justice into law and equity, and the provision of different courts for different classes of cases. He demanded the creation of public prosecutors and of advocates of the poor. He would have been pleased by a recent event, when a Vacation Judge swimming in the sea was overtaken by a barrister who made an *ex parte* application for an interim injunction two hundred yards from the shore, an application which was immediately granted. Next to the reform of procedure, codification was Bentham's remedy for the confusion and massiveness of the law; and the practice of codification has steadily progressed in England, though in forms that would have filled the philosopher with horror and dismay.

That is the polity of the great Utilitarian philosopher and lawyer. To us to-day practically the whole of it in principle, if not in effect, is admitted. It makes quite dull reading. The obvious is dull. But if the obvious be dull, the impossible is not dull. It is a tale of heroic adventure; for when Bentham set forth his polity all these things were impossible, absurd, ridiculous. Great intellects waived them away. What could any sensible person think? Why, Bentham must be a maniac, or at best an idealist, a Platonist, a man who trod the clouds, an opium-eater who in the filthy den of this dirty world dreams of God in his new heaven. That was how men, good men, thought of what seems obvious to us now. It is tempting to believe that Bentham was really an idealist, a Platonist, a man who saw the pattern of the Mount laid up in heaven. But he saw his task, an immeasurable and impossible task; and he so set the labourers to work that almost from the very day of his death on June 6, 1832, at the age of eighty-four, the great task of cleansing public and private life, and of constructing once more on traditional lines the forces of an indomitable people, went steadily forward.

Many men stand on Mount Pisgah and see in the dim distance the land of promise. So stood Voltaire and Bentham. Their fate was to see it with their eyes but they were not to go over to possess it. Yet they prepared the way for the fulfilment of those glorious visions they themselves were never destined to realise. These visions did not spring from a happy home, for both endured the clash of the two generations. Voltaire's sagacity in the days to come rendered him alive to the circumstance that the professional and middle classes are a worse enemy of liberal opinion and are more intolerant than the old aristocratic order, yet Bentham and he came from middle-class homes. They fell in love, but they never married. Both enjoyed the joys of country life, and were sensitive to the beauties of a noble landscape. "I was born," acknowledges Voltaire, "to be a faun or creature of the woods; I am not made to live in a town." They were most regular in sitting at their desk, and were unwearied in giving forth to the world masses of manuscripts. They were patient in awaiting the fruition of their long labours through the press and the pamphlet they so steadily used. Both travelled over the face of Europe, and seemingly their travels bestowed but little impression on either. Both lived to be eighty-four, and became institutions in France and England respectively, owing no scanty portion of their power to their length of days. For they were able to impose their opinions on more than two generations. Comte questions if Voltaire had been as clear-sighted and active as he was, and yet had lived only fifty years, whether Voltairism would have struck root, and neither might Benthamism. The genius and the longevity of Voltaire and Bentham bestowed on them an influence on the destiny of mankind seldom surpassed. Voltaire said of Montesquieu that humanity had lost its title-deeds, and he had recovered them. Voltaire himself and Bentham also helped in splendid fashion to recover these title-deeds of humanity.

The ideas of Voltaire and Bentham were in the air, and they rendered much of their service in bringing these ideas to mother earth. "Voltaire," sneered an enemy, "is the very first man in the world at writing down what other people have thought." It was a distinction enjoyed by Bentham every whit as much as by Voltaire. They contributed to the augmentation of the happiness of mankind and to the diminution of its pain. Remarkably enough, each refused to appeal to the spirit of asceticism. Fair play was the very breath of their nostrils; and what Voltaire accomplished for the individual Bentham accomplished for the race. Voltaire executed the social revolution he never planned, Bentham the legal revolution he planned. They were, in varying degree, among the greatest of overthrowers. Their labours were largely carried out through the agency of their friends, and these friends they did not always succeed in keeping. They were suggestive stimulators, not mere preceptors; they influenced others through themselves in others, sometimes with fortunate, sometime with unfortunate, effects. The quarrels of Bentham with his circle are not so notorious as those of Voltaire, yet quarrels there were. The two men, by their writings, incurred the enmities of kings. They exhibited neither serenity of mind nor composure of spirit. Sharpness and scornfulness characterised their analytic mind which felt little reverence and denied mystery, reducing the whole of creation to a sum in mathematics. Their generosity was unbounded. Both practised the Aristotelian spirit of magnificent expenditure.

The two philosophers lived in large degree the life of recluses. They were, however, recluses with marked social tastes, gathering congenial friends around them in their solitude. They were men of thought rather than men of action, with distinct leanings to the world of affairs. Did not Gibbon describe Boethius not as stooping, but rather as rising, from his life of placid meditation to an active share in the imperial business? This imperial business attracted Voltaire and Bentham, and the former offered his services to Fleury and Choiseul in turn, not to speak of Frederick the Great. As neither Voltaire nor Bentham was successful in obtaining public office, their labours necessarily wore a negative form, though we must not forget the fact that negation is an element in reformation. They undermined the traditional authority of men, and this work of undermining was essential for the improvement of the world at large. The false notions of the Tribe, the Market, and, above all, the Cave were the subject of their mocking laughter. They questioned the past, a thing in itself then almost unheard-of. They communicated their questionings to others, and spread the inquiring spirit. Bold and inquisitive conceptions began to filter down to the average man. For authority they substituted reason— and sometimes their own authority. Sinister interests, whether they were preferences of class or creed, of pride or prejudice, were abhorrent to them, so abhorrent that they failed to render justice to any of them. In their exaltation of judgment even above sympathy, and of robust worth above any rose-water virtue, in their catholic yet discriminating helpfulness, they are fundamentally the same. The military spirit was conspicuously wanting in them: "gloire" and "victoire" evoked their emphatic protests.

The utter detestation of tyranny, in its manifold forms, is common to Voltaire and to Bentham. Nor did they conceal their hatred in their hearts: it was known of all men. To combat injustice proved the passion of their lives, and Voltaire wrote himself an epitaph which will serve for both, "*J'ai fait un peu de bien: c'est mon meilleur ouvrage.*" The cruelty of the Law Court, in the eyes of each, was abominable, to be rooted out at all costs. The passion of justice had taken possession of them. Hateful atrocities, perpetrated by a tribunal of justice, were frequent in France and England. The very thought of such atrocities burnt into their souls, destroying their peace of mind. Their passionate denunciation of these invested them with a quality which virtually constituted them a fresh and living force. D'Alembert gave Voltaire an account of the execution of the unfortunate La Barre, and Voltaire was so horrified that he wrote: "This is no longer a time for jesting: witty things do not go well with massacres. What? These Busirises in wigs destroy in the midst of horrible tortures children of sixteen! And that in the face of the verdict of ten upright and humane judges! And the victim suffers it! People talk about it for a moment, and the next they are hastening to the comic opera; and barbarity, become the more insolent, will to-morrow cut throats juridically at pleasure. Here Calas broken on the wheel, there Sirven condemned to be hanged, further off a gag thrust into the mouth of a lieutenant-general, a fortnight after that five youths condemned to the flames for extravagances that deserved nothing worse than Saint Lazare. Is this the country of philosophy and pleasure? It is the country rather of the Saint Bartholomew massacre. Why, the Inquisition would not have ventured to do what these Jansenist judges have done!" Bentham's last thoughts were with the slave, the hope of his emancipation. Voltaire's last writing was a line of rejoicing to young Lally, that their efforts had been successful in procuring justice for the memory of one who had been put to death unjustly.

No man, pointed out Cromwell, goes so far as he who does not know whither he is going. Accordingly, Voltaire and Bentham travelled far, but their journey was a long one. "I now perceive," Voltaire wrote the year before his death, "that we must still wait three or four hundred years. One day it cannot but be ,that good men win their cause; but before that glorious day arrives how many vexations have we to undergo, how many dark persecutions, without reckoning the La Barres, of whom from time to time they will make *autos da fé.*" There is a divine event towards which the whole world is moving, but it is still far off, still slow coming. A measure of success was vouchsafed to Voltaire and to Bentham. Still, their work was incomplete. In literature the crown of success falls to many. Gibbon is not the only historian to conclude his life's work in such calm detachment that he may meditate upon the last sentence among the acacias in a starlit garden at Lausanne. In life it is otherwise. The thoughts of Voltaire and Bentham were occasionally bitter when they saw that their labours were not destined to completion. What were the last thoughts of Raphael that Good Friday, nearly four hundred years ago, as he gazed on his "Transfiguration"? It is the fate of the worker in the service of humanity that he sees his toil unfinished. A Voltaire, a Bentham, shatters an old building standing in the way. The century succeeding has succeeded in raising a stately edifice.

The attitude of Voltaire and Bentham to theology was not unlike, and their object undoubtedly was *Ecrasez l'infâme.* The cruelty and the obscurantism of theology in their day moved them to scorn. They were as eager to clear the mind of cant, as to exalt the spirit above the letter. The quarrels of the theologians added to this feeling. "Now," wrote Voltaire in 1768, "a revolution has been accomplished in the human mind that nothing again can ever arrest. They would have prevented this revolution, if they had been sage and moderate. The quarrels of the Jansenists and Molinists have done more harm to the Christian religion than could have been done by four emperors like Julian." What Voltaire and Bentham saw wrong with the Church they saw with painful clearness: what they saw right—but could they see what was right? Both men were blind or were blinded to the saintly souls and to the Master who inspired their saintliness. "The love of Christ constraineth us"—so humanitarians like William Wilberforce and John Wesley could testify. So could neither Voltaire nor Bentham testify. The joy of holiness was not felt by either. It is characteristic of them that they pass by the conception of a corporate body, the Church or any other.

Toleration was a virtue that our two thinkers held in reverence, though they did not invariably exhibit it to right-minded clergy. To the wrong-minded they proved both intolerant and contemptuous. It is lamentable, however, to observe the scanty sympathy they received from the Church of France and the Church of England respectively in their noble humanitarian labours. Unconsciously they were animated by the spirit of Christ, and served Him better than some conscious Christians. In their own manner—peculiar as it often was—Voltaire and Bentham cared for the needy. In a vision of the judgment day, the King will say to them on His right hand:

"Come, ye blessed of My Father, inherit the kingdom prepared for you from the foundation of the world:

"For I was an hungred, and ye gave Me meat: I was thirsty, and ye gave Me drink: I was a stranger, and ye took Me in:

"Naked, and ye clothed Me: I was sick, and ye visited Me: I was in prison, and ye came unto Me."

Voltaire and Bentham had in no mean measure rendered

this service from the giving meat to the hungred, to the visiting of the captive. Their labours were Christ-like, and the light denied to them here we pray may be given to them hereafter.

References

Albee, E. A.   *A History of English Utilitarianism.* (New York, 1902.)
Atkinson, C. M.   *Jeremy Bentham: his life and work.* (London, 1905.)
Bowring, J.   *Bentham's Collected Works.* Vols. XI and XII. (Edinburgh, 1838–43.)
Brougham, Lord.   *Works.* (London, 1859–62.)
Cambridge History of English Literature. Vol. XI. (Cambridge, 1914.)
Colls, J. F.   *Militarianism Unmasked.* (London, 1844.)
Davidson, W. L.   *Political Thought in England. The Utilitarians from Bentham to J. S. Mill.* (London, 1915.)
Davis Carless, H. W.   *The Age of Grey and Peel.* (Oxford, 1929.)
Dicey, A. V.   *Law and Opinion in England.* (London, 1914.)
Edinburgh Review. Vol. XXIX, 1817; Vol. LXXVIII, 1843.
Graham W.   *English Political Philosophy.* (London, 1914.)
Guyau, M.   *La Morale Anglaise Contemporaine.* (Paris, 1900.)
Halévy, E.   *La formation du radicalisme philosophique. La jeunesse de Bentham.* (Paris, 1901 ff.)
Halévy, E.   *Thomas Hodgskin (1787–1861).* (Paris, 1903.)
Hazlitt, W.   *The Spirit of the Age. Works.* Vol. IV. (London, 1902.)
Höffding, H. A.   *A History of Modern Philosophy.* (London, 1900.)
Holdsworth, W. S.   *A History of English Law.* Vols. VII and VIII. (London, 1922 ff.)
Kenny, C. S.   *Law Quarterly Review.* Vol XI, 1895.
Lundin, H. G.   *The influence of Jeremy Bentham on English democratic Development.* (Iowa, 1920.)
MacCunn, J.   *Six Radical Thinkers. Bentham, J. S. Mill, Cobden, Carlyle, Mazzini, T. H. Green.* (London, 1910.)
Macdonell, Sir J. and Manson, E.   *The Great Jurists of the World.* (London, 1912.)
Mill, J. S.   *Dissertations and Discussions.* Vol. I. (London, 1859–75.)
Mohl, R. von.   *Geschichte u. Literatur der Staatswissenschaften.* Vol. III. (Erlangen, 1855–58.) Vol. III, No. 18, p. 610 ff.
Phillipson, C.   *Three criminal law Reformers: Beccaria, Bentham, Romilly.* (London, 1923.)
Paul, H.   *Men and Letters.* (London, 1901.)
Pringle-Pattison, A. S.   *The Philosophical Radicals.* (London, 1907.)

References

REYBAUD, L. *Etudes sur les Reformateurs ou Socialistes Modernes.* Vol. II. (Paris, 1843.)

SAINT-AMAND. *Notice sur les ouvrages de J. Bentham, suivie d'une analyse des pièces relatives à la codification.* (Paris, 1826.)

SIDGWICK, H. *Miscellaneous Essays and Addresses.* (London, 1904.)

SIEGWART, A. *Bentham's Werke u. ihre Publikation.* (Bern, 1910.)

STEPHEN, Sir J. F. *Horae Sabbaticae.* Series 3. (London, 1892.)

STEPHEN, Sir L. *History of English Thought in the Eighteenth Century.* (London, 1881.)

STEPHEN, Sir L. *The English Utilitarians.* (London, 1900.)

WALLAS, G. *The Political Science Quarterly.* March, 1923; *Contemporary Review*, March, 1926.

Westminster Review. Vol. XIV (1827.)

WILLIAMS, A. T. *The concept of equality in the writings of Rousseau, Bentham and Kant.* (New York, 1907.)

WILSON, Sir R. K. *Modern English Law.* (London, 1875.)

Chapter III.

JAMES MILL AND MIDDLE CLASS DEMOCRACY

"I was the spiritual father of Mill," declared Bentham, "and Mill the spiritual father of Ricardo." Such a declaration is a statement of fact, for the intellectual relationship between Bentham and James Mill was just as close as that between James Mill and his son John. Nor did the man that Bentham influenced change his life. As James Mill was in the beginning of his days, so he was in the end of them. He generally accepted the Benthamic doctrine as the truth, the whole truth, and nothing but the truth. Like Bentham, Mill steadily believed in the excellences of the middle class, the class whence Bentham sprang, and the class to which James Mill had risen. It was the class, in James Mill's judgment, which possessed the "largest share of sense and virtue," and was most connected with other classes.

If the power of the master over the disciple was overpowering, that of the disciple over the master was no less overpowering. He supplanted Romilly, the contemporary of Bentham, in the inner circle. If Romilly represented the master in the House of Commons, Mill represented him on the press, and it was easy to think that an article might be important, whereas a speech might be possibly unimportant. A Scot, Mill possessed the aggressive and militant as well as the industrious qualities of his race. Bentham had been an influence, and James Mill went far to turn this influence into a school of thought which was to exercise a vast influence on the growing movement for parliamentary reform. Mill believed with all his heart—or with such an outline of an heart as he possessed—and with all his mind in the Utilitarian philosophy, and he could see its far-reaching effects. If Bentham pleaded for the reform of law as an aid to the weal of mankind, Mill could also see that Malthus, by his principle of population, was also working for this weal. A servant to Bentham, Mill was a master, a tyrant, to everyone else. A tyrant at home, he bullied his children. A tyrant abroad, he bullied the Benthamic circle. He drove

Bentham himself in directions, political directions, in which at first he had never meant his steps to wander.

James Mill (1773-1836) came from the home of a Scots' shoemaker where there were plain living and high thinking. The lad showed that he possessed brains, and he attended Montrose Academy, where he had for a school-fellow, Joseph Hume. He acted as tutor to Wilhelmina Stuart, Sir Walter Scott's early love, and with the Stuarts he always remained on friendly terms. He entered Edinburgh University in 1790, and bestowed particular attention on Plato and philosophy. We can feel sure that it was the reasoning and clarifying powers of Plato that attracted him, not the imaginative genius. Dugald Stewart's lectures he admired. In the days to come he was to hear the speeches of Pitt and Fox, but Stewart's lectures he deemed more eloquent. In 1794 his divinity studies commenced, and lasted four winters. He delivered the usual homilies before his professors, and he preached. "I've heard him preach," declared Sir David Brewster, "and no great han' he made o't."

In company with Sir John Stuart he set out in 1802 for London, there to make his way by his pen. Seemingly, he was no more particular than most journalists as to the politics of the papers to which he contributed. For we find that the future advanced politician wrote for the *Anti-Jacobin Review*, a strong Tory organ. He translated books and wrote articles for the *Encyclopaedia Britannica*. For four years he edited *St. James's Chronicle*, which professed to survey the literary, scientific, and philosophical publications of the day. Hard work he knew; holidays he never knew. As he was earning about £500 a year he thought himself justified in marrying Harriett Burrow. Literary work, however, vanished, and the question of ways and means proved serious. He toiled as terribly as Raleigh. Writing for periodicals was a crutch, not a support, yet a support it had to be. His son John observes that nothing could be more opposed to his father's later principles than marrying and producing a family of nine under these circumstances. The marriage was not happy. The husband failed to find the intellectual companionship on which he set store; and the wife, the social on which she in her turn set store.

In 1806, for reasons difficult to divine in an Utilitarian, Mill began to compose his *History of India*, which was to occupy him for the next twelve years. It was to win for him that independent position for which he longed. In 1814 he told Place that he was working at the *History* from 5 a.m. to 11 p.m. When at Ford Abbey with Bentham his regular day's work began at 6 a.m. and lasted to 11 p.m., and the only break in that time was the three hours he gave to teaching his children and the couple of short walks which sufficed for recreation. He worked with a will, sparing no pains, shirking no difficulties. The *History* was, in fact, a manifesto of the school to which its author belonged. The causes, courses, and consequences of events form the matter which he seeks to expound. Social phenomena and the laws regulating them are to be examined, and the light they shed on India—and Utilitarianism—is not to be set aside. The lives of kings, the results of battles, are of small moment compared with the essentials of history. The preface points out: "But we can show how they lived together as members of the community, and of families; how they were arranged in society; what arts they practised, what tenets they believed, what manners they displayed; under what species of government they existed; and what character, as human beings, they possessed. This is by far the most useful and important part of history." It is a conception entirely in keeping with that of Voltaire in his *Essai sur les Moeurs*, and is entirely out of keeping with the whole train of thought of Bentham. No doubt Mill insists that in proportion as a nation is civilised it maintains the principle of utility as the object of all its efforts. If Voltaire influences him, so does Condorcet, for Mill is anxious to hold before us the hope of progress, the perfectibility of the race. Malthus had no doubt set forth doubts on the probability of reaching this goal, but reached it must be.

While the *magnum opus* was progressing, Mill was meeting friend after friend. Prominent among them was David Ricardo who meant to Mill what Mill meant to Bentham. Others in his circle were Sir Samuel Romilly and Henry Brougham, who were also friends of Bentham; Joseph Hume, the schoolfellow of Mill; Francis Place the tailor who preferred to agitate behind the scenes; George Grote, the historian of Greece; John Austin, the founder of Utilitarian jurisprudence; General Miranda, who was seeking to emancipate Venezuela from Spanish rule; and William Allen, the Quaker humanitarian. Through men like Allen it was easy to bridge the gulf which separated the Utilitarians and the Evangelicals. The Zachary Macaulay type could meet the Mill type in active work, though not in contemplative thought. If theology meant little to Bentham, it came to mean little to Mill. Bentham's *Church-of-Englandism and its Catechism Examined*, and his anonymous book on natural religion, criticised dogma destructively. Like Napoleon, as a legislator Bentham had to find a place for religion. His attitude became Gibbonian. To him all religions were equally useful so far as they inculcated obedience to the law, useless if they did not do so.

A born Scot, with all implied by this, and trained for the Presbyterian ministry, with all which that also implies, James Mill had early in life rejected "not only the belief in revelation, but the foundations of what is commonly called Natural Religion." But the "dominant chords" had been too strongly struck; the iron had entered into his soul. For throughout his own life he was possessed by the despairing gloom, the austere fanaticism, the moral power, of his first—nay, his only—creed. That creed has driven more than one noteworthy follower into reaction; but we know none which presents with equal completeness the type of the ex-Calvinist. The Christianity which Mill rejected appears never to have overpassed the rigid but powerful dogmatism with which Calvinism is popularly associated. Omnipotence and hell, each taken in its crudest sense, as if the terms referred to something tangible and visible, were all the elements that he read in the Christian scheme. This skeleton of dogma, from which the idea of God as love was wholly absent, and which, as a true expression of their creed, St. Augustine and Calvin would have put aside with compassionate contempt, seems again to have been all of Christianity that he found in Butler's *Analogy*, to the amazing force of which he bore witness. Feeling with a sensitiveness which sprang from the best side of his nature, the often "unfelt oppressions of the world," the wrong and misery under the sun, he concluded with a leap that as he could not reconcile to himself the contemporaneous existence of God, all-knowing and all-powerful, and of Evil, his sole refuge lay in the denial that any solution could be found. As a superstition, he repudiated also the idea which "attributes a pretended perfection to the order of nature and the universe." Thus thinking, he repudiated all inquiry into the origin and causation of the world, all questions of the whence and whither, as hopeless and inscrutable, accepting Agnosticism as his only possible creed; too honest to think the existence of God deniable; at once disbelieving and trembling at the sight of the evil all around him.

By his son's account, James Mill stood in the mournful position of one who found himself surrounded by sin and suffering, for which he could see neither cause nor compensation, neither beginning nor ending. The world, in his eyes, was a battlefield in darkness, where aristocrats and priests, "enemies of the human race," were contending with the utilitarian and association philosophies, the forlorn hopes for possible light and happiness. The Calvinist inferno, from which he rightly revolted, was hardly a more dismal spectacle than this. His son deeply admired him, and yet in his *Autobiography* his father appears as a man suffering perpetual eclipse, the darkness, not of intellect, but of despair, and as one lying under the shadow of Ahriman. "He thought human life a poor thing at best, after the freshness of youth and of *unsatisfied curiosity* had gone by"—the noble and enduring interest of physical, historical, or literary investigation, which in itself has animated so many lives, being apparently nothing in his eyes but boyish inquisitiveness. "This was a topic on which he did not often speak; but when he did it was with an air of settled and profound conviction. He would sometimes say that if life were made what it might be by good government and education, it would be worth having: but he never spoke with anything like enthusiasm even of that possibility." Temperament and views of this nature inclined Mill naturally to look to the philosophy of Greece, or, rather, to the recorded sayings of her philosophers, as an ethical code.

The son curiously describes him as "partaking of the Stoic, the Epicurean, and the Cynic." There is something almost pathetic in J. S. Mill's attempt to dignify with these great names his father's crude ex-Calvinism. But what are we to think of an eclecticism which presents a Stoic without his belief in Providence and an Epicurean without his belief in pleasure? The *Autobiography*, however, testifies to James Mill's ideal of virtue which, within its limits, was high; his passion for the good of others, which was strong; and his love of justice, which was intense.

It is not wonderful that a general sternness should have marked this singular man in relation to his fellow-creatures. His creed was obviously the child, not of reason, but of sentiment; it reflected the gloom of his nature, while deepening it. His wife's name is absent from the *Autobiography*. The son unwillingly admits that "the element which was chiefly deficient in his moral relation to his children was that of tenderness." He argues that his father really possessed "much greater capacities for feeling than were ever really developed." This may have been; but the reason to which he ascribes the want of development is of little force. It was simply one part of the theory which James Mill's Puritanism had embraced. Such was his severity that his son never loved him tenderly; and such his despotic attitude towards opinions differing from his own that long after the son (then in the maturity of his powers) was unable "to speak out his mind on the subject" of his philosophy on points on which he dissented from the father.

The impartial *History of India* at last appeared in three volumes at the end of 1817. In the preface the author set down his ideal of history and the laws governing its course, and he characteristically argued that the fact that he had never been in India was an advantage, for he was unbiased. His master, Bentham, had been unable to learn from travel, and we doubt if the disciple either could or would have learnt. Utilitarianism was so much a part of the mental furniture of the man that we wonder if he could have appreciated the importance of Hindoo ways and works. Bentham, after all, had been a recluse, and he had legislated for the race. Mill was a recluse, and why should he not write the history of a portion of the race? Blue-books and statistics gave him the bones of the Hindoo, but could they give him the flesh and blood with which to clothe the skeleton if it were to live? This attitude of Mill towards Indian problems has been at the bottom of some of our mistakes in the East. On the fortunes of the Hindoos it has played its part. On the fortunes of Mill it also played its part. There was a vacancy in the India Office, and Ricardo and Hume exerted themselves on behalf of their friend. Mill was appointed Assistant to the Examiner of India Correspondence in the revenue department, with a salary of £800 a year in 1819. At last the Scotsman had secured his independence after a sojourn of seventeen years in London. In 1821 he became Second Assistant with £1000 a year; in 1823 Examiner with £1200 a year; and in 1830 Examiner with £1900, which in the year of his death was raised to £2000. The philosopher had realised the Platonic dream in 1830, the culminating point of his career: he was king, but his kingdom lay in India. In England his official position, of course, debarred him from all active interference in the world of politics. Like Bentham, though for a different reason, at home he was obliged to stand outside Parliament. The passing of the Reform Bill saw such friends in the House as Grote, Strutt, Charles and Hyde Villiers, Buller, Marshall, and Roebuck.

Direct influence was sometimes taken from the thoughtful till the appearance of the leading quarterlies gave them another opportunity. The power of these when the nineteenth century was young illustrates the vast change that has come over literary conditions in our own time. The directing classes, among other elements of discipline now departed, then undoubtedly had this: that they were more or less compelled to read the same books, to discuss the same themes, to assess the same authors. An average article then had a far more vigorous existence than an average book has with us. In a comparatively limited circle of cultivated people of a certain position in society an article was discussed long before its birth. When it appeared it was pronounced upon. The justly elated author insisted upon eliciting an opinion as to its merits up to the very verge of his acquaintance. It formed the subject of unlimited correspondence; and its republication was seriously contemplated for two whole seasons, by which time the author was canvassing another serious effort.

This literature was pre-eminently written by gentlemen for gentlemen, and the gentry took it as solemnly as nourishing food, upon which they counted for the sustentation of opinions, prejudices, and aversions. The impossibility in a bipartite nation, of getting all ideas properly sorted within a single cover, made it necessary that there should be two quarterlies. Before 1802 there had been two standard reviews in England, the *Monthly* and the *Critical ;* but far from being written by gentlemen for gentlemen, these were written by unpresentable denizens of Grub Street for the publishers, who regarded them primarily as mediums of advertisement for their particular wares. If a man of quality by any chance wrote for one of these reviews he felt it hardly seemly to take money for it; the pay was two guineas a sheet of sixteen, or, in some cases, thirty-two pages. All this was changed, the pay raised to ten guineas and more, the poor hacks transmuted to Whig mandarins, the number of readers quintupled in number and decupled in influence, by the fairy wand of Jeffrey and his versatile team of exultant Edinburgh reviewers.

Disgust was soon excited, as was natural, among the Tories by the strident partisanship of the blue and buff organ; and in 1808 a grand scheme of opposition was set on foot to oppose "the proud critics of Edinburgh," and to discharge an unexpected "bomb into their midst." Scott was the prime mover, along with John Murray, while Gifford, Southey, Ellis, Rose, Canning, Croker, Barrow, Lockhart, and others were enlisted in an attempt which could hardly fail to be arduous, for the *Edinburgh* had just struck its roots firmly and was improving with every number. Yet the *Quarterly* made steady progress. In 1817 we learn that Murray was already printing 10,000 of "the greatest of his works." In 1826 Lockhart is the new editor. He was paid a thousand a year, apart from his articles, and the unique *entrée* which his position gave him in London society, though Scott took care to warn him to "be devilish careful" of the start he made, and to be sure to avoid the raffish set on the one hand, and the slippered set on the other. The tendency for the rest of the nineteenth century was to limit the articles in number and increase them in amount, as they were certainly augmenting in interest. In the forties the *Quarterly*, with a circulation of near 20,000, is at its prime. The literary quality of the articles and their magisterial authority gave them a power now hard to credit. There has been a change in the position of all such magazines due not to any diminution of their intellectual activity, but to such complicated and indefinable forces as the over-multiplication of books and magazines, libraries and publishers, the decreased numerical ratio of highly cultivated readers and booksellers to the total number of the reading public, and to the increased complexity of literary and social defluents and cross-currents.

In the twenties the Whigs had the *Edinburgh Review*, and the Tories the *Quarterly Review*. Neither organ of public opinion was open to the Utilitarians, who were naturally desirous of venting their views among the readers to whom they wished to appeal. Bentham supplied the funds, and in April, 1824, the first number of the *Westminster Review* appeared. The Utilitarians, who were, on the whole, radical, despised the Whigs as trimmers, and half-hearted in their advocacy of parliamentary reform. James Mill's official position prevented his undertaking the editorship, but his son John could—and did—write. At last the Utilitarians had an organ of their own, and it inevitably attacked the *Edinburgh Review* and the *Quarterly Review*. Its life was not long, but during its existence James Mill had the feeling that he was in no mean measure setting forth principles on which the public required instruction. The proprietor, Bentham, and the influencer, Mill, did not always see eye to eye. The former was amiable and unassertive, the latter unamiable and self-assertive. Disguise it as we will, love lay at the bottom of the creed of Bentham, but did it lie at the bottom of the creed of Mill? Bentham declared—and who knew Mill better?—that Mill's political faith arose less from his love for the many than from his hatred of the few. According to Vauvenargues, great thoughts come from the heart, but do they come from a heart with a hate in it? Mill's upbringing, in spite of the kindness of Sir John Stuart, led him to take a consistently harsh view of the upper classes. Though the shoemaker's son became middle class, yet he never wholly cast off that radicalism that characterises so many shoemakers.

The early days of Mill had been simple, and his Utilitarianism did not induce him to regard life as complex. Pain and pleasure covered most of it, if not all of it. He knew the views of Stewart, his old teacher, and Stewart's successor, Brown. Locke and Hume, and particularly Hobbes and Hartley, had left their mark upon him. He was aware of the speculations of Condillac and the French ideologues, but was unaware of those of the German thinkers. In 1817 Place drew his attention to an article on Kant. Mill then tells Place that he has begun to read *The Critique of Pure Reason*, and he writes, "I see clearly enough what poor Kant would be about, but it would require some time to give an account of him." On December 6th, 1817, the hard-working man wishes he had time to compose a book which would "make the human mind as plain as the road from Charing Cross to St. Paul's." In 1829 he was to compose his *Analysis of the Phenomena of the Human Mind*, and readers of it did not find it quite so plain as the road from Charing Cross to St. Paul's. In it he lays stress on the principle of association. By it he resolves our complex feelings or emotions into simple or elementary feelings. The consideration of pleasurable and painful sensations forms the groundwork of his book, and he shows how association connects them in our minds with their causes. From actual sensations and their actual causes we arrive, by repetition, at the formation of these sensations and their causes. Out of these conjunctions arise our ideas of wealth, power, dignity, and their contraries. When members of the race cause pleasure or pain we entertain feelings towards them, which correspond to such social pleasures as friendship, family, country, party, and their contraries. He takes the standpoint that *penser c'est sentir*, transforming ideas into sensations, and he is anxious to show that human desires correspond to a definite measurable thing. It may be utility in ethics, or value in political economy, or self-interest in politics. A moral or other pathometer he is determined to find.

The æsthetic development of the principle of association leave one dissatisfied. According to Mill, the sensations we immediately derive from colour, form, and sound are in themselves absolutely indifferent, and only become interesting by association with ideas. The association, we learn, in every case, and the association alone, is the cause of beauty: there is no underived beauty of colour. Who will agree that there are no direct physical sensations of pleasure derivable from music? Who will believe that the pleasure derivable from the Passion music of Bach is due to its association with pleasurable ideas? Who will believe with Mill that the train of ideas associated with the form of the Venus de Milo, and this alone, induces us to call it beautiful, and justifies us in so calling it? The truth is that no Benthamite left much room for the play of the imagination. True, Bentham was passionately fond of music, though he thought poetry misrepresentation. Mill condemned the drama, thought little of Shakespeare, and less of actors, quoting approvingly Johnson's disparaging remarks on Garrick. The result is that there is a dryness in all Mill writes which must be experienced by a perusal of his books in order to be understood.

The association of Mill with Bentham failed to drive away his dryness, yet he turned his master into an advanced reformer. The conservatism of Bentham is replaced by a growing radicalism. If, as Mill maintained, man is capable of perfectibility, how dare we limit his progress? In an article in the *Edinburgh Review*, January, 1809, Mill, while treating of the South American republics, advocates the theory of representative government based on the principle of utility. The writer tends to approximate to the Whig position more than perhaps he realises. On September 10th, 1819, he realises it, for he writes to Napier: "You need be under no alarm about my article 'Government.' I shall say nothing capable of alarming even a Whig, and he is more terrified at the principles of good government than the worst of Tories. I would undertake to make Mr. Canning a convert to the principles of good government sooner than your Lord Grey and your Sir James Mackintosh." Opportunist Mill was, and opportunist he remained. In an article he wrote in 1836, he practically pleaded for the monarchical authority—if it freed itself from aristocratic control and identified itself with popular interest which, of course, meant middle-class ones. Men of genius are generally ahead of their time, and Mill was barely abreast of it.

To the follower of the utilitarians it is significant that Mill's article on "Government" appeared in the *Encyclopædia Britannica* in 1820, and the Reform Bill was passed in 1832. One point of agreement we can readily allow. The Bill was as middle class as the article. J. S. Mill thought it "a masterpiece of political wisdom," and A. Bain "an impelling and a guiding force." The *advocatus diaboli*, Macaulay, in his attack upon it, taunts the Millites for holding it to be "perfect and unanswerable." Be it remarked that the editor of the *Encyclopædia* was Macvey Napier, a sound Whig. In thirty-two pages Mill sets forth a clear and condensed view of the principles of politics. The test of government is, of course, the Utilitarian one. The greatest happiness is induced by "assuring to every man the greatest possible quantity of the produce of his own labour." Accordingly, men unite and delegate to a few the power required for protecting all. This means a government which essentially is an association of men for the protection of property. There must be guardians; but who shall guard the guardians? "All the difficult questions of government relate to the means of doing so."

How is this to be accomplished? The power of protection —here Mill follows the old theory—may be entrusted to the whole community, to a few, or to one; that is, we may have a democracy, an aristocracy, or a monarchy. In none of these three are the requisite securities to be found. "The law of human nature" is that "a man, if able, will take from others anything which they have and he desires," a position sufficiently Hobbeian. *Homo homini lupus* is still the rule. Democracy is unwieldly and impracticable. Aristocracy suffers from the lack of motive to intellectual application on the part of its members, and from the inevitable drawback that there is the natural disposition of men to prey upon those under them. Monarchy suffers seriously from the same ills. The writer is still at work on his *History of India*, and he invokes Clio to aid him in the position he assumes. An English gentleman, he says, is a favourable specimen of civilisation, yet glance at his treatment of the West Indian slave. He endorses Montesquieu's view that every one who has power is led to abuse it. In fact, Mill thinks that all power essentially implies abuse. He entertains, however, little sympathy with Montesquieu's theory of the checks and balances in our constitution. He sees plainly that there cannot be three co-equal powers working in mutual antagonism; two would swallow up the third, and, if one of these could not be master of the second, they would agree to some division of the spoil.

Where are we to look? The "grand discovery of modern times" is the representative system, the only security for good government. He analyses the principles of a sound representative body. First, without fixing on a term of years, the duration of the power of its members is to be limited, though there are grave disadvantages in too frequent elections. The representation must be so wide that the interests of the choosing body shall be the same as the interests of the whole community. There are, of course, limitations on the suffrage, and obviously we may strike off those individuals whose interests are indisputably included in the interests of others. Those of the children are included in their father's, and those of the woman in her father's or in her husband's. Unlike Bentham and unlike his own son, Mill lays down that: "In this light, *women* may be regarded, the interest of almost all of whom is involved either in that of their fathers or in that of their husbands." This was to prove a hard saying to the younger generation of utilitarians.

The desirable mental qualities in the electoral body are years, property, profession or mode of life. He suggests a high figure for years. All men under forty may be omitted without mischief, for "the great majority of old men have sons whose interests they regard as an essential part of their own. This is a law of human nature." There is, he proceeds to add, no danger that men above forty will aim at the reduction of "the rest of the community to the state of abject slaves." He is in a dilemma on the qualification for property. Will not a high qualification constitute an aristocracy of wealth? Will not a low one be as good as none? There is no satisfactory principle here to guide us. Sir James Mackintosh in the *Edinburgh Review* had advocated that each great class and profession in the country should have a certain proportion of representatives in the House of Commons: landlords, of course; merchants and manufacturers; officers of the Army and Navy; lawyers; and men of letters. In the opinion of Mill, "the real effect of this motley representation would only be to create a motley aristocracy; and to insure that kind of misgovernment which it is the nature of an aristocracy to produce, and to produce equally, whether it is a uniform or a variegated aristocracy." What is left? A perfect representative system. First, will it not destroy the Monarchy and the House of Lords? He replies that it will not destroy the Monarchy, for the king is left with the administration, which the representative body checks and controls but does not undertake. If a second chamber is vital, and if the hereditary landowners are the best class for that chamber, then a body of representatives will, doubtless, establish such a chamber. Here is cold comfort for the peers. Second, are the people capable of acting agreeably to their interests? This forms the strength of the aristocratic party. Mill's reply is that if the community does not act according to its interests, the prospect of mankind is indeed deplorable. The aristocracy is sure to take care of itself. If the people do not, the remedy is, enlighten them and enlighten them, at once. The ballot is to be secret.

Neither an aristocratic body nor a popular one is suitable to possess political power. The conclusion is irresistible. "There can be no doubt that the middle rank, which gives to science, to art, and to legislation itself, their most distinguished ornaments, and is the chief source of all that has exalted and refined human nature, is that portion of the community of which, if the basis of Representation were ever to be extended, the opinion would ultimately decide.

Of the people beneath them, a vast majority would be sure to be guided by their advice and example." In the article on colonies we glean that their good is to give places to members of the ruling class; and John Bright, a typical member of the middle class, attributed the continuance of the diplomatic service to this very reason. In the eyes of Mill, colonies are a grand source of war, and of additional expense in war; and they create and increase patronage and the means of corruption to the government at home. To-day the one place open to the sons of the middle class is the Civil Service, Colonial and Home, and, perhaps if Mill could have foreseen this, he would not have condemned colonies so vigorously. What he would have said at the existence of a middle class which every politician ignores save for taxable purposes, we tremble to think. The irony of history is keen. Mill lays down principles leading to the enfranchisement of the middle class, and his are the very ones to lead in the long run to universal suffrage. A glimpse of this is afforded to Macaulay in his attack on Mill; for Macaulay asks: "Will the people act against their own interest? Or will the middle class act against its own interest? Or is the interest of the middle class identical with the interest of the people? If any one of the three be answered in the affirmative, his whole system falls to the ground. If the interest of the middle rank be identical with that of the people, why should not the powers of government be trusted to that rank." With a foresight deeper than Mill's, Macaulay finally points out that "the system of universal suffrage, according to Mr. Mill's own account, is only a device for doing circuitously what a representative system with a pretty high qualification would do directly."

Lord Lansdowne "had been much struck by the articles" Macaulay wrote against Mill's "Government," and in consequence of them he offered their author his seat in Parliament. They exercised also an influence on J. S. Mill, who ascribed to them the creation of an epoch in his intellectual history. James Mill's method had been the deductive one, Macaulay's the inductive or historical. Macaulay remarks that the "Government" article is so abstract that, but for two or three passing allusions, it would not appear as if Mill were aware that any rule existed among men. Monarchs and aristocrats may be—or may desire to be—as self-seeking as Mill makes them out to be, for he has chosen to look only at one half of human nature. Take the reigns of Philip II, or Louis XV, or the Emperor Paul. The desire of the good opinion of others and the pain of public hatred and contempt restrain princes as well as peers. In fact, Mill suffers from the adoption of the *a priori* method as well as from the dryness of his style. Mill, in the eyes of Macaulay, proposes to discover what governments are good; and, finding that experience gives no clear answer, throws experience aside and appeals to absolute laws of human nature. One such "law" asserts the beatitude, Blessed are the strong, for they shall prey on the weak. Mill thereupon jumps to the conclusion that all governments save those of the middle class must be oppressive, and rule by sheer terror. Yet some despotisms work well while some work badly. The eighteenth century was the age of the enlightened despots. There are the shining names of Joseph II, Catherine II, and Frederick II. Nor can we pass by such names as Charles III of Spain, Joseph of Portugal, Amadeus III and Gustavus III of Sweden, Christian VII of Denmark, Charles Frederick, Margrave of Baden, Maximilian Joseph and Charles Theodore of Bavaria, Frederick Augustus, Elector of Saxony, and the Grand Duke of Tuscany. Ministers like Pombal, Tanucci, Aranda, Blanca, and Bernstorff deserve honourable mention on any bead-roll of the benevolent despots. In a word, Mill assumes terrible consequences deducible from the selfishness of rules "if nothing checks." Macaulay supplies some checks. Bentham had laid such stress on the sinister interests of the motley aristocracy, the landowners, merchants, manufacturers, officers, lawyers, and *littérateurs* that he passed by the checks due to good opinion, public hatred and contempt. Nevertheless these checks actually worked. Macaulay shows the absurdity of transferring the legal to the political sovereignty. Parliament may, as he says, make a law that every gentleman with £2000 a year may flog a pauper with a cat-of-nine-tails whenever he pleased. Nevertheless, as the first exercise of such a power would be the "last day of the English aristocracy," their power is, in fact, strictly limited.

It was open to Mill, as his son suggests, to meet the criticism of Macaulay by lowering his claims. If the article on "Government" were supposed to be strictly scientific, Macaulay was justified in his strictures. But what if Mill were simply analysing tendencies? What if for that purpose he assumed that checks were non-existent? What if Macaulay were an empiricist and Mill a reasoner who simplified his argument for the purpose of reaching definite conclusions? When these conclusions had been reached, then the omitted "checks" could be considered. In his Indian evidence Mill showed himself well aware of the qualifications necessary before his principles applied. Nor did he exercise his office as correspondent in the revenue department for seventeen years for nothing.

Mill falls back on the selfishness of mankind. Will not this selfishness at any given moment lead the majority to plunder the rich and to disregard the interests of their own successors? In reply to Macaulay, he suggests that his opponent foresees a reign of terror as a necessary outcome of the extension of the franchise. "We say again and again," Macaulay retorts, "that we are on the defensive. We do not think it necessary to prove that a quack medicine is poison. Let the vendor prove it to be sanative. We do not pretend to show that universal suffrage is an evil. Let its advocates show it to be a good." The Chartists' petition in 1842 demanded universal suffrage. Macaulay thought then that universal suffrage would be incompatible with the "institution of property." His view was that if the Chartists acted on their principles we should witness "something more horrible than can be imagined—something like the siege of Jerusalem on a far larger scale." The most he could hope for would be a military despotism, giving a "sort of protection to a miserable wreck of all that immense glory and prosperity." With as much confidence in the virtue and the wisdom of the middle class as his opponent, Macaulay had yet suggested, in reply to Mill, that if his opponent were correct in his outlook, and "Government" came from the ideal to the real, "literature, science, commerce, manufactures" would disappear, and a "few half-naked fishermen would divide with the owls and foxes the ruins of the greatest of European cities."

The attacker and the attacked felt distinctly strongly in favour of the liberty of the press. Mill willingly admits—here the official speaks—that exhortations to obstruct the operations of government *in detail* should be deemed offences; but if directed against government generally, they should not fall into this category. General disapprobation of the government is unobjectionable: disapprobation with civil commotion for its end is objectionable. In punishing offenders of the latter type, the thing to avoid is vengeance. In the work of the obstruction of the government in detail, a distinction is to be drawn between those exhortations that are direct and explicit and those that are indirect and implicit. The former ought to be punished. Such a limitation on the liberty of the press is obvious, but the ideal he dwells on is the power of freely expressing oneself. The right to bestow censure in the institutions of government is vital for the good of the people. Characteristically, he holds that the press is abused when the rulers receive undeserved praise. In a curious essay Mill wrote on the principles of toleration in the *Westminster Review* in July, 1826, he takes as his motto the words of Whichcote, "I would rather meet with a true philosopher, a considerate mind, one that hath searched and examined, one that hath thought upon and submitted things to discussion—I had rather be in that man's company than in his that will entertain me with delights of the sense. For to please the mind, to satisfy a man's understanding—this is worthy of a man—this is entertainment." The reality of toleration is forcibly handled, and the ex-divinity students ends the matter with these words: "Of all classes of men, the clergy, as a class, are the most constant and the deepest offenders against the virtue of rightly dealing with evidence, it follows, that of all classes of men living, the clergy are the most remarkably destitute of faith, in other words, are of all men living, the greatest infidels."

The Church, according to Mill, was a decidedly curious one, and we wonder if Newman ever read such an amazing conception of it. Had he done so, it would have furnished another reason for his dread of liberalism. The regular services of the Church of England are drastically handled, Holy Communion being considered as a ceremony, and an ill-fitted one at that. He admits—here speaks the licensed Scots divinity student—that a discourse of the right sort, delivered on the day of rest to the assembled parishioners, would have happy effects, but how often it has not? The prevailing doctrine of future punishments, he thinks, reduces the Deity to the level of an atrocious savage. He forgets Heine's great *obiter dictum* that as is a man, so is his God. The ceremonies of Baptism, Marriage, and the Burial of the Dead are all dismissed as worthless, and that of Baptism is vicious in doctrine.

What is the remedy? First of all, a more equal distribution of work among the clergy by equalising parishes. Next, to secure men of education and character, they should receive sufficient pay. The mode of their appointment is left unsettled. Is the mode of their superintendence to be by individuals (bishops) or by assemblies, as in Scotland? He allows that the Scots system has worked well, but favours a modified system of personal inspection. The great lords are not to be inspectors, but is there no question of sinister interest in the men of whom Mill approves? These lay inspectors are to have £1000 a year, and the highest income of the parish priest is to be £500 a year. All are to be paid by salary, not by rent or tithes from land, a system he strongly condemns, though it is still in force in the Church of England. Of course there is to be no doctrinal dogma. Obviously this will, in Utilitarian eyes, at any rate, be a truly Catholic Church. Will not all share its services? Will it not provide the true conception of a State religion? For the clergy, in their addresses, will have no other object than to assimilate the minds of their hearers to Him who is the perfection of wisdom and benevolence. Dissenters will no longer be branded as "enemies" and men of "guilt." Thereby religion, which ought to be a principle of love, has been converted into a principle of hatred. Dissenters will, however, turn to this Catholic Church. There would be no schism when men had nothing to scind about.

The clergy are to diffuse all incitements to happiness: they are to supply all inducements to good conduct. Rules for these desirable ends cannot be laid down. Tests can, however, be applied for results, and these will be premiums for the minimum of crimes, of law-suits, of pauperism, of ill-educated children. In addition to moral addresses, there is to be instruction in science and useful knowledge. Such branches of political science as political economy and the conditions of good government are to be promoted. To teach the maxims of justice and the theory of protection of rights—less is said about duties—, the elements of jurisprudence are valuable. The assembling of all the families on Sunday, clean and well-dressed, produces an ameliorating effect. An Agnostic lady of our acquaintance, actuated by motives like these, compels her maids to attend Church on Sundays, on the ground that thereby she secures a change of clothes on their part.

Memories of the Scots' Sabbath suggest to Mill that there should be social amusements, though old association inclines him to those of a mild nature. A generation like ours will not take kindly to the suggestion that sports involving bodily strength are not well adapted to the promotion of brotherly feelings. Still, there are to be music and dancing, though the modern forms of dancing are frowned upon by anticipation, for is not dancing to represent parental, filial, and fraternal affections? One can draw deductions from this idea as to the failure of the philosopher's marriage. His ideal in dancing is to avoid all tendency towards lasciviousness, his Scots' Puritanism thereby appearing. In spite of his contempt for Holy Communion, there is to be a conjoint meal on Sunday, renewing the Agapai, the love feasts, of the early Christians; but there are to be no intoxicating liquors. Larévellière-Lépeaux observed to Talleyrand that it was quite easy to start a Church, but the difficulty was to secure adherents. How could he attract them? "Still," retorted the former prelate, "there is one plan which you might at least try; I should recommend you to be crucified and to rise again the third day." Mill's Church was to have been a glorified Mechanics' Institute, but had it any attraction? He himself never started a branch of it, and it is safe to prophesy that a branch of it never will be started. The religious faculty in him became as atrophied as the æsthetic faculty.

Mill is a securer guide in the world of fact than in the world of religion. His *Elements of Political Economy* appeared in 1821, and is so abstract as to suggest that he deemed all illustrations from life as quite irrelevant. In sheer abstractness he suggests his spiritual son, Ricardo. With his feeling for the Physiocrats, did he not mean Ricardo to be the Quesnay of England? Malthus and Mill influenced Ricardo deeply. Classical political economy comes to him from Malthus, and a deductive and reasoning method comes to him from Mill. In spite of differences Mill was attached to Bentham, and his dry heart came near to feeling true affection for Ricardo. His death in 1823 moved him to a degree which astonished his circle, accustomed only to his stern exterior.

According to the *Elements*, the wealth of a country is its annual produce and not its capital. Practically, Mill defines capital as instruments and materials, whether accumulated into a stock or not. He assumes that the circulating capital of a country, or perhaps the whole capital, circulates or is consumed and reproduced once a year. In his first edition he pays little attention to the laws regulating the production of commodities, though in his second he expounds the advantages of the division of labour and the nature of capital. He recognises the law of diminishing returns, repeatedly speaking of it as if it were not only a general rule, but an invariable rule, except in cases where colonists from civilised countries "have the power of cultivating without limit the most productive species of land."

Ricardo analyses the laws of distribution into those regulating rent, profit, and wages, and Mill follows this example. In rent he stresses the law of diminishing returns. Land once brought into cultivation, he explains, is more valuable than uncleared land. Rather than clear fresh land, a man will pay an equivalent for the cost of clearing, yet this "is not a payment for the power of the soil, but simply for the capital bestowed upon the soil." In his desire to support the position of the capitalist, he justifies the existence of profits. At the same time he exhibits a desire to assimilate the position of the capitalist with that of the labourer. He asks the question: What determined the quantity in which commodities exchange for one another? His answer is Quantity of labour, a truly Ricardian answer. When the natural tendency of population to increase faster than capital works normally, and has time to make itself felt, wages will fall to a level which will only afford the means of rearing a family which is not "numerous." He has nothing to say about the causes of differences in wages.

The article on "Government" and the *Elements of Political Economy* were written with a practical end in view, and that end the installation of politicians imbued with Utilitarian views. The theory of production and the theory of distribution were admirable weapons for propaganda. The theory of production imbued the employer with distrust of all efforts of the State to look after labour. The Poor Law had been devised for that purpose, and the Act of 1834 attests the abuses of the old Poor Law. The political economists then came to teach that capital was what really set industry in motion, what really supported labour. The Ricardian theory of distribution depicted the growth of rent at the expense of the community. Soils of a steadily lower class were being cultivated, with the result that rent was no less steadily increasing. Was it not easy in the near future to depict the landlords as men drawing a tribute stained with blood? With such an argument, what hope was there of a continuance of the Corn Laws? There was every opportunity afforded to the manufacturers to show what an odious class the landlords were, and right well were Bright and Cobden to use their opportunity. Writers like Mill and his disciple Ricardo considered wealth as consisting of objects with exchange value, not as objects concerning the welfare of the persons concerned. They could see, and see quite clearly, the changes wrought by the capitalist in the Industrial Revolution, but how these changes affected the toiler was by no means so clear. The aim of Mill was to increase the exchange value of the property of the middle class, which he honestly believed was for the benefit of the country. The aim of the toiler was to increase the material welfare of his class, and the improvements in the world of industry impelled him to note if an alteration in the laws of distribution were not to his advantage. Obviously, Mill and Ricardo were not in the least contemplating this situation.

From 1760 to 1785 there was a remarkable set of inventions and improvements. Brindley's canals, Watt's steam-engine, Cort's processes of puddling and rolling iron, and Roebuck's method of smelting it came into operation. The spinning-jenny, the carding machine, and the power-loom, thanks to the services of Hargreaves, Crompton, Arkwright, Cartwright and others, became more efficient. The north of England had taken but a small share in our history up to the accession of George III, though ever since that date it has won a gradually increasing paramountcy. There were more changes in England from 1760 to 1785 than probably took place from 1066 to 1760. The large factory, with the tall chimney, and the black smoke appeared, and the men in them aspired to be more than mere hands. In the India Office, Mill heard the mutterings of the storm. In October, 1831, he wrote in grave agitation to Francis Place, fashionable tailor and unfashionable agitator, concerning a deputation, "from the working classes," who had been preaching communism to Black, the editor of the *Chronicle*. Place soothes Mill by replying that "the men who called on Black were not a deputation from the working people, but two out of half a dozen who manage, or mismanage, the meetings of the Rotunda. . . . The doctrine they are now preaching is that promulgated by Hodgskin in a tract of 1825." In turn, Mill wrote to Brougham on September 3rd, 1832: "The nonsense to which your Lordship alludes about the rights of the labourer to the whole produce of the country, wages, profits, rent, all included, is the mad nonsense of our friend, Hodgkin (*sic*) which he has published as a system, and propagates with the zeal of perfect fanaticism. These opinions, if they are to spread, would be the subversion of civilised society; worse than the overwhelming deluge of Huns and Tartars." He tells Brougham that he entertains little fear of the propagation among the common people of any doctrines hostile to property were it not for two circumstances. One is the currency agitation, the question whether or not there should be a return to the payment of gold suspended during the Napoleonic Wars. The other is "the illicit, cheap publications, in which the doctrine of the right of the labouring people, who they say are the only producers, to all that is produced, is very generally preached. The alarming nature of this evil you will understand when I inform you that these publications are superseding the Sunday newspapers, and every other channel through which the people might get better information."

The remarkable matter is that the fountain of this agitation was Ricardo himself. According to Adam Smith, labour is the real measure of the exchangeable value of all commodities. According to Ricardo, the real price of a commodity depends on the greater or less quantity of labour which must be employed to produce it. He constantly takes no notice of capital, mentioning labour only, and seeks to justify his practice by treating capital as accumulated labour. Many who read his writings—and more who heard of their teaching—ignored this accumulated labour. The outcome was that men took Ricardo's statements as he often expressed them in disregard of the share taken by capital. The conclusion reached was that the real price of a commodity depended on the amount of labour. The next conclusion was, Why should not labour have the sole right to the whole of what it produced? If other classes received share in this, it was clearly unearned, and the notion of the unearned increment is plain in the writings of Thompson, Hall, Gray, and Bray, as well as in those of Hodgskin. These writings mainly appear in the twenties and thirties of the nineteenth century, and they are in fundamental agreement in the demand for social justice. Their authors do not always discriminate between the right to subsistence and the right to the whole produce of labour, though the former appears to be the right to which we are now tending. Once the worker grounds his claim on equity, he gravitates towards pure communism. He unmistakably felt that remedial measures, if not revolutionary ones, were required. Among these remedial measures we class Trade Unions, Co-operation, and Factory Legislation. Among these revolutionary measures we class the Socialism advocated by Thompson, Hall, Gray, Bray, and Hodgskin. Nor can we pass by the circumstance that the revolutionary measures, as well as the remedial ones, are definitely English, anticipating the ideas of Marx by at least a generation.

William Godwin is the father of the Socialism of our day, moulding the opinion of many who had never glanced at a page of his writings. His *Inquiry concerning Political Justice and its Influence on General Virtue and Happiness*, had appeared in 1793. All government, he contends, is evil and unnatural, while society is good and natural. Neither society nor individuals possess any rights. For property, the root of all evil, he substitutes a system of equal property, distributed according to want or "the capacity of the subject." His plan requires "no restrictions or superintendence whatever." We leave the real behind us and soar to the ideal. "It grows out of a simple, clear, and unanswerable theory of the human mind, that we first stand in need of a certain animal subsistence and shelter, and after that, our only true felicity consists in the expansion of our intellectual powers, the knowledge of truth, and the practice of virtue." How he was to combine his rejection of the communistic state with his acceptance of the right of subsistence and of an individualistic industrial organisation does not emerge. His dreams, nevertheless, moved men, and continue to move them.

The Saint-Simonians and Proudhon moulded the thoughts of Rodbertus, while the early English socialists, particularly William Thompson, moulded those of Marx. The labours of Thompson are much more fundamental than those of Marx. An Irish landlord, Thompson had been, so he tells us, "living on what is called rent, the produce of the labour of others." A pupil of Bentham, "who has done more for moral science than Bacon did for physical science," he describes himself as merely working out the applications of his master's principles. He sought to maximise happiness and minimise pain. Bentham, Godwin, Ricardo, and Owen, the philanthropic employer, all left their impress on him. Thompson prefers the voluntary methods of Godwin, and entertains high hopes of the development of the intellectual side of human nature. He is, however, a communist rather than an individualist. Ricardo's views on labour colour his writing when he lays down that "wealth is produced by labour; no other ingredient, but labour makes any object of desire an object of wealth. Labour is the sole universal measure, as well as the characteristic distinction of wealth." Labour with Ricardo means ordinary labour and capital as well; but when Ricardo set the example of discarding capital, why should not Thompson follow this example? Give the word labour its popular meaning, and on Ricardian principles, as interpreted by Thompson, we at once have modern Socialism. True, Ricardo had in his mind the accumulated labour he called capital, but who else had it in his mind? The Ricardian qualifications were conveniently left to the one side, and the outcome was that the average man carried away the impression that the labourer did the work, while the capitalist and the landlord enjoyed the proceeds. The last influence on Thompson's mind was Owen, and he furthered the formation of Owenite Co-operative Societies with all his Irish enthusiasm.

The drift of the toiler who bases his claims on equity is apparent in the advice Thompson tenders the distressed Spitalfields weavers. "Would you like," he asks, "to enjoy yourselves the whole products of your labor? You have nothing more to do than simply *alter the direction of your labor*. Instead of working for you know not whom, *work for each other*." In 1824, he holds that if any departure is made from the principle of securing the whole product to labour, it should be in the direction of equality, though such a departure "ought scarcely, if ever, to occur." After 1830, he spent his efforts in the advocacy of communistic societies of the Owenite type, leaving the bulk of his property for that purpose. He abandons the idea of security for the idea of equality, championing the rights of women and the equal freedom of the sexes. He is the Utilitarian turned Socialist.

In his *Inquiry into the Principles of the Distribution of Wealth most conducive to Human Happiness*, 1824, Thompson investigates the natural laws governing distribution. He argues that it is the unnatural and unjust distribution which checks production. Capital is unproductive of any new values: labour produces the additional value. He rests himself on what he conceives to be the Ricardian position that all value in exchange is derived from labour alone. "The productive labourers," according to Thompson, "stript of all capital, of tools, houses, and materials, to make their labor productive, toil from want, from the necessity of existence, their remuneration being kept at the lowest compatible with the existence of industrious habits." The inference is perfectly plain. The labourer receives only the smallest possible return compatible with existence, the amount falling to Lassalle's iron law of wages. He creates the remainder of the value which enriches the pockets of the landlord and the capitalist. Surely to him who has wrought to produce the value should belong the total reward of his effort, yet under the existing social *régime* nothing of the sort takes place. With Adam Smith and Ricardo in their unguarded moments, Thompson claims that rent and profits are deductions, unjust deductions at that, made by the owners of land and capital. He favours distribution according to needs, the right to subsistence. His *Inquiry into the Principles of the Distribution of Wealth most conducive to Human Happiness* raises the question of the right distribution of wealth to that high position it then held, and holds even more insistently at the present moment.

Charles Hall was a physician who met in his daily round the misery of mankind. What is the root cause? It is, in his opinion, civilisation, and he writes in 1805 his book on *The Effects of Civilisation on the People of the European States*. He gives us his personal observations on the effects of the Industrial Revolution, and he does so with a hold on facts and a restraint on his indignation that mark off his book from Marx's *Das Kapital*. What Godwin means by the effects of property, a certain legalised inequality, Hall means by civilisation. He defines civilisation as that state of society in which, on the one hand, science, knowledge, trade, and manufactures flourish, while, on the other hand, the large majority of the population is poor, or sinking into poverty. He estimates that eight-tenths of the population only receive one-eighth of all the wealth they produce, while two-tenths, who produce nothing, receive seven-eighths as rent and interest. Out of an eight hours' day, were such a day then conceivable, the poor man works but one hour for himself, and works the other seven for the idle rich. The French had suffered from the *corvée*, and the English were suffering from a disguised *corvée*. His thesis is that wealth is power over the labour of the poor, leading, under the *régime* of the manufacturer, to inequality and oppression. What is the remedy? He has no precise one. He simply lays down principles. Firstly, every man shall labour so much only as is necessary for his family; secondly, he shall enjoy the whole fruits of his labour. He proposes the abolition of the English law of primogeniture and the prohibition, or the heavy taxation, of the manufacture of luxuries. The more equal distribution of land is his main solution, though he leans to it in a tentative spirit. The State is to own the land, to allot it to families in proportion to their numbers, and on the extinction of any family the allotment reverts to the State. As families increase at different rates a redistribution shall from time to time take place. In this fashion we have community of property with an individualistic system of production and family life. But what if population increases faster than the means of subsistence? There is the spectre evoked by Malthus. Godwin contrives not to see this spectre when he talks of the "triumph of mind over matter." Hall, as a physician, has too often seen the triumph of matter over mind, yet he thinks that the fear of over-population is a distant one. It is an enormous gain if we can "lay the reprieve at one hundred years." In the meantime political action may extend this physical limit. Adopt "nature's remedy, colonisation," and "marriage may be regulated by law," a position to which we may come when Socialism gains the ascendant. *The Effects of Civilisation on the People in European States* was a cry from the human heart. It was more than a cry, for it was based on a fine survey of the course of history, poignantly inspired by the intensity and the sincerity of its author.

In 1825, John Gray published his *Lecture on Human*

Happiness, being the first of a series of Lectures on the Causes of the existing evils of Society. Nominally, it advocates Owen's schemes, though really it sets forth an argument of the laws of distribution similar to that of Dr. Hall's statistical one. The Industrial Revolution has not impressed him as it did Hall, for he contemplates that simple society of small producers just then being replaced by the complex society of the manufacturing age. Gray contends that there is no just title to land. "The foundation of all property is LABOUR, and there is no other just foundation for it." "The interest of money is another mode of obtaining labour without giving any equivalent for it." "*What does the productive labourer obtain for that portion of the produce of his industry which is annually taken from him by incomes obtained by the lenders of money?* He obtains NOTHING! Then, we ask, is a man the natural proprietor of the produce of his own labour? If he is not, what foundation is there for property at all? . . . If he is, . . . there is no justice in requiring interest for the use of money?" Nor is Gray's censure of the unproductive services of the lender, the landlord, and the capitalist so foolish as it sounds, for had not Adam Smith and David Ricardo, to say the least, lent him countenance? No doubt his tone is militant, but the situation of the worker, in his opinion, called for militancy. At the same time we note his depreciation of force, even admitting that his criticism of "the established customs of the country" has been an unpleasant task, forced upon him.

Thomas Hodgskin was a young naval officer who had studied Locke, Adam Smith, and Ricardo. Locke indeed had anticipated his two successors in holding the labour theory of the value of commodities. Hodgskin seems to have anticipated Marx's theory of surplus value, and proposed writing a book on it till Place dissuaded him from this project, and indeed Marx quotes him. He adopted the principles of Ricardo, and gave them a Socialist turn, a comparatively easy matter to do. Hall had been stimulated to thought by contract with his patients, Hodgskin by the public movements of the twenties. Thanks to Joseph Hume's Committee, the Combination Laws of 1824 had been repealed. In spite of this repeal there had been a development of trade union activity, followed by strike after strike. In 1825 another Committee sat to consider the re-enactment of the old anti-combination laws. Place, by his generalship, averted this, and the new Act of 1825, while imposing certain restrictions, left the right of agreement and discussion in wages questions substantially unimpaired. In 1825, Hodgskin wrote *Labour Defended against the Claims of Capital; or the Unproductiveness of Capital proved with reference to the Present Combinations of Journeymen, By a Labourer*. He examines the necessity of protecting capital, concluding that the benefits attributed to capital really arise from co-existing skilled labour. Has capital any just claim to the large share of the national produce it takes? "This large share ... is the cause of the poverty of the labourer; and he ventures to assert that the condition of the labourer can never be permanently improved till he can refute the theory, and is determined to oppose the practice, of giving nearly everything to capital." Capital is a flow, not a fund. "As far as food, drink, and clothing are concerned, it is quite plain that no species of labourer depends on any previously prepared stock, for, in fact, no such stock exists; but every species of labourer does constantly, and at all times, depend for his supplies on the co-existing labour of some other labourers." "All the effects usually attributed to accumulation of circulating capital are derived from the *accumulation and storing up of skilled labour*." He admits that fixed capital is stored, but "fixed capital does not derive its utility from previous, but present labour."

Hodgskin fully recognises that the inventor deserves his reward, but so does the artisan who uses the invention. He is far ahead of Marx and the economists in distinguishing between the functions of the capitalist and the *entrepreneur*. If in this respect he goes forward, he falls back for support on Ricardo. He claims his authority for the truth of the iron law of wages, for the position that "the exactions of the capitalist cause the poverty of the labourer." He allows competition in wages and combination against capital. The classical economists, Adam Smith particularly, inspired him to write *The Natural and Artificial Rights of Property Contrasted*, 1832, and in it there is explicit the anarchism implicit in that Physiocratic influence which permeates the *Wealth of Nations*. There is no proposal contained in this book of Hodgskin's, though this is quite common in anarchical writings. His real desire is to reform the law of property, not to destroy it. There are many rhetorical flourishes. We read that "the law of nature is that industry shall be rewarded by wealth, and idleness be punished by destitution; the law of the land is to give wealth to idleness, and fleece industry till it be destitute."

In *Labour's Wrongs and Labour's Remedy: or the Age of Might and the Age of Right*, 1839, John Francis Bray has much to say about the laws of nature. Among these laws are equality of men, equality of rights and duties, and common ownership of the soil. Of course it is labour alone that bestows value. Inequality of possessions is the fundamental cause of the wrongs of labour. Long before Marx he insists that as "all profit must come from labour . . . the gain of an idle class must necessarily be the loss of an industrious class." He is as weak on the theory of money as so many Socialists are, thinking it quite practicable to issue paper money against the whole mass of national property. He is contemptuous of the Whig remedies for the social *malaise*, Free Trade, machinery, emigration, and the rest of them. He pierces the fallacy of the wage-fund theory, and notes the failure in this day of the trade unions. Universal Labour and Equal Exchanges form his panacea. "Every man has a right to do what he likes, *provided the so-doing interferes not with the EQUAL rights of his fellow-men*." Thereby he believes he excludes property in land and includes a right to the whole produce of labour. "Equal labour of all kinds should be equally remunerated . . . inequality in the value of labour to society is no argument for inequality of reward." According to Ricardo, so Bray teaches us, "it is not to any one commodity, or set of commodities, but to some given *quantity of labour*, that we must refer for an unvarying standard of real value. Here is a recognition of the principle that real value is dependent on labour; and the only inference we can draw from it is that all men who perform an equal quantity of labour ought to receive an equal remuneration."

The communism of Bray requires no demonstration. To him "the present crisis is no more than a natural movement attending the course of things—it is but one move of that mighty ocean of events, the billows of which have rolled on from eternity, and will progress in unchecked power for ever . . . it was advancing even when polished Greece and Rome degenerated into semi-barbarism—it was coming on when the French Revolution took place . . . and it is at this moment passing before our eyes and bearing us along, destroying and reinstituting political and social institutions of every character and kind. The present is not a merely local movement, it is not confined to country, colour, or creed—the universe is the sphere in which it acts . . . and whatever may be its immediate prospect, there are to be seen harbingers of brighter and better times. The light of Mind is beaming through the gloomy boundaries of the Age of Might, and ushering in the Age of Right."

References

BAIN, A. *James Mill, a biography*. (London, 1882.)
BEER, M. *A History of British Socialism*. Vol. I. (London, 1920.)
BOWER, B. S. *Hartley and James Mill*. (London, 1881.)
CANNAN, E. *A History of the Theories of Production and Distribution in English Political Economy*. (London, 1903.)
DAVIDSON, W. L. *Political Thought in England. The Utilitarians from Bentham to J. S. Mill*. (London, 1915.)
FAWCETT, Mrs. *Life of Sir William Molesworth*. (London, 1901.)
GODARD, G. *George Birkbeck, the Pioneer of Popular Education*. (London, 1884.)
GROTE, Mrs. *The Personal Life of George Grote*. (London, 1884.)
GROTE, Mrs. *The Philosophical Radicals of* 1832. (London, 1873, mainly Molesworth's work.)
GUYAU, M. *La Morale Anglaise Contemporaine*. (Paris, 1900.)
HALÉVY, E. *La formation du radicalisme*. (Paris, 1901 ff.)
HALÉVY, E. *Thomas Hodgskin (1787–1861)*. (Paris, 1903.)
LOWENTHAL, E. *The Ricardian Socialists*. (New York, 1911.)
MENGER, A. *The Right to the Whole Produce of Labour*. (London, 1899.)
MILL, J. S. *Autobiography*. (London, 1867.)
STEPHEN, Sir L. *The English Utilitarians*. (London, 1900.)
WALLAS, G. *Life of Francis Place*. (London, 1898.)
WHITAKER, A. C. *History and Criticism of the Labour Theory of Value*. (Columbia University Press, 1904.)

Chapter IV.

OWEN A PRACTICAL SOCIALIST

SIX Englishmen, Godwin, Thompson, Hall, Gray, Hodgskin, and Bray, had been so stirred by the horrors of the Industrial Revolution as to advocate what were then regarded as revolutionary remedies which to-day we should call Socialism, and the amazing matter is that the fount of the inspiration of five of them is the classical economist, Ricardo. These men talked: it was reserved for Robert Owen to act, and he, like them, was also inspired by Ricardo. The agitation for the right of combination on the part of working men in 1824 and 1825 afforded them all an opportunity for airing their views, and it is more than a coincidence that Thompson, Gray and Hodgskin published books in 1825. The three men worked separately and independently, and their one point in common was that they owed much to Ricardo. Owen's name and fame were to give the writings of these six men a greater currency than perhaps they might have obtained, but the man who was really read was not these six, but Ricardo himself. In his *History of Co-operation*, Holyoake tells us that "it was the year 1825 which saw co-operative views—which since 1812 had been addressed by Mr. Owen to the upper classes—first taken up by the working classes." Co-operative papers and co-operative societies scattered abroad the Ricardian doctrines till then known only to the elect like James Mill. This is particularly true of 1830, when the Owenite movement drifted towards Socialism. "For fourteen years" (after 1830), concludes Holyoake, "co-operation has to be traced through Socialism." Behind Owen lies Thompson and his school. Chartism, as well as Socialism, finds shelter under the protection of Owen's name. The remarkable matter is that Owen was distinctly of the bourgeois type, yet, like Saint Simon in France, he popularised a movement from which he shrank. The reason of this is not far to seek. The six had not succeeded in business, and for the average Englishman they were probably quite decent people, but undoubtedly cranks. Owen proved a huge success in business, and certainly, tried by that test, there must be something in his views that was not found in those of Thompson and his fellow-thinkers.

Robert Owen (1771-1858) was born at Newtown, in Montgomeryshire; his father was a working sadler and kept a small shop. The boy was very precocious; at the age of seven, having learnt the little that the schoolmaster could teach him, he became an usher, nor did he ever have any more formal education. His home was not so Puritan as Bentham's or Mill's, and as the lad was an omnivorous reader he devoured *Robinson Crusoe* and Richardson's novels as well as Young's *Night Thoughts* and Bunyan's *Pilgrim's Progress*. Unconsciously, the last impressed him as *Télémaque* impressed Bentham, for he was to be a pilgrim all his days. There are few great Welshmen, yet Thomas Cromwell—or Williams—inaugurated one social order and Robert Owen another.

At ten Owen set out for London, on his own initiative, to seek his fortune, with forty shillings in his pocket; and within six weeks he found it. For a Ludgate Hill lace-dealer procured for him the offer of a place with a big draper in business at Stamford. The boy was to be apprenticed "for three years—the first without pay, the second with a salary of eight pounds, and the third with ten pounds, with board, lodging, and washing in the house." "These terms," Owen writes in his autobiography, "I accepted, and being well found in clothes to serve me more than a year, I, from that period, ten years of age, maintained myself without ever applying to my parents for any additional aid." This strangely self-reliant child was father of the man. The most striking of Owen's qualities was his supreme self-confidence; it was not of an offensive, bullying kind, being allied with an equally supreme gentleness and tolerance of opposition, but it was absolute, unshakable, immovable. In after years he never doubted that the times were out of joint, that he was born to set them right, and that he was on the point of succeeding. One scheme after another might fail and come to nothing, supporters might leave him and friends become estranged, opponents and events might prove him wrong; he remained unmoved, serenely convinced that he alone was right, and that his projects were about to usher in the millennium at once and on the spot where he was. It is evident that he began life with this temperament, and that all his early experiences fostered it. As a child he was never corrected but once, when he gave his mother a wrong answer through failure to hear her question. Having given his answer, he could not bring himself to alter or acknowledge his mistake, even though he were beaten to death for it. That was Robert Owen at seven years of age, and that was he at eighty-seven. He always thought for himself and went his own way; his natural assurance was monumental, and for many years events conspired to strengthen it. When he was twelve or thirteen, a draper's apprentice in a small country town, he wrote to Pitt on the question of Sunday observance, and shortly after the Government issued a proclamation on the subject. At this mature age he read and pondered on religion in the intervals of attendance on the counter; and the result was that "with the greatest reluctance and after long contests in his mind," as he gravely tells us in his autobiography, he "was compelled to abandon his first and deep-rooted impression in favour of Christianity." The same profound reflections taught him that all religion was founded on error, and must be given up, to be replaced by "the spirit of universal charity"; but where that came from does not seem to have been considered.

At Stamford he met with an employer, Mr. McGuffog, of the same type as himself. McGuffog had been originally a Scots pedlar, and had commenced life with a few shillings and a basket, which in a short time he changed for a pack, ultimately becoming a rich trader. The apprentice was as hard-working as his master, and never during his long life drank intoxicants or smoked tobacco. He was, in fact, a thoroughly model young man, and remained so.

The ideas of the French Revolution were in the air. Wordsworth, Coleridge, and Southey were scattering them abroad, but there is no evidence that such thoughts stirred the business man in the least. His main task was quite obviously that of making his way, and make his way he undoubtedly did. Thanks to John Wesley, the thoughts that created the political revolution of France in 1789 created the religious revolution of England. No doubt it stirred Owen to denounce creeds, yet even in his denunciation he remained a religious man. The Industrial Revolution was to absorb his thoughts, for he moved to Manchester.

Facts are eloquent on the change that was taking place in the north. In 1701 the amount of cotton imported into Great Britain was 1,985,868 pounds, and in 1800 it was 56,010,732 pounds. The value of our cotton exports in 1701 was £23,253, and in 1800 it was £5,406,501. The spinning-wheels and looms at the beginning of the century had been worked at home, but the great inventions transferred them to the factory. Hargreaves's spinning-jenny, Arkwright's water frame, and Crompton's mule were the main agents in this transference. The slow handloom, however, could not overtake the rapidity with which the mule and the water frame produced cotton twist. For this purpose Cartwright devised his loom worked by mechanical power, and Watt's steam engine was there to provide this mechanical power. Man power was to be employed as relentlessly as mechanical. "An eminent manufacturer of that age," writes Dr. Aikin, "used to be in his warehouse before six in the morning, accompanied by his children and apprentices. At seven they all came to breakfast, which consisted of one huge dish of water pottage, made of oatmeal, water, and a little salt, boiled thick and poured into a dish. At the side was a pan or basin of milk, and the master and the apprentices, each with a wooden spoon in his hand, without loss of time, dipped into the same dish, and thence into the milk pan, and as soon as it was finished they all returned to their work." The employed were not the only slaves of the Industrial Revolution. The masters were victims as well as the men.

According to Louis XIV, in war it is the last *louis d'or*

that wins. Michelet improves on this *obiter dictum* when he narrates the twenty-two years' struggle between France and England. "When the English manufacturers warned Pitt," he records, "that owing to the high wages they had to pay their workmen, they were unable to pay their national taxes, Pitt returned a terrible answer: 'Take the children.' That saying weighs like a curse upon England." Pitt of course never uttered this remark. The children of the poor, however, have always had to work for their living before the Industrial Revolution, and after its coming. The horrible thing is that before the quarter of a century from 1760 to 1785 they worked as a subordinate factor, whereas after that time they worked as a main one. Till mechanical power was developed, hand power was employed, and this hand power came from the children. The parochial authorities had many unwanted children, and they naturally were glad when the factories came to absorb them. From seven to twenty-one the children came to the mills to spend that portion of their existence in monotonous toil. The mills worked normally fifteen hours a day, and in them work never ceased. A shift of night children took the place of the day children. On Sundays some were employed from 6 a.m. till 12 in cleaning machinery. Inevitably the overworked children easily fell victims to disease. An epidemic of putrid fever at Radcliffe in 1784 drew attention to the plight of these apprentices. On the recommendation of Dr. Percival, a doctor as noble as Hall, the Manchester magistrates passed a resolution that in future they would refuse to sanction indentures of parish apprentices to cotton mills where there was night work or day of more than ten hours. Other northern magistrates passed similar resolutions, but as the children did not come from their districts, little was done for these tiny victims. Epidemics of putrid fever in cotton factories still continued. The first Sir Robert Peel had mills where children suffered, and in 1784 and 1796 the magistrates had complained of their suffering. Peel inquired into the matter, and stated that "having other pursuits, it was not often in my power to visit factories, but whenever such visits were made I was struck with the uniform appearance of bad health, and in many cases stunted growth of the children; the hours of labour were regulated by the interest of the overseer, whose remuneration depending on the quantity of work done, he was often induced to make the poor children work excessive hours, and to stop their complaints by trifling bribes."

The outcome of Peel's notice of the condition of the children was the Act of 1802 "for the better preservation of the Health and Morals of Apprentices and others employed in cotton mills and cotton manufactories," and Wilberforce, the abolitionist, successfully altered the last words to "cotton and other mills,—and cotton and other manufactories." This Act laid down that all cotton or woollen mills must be kept clean and airy; the children were not to work more than twelve hours a day, exclusive of meal times, and these twelve hours were to be between 6 a.m. and 9 p.m. Except in the case of the bigger mills, night work after June, 1803, was prohibited. Provision was made for secular and religious education. Employers in Manchester and elsewhere emphatically protested that the Act was "prejudicial to the Cotton trade" and also "impracticable." In spite of this protest the Justices of the Peace were to appoint a magistrate, unconnected with the mills, and a clergyman to see that these provisions were enforced, but what power had these two? When a West Indian slave-master heard of the hours of the children he was astounded. "Well," he observed, " I have always thought myself disgraced by being the owner of slaves, but we never in the West Indies thought it possible for any human being to be so cruel as to require a child of nine years old to work twelve-and-a-half hours a day; and that, you acknowledge, is your regular practice." The children were victims as well as the masters.

In the meantime Owen had been pursuing his markedly successful career. He had gone to Manchester to work in the cotton mills at sixteen, started cotton spinning with a partner at eighteen, had a factory of his own at nineteen, and earned three hundred the first year. He inquired minutely into the mechanism of the machinery and—what was then rare—into the mechanism of the men, women, and children who handled this machinery. "I can make manufacturing pay," he said to himself, and was shortly to say to others, "without reducing those whom I employ to misery and moral degradation." For he anticipated modern doctrines on environment by generations. In season—and out of season, we are afraid—he never ceased to lay down that "man's character is made for him and not by him." He staunchly taught that, if men were to do good work, they must have a suitable moral and physical environment. As practised by him, it was a commercial creed consistent with profit. He then became the manager of a large mill, and soon after partner in the business. At the Manchester period of his life he seems to have had more regard for money than he afterwards showed, and he always made a keen bargain for himself; but his success as a manufacturer was due more to industry, assiduity, and some mechanical ingenuity than to what is called business aptitude. Here is how he set to work at twenty. "I looked grave, inspected everything very minutely, examined the drawings and calculations of the machinery as left by Mr. Lee, and these were of great use to me. I was up with the first in the morning, and I locked up the premises at night. I continued this silent inspection and superintendence day by day for six weeks, saying merely 'yes' or 'no' to the questions of what was to be done or otherwise, and during that period I did not give one direct order about anything. But at the end of that time I felt myself so much master of my position as to be ready to give directions in every department." Blessed are the self-reliant, for they shall succeed.

At Manchester, Owen met Dalton, the discoverer of the atomic theory, and he met Coleridge, who "solicited permission to join our party, that he might meet me in discussion, as I was the one who opposed the religious prejudices of all sects, though always in a friendly and kind manner, having now imbibed the spirit of charity and kindness for opponents, which was forced upon me by my knowledge of the true formation of character by nature and society." Of the subjects under discussion we glean nothing save that "Mr. Coleridge had a great fluency of words, and he could well put them together in high-sounding sentences; but my few words, directly to the point, generally told well; and though the eloquence and learning were with him, the strength of the argument was generally admitted to be on my side." Again we say, Blessed are the self-reliant.

The economic Socialism of Godwin, Thompson, and his school was not in the mind of the young manufacturer. Life, not books, was to be his teacher. He was not satisfied —how could he be?—with the conditions of the cotton mill. When twenty-seven, he visited Glasgow, meeting Miss Dale, the daughter of David Dale, the well-known Glasgow banker and religious leader. She suggested that he should pay a visit to her father's big cotton mills at New Lanark. Owen paid the visit, recording that "of all places I have yet seen I should prefer this in order to try an experiment I have long contemplated, and have wished to have an opportunity to put in practice." At the time Miss Dale owned on meeting Owen, "I do not know how it is, but if ever I marry, that is to be my husband." Her father's hostility was at last overcome, for their religious opinions clashed, and Owen, at the age of twenty-eight, married her. Her father possessed the New Lanark Mills, which were to be the scene of Owen's first social experiment. They were bought, as part of the marriage settlement, by Owen and his partners, and in January, 1800, he became resident managing director.

His books, *A New View of Society, or, Essays on the Principle of the Formation of the Human Character, and the Application of the Principle to Practice*, his *Observations on the Effect of the Manufacturing System, with Hints for the Improvement of those Parts of it which are most injurious to Health and Morals*, and his *Address delivered to the Inhabitants of New Lanark . . . at the opening of the Institution established for the Formation of Character*, and his *Peace on Earth . . . Development of the Plan for the Relief of the Poor, and the Emancipation of Mankind*—there are many other pamphlets—appeared in 1813, 1815, 1816, and 1817 respectively. The ideas contained in them had long been in his mind. He was one of the most original of men, too original to have much respect for experience; therein lay his strength and weakness. His inspiration was in himself, and he does not seem to have cared a straw what any one else thought except in so far as support was necessary for the immediate practical realisation of his visions on which he was self-reliantly bent.

During the twenty-five years he spent at New Lanark he developed his theories; and the practical success that attended his efforts, limited as they were by his successive partners, confirmed his confidence in the correctness of his own judgment. His writings became widely known, and he was brought into contact with thinkers and men of mark. His books were the matured expressions of the ideas he had formed as a child. The fundamental conceptions were the paramount influence of environment, as it is now called, and the consequent denial of moral responsibility, of praise and blame. From this standpoint the regeneration of mankind is the simplest thing in the world. Change the environment, and the millennium is thereby attained. Active practical Socialism of all degrees is based upon this notion, and Robert Owen was its real father, though the name was not then invented. He stands apart from economic Socialism; there was none of it in his blood, so to speak, in its intellectual pedigree, which really began with Godwin, and was continued by Thompson and his school. Nevertheless, Owen's was the force which gave it actuality. It was New Lanark which caught the public eye and ear; it was New Harmony and the Labour Exchanges that gave concrete expression, understanded of the people, to the aspirations labelled Socialism, and brought the vision within grasp; it was the flood of Owen talk that set everyone agog looking for the millennium, and once for all made the idea of salvation by material means real and familiar. It is sad to a degree to read the fevered success and utter failure of the Owenite schemes, followed by the later propaganda of their author, more or less aberrant, less and less regarded, but ever hopeful to the last, when he died at the age of eighty-seven. It is a pathetic story, on the face of it, a story of great efforts and great failure in the New World as in the Old. And yet there is another view. Owen himself was neither conscious of failure nor sad, and perhaps he was right. Blessed indeed are the self-reliant. There is hardly an item in the whole modern programme of social endeavour to-day, apart from religion, which he did not initiate, promote, or suggest; and the gospel of salvation by material means, which is his gospel, gains ground everywhere at the expense of all other gospels. His turn has come round again.

Malthus, Bentham, and James Mill had left their influence on the world of thought, and it is true to say that Owen also left his influence. His writings, however, would have perished had it not been for the fact that their author had been an enterprising and successful business man. New Lanark appealed to many who would not have opened the pages of *A New View of Society*. Like other socialistic schemes of his day, following in the steps of Plato, Owen set up a factory in the country, and his was at New Lanark. At first he had not a free hand, for there were other partners. Fortunately for Owen's set purpose to turn his factory into a laboratory where he could try experiments in education and moral and physical reform, his four partners lived elsewhere. They, intent on viewing the factory as a business concern, objected to his building new schools. In the end he was obliged to buy them out. The profit for four years had been no less than £160,000, fine profits even for those days, and Owen had the natural satisfaction of feeling that his philanthopy paid in this world as well as the next—if there was a next. In the new deed of partnership he insisted on having a freer hand, and its terms were that "all profits made in the concern beyond five per cent. per annum on the capital invested shall be laid aside for the religious, educational and moral improvement of the workers, and of the community at large."

There had been benevolent despots among the ranks of sovereigns and their ministers during the eighteenth century, and Owen was to be a benevolent despot seated not on a king's throne but on an employer's chair. He thought alone, he directed alone, and his men were to receive the orders he transmitted to them. He never asked them for ideas: he did ask them for obedience—obedience of the unquestioning type. His workmen and their children felt the simplicity and the goodwill that radiated from him. During his early life he had the supreme misfortune never to have known failure—that jade we all meet sooner or later. Owen met her later, too late to temper his autocracy and his self-complacency. Thompson, the Master of Trinity College, Cambridge rebuked Mr. Gerald Balfour, when an undergraduate, with the words, "None of us are infallible—not even the youngest." None of us are infallible—not even the oldest, as Owen was to find out. This meant that he was incapable of learning either from books or from life, and this lack of teachableness peeps out in manifold fashion.

When he was beginning his labours at New Lanark he could allow for the hindrances which crossed his path, for the factory was realising a profit; and once the men began to realise this, their increased wages would dispel troubles. The terrible evils of the Industrial Revolution were with him, and there were other ones as well. The people were of a low type, drawn from the refuse of the social system, and there were also four to five hundred unfortunate parish apprentices, aged from five to ten. Like the rest of the hands, they worked thirteen hours a day, with an hour and quarter allowed for meals. Owen resolutely made up his mind to engage no more of these pauper apprentices.

On assuming command of New Lanark with its 1,300 souls, Owen tells us that drunkenness and immorality were very prevalent. Thieving was common in every department of the works; housing conditions were disgusting, and, as sanitation was unknown, filth was everywhere, both in the houses and in the streets of the village. As a stranger Owen was not popular, and his popularity was not increased by his attempts to cure the evils from which the village was suffering. He allowed no public-houses, though there were many at Old Lanark, a mile away. He closed all the petty shops, replacing them by stores owned by the firm where all necessaries were sold at cost price. He supplied whisky, but it was good whisky, not the poison the people had been consuming. Families had had only one room, and he gave them two. Refuse at the cottage door he had carted away; and the cleanliness of the outside of the cottage he carried inside, and carried it inside successfully, though this success came only after the lapse of years. He persuaded the men to appoint a visiting committee, whose members were to endeavour to raise the deplorably low standard of cleanliness, which Owen regarded as next to godliness, to a high one.

The improvement of conduct in the factory was by no means an easy task, and the method Owen employed deserves to be set down. "That which I found to be the most efficient check upon inferior conduct was the contrivance of a silent monitor for each one employed in the establishment. This consisted of a four-sided piece of wood, about two inches long and one broad, each side coloured—one side black, another blue, the third yellow, and the fourth white, tapered at the top, finished with wire eyes, to hang upon a hook with either side to the front. One of these was suspended in a conspicuous place near to each of the persons employed, and the colour at the front told the conduct of the individual during the preceding day to four degrees of comparison. Bad, denoted by black and No. 4; indifferent by blue, and No. 3; good by yellow, and No. 2; and excellent by white, and No. 1. Then books of character were provided for each department, in which . . . I had the conduct of each registered . . . for every year they remained in my employment. The superintendent of each department had the placing of these silent monitors, and the master of the mill regulated those of the superintendents in each mill. If anyone thought that the superintendent did not do justice, he or she had a right to complain to me, or, in my absence, to the master of the mill. . . . At the commencement of this new method of recording character, the great majority were black, many blue, and a few yellow; gradually the black diminished and were succeeded by the blue, and the blue were succeeded by the yellow, and some, but at first very few, were white."

Evidently the plan worked, and worked doubtless because the men found the fairness of it, for fairness does enlist the whole-hearted sympathy of the worker. The author of this book once had the good fortune to be chaplain to the Royal Hibernian Military School, Dublin, and there lads were given stripes on their left arm for good conduct, and not a few were to be found with the maximum number of these stripes. Behind the stripes lay the springs of good conduct which went to the making of the future man. Owen realised this, and his own words of realisation rivet our notice. "The experiment at New Lanark was the first commencement of practical measures with a view to change the fundamental principle on which society has heretofore been based from the beginning; and no experiment could be more successful in proving the truth of the principle that the character is formed *for* and not *by* the individual, and that society now possesses the most ample means and power to well form the character of everyone." It was a principle which Owen was always impressing on people, and indeed it formed the ground-work of his educational schemes for children as well as for their parents. Nor was he one of that common breed of man who can talk of principles and cannot apply them. In an age when low wages and long hours were the order of the day he preached the gospel of high wages and short hours, and, amazing to relate, he made his venture pay. In the time of his father-in-law, Dale, a most humane employer, there had been a working day of eleven and three-quarter hours. His partners forced Owen to raise these hours, after 1800, to fourteen hours a day. Owen had reduced them in 1816 to ten and three-quarter hours, and even this shortened time he believed to be too long. As he told the Parliamentary Committee of 1816, he had set up a ten-hour day as the ideal. Nor did he shorten wages when he shortened hours. Half the work in the mills was paid by piece, and yet by increased output the wages did not fall. In 1817 the operatives tendered an address of thanks to Owen, on the anniversary of the introduction of the shorter hours, and proposed to present him with a piece of plate, which he refused to accept.

In 1818 the New Lanark operatives signed a petition to the House of Commons in favour of the Factory Bill then under consideration. In it they claimed that they did more work in ten and three-quarter hours than others in twelve or thirteen. The causes of this were the obvious ones of their increased zeal and activity. Owen did not venture to give the House precise details on these matters. He was right in thinking that the men rendered more efficient service, yet it is perfectly clear that he reckoned any slight increase in the cost of production as insignificant compared with the improved health and education of the workers themselves. His conviction was that the manufacturers would not lose by the shortened hours of production, for such hours would "hardly make any perceptible difference in the prime cost of any article."

Success did not come in a day, yet from the first there was progress. If there were many men with black wood beside them, there were some, and an increasing number, with white. In 1819, Mr. Baines, of the *Leeds Mercury*, came with a deputation to report on what they saw in New Lanark. "Mr. Owen's establishment," according to the report, "at New Lanark is essentially a manufacturing establishment, conducted in a manner superior to any other the deputation ever witnessed, and dispensing more happiness than perhaps any other institution in the kingdom where so many poor persons are employed. . . . In the education of the children the thing that is most remarkable is the general spirit of tenderness and affection which is shown towards them, and the entire absence of anything which is likely to give them bad habits—with the presence of whatever is calculated to inspire them with good ones. The consequence is that they appear like one well-regulated family, united together by the ties of the closest affection. In the adult inhabitants we saw much to commend. In general they appeared clean, healthy and sober. Intoxication is almost unknown." The deputation witnessed this success in 1819. Owen had been hard at work at his task of regeneration since 1800, and the turning point was not reached till 1813. His *Statement Concerning the New Lanark Establishment* and his *New View of Society: or, Essays on the Principle of the Formation of the Human Character*, had appeared in 1812 and 1813 respectively. What he laid down in them he had at last in 1813 the power to carry out, for he was freed from the irksome restrictions of his non-resident partners. He had improved the environment of his men, and they had responded to this improvement. Clearly, it was possible to inaugurate a new social order. In his

Address to the Inhabitants of New Lanark on New Year's Day, 1816, he was able to speak what his hearers knew to be true. "My attention was ever directed to remove, as I could prepare means for their removal, such of the immediate causes as were perpetually creating misery amongst you; and which, if permitted to remain, would to this day have continued to create misery. I therefore withdrew the most prominent incitements to falsehood, theft, drunkenness, and other pernicious habits with which many of you were then familiar; and in their stead I introduced other causes, which were intended to produce better external habits; and better external habits have been produced. I say 'better *external* habits,' for to these alone have my proceedings hitherto been intended to apply. What has yet been done I consider as merely preparatory."

His monitors from black to white had accustomed men to the notion that they could improve, and that was a novel notion to many of them. The sense and the simplicity with which he urged this and other reforms swept the operatives along with a master who obviously cared for their welfare. Nor did he hesitate to furnish them with proof of this attitude, proof that none could gainsay. Our use of the unrestricted right of search at sea led to trouble with America in 1806, just as it did from 1914 to 1917. The Americans retorted by an embargo on the export of cotton, with the result that its price soared. Owen and his partners found themselves obliged to close down, but during this closing down for four months, full wages, at a cost of £7,000, were paid to all. Owen's influence after 1806 was magical. Nor did he believe in punishment. At first indeed he had to fine men for drunkenness, and to dismiss the habitual drunkards. This passed away, and it seems clear that the personality of the thoughtful manager mastered the men. Moral suasion works—if it is supported by so dominant a personality as Owen's.

If the environment improved, the man improved. What Owen believed abroad he carried out at home. His son Robert records that, in infancy, he had the habit of screaming long and loud whenever he was denied anything he wanted. "When the child screams from temper," said his father, who was devoted to him, "set him in the middle of the nursery floor, and be sure you don't take him up till he stops crying." "But, my dear, he'll go on crying by the hour." "Then let him cry." "It may hurt his little lungs, and perhaps throw him into spasms." "I think not. At all events, it will hurt him more if he grows up an ungovernable boy. Man is the creature of his circumstances." The cure was tried, and, after a few repetitions, it was effective. "The infant culprit," commented the lad Robert in the days to come, "had learned a great lesson in life—submission to the inevitable." The father became engrossed with the part taken by environment, and was what Hazlitt called him, "a man of one idea." He had humanity enough when he married, but he turned into a humanitarian. He resembled increasingly a mass of energy driven by gigantic purpose, turning all who came his way to that purpose, and throwing to the one side those who refused to subserve its wants. Children he regarded partly as "passive compounds," and men shared this quality. Though he spoke to his teachers of his children, of the need of studying the mind of each boy or girl, in practice it is to be feared that moulding was the order of the day. If the child's mind was "plastic," the spirit of universal charity was to be inculcated. If it was not "plastic," still the spirit of universal charity was to be inculcated.

Bell and Lancaster had in the opening decades of the nineteenth century busied themselves with the education of children, employing monitors to carry out the actual teaching. Owen was clear-sighted enough to discern that the monitorial system had been driven to excess. By this plan children might be taught the elements of education, and in Owen's judgment "yet acquire the worst habits, and have their minds rendered irrational for life." Memory might be cultivated at the expense of the reason. In an age of parish apprentices, it is wonderful to meet with one employer who sees that by the premature labours of children, the parents "sacrifice not only future pounds, but also the future health, comfort, and good conduct of their children." Interest the children as well as instruct them: enlist their imagination more than their memory. In such fashion you will lay a foundation on which the boy or girl can build in the days to come.

Education was to be for all, not merely as then for the children of the well-to-do. For we must remember that there was no system of national education in Owen's day. A career opened to talents, the talents of all, was his ideal. Not for a moment did he think that all men are equal, but he did think that their children should possess the opportunity of being trained to good citizenship. He was keen-sighted enough to know that if ever there was to be an inauguration of a new society, education must be universal; no child should be excluded from its benefits. Utilitarian ideas were in the air, and their presence is felt in such a statement as that "general bodily and mental differences between inhabitants of various regions are wholly and solely the effects of education." It is a sentiment to which Bentham and Mill would readily have subscribed, but is it a sentiment with any hold on reality? Owen stood on surer ground when he taught that the rivalries of class and creed, of country and cosmopolis, would tend towards reconciliation—if only the rising generation were impregnated with his ideas of peace and goodwill. Nor did he hesitate to lay down ideals perilously near those of Napoleon and Treitschke. Beyond question "the governing powers of all countries should establish rational plans for the educational and general formation of the character of all their subjects. These plans will be devised to train children from their earliest infancy to *think* and act aright, for which purpose they must be prevented from acquiring habits of falsehood and deception." Such is the teaching of *A New View of Society*. His view was that "children may be formed *collectively* into any human character."

Owen, like Bentham, persistently overrated human nature. His own life had been free from struggle and failure to such a degree that he thrust to the one side what the Church calls original sin and what science calls inherited tendencies. It is a grave omission, and his constant optimism is simply explicable by this omission. Just as a mechanical age infected Bentham when he constructed his Panopticon, so it infected Owen when he constructed his theory of the influence of environment. Society, in his judgment, was simply a machine with wheels transformable at will. His *New View of Society* is one in which he speaks of the "new machinery" which he proposes to employ, and similarly in education he does not hesitate to speak of the power to "manufacture characters." He pays a lip service to individuality, yet at the back of his mind there lies the idea that as his mills turn out cotton, so his schools turn out men and women. The one creates fabrics: the other fabricates creatures who are scarcely individual men and women. Nor is this a conception which has passed away like the mills of New Lanark. For what the Owenite schools were to carry out, the Socialist still fondly hopes that the schools and the State will now carry out. There is abroad a mechanical conception of the functions of the State akin to Owen's, and these conceptions ask for a uniform education which will turn us all out on the same pattern as the machine does. The outstanding omission of Owen vitiates part of his conception: there is a deal of human nature, as the common saying has it, in all of us, and this nature falls a victim sometimes to original sin or inherited tendencies, call it what you will. Still, there is more in Owen's supposition than is sometimes imagined. "Let us suppose an exchange of any given number of children to be made at their birth between the Society of Friends, of which our worthy guest, Joseph Lancaster, is a member, and the loose fraternity which inhabit St. Giles's in London; the children of the former would grow up like the members of the latter, prepared for every degree of crime, while those of the latter would become the same temperate good moral characters of the former." In spite of everything, environment remains the master of us all.

No child at New Lanark came to school till he was five, and beside ordinary instruction, stress was laid on morality in the large sense. The lesson never lasted more than three-quarters of an hour. In the Infant School work was done on the lines of Pestalozzi: it was a real kindergarten. Maps, pictures, and natural objects were all employed in order to render every subject attractive. There were no prizes for industry or good conduct; and there was no punishment for idleness or disobedience. And the astounding thing is that this system worked. It had worked with the operatives in the factory, and it worked with their children in the school. Can we offer a stronger testimony to the overpowering personality of the presiding genius of New Lanark? The respect of the parents was sustained by the fact that they contributed their modest payment of threepence a month for each child. Among the evils done to education in our day, few have been productive of so much mischief as "free" education. The parents of Owen's day looked up to education: the parents of our day look down on education. The self-reliant Owen rendered homage to the natural feeling of the father that he is paying for the education of his family: the self-reliant State renders no such homage. The result is that contempt for education felt to-day by so many working-class fathers and mothers. The child leaves school at fourteen, and he often leaves something he dreads or, at any rate, dislikes. In this respect Owen was infinitely wiser. Besides, he was able to issue an effective appeal to his fellow-manufacturers. "Like you," he drily wrote in his *Address to the Superintendents of Manufacturies*, "I am a manufacturer for pecuniary profit." Surely every employer realised the need of the latest machinery and the attention to be paid to it. "If, then, due care as to the state of your inanimate machines can produce such beneficial results, what may not be expected if you devote equal care to your vital machines, which are far more wonderfully constructed?" His experiments with men and children attested that "the time and money so spent, even while such improvements are in progress only, and but half their beneficial results attained, are now producing a return exceeding 50 per cent., and will shortly create profits equal to cent. per cent. on the original capital expended in these mental improvements."

A wider audience than that of the manufacturers was opening before Owen. His early writings, combined with profits earned at New Lanark, commanded respect from many who would have disdained his plans as chimerical. He interviewed Lord Liverpool, the Prime Minister, who introduced him to Lady Liverpool in order that she might express approval of his pamphlets. In 1814 Lord Sidmouth, the Home Secretary, not only expressed his own sympathy, but undertook to circulate the pamphlets among the leading Governments and learned bodies of Europe and America. Copies were sent, at Sidmouth's suggestion, to all the English bishops, and, later, at the request of the Archbishop of Armagh, to the Irish ones. John Quincy Adams, the American Ambassador, next asked for copies for the Governors of all the States in the American Union. At Elba even Napoleon received a copy, read it, and found leisure to pursue inquiries about the author. The Duke of Kent, Queen Victoria's father, gave hearty support. The Archbishop of Canterbury, Dr. Sutton, invited Owen to Lambeth in order to hear him read manuscript essays, expressing a desire that he might correspond with Owen. Bentham had been a partner in New Lanark, and in his circle there were such sympathisers as David Ricardo and James Mill, Francis Place, and Sir James Mackintosh. In the older generation there were William Godwin and Thomas Malthus. Among Owen's other acquaintances were Brougham, Clarkson, Wilberforce, Zachary Macaulay, father of the historian, and other philanthropists. In the visitors' book at New Lanark were recorded from 1815 to 1825 no less than 20,000 names. These included such distinguished strangers as the Duke of Holstein and his brother, who stayed several days with Owen for the purpose of thoroughly understanding the machinery of the system of education, the Grand Duke Nicholas, afterwards Emperor of Russia, Princes John and Maximilian of Austria, many foreign ambassadors, and among them Baron Just, ambassador from Saxony, whose sovereign presented Owen with a gold medal as a mark of his approval.

New Lanark was to serve more than Scotland. It was to be a model village which was to serve England and the world as well. In his *Report to the Committee of the Association for the Relief of the Manufacturing and Labouring Poor*, 1817, and in his *New Existence of Man on the Earth*, 1854, Owen adumbrates his plan for the much-needed regeneration of society. He imagines a New Lanark very much like the one in existence with from 500 to 2000 people in it, settled on land from 1000 to 1500 acres. Mutual voluntary co-operation is to be the rule. All are to live in buildings on three sides of a square, and each family is to have four rooms. The building in the centre of a square is to contain a common kitchen, a common mess room, schools, library, and a lecture hall. Each family cares for its children till the age of three, when they are sent to the dormitory on the fourth side of the square. Their parents are to see them at meals and "all other proper times." The object of this is the paramount one of ensuring the due formation of their character from an early age. Sympathies now confined to the family are to overflow to the community. This community of interest supplies the incentive to industry. For "a man is not likely to work with less zeal for a society in which he himself has a direct interest than for a master in whose prosperity he has no concern." The parish, the country, the State, can establish these communities. The surplus labour of their members is available for themselves. We never get far from Ricardo. The *Report to the County of Lanark* opens with the confession that "manual labour, properly directed, is the source of all wealth and of national prosperity." The trouble is that "the existing arrangements of society will not permit the labourer to be remunerated for his industry, and in consequence markets fail." Once Owen's model villages are started "there will be no desire or motive for individual accumulation of wealth": all will have enough. The toiler will at last come into all his own. Often quoted lines in *The Poor Man's Guardian*, 1831, disclose the situation:

> Wages should form the price of goods;
>   Yes, wages should be all,
> Then we who work to make the goods
>   Should justly have them all.
>
> But if their price be made of rent,
>   Tithes, taxes, profits all,
> Then we who work to make the goods
>   Shall have—just none at all.

Owen's views were not so naive as the writer of this poem, for he clearly perceived the director—himself. He, however, saw that it was the duty of society to provide employment for its members, and his model village is the outcome of his thought. His *Villages of Co-operation* were to solve the problem of the unemployed by providing markets.

Opposition came from the Malthusians, the Radicals, and the Church. The Malthusians were afraid of the growth in population; the Radicals were afraid of the increase in taxation due to the adoption of the *Villages of Co-operation*; and the Church was incensed by the vigorous fashion in which the reformer denounced religion in 1817. This year indeed marks a turning point in his career. The Church, with her belief in original sin, did not take kindly to the view of her opponent that the making of virtue and vice lay completely in the hands of men. In spite of Locke and Owen, she held that the mind of a child was not a *tabula rasa*. Character-building was not the easy task Owen had imagined in his schemes of education. He broke with the Church, and her archbishops and bishops, to their loss and his, consulted him no more.

Bishop Butler once astonished his chaplain by asking him the question, Can a nation go mad? It certainly seems as if England went mad in 1817, and in 1819, for, frightened by the growing discontent, her rulers turned not to make use of a remedy, but to use force. A change came over the country, and the Six Acts were the outcome of this disastrous change. The atmosphere had subtly altered, and Owen was no longer to meet with supporters in high station. Radicals like Cobbett and Hunt continued their opposition to his plans. The tide in Owen's affairs had not been seized, and for the last forty years of his life the word failure is written across them, failure in his own generation to meet with success in ours. Abroad his fame still stood at a lofty level, for, curiously enough, he visited Paris in 1817 to meet with a reception almost as triumphal as Bentham's. The Duke of Kent gave him introductions. He travelled to Paris with Pictet and Cuvier the naturalist on a French frigate. He interviewed Louis Philippe, then Duke of Orleans, and the French Prime Minister, who, on his acquaintance with his ideas, pronounced them fine but premature. He also met Alexander von Humboldt and

La Place. In Switzerland he met Sismondi, and examined carefully the educational establishments of Oberlin, Pestalozzi, and Fellenberg. In spite of these acquaintances abroad and of their diminishing number at home, the Committee of Investigation, with the Duke of Kent as chairman, appointed in 1819 to examine his *Villages of Co-operation*, gave them favourable consideration. The sum of £100,000 was required, and this large sum, combined with the abandonment of Owen by the bishops and the opposition of the Radicals, stood in the way of their practical adoption. In drawing up this report the Committee was influenced by the fact that Owen offered to be superintendent of the village, and that he pledged himself that the interest on the capital should be paid.

The Old World had failed Owen, but there was still the New. His model village was New Harmony in Posey County, Indiana. Coleridge, Southey, and Wordsworth had dreamed their dream of a Pantisocracy on the banks of the Susquehannah on the morrow of the French Revolution. With his invincible optimism Owen bought New Harmony from the Rappites in 1825, confident that the failure of the past would be more than redeemed by the success of the present. The Rappites were the followers of George Rapp, a Wurtemberg farmer who set out in 1803 for America as the land of religious freedom. His little community was composed of pious German peasants, sober, thrifty, industrious, and celibate. The soil brought forth luxuriantly. Cornlands and homes, orchards and vineyards sprang up as if by magic. In April, 1825, Owen bought the village of New Harmony, with all its industries and 20,000 acres of land for £30,000. The fame of the buyer in the New World attracted recruits on all sides, and in October he had nine hundred of them, good, bad, and indifferent. Here, however, was an environment untainted by the Industrial Revolution. Surely man here was master of his fate, captain of his soul.

In his *Discourses on a New System of Society*, which opened his American campaign, it is pathetic to note how it recalled the title of his 1813 pamphlet, *A New View of Society*. There is nothing new in his writing. As his message was in the beginning, so it is now. Environment has been altered, and all other desirable results flow therefrom—if the inhabitants of New Harmony really desire them. The old *régime*, "the whole trading system," is essentially "one of deception." From principles he comes down to practice. Of course he is the founder and sole proprietor, and as such he appoints a committee of management, with the proviso that at the end of the first year the members shall elect representatives on this committee. The Society is open to all the world, except "persons of colour." As the colour bar does not appear before the French Revolution, this is an early date to meet it. The members accept no pecuniary liability. They are to bring their own furniture and effects; they are to work, under the direction of the committee, at a trade or occupation. For the useful work done a credit is to be set against the name of each at the public store, and against this credit a debit is to be entered of the goods supplied. At the end of the year the balance is placed to the credit of the member; but he cannot, unless the committee consent, withdraw any part of it in cash. At the end of three years he buoyantly hoped the members would constitute a Community of Equality, "and so for ever bury all the evils of the old selfish individual system."

The motto of the *New Harmony Gazette* was, "If we cannot reconcile all opinions, let us endeavour to unite all hearts." Owen returned to Europe, leaving his sons to manage as best they could. Building and fitting up houses stared them in the face, and they were at their wits' end to know what to do. On his return in 1826, Owen restated the objects of New Harmony. Article No. 1 prescribes the title "The New Harmony Community of Equality." Article II runs, "All the members of the Community shall be considered one family, and no one shall be held in higher or lower estimation on account of occupation. There shall be similar food, clothing and education, as near as can be, furnished for all according to their age and, as soon as practicable, all shall live in similar houses, and in all respects be accommodated alike. Every member shall render his or her best service for the good of the whole."

Owen was now fifty-five, an age when illusions are shed, and yet he remains as hopeful as when he was twenty-five. He divided the little community into the six departments of agriculture, of manufactures, of literature, science, and education, of domestic economy, of general economy, and of commerce. Social inequalities, religious differences, and national idiosyncracies combined to create disunion. The concerts, the weekly dances, and the social intercourses failed to attain the spirit of community or equality. Maclure broke off from the parent society on religious grounds. Captain Macdonald refused to accept the constitution because it involved elections and representative government, and these are fatal to the free spirit of community and equality. In three years New Harmony was a failure. Nor are the causes of this difficult to discern. Social, religious, and national distinctions stood in the way. The Rappites had not permeated the newcomers with their spirit, for they left for a fresh colony of their own. The issuing of invitations to all comers was a mistake, for some came who were quite unsuitable. The sharper and the speculator duly appeared as well as the visionary. Moreover, Owen himself for part of the time had been absent. New Lanark had succeeded because he was present: New Harmony failed because he was absent. It was not his principles which created this enormous difference: it was his personality, and this he persistently refused to recognise. This is to his credit as a man, to his discredit as a thinker.

It is remarkable to see how much he had hoped from the Rappites, and yet he ignored the spirit of religion in them that created all the difference between them and the sharper and the speculator. The religious motive and the business motive are the two great ones which drive mankind. Owen admitted the one, and refused to admit the other. He allowed no outlet for the ambitious, the money-making. In a word, he called for the spirit of self-sacrifice, which is inherent in all religion, and yet he attacked the Church. The mediaeval monastic orders succeeded because they turned this spirit to admirable account, and the same spirit is present in all bodies of this class, succeeding in the present. The Oneida Community was a case in point.

It was founded on a democratic basis, refusing to accept celibacy. A clear-headed member of it summed up the case against Owen. "There are only two ways," he remarked, "of governing a Community; it must be done either by law or by grace. Owen abolished law, but did not establish grace."

On his return home, the movement for the reform of Parliament was growing, yet this movement left him unaffected. His diagnosis of the body politic was that it was suffering from ills social and economic, and for these parliamentary reform could afford no remedy. He was never more occupied in England than from 1829 to 1832, but the field of his activities was the idea of Labour Exchange, the Builders' Guild, or even co-operation. A Reformed Parliament would be one of capitalists, and what would they care for ideas like his? He was against Parliament because he instinctively realised that Parliament was against him. Besides, his autocratic methods had nothing in common with the freedom demanded by representative government. Reform was something he was to impose from above upon the mass of mankind. No member of the reformed House of Commons would listen to the part he deemed environment should play. The average M.P. is a creature of compromise, whereas Owen was content with no measures falling short of his ideal. He would much rather have no bread than half a loaf; yet if the idealists move the world, it is often enough the half loafers who put these ideals into practice.

The disappearance of rent and interest appealed to Proudhon as it appealed to Owen. Proudhon's plan is to found a national bank which will allow gratuitous credit. Who will pay money when the freedom of credit enables him to secure a loan? How did Proudhon provide this gratuitous credit? By the issue of a paper currency which all members of the bank association shall be bound to accept as payment. The bank converts the note into coin, as the note is simply an order on the members of the bank association to deliver to the holder goods and services of specified amounts. Owen's Labour Exchange, which opened in 1832, is based on a similar idea. The unit of value is an hour's time, worth sixpence in metallic money.

The Labour Exchange converts the goods into a note which specifies the number of hours they are worth. As one man may spend more hours than another, the unskilful than the skilful, a test is to be applied by reckoning the amount of hours an average workman will take to execute the task. The price of the material is to be calculated in money at the market price. Add to this price the time spent and a penny in the shilling for the expenses of the Exchange, and you have the price of the article made. Then divide the total in pence by six, the unit. Thus if the material cost 8s., if the time amounts to six hours of skilled labour at 1s. an hour, this is equal to 6s., the commission of 1d. a 1s. is roughly equal to one shilling. The total is 15s. which at 6d. an hour is equal to 30 hours of labour time.

Is the quantity of labour required easy to determine? Plainly, it is not, and for the short period the Labour Exchange actually worked, the declaration of the labourer was normally accepted. For Owen started the Labour Exchange as a private undertaking, quite recognising that the State ultimately must take it up—if it were to prove a success. In such a simple society as New Lanark or New Harmony it might have worked, but it certainly refused to work in England, New or Old. A tailor of the sharper order took to the Exchange a coat and pair of trousers, and received the full market value for his labour on what proved to be misfits. The receipt of provisions gave rise to inconvenience. A baker undertook to supply bread to the Exchange, if he received half cash and half notes in payment. A Southampton merchant offered a hundred tons of potatoes, expressing his willingness to accept labour notes in exchange. In the seventeen weeks ending December 22, 1832, the deposits represented 445,501 hours and the exchanges 376,166 hours, leaving a balance of stock in hand representing 69,335 hours or £1733 7s. 6d. William Lovett, the store-keeper of the First London Association, sums up the chief causes of the failure of the Labour Exchange. They were the religious differences, the want of legal security, and the dislike entertained by the women to the confinement of their dealings to one shop.

In 1833, Owen addressed the annual meeting of the

Builders' Guild, enunciating once more that "labour is the source of all wealth." His newspapers urged the formation of a General Union of the Productive Classes. His own incessant activities led to a phenomenal growth of Trade Unions in 1834. Here at last he seemed to read the true path leading to industrial, not political, democracy. He inspired the industrial democrats with the hope that the future belonged to them. He had had six departments at New Harmony, and now he proposed more. Each Trade Union was to be transformed into a national one to carry on the employment with which it was associated. The Agricultural Union was to take possession of the land, the Miner's Union of the mines, the Textile Unions of the mills. William Benbow, an enthusiastic disciple, saw in the whole process the possibility of the general strike. For in 1831 he advocated what did not happen till May, 1926. Owen deprecated strikes, for he saw the possibility of doing without violence. The inauguration of the new moral order was not to take place through the instrumentality of the strike, but through the joint action of all the Trade Unions. Owen always found it hard to work with people: he could order them, a wholly different matter. His assistants in his plan of the joint action of all the Trade Unions were Morrison and J. E. Smith, and he quarrelled with both men. "He thinks," owned Smith, "that he can lead the people—he is not aware of the odium which attaches to his name. He is too full of himself to see it, and we have always been suppressing his name and his articles as much as possible. He cannot brook this any longer, and seeing that he cannot get everything his own way, he is going to start a new paper under the name of the *Union Gazette*, which he expects will swallow up all others. He means to work behind the curtain, and yet to be dictator. Now our move is to prevent this dictatorship, for we know it cannot be tolerated." By the end of 1834 Consolidated Unionism had perished. It had gone the way of New Lanark, New Harmony, the "Villages of Co-operation," the vast educational schemes, the Labour Exchange, and many another project. Others might be daunted: he remained undaunted. Blessed, beyond measure, are the self-reliant.

Politics he had despised, yet he even turned to them in 1847 when he issued an election address, advocating a graduated property tax, the abolition of all other taxation, free trade with all the world, national education for all who desired it, national beneficial employment for all who require it, the freedom of religion, national military training to protect our country against foreign invasion, and a national circulating medium capable of increase or diminution as wealth for circulation increased or diminished. The old ideas remain in force. It is perhaps needless to add that he did not go to the poll. Nor is it possible to avoid noting his influence on Chartism. Like Owen's schemes, it failed most unmistakably. The disenchanted Owenite, like Lovett, naturally turned to the Chartist cause. Radicals, like Place, welcomed Lovett and his friends when they came to his tailor's shop in Charing Cross to discuss universal suffrage and the ballot. The year 1838 marks the period when the Trade Unions shrank from Chartism. The prosperous operatives did not stand shoulder to shoulder with their "more distressed brethren." As a matter of fact the Chartists were hungry, and many of their meetings simply testified this fact to the audience. True, there are exceptions to this statement, and Bronterre O'Brien is undoubtedly one. He was a follower of Owen and a student of the French Revolution. He meant to combine the ideals of the socialism of Owen with the Jacobinism of Robespierre. After 1838 Chartism undergoes its decline and fall. Its centre had been in the provinces, but not in London; in the north, but not in the south. Yet even Carlyle took Chartism at its face value, vastly exaggerating its real position. The fear of 1817 and of 1819, testified by the Six Acts, had not been wholly forgotten, yet such a fear in 1838 or dread of the Chartist riots of 1839 was a vain one. The men who wanted a higher wage than the pittance they received, and shorter hours than the fourteen they often worked, were not Socialists: they were simply toilers suffering from the horrors, named and unnamed, of the Industrial Revolution. For this reason Napier handled the Chartist rising in the north in 1839 with consummate ease as well as with consummate tact. Would he have handled an Irish mob with similar ease? Or a French mob? We take leave to doubt it. It is curious to note how the Chartists imitated part of the belief of Owen in the shortness of time required for their changes. He felt it possible that the transition from the "Old Immoral World" to the "New Moral World" would be like the shifting of scenery between the acts of a play. O'Connor, the Chartist leader, wrote that "Six months after the Charter is passed, every man, woman and child in the country will be well fed, well housed, and well clothed." In the Place manuscripts for 1836 it is similarly recorded: "Mr. Owen this day has assured me, in the presence of more than thirty persons, that within six months the whole state and condition of society in Great Britain will be changed, and all his views will be carried fully into effect." When the philosopher Diderot, after many hours of enthusiastic eloquence, finally asked his patron why she was not carrying out his reforms, the Empress Catherine replied, "Ah, my dear friend, you write upon paper, the smooth surface of which presents no obstacle to your pen; but, I, poor Empress that I am, must write on the skins of my subjects which are sensitive and ticklish to an extraordinary degree." What the Empress realised, the visionary never realised.

There is a deeply marked Celtic strain in Robert Owen and Charles Fourier. Each was the son of a tradesman, born the same year, and each carried the marks of his class with him. The lives of both attest a rare devotion to the convictions they held dear. True, there is as much folly in Fourier's imaginings of a millennium of seventy thousand years as in Owen's naive faith in phrenology. Yet these accidentals cannot disguise the simplicity, the kindliness, and the disinterested devotion of the two men. They might belittle self-sacrifice, yet two more self-sacrificing men it would be hard to find. In their philosophy the family and marriage tend to disappear, for only thus is it possible to suppress individualism in favour of communism. Both based their systems on logic and science rather than on feeling and impulse, deducing laws of progress plain to them though not to other people. No one, not even Condorcet, entertained more sanguine confidence in the possibilities of human progress than Owen and Fourier. God had done all things well had it not been that man misunderstood and thwarted His benevolent purpose. To Fourier there was an ever-present power in the world that draws men together, and to Owen this was universal charity. This power was to be exercised, in the view of both thinkers, in small communities. What Owen had endeavoured to carry out at New Lanark and New Harmony, Fourier had endeavoured to carry out on an estate near Versailles. They were eager, energetic, and enthusiastic, and they could inspire eagerness, energy, and enthusiasm in others. Both were insistent in emphasising the practical worth of their theories. They could heal the sickness of society; they could further the welfare of humanity. They were no dreamers of vain dreams. Mystics in some respects they might be, but were there not such practical mystics as Catherine of Siena and Oliver Cromwell? They were not among the greatest of men, but they hold a very high place in that secondary order of intellects which have perhaps more often heralded the wider resolutions of human action, not thought. They launch not their generation but ours upon new courses because they penetrate its vague cravings, formulate its floating sentiments and ideas, and give practical direction to its energies by setting more or less clearly before it the goal it unconsciously desires. True, their divination was not invariably correct. Owen and Fourier, little as perhaps they realised it, lived to some extent in the pre-industrial age. They survey "Villages of Co-operation," and the possibility of the huge towns of present-day France and England never seems to have crossed their ken. Nor can we fail to be struck with the resemblance of the parallelogram in which Owen arranged his model village with its 500 to 2000 souls and the kindred phalange of Fourier with its 400 to 2000 souls. The new world was to come for both, but it was to come peacefully. Each held with a faith nothing could shake that one honest experiment in communal living according to the principles he laid down would be absolutely sufficient to convince the world of the soundness of his views. For Owen the millennium was to dawn within six months, and for Fourier within ten years. At least their hopes, vain as they proved to be, conferred one benefit on the world: they saved it from the violence of revolution, and we, who have lived through so many revolutions since March, 1917, will reckon this to them for righteousness. By faith Owen and Fourier sojourned in the land of promise, though it is passing strange to glean from them that our salvation is to be won by material means. It is the most popular of gospels, but is it the truest?

References

The National Library of Wales issues an exhaustive *Owen Bibliography* (2nd ed., 1925).
BEER, M. *The History of British Socialism.* Vol. I. (London, 1920.)
BOOTH, A. J. *Robert Owen, the founder of Socialism in England.* (London, 1869.)
COLE, G. D. H. *Robert Owen.* (London, 1925.)
DOLLÉANS, E. *Individualisme et Socialisme.* (Robert Owen, 1771–1858.) *Avant-propos de E. Faguet.* (Paris, 1907.)
DOLLÉANS, E. *Le Chartisme, 1830–48.* (Paris, 1912–13.)
FABRE, A. *Un Socialiste pratique.* (Robert Owen.) *Avec introduction par Charles Gide.* (Nîmes, 1896.)
FAY, C. R. *Life and Labour in the Nineteenth Century.* (Cambridge, 1920.)
HOLYOAKE, G. J. *Life and Last Days of Robert Owen of New Lanark.* (London, 1871.)
HOLYOAKE, G. J. *The History of Co-operation in England.* (London, 1875.)
HOVELL, M. *The Chartist Movement.* (London, 1918.)
HUTCHINS, B. L. *Robert Owen: Social Reformer.* (London, 1912.)
JOAD, C. E. M. *Robert Owen: Idealist.* (London, 1917.)
JONES, L. *The Life, Times, and Labours of Robert Owen.* Edited by W. Cairns Jones. (London, 1900.)
LOCKWOOD, G. B. *The New Harmony Movement.* (New York, 1905.)
MCCABE, J. *Robert Owen.* (London, 1920.)
MARTINEAU, H. *Biographical Sketches.* (London, 1869.)
OWEN, R. *The Life of Robert Owen.* Vol. I (to about 1822). (London, 1857–58.)
OWEN, R. D. *Threading my Way.* (London, 1874.)
PACKARD, F. A. *Life of Robert Owen.* (Philadelphia, 1866.)
PODMORE, F. *Robert Owen: a Biography.* (London, 1923.)
REYBAUD, M. R. L. *Etude sur les Réformateurs Contemporaines.* Vol. I. (Paris, 1849.)
ROSENBLATT, F. *The Chartist Movement in its Social and Economic Aspects.* (New York, 1916.)

SARGANT, W. L. *Robert Owen and his Philosophy.* (London, 1860.)
SELIGMAN, E. R. A. *Robert Owen and Christian Socialism.* (Boston, 1886.)
SIMON, H. *Robert Owen: Sein Leben u. seine Bedeutung für die Gegenwart.* (Jena, 1905.)
SLOSSON, P. W. *The Decline of the Chartist Movement.* (New York, 1916.)
WATTS, J. *Robert Owen the Visionary.* (Manchester, 1843.)
WEBB, S. and B. *History of Trade Unionism.* (London, 1920.)
WEST, J. *A History of the Chartist Movement.* (London, 1920.)

Chapter V.
COLERIDGE THE PHILOSOPHIC CONSERVATIVE

DURING the opening years of the nineteenth century Burke occupied a paramount position in the political heavens. In spite of the years 1817 and 1819, the years of reaction, this luminary was beginning to stand in danger of eclipse. As his sun was setting, the sun of Bentham and the Utilitarians was mounting in the heavens, and from 1825 onwards was replacing the former luminary. During the twenties and the thirties a lesser Burke was questioning Utilitarian ways and works, and this questioner was Samuel Taylor Coleridge (1772–1834). He was born the same year as Owen and Fourier, a year after Scott, and two years after the friend he influenced and who was to influence him, Wordsworth.

Coleridge was the tenth and youngest son of the Vicar of Ottery St. Mary, near Exeter, a man of learning and simplicity, often compared by his son to Parson Adams. At the age of three the lad went to school. "By the infusion of certain 'jealousies into my brother's mind,'" he tells us, "I was in my earliest childhood huffed away from the enjoyments of muscular activity to play to take refuge at my mother's side on my little stool, to read my little book, and to listen to the talk of my elders. I was driven from life in motion to life in thought and sensation. I never played except by myself, and then only acted over what I had been reading or fancying, or half one, half the other, with a stick cutting down weeds or nettles, as one of the Seven Champions of Christendom. Alas! I had all the simplicity, all the docility of the little child, but none of the child's habits. I never thought as a child, never had the language of a child." In 1782 he went to Christ's Hospital where he remained over eight years. There Middleton, afterwards Bishop of Calcutta, protected him and there he met Lamb, his friend. His precocity is evident by his reading Plotinus and Synesius as well as Voltaire. The last tempted him to infidelity, which the headmaster, Dr. Bowyer, cured with a flogging. Coleridge's taste for wandering off the beaten track was manifest. "I never," owned Sir Walter Scott, "knew a man of genius that could be regular in all his habits; but I have known many a blockhead who could." Yet it was not genius that mastered Coleridge: it was his weakness. He was to write to his own *apologia pro vitâ suâ* in his *Table Talk*. In it we learn that "there are two sides to every question." Some critics may prefer to "dwell on the foolish, perplexing, imprudent, dangerous, and even immoral, conduct of promise-breach in small things, of want of punctuality, of procrastination in all its shapes and disguises." Others, however, will "take him in his whole—his head, his heart, his wishes, his innocence of all selfish crime—and a hundred years hence, what will be the result? The good—were it but a single volume that made truth more visible, and goodness more lovely, and pleasure more akin to virtue, and, self—doubled more pleasurable! and the evil—while he lived, it injured none but himself; and where is it now? in his grave. Follow it not thither."

Coleridge entered Jesus College, Cambridge, the college of Malthus, in 1791, becoming exhibitioner and foundation scholar. He was one of the four selected candidates for the Craven scholarship in 1793 when all were pronounced equal, and it was awarded to the youngest, S. Butler. From his childhood he was puzzling out answers to the question, What can we know? His views in religion turned him to Unitarianism, and in politics to republicanism. He opposed property, he opposed the aristocracy, and he opposed the clergy. He opposed property on moral grounds; he opposed the aristocracy from a sense of the nobility of man; and he opposed the clergy from motives of religion. "Away with the superfluous harmful crutches of virtue." In 1793 a Unitarian Fellow of Jesus, Frend, was tried for too liberal views in politics and Unitarian opinions in religion; and Coleridge warmly espoused the cause and its holder. The Master of Jesus remonstrated with Coleridge for his advanced ideas; and he was getting into other difficulties like debt. Suddenly he enlisted in the 15th Dragoons, where he proved an incapable horseman, and was discharged in 1794. He had no grip on the architectonics of life, and signally lacked the ability to turn his rare gifts to his own practical account.

Opium added to his weakness, a weakness which he finally overcame. A man may be addicted to strong drink—or even to narcotic drugs—and yet avoid failure and retain his self-respect. The cases of Byron during his Venetian period and of Lamb will occur to every one; and there are many others. In Coleridge's case the addiction to opium was not the disease, but the remedy with which he sought to palliate and alleviate a disease which he felt to be well nigh incurable. For the malady itself we have no name in English; but the French know it, and are continually remarking it in those neurasthenic Russian writers who revolve helplessly in the vicious circle of Slav pessimism. They call it *impuissance de vivre*, meaning thereby a certain incapacity to face the facts of life and adapt onself to its hard unalterable conditions. One may often see an example of it in the position of a weak and sensitive boy, the unresisting victim of oppressors at a rough public school.

Coleridge suffered from this *impuissance de vivre*, and yet he had set a noble vision before him, the pursuit of truth at all costs. He never felt satisfied with himself, and had it pleased God to give him the choice between truth and the restless search for it, he would, like Lessing, have bent his knee modestly before the search. "Father, give; the pure truth is only for Thee alone! Not truth itself, the possession of which a man has, or thinks he has, but the earnest effort to gain it, makes the worth of the man." He felt forced to expound his theories. He asked Lamb whether he had ever heard him preach. "I never heard you do anything else," was the answer. It is deeply significant that the two chief English critics of the nineteenth century, Coleridge and M. Arnold, should have been constrained to preach and to popularise. Each realised that he had a humanising task to perform, and each disdained any unwillingness in setting about it.

In 1794 Coleridge visited Oxford, and there met Southey for the first time, and the acquaintanceship ripened into friendship, exerting a healthy influence on a man who suffered from *impuissance de vivre*. At Bristol he met the Frickers. Lovell had married one sister, Southey was engaged to another, and Coleridge became engaged to a third. Southey fetched Coleridge to Bristol where he gave sundry lectures on political and religious subjects, some of which were published in 1795 under the title *Conciones ad Populum* and *The Plot Discovered*. If any one takes the trouble to compare these writings with his later ones, the continuity of thought is evident, though the course of the French Revolution altered him as deeply as the Revolution itself altered Burke. Southey, like Coleridge, was a poet, a philosopher, and an enthusiast for the French Revolution. Southey, like Landor, signified his republicanism by his dress. Coleridge's wide reading, fertile imagination, and charm of voice and manner rendered him a fascinating companion. Among the airy creations of his brain was the project of Pantisocracy, or immigration to America. Cowley intended to retire to the New World with his books. Plotinus asked Gallienus to grant him a deserted town in Campania which he might people with philosophers.

At Bristol, Coleridge had taught, like Owen, that vice is "the effect of error, and the offspring of surrounding circumstances; the object therefore of condolence, not of anger." In a new world there would be a totally different environment. The modern Pantisocrats were to reclaim the forest, build for themselves, till the ground, and yet find time for poetry: they were to combine the innocence of the patriarchal age with the refinements of European civilisation. Southey was fascinated by the idea. In America he would sit unelbowed by kings and aristocrats. The Garden of Eden was to be renewed on the banks of the Susquehannah. Coleridge selected the river partly for its association with Wyoming, partly for the poetic sonorousness of the name. Of its exact position he was uncertain. "It is a grand river in America," was the reply he vouchsafed to give to geographical inquirers. The Pantisocracy exacted marriage, and this was the only practical step the brethren took to comply with its requirements. On the strength of a promise of a guinea and a half for every hundred verses, Coleridge in 1795 married Sara Fricker, and passed a long honeymoon of perfect bliss at Clevedon. To his marriage, though not to his wife, may be traced the embarrassments of his life—he had no means, and no persistence in the art of acquiring any. He was one of those sanguine men who never was, but always to be blessed, and that by some ideal formula of his own devising. The absurdity of his Pantisocratic scheme was wont to draw a smile from him in late life; but to his latest day the theory of it coloured his thoughts and aspirations. The young man who has once seen the vision of the ideal is never the same. After the vision of the burning bush Moses was never the man he was before.

The humanitarian impulse was a work in poetry as in life. Mallet had been stirred by compassion for the suffering poor, Thomson by the spectacle of a man frozen in a snowstorm, Akenside felt for unhappy lovers, Gray for the evils threatening the schoolboy, Shenstone for the negro slave, and Goldsmith for the misery of the deserted village, Cowper and Burns had extended the range of sympathy to animals. Wordsworth's *Peter Bell* was to glorify that faithful animal, the ass. Coleridge anticipated him in his lines "To a Young Ass, its mother being tethered near it." The world was ringing with revolutionary watchwords of a universal philanthropy, and Coleridge ventured to address publicly a lowly animal as

> Innocent fool! thou poor despised, forlorn!
> I hail thee brother—spite of the fool's scorn!

Did not Coleridge represent the characteristic tendencies of the day? He laboured to found a philosophy of history; he laboured to convert criticism into a science; he combated that literary bigotry, confirmed by social panic, which confounded novelty with subversion. Politically the new forces threatened the existing organisation of society. In France a terrible grandeur is given to the work of destruction by the concentrated enthusiasm of unanimity. In the poetry both of man and of nature Coleridge struck a new note, and he struck it with no faltering hand. Pope treats nature as a mighty plan of which the great First Cause was the author. To her charms he is blind; he is never a lover, rarely an admirer. But, as the eighteenth century advanced, poetry passed from court and city into a larger and purer air, which inspired a stronger feeling for the natural world than the faded sentimentalism of pastorals or the dainty interest of scholars. The revolt against artificial conventionalities of representation, the growing sympathy with rustic life, the spell of the law of nature, led men to invest nature with mortal attributes and worship in her sequestered shrines. The idea of nature as a living personal being inspired the reverence of Wordsworth, stirred the introspective mind of Coleridge, and culminated in the sensuous passion of Keats. It was, however, the subjective side of the poetical movement which Coleridge most strongly represented. Pope studied men rather than mankind, classes not humanity. His was a critical interest in fashionable persons of the day. But Cowper and Burns were poets of the people. Their sympathy with suffering is passionate; they raise their cry against oppression, stir the poor to a sense of their own dignity, value at their true worth the gold and the guinea stamp. It was but a short step further to the conception of universal humanity, the brotherhood of nations which Coleridge hoped to see realised in the French Revolution. Didactic poetry contented a cold philosophic age. Yet amid the stir and ferment of Coleridge's day, when men thought and felt intensely, lyric verse at once found her cradle and held her festival.

Wordsworth described the feeling of the time:

> Bliss was it in that dawn to be alive,
> But to be young was very heaven, oh, times
> In which the meagre stale forbidding ways
> Of custom, law, and statute, took at once
> The attraction of a country in romance.

His feelings and his imagination, Coleridge declares, did not remain unkindled, "and I confess I should be more inclined to be ashamed than proud of myself if they had. I was a sharer in the general vortex, though my little world described the path of its revolution in an orbit of its own." France commanded his allegiance, and when England took up arms against the Republic, he, like Wordsworth, was smitten with grief and shame. Mysticism and religion drove him to express his sympathy with France in the poems of 1794 and 1795, though the reaction is plain in the poems of 1797. He exults in the gathering storm which shall sweep away distinctions of race, caste, and rank. In the morning of hope there shone before him

> A glorious world
> Fresh as a banner bright, unfurled
> To music suddenly.

The most important of the Juvenile Poems, *Religious Musings*, forms a curious commentary on his mind. In religion he is a Unitarian; Priestley is his "patriot, saint, and sage," yet the poem is elevated by the deep tone of religious awe, which eventually changed the current of his ideas to the Church of England. In philosophy he is a materialist, and a disciple of Hartley, "wisest of mortal kind." But, above all, politics are the inspiration of the poem which shows but little sign of his coming power. The finest passage is an apostrophe to the "numberless children of wretchedness," whom he bids "rest awhile" and await their coming deliverance. He sees France quivering with the effort of the destined deliverer to burst from the cell, where sits

> The old hag, unconquerable, huge,
> Creation's endless drudge, black Ruin.

The sonnets glow with the same political fervour. He glories as champions of freedom in Kosciusko, Erskine, Priestley, or attacks Pitt as the Iscariot of his country, or laments the apostasy of Burke—

> Whom stormy Pity and the cherished lure
> Of Pomp, and proud precipitance of soul
> Wildered with meteor fires.

The noble ode to *France* is inspired by the disappointment of his hopes. It opens with a stirring appeal to all that is freest in nature to bear witness to his deep worship of "the spirit of divinest liberty," and to his hopes and fears

> When France in wrath her giant limbs upreared,
> And, with the oath which smote air, earth, and sea,
> Stamped her strong foot and said she would be free.

It closes with the melancholy confession how profitless had been his pursuit of liberty in any "form of human power." His belief in humanity broke the ties of patriotism; he had cursed England as the enemy of freedom. Nor did the horrors of the Revolution check his ardour. He still looked beyond the storm-clouds to the light on the horizon. When France appeared as the enslaver of Switzerland, when the orient flush proved not to be the holy flame of liberty but the baleful star of Napoleon, his hopes were extinguished. He had looked at the Reign of Terror as if in a dream. The dream passed away, and he shuddered at the realities of his waking vision. His disappointment was embittered by the sense of confidence betrayed; his patriotism was revived by the attack on England. The shock chilled his poetic impulse; it also caused a recoil in his political opinions. He had never been an extreme Jacobin, but he perceived that the new despotism in France was but the old writ large. His worship of liberty combined with his hatred of atheism and love of the soil of his country to develop the patriotism always latent in him.

In 1796 Coleridge started a periodical *The Watchman*, which enjoyed but a brief existence. In the second issue he records, with delightful naïveté, "an essay against fast-days, with a most censurable application of a text from Isaiah for its motto, lost me near five hundred subscribers at one blow." He alienated his revolutionary supporters by his support of bills gagging the press, "which, whatever the motive for their introduction, would produce an effect to be desired by all true friends of freedom, as far as they should contribute to deter men from openly declaiming on subjects, the principles of which they had never bottomed, and from pleading to the poor and ignorant instead of pleading for them." At the same time the editor of *The Watchman* urged that national education and a concurring spread of the Gospel were the indispensable conditions of any true political amelioration. Burke's *Letter to a Noble Lord* he avows to be "as contemptible in style as in matter— it is sad stuff." The collapse of *The Watchman* allowed him to turn from politics to poetry. Wordsworth and he wrote the *Lyrical Ballads*, published in 1798. Coleridge's contribution to it was the *Ancient Mariner*. In the winter of the preceding year he had written the first parts of *Christabel* and *Kubla Khan*. These three are far above all his other poems. They are new creations. The other poems are nothing of the sort. Some of them are good poetry such as other men could write, and some read like bad prose. Like Wordsworth, and unlike Shelley and Keats, he often could not distinguish between the subject-matter proper to poetry and the subject-matter proper to prose, and this not merely in his declining years, but also in the prime of his power.

Wordsworth, as we know, suffered from a kind of stupidity which only inspiration could enlighten. He had no tact, no discretion, no literary contrivance. On the other hand Coleridge's best verse is full of tact and discretion and literary contrivance. The effects of the *Ancient Mariner* are as surely calculated as those of any poem in the language. Keats himself never wrote so many lines of pure poetry without any lapse of misjudgment. Yet it is remarkable that whereas Wordsworth and Shelley put all their interests and powers of their minds into their best poems, a great part of Coleridge's thought and learning and humanity never found their way even into *Christabel* or the *Ancient Mariner*. There is no sound of the French Revolution in their music, nor is there any inspired meditation on the purposes of life. They are full of nothing but wonder at the world in which magical new gleams have taken the place of the cold light of reason, in which the wind has shifted suddenly from east to west, changing the colour of the earth and filling the sky with a mysterious conflict of cloud and sunlight. They are pure bird-songs of the romantic spring; and *Kubla Khan* is the skylark's song of its summer, rising up and up in aimless delight, till it breaks off sharp because it can mount no higher. Yet we know that Coleridge was a philosopher from his childhood, and that in his youth "he nerved his heart and filled his eyes with tears, as he hailed the rising orb of liberty." Sometimes, it is true, thoughts of liberty inspired his verse, as in the Ode on France; but even in that the finest part is the pure romantic exaltation of the first stanza. When he begins to write of the Revolution, and to explain his own attitude towards it, he descends through rhetoric towards prose. Sometimes there are lines of inspired meditation also in his philosophic verse; but the best of it, like the best even of the Ode on France, is far below the *Ancient Mariner*, while the worst of it is far below plain prose.

Dowden has pointed out the fact that there was so imperfect an alliance between the poet and the thinker in Coleridge is one cause why his output of perfect verse was so scanty: fifty pages will include it all. This is true no doubt. But why is this alliance so imperfect? The doses of opium will not explain it, for they were an effect rather than a cause, and began after he had written much of his best poetry. The reason is to be found in certain defects of the philosophy, which were the results of infirmities rather moral than intellectual in Coleridge's mind, infirmities which turned fatal through cruel circumstance. There are many people, of course, who think that poetry has nothing to do with philosophy, and Dowden said that some will offer up fervent thanks because Coleridge's philosophical systems ceased to enter into his poetry. Yet if a poet philosophises at all, his philosophy should be the raw material of his poetry. It was so in the case of Wordsworth, and often it remains raw material in his verse. But it was not so in the case of Coleridge, and the reason was that his philosophy had no connexion with his conduct. "Scarce a thought," says Hazlitt, "can pass through the mind of man, but its sound has at some time or other passed over his head with rustling pinions." Yes, the thoughts came thick and fast, but only the sound of them lingered in his brain. They never made their home in his mind or grew there into principles. He could not choose between one theory and another, because he tested none of them in action. He was but a connoisseur in wisdom, wandering, like a tourist, through all regions and cities of thought, but never finding an abiding place in any of them. Hazlitt has written that no one can think or write about Coleridge without considering why "all this mighty heap of hope, of thought, of learning and humanity . . . ended in swallowing doses of oblivion and in writing paragraphs in the *Courier*." Coleridge himself, more than once, in the poem written after Wordsworth's recitation of the Prelude, and again in *Work without Hope*, has told us how passion and thought both ran to waste in his life until both were impotent:

> Yet well I ken the banks where Amarantha blow,
> Have traced the fount whence streams of nectar flow.
> Bloom, O ye Amaranths bloom for whom ye may,
> For me ye bloom not! Glide, rich streams away!
> With lips unbrightened, wreathless brow, I stroll:
> And would you learn the spells that drown my soul?
> Work without hope draws nectar in a sieve,
> And hope without an object cannot live.

Here he tells us that his passion for beauty had grown impotent, as it always must when youth departs, unless it is strengthened by thought. But Coleridge's thought was disconnected from his passion, and seldom became poetry; because poetry, like action, issues from a man's whole life, and philosophy cannot be heightened into poetry until it has grown to be a part of the poet's life, and not merely a game of his intellect. It must be felt as well as thought; it must turn from a theory into a faith. For Coleridge it remained always a game, an idle and delusive exercise of his mind; and at last it became, not work, but play without hope.

We have said that his impuissance was inborn. From the first he would rather think than act. Lamb called him at school an "inspired charity boy," and this, in another sense, he remained all his life, expecting inspiration as a gift rather than trying to earn it by action. But, to add to his native infirmity, life was very hard upon him. When we feel inclined to reproach him or Wordsworth or Southey for losing the generous ardour of their youth, we should try to imagine to ourselves what hopes the Revolution raised in their minds, and what it meant to them when those hopes were "quenched in darkness and in blood." Wordsworth has told us in the Prelude that the worst of it was the outbreak of war between England and France, for that set up a conflict in his mind that nothing could reconcile.

> Not in my single mind alone I found,
> But in the minds of all ingenous youth,
> Change and subversion from that hour. No shock
> Given to my moral nature had I known
> Down to that very moment; neither lapse
> Nor turn of sentiment that might be named
> A revolution, save at this one time.

Coleridge, in the Ode on France, gives another reason for his despair:

> Are these thy boasts, champion of humankind?
> To mix with kings in the low lust of sway,
> Yell in the hunt, and share the murderous prey;
> To insult the shrine of Liberty with spoils
> From free men torn; to tempt and to betray?

In any case the two poets were differently affected. Wordsworth's will triumphed over the shock. He made his choice and regained his tranquillity. He built up a new faith out of the ruins of the old. Yet even for him "the second temple was not like the first." The constitution of his poetical mind never recovered from the shock it had suffered, though his prose mind effected a recovery. Like Wordsworth, Coleridge feared for the order and continuance of civilisation, but, unlike Wordsworth, he feared also for himself. One has only to read the *Biographia Literaria*, written when reaction was everywhere triumphant, to see this.

In that book, Coleridge is almost abjectly eager to prove that he is no Jacobite and never has been one. He abjures all his religious errors and consents to reaction. Writing in 1816 he says that "the hand of Providence has disciplined all Europe into sobriety, as men tame wild elephants, by alternate blows and caresses." Still his consent is given, not by his heart and mind, but only by his fears. He is for ever explaining and justifying himself both to the revolutionaries whom he has left and to the reactionaries whom he cannot join. But his explanations are negative. He is not a Jacobin; but what he is, what he wants or hopes or believes, he cannot quite say. Now many men could rest comfortable in such a state of negation, but not Coleridge. He was not born to be satisfied with things as they are, especially as they were between 1815 and 1830. He was born, like Shelley, to enormous hopes and visions of extreme delight; and for a short time in his youth these hopes touched the earth itself with gold. But even then they came only like chance fair weather to his soul, and he received them passively as a plant takes sunlight. In a few years they came no more in poetry; their very source was darkened, and much of Coleridge's object in life was gone. He became "the hooded eagle among blinking owls," in poetry with inspirations in his political writings.

Coleridge cannot ever again enjoy the vogue as a thinker, almost as a prophet of wisdom, which he possessed between 1820 and 1850. That position was partly due to the brilliant personal gifts of a man whose talk had stimulated the intellectual life of a whole generation, which inevitably repaid him in the natural coin of discipleship, unstinted gratitude, and unquestioning loyalty. Party spirit, ecclesiastical and political, had also, of course, something to do with it. When the one sinner that repented was such a one as Coleridge, it was natural that Churchmen should rejoice over him as over a converted Saul, and Tories exalted his wisdom as their fathers had exalted the Burke of the *Reflections on the Revolution in France*. And, in the religious sphere at any rate, the Oxford Movement, representing, just as he did, the restoration to authority of the Fathers and of the great seventeenth century divines, and the dethronement of Paley and the mechanic school of theology, came to bestow upon him the vogue of success in addition to that of mere celebrity. But parties change and party idols are rapidly forgotten. The philosophic Conservatism of Burke is no longer, unfortunately, a very visible force in politics. The Oxford Movement is very visible in theology, yet its first force has witnessed the spending of some of it in the ritualistic follies of its less intelligent offspring or in the solution of the critical and social problems which it ignored. It is plain, then, that the fame of Coleridge cannot now receive much support from the parties in Church and State who maintained it in his life and after his death. He suffers as well from a more honourable cause. The mind of Coleridge, so far as it did not belong to poetry, came to do three things. It came to deliver English thought from the exclusive domination of the literary ideals of Pope, from that of the theological ideals of Paley, and from that of the philosophical principles of Locke and Hume. And it did them all. At least they are all now done. And like the general whose victories destroyed his own importance by restoring peace to his country, Coleridge suffers from his very success.

In order to preserve Coleridge's gifts for literature the Wedgwoods settled an annuity of £150 a year on him. Journalism eked out his income, and from 1798 to 1802 he contributed 83 poems and 55 prose articles to the *Morning Post*. He was to send the editor what he liked, in verse or prose, and he was to be paid a guinea a week. The articles are very much to the point. On December 31st, 1799, he assails the new constitution established by Napoleon and Sièyes on the foundation of the Consulate, with its eighty senators, the "creatures of a renegade priest, himself the creature of a foreign mercenary, its hundred tribunes who are to talk and do nothing, and its three hundred legislators whom the constitution orders to be silent." What a ludicrous Purgatory, he adds, "for three hundred Frenchmen!" He argues against the rejection by our ministers of the French proposals of peace in 1800, holding that the French were sincere in advancing this proposal. Alas! years later Napoleon admitted in his Memoirs that he was insincere in soliciting peace. "I had need of war; a treaty of peace . . . would have withered every imagination." And when Pitt's answer arrived, "it filled me with a secret satisfaction." Coleridge characterises Pitt with perverse political judgment, simply allowing that he owed to his father the sedulous rhetorical training which resulted in "a premature and unnatural dexterity in the combination of words." The wrath of the First Consul against Coleridge is supposed to be excited by his contributions to the *Morning Post*. On a voyage home from Malta, where he had been acting as secretary to the Governor, the vessel with him on board was chased by a French ship. This so alarmed the captain that he compelled Coleridge to throw all his papers overboard, nor is it far-fetched to believe in the truth of this tale. For Fox—and Napoleon would pay attention to any of his remarks—had declared in the House of Commons that the rupture of the Peace of Amiens had been due to essays in the *Morning Post*. The man who shot Palm and attacked Madame de Stael would not have deemed a man of Coleridge's reputation in letters beneath his vengeance. His dread of Napoleon gradually deepened. On the renewal of the war he supported it as a struggle for liberty. The peace party seemed to him not anti-ministerial, but anti-national. His patriotism stands contrasted with his early cosmopolitanism.

In 1816 Coleridge published *The Statesman's Manual; or the Bible the best Guide to Political Skill and Foresight: A Lay Sermon on the Distresses of the Country, addressed to the Middle and Higher Orders.* In it he blends his religious appeals with political and economical arguments. There is an effective analysis of the various artifices by which most orators delude their hearers. Occasionally he drops pregnant remarks. "The mere appeal to the auditors, whether the arguments are not such that none but an idiot or an hireling could resist, is an effective substitute for any argument at all. For mobs have no memories. They are nearly in the same state as that of an individual when he makes what is termed a bull. *The passions, like a fused metal, fill up the wide interstices of thought and supply the defective links; and thus incompatible assertions are harmonised by the sensation, without sense of connection.*"

At Bristol he lectured again in 1818, and published his lectures in *Essays on his own Times*, describing the "oppositionists to things as they are," the "democrats" of his day. He divides them into four classes. The first is composed of men of small education and little disposition to arduous thought, who yet feel vaguely that something is wrong, and will give an indolent vote for reform provided they are not too much frightened by news from France. The second are the men who undertake violent revolutions: hunger drives them to do it. Coleridge discerns signs in the state of the English poor, showing that they are drawing near to this danger-point. The third class is composed of those who pursue freedom because it means profit to them. Their main desire is the abolition of the privileged orders, the pulling down of whatever is above them. They do not, however, believe in plans for the amelioration of the lot of the poor: these are the dreams of idle visionaries. Equality of rights is all that men can claim. Yet, in Coleridge's opinion, equality of rights become an empty phrase when used to justify a blind struggle for economic power. "It is a mockery of our fellow creatures' wrongs to call them equal in rights, when by the bitter compulsion of their wants we make them inferior to us in all that can soften the heart, or dignify the understanding." The last class includes the calm, pure-minded followers of a rational idea of the good life for all. They alone, we learn, can lead a successful revolution.

Coleridge did not content himself with phrases. He wrote two circulars on behalf of the Factory Act which Peel introduced in 1818. How little *laissez-faire* weighed with him is clear from the letter he wrote to Crabb Robinson on May 3rd: "Can you furnish us with any other instances in which the legislature has interfered with what is ironically called 'Free Labour' (i.e. dared to prohibit soul-murder on the part of the rich, and self-slaughter on that of the poor!) or any dictum of our grave law authorities from Fortescue to Eldon; for from the borough of Hell I wish to have no representatives." On May 2nd, 1818, he wrote to J. H. Green who endeavoured to act to his master the part in some measure assumed by Dumont to Bentham: "The Cotton-children Bill (an odd irony to children *bred up in cotton*!) which has passed the House of Commons, would not, I suspect, have been discussed at all in the House of Lords, but have been quietly assented to, had it not afforded that *Scotch* coxcomb, the plebeian Earl of Lauderdale, too tempting an occasion for displaying his muddy three-inch depths in the gutter of his Political Economy. Whether some half-score of rich capitalists are to be prevented from suborning suicide and perpetuating infanticide and soul-murder, is, forsooth, the most perplexing question which has ever called forth his *determining* faculties, accustomed as they are *well-known* to have been, to grappling with difficulties."

Coleridge's *Table Talk* for March 17th, 1833, and June 23rd, 1834, show that the views of 1818 were not transient. The much-vaunted science of Ricardo and James Mill was, after all, "solemn humbug." The patriot within Coleridge believed that this so-called science presented problems without theorems, "the direct tendency of every rule of which is to denationalise, to make the love of our country a foolish superstition," a position hard for the Utilitarian to deny. On August 12th, 1832, he asks in his *Table Talk*: "Is it not lamentable—is it not even marvellous—that the monstrous practical sophism of Malthus should now have gotten complete possession of the leading men of the kingdom? Such an essential lie in morals—such a practical lie, in fact, as it is too! I solemnly declare that I do not believe that all the heresies, and sects, and factions, which the ignorance, and the weakness, and the wickedness of man have ever given birth to were altogether so disgraceful to man as a Christian, a philsopher, a statesman, or citizen, as this abominable tenet." The emancipation of the negro he regards in the light of staking "the tranquillity of an empire, the lives and properties of millions of men and women, on the faith of a maxim of modern political economy!" Colonisation is "not only a manifest experiment, but an imperative duty in Great Britain. God seems to hold out His finger to us over the sea. But it must be a national colonisation." Machinery has cheapened production, but it has not cheapened the necessaries of life. "The vast increase of mechanical powers had not cheapened life and pleasure to the poor as it has done to the rich. In some respects, no doubt, it has done so,—as in giving cotton dresses to maid-servants, and penny gin to all. A pretty benefit truly!" The scorn of Burke for the sophisters, economists, and calculators is his. You may buy, as you think, cheaply, but what if you are buying dearly? You may reduce the price of an article from eightpence to sixpence, "but suppose, in so doing, you have rendered your country weaker against a foreign foe; suppose you have demoralised thousands of your fellow-countrymen, and have sown discontent between one class of society and another, your article is tolerably dear, I take it, after all? Is not its real price enhanced to every Christian and patriot a hundredfold?"

Bentham and Owen had been moved to action during the Industrial Revolution, but they spoke from a more or less Radical position. Bentham had assumed the truth of Political Economy, an assumption questioned by Owen and now by Coleridge. As a philosophic Conservative he was anxious to right the wrongs of the poor. To him the outcome of their neglect meant that Radicalism his soul abhorred. "When the Government and the aristocracy of this country had subordinated persons to things, and treated the one like the other—the poor, with some reason, and almost in self-defence, learned to set up rights above duties." As a Churchman his Catechism had taught him to set duties above rights. *The Statesman's Manual*, imperfect as it was, had inculcated the same lesson. The black slaves of the West Indies stirred Wilberforce to indignation: the white slaves of England stirred Coleridge to indignation. The soothing maxim of *laissez-faire* failed to afford him comfort. A Ricardo might assure him with the words, "all things find their level." Yes, but what about the misery and degradation endured by the poor in this painful process? Goods might find their level of price. Did human beings readily find it? "But persons," he vigorously asserts, "are not things, but man does not find his level." The Industrial Revolution was shifting folk to the north, and was allowing the growth of a larger population. Such a gigantic movement attested the truth that men "ought to be weighed, not counted." Granted that the tall factories had taken their due share in the winning of the war against Napoleon, but what about the condition of the toilers in these factories? The addition to the material wealth of the country was enormous, yet was the addition to the moral wealth in any wise commensurable? The standard of cotton dresses and gin emphatically did not apply. The production of wealth was progressing, but Coleridge was more concerned with its equitable distribution. "We have," he declared with passion, "game laws, corn laws, cotton factories, Spitalfields, the tillers of the land paid by poor rates, and the remainder of the population mechanised into engines for the manufactory of rich men; yea, the machinery of the wealth of the nation made up of the wretchedness, disease, and depravity of those who should constitute the strength of the nation." The heart of the humanitarian which beat for the fate of the lowly animal beat for the fate of the lowly man. He disdained Whig measures of parliamentary reform as deeply as Owen himself. "It is a mockery of our fellow creatures' wrongs to call them equal in rights, when by the bitter compulsion of their wants we make them inferior to us in all that can soften the heart, or dignify the understanding."

The new age was a mechanical one with which Coleridge

exhibited but scanty sympathy. He discerns its beginnings in Kepler and Newton, in Locke and Hartley, yet its long lineage in no wise reconciles him to it. What the scientists and the moralists taught was supported by the politicians. True, once upon a time Coleridge had been a necessitarian, but from those days he shrank back with horror. He shrank back scarcely less from the moralists who taught that virtue simply depended on a calculation of the degree of happiness or pain entailed by the act of the will. Accordingly, he denied that the State can construct its government of men on the plan that they are as mechanical as the machines they work. He was a mystic: he was not a materialist. Mysticism came to him through the writings of Jacob Boehme and George Fox, and he could not believe that man liveth by bread alone. As his metaphysics were a recoil from the dominant sensationalism lying behind utilitarianism, so in morality he preached a crusade against fashionable ethics. He had been to Germany and he had read Kant. He had been moved, as we all know, by the starry heavens above and the moral law within. Man indeed looks outward before he looks inward, and both outward and inward before he looks upward. Duty spoke to Coleridge, at any rate, in his writings, with the sound of a trumpet. Paley's school reduced virtue to expediency, made utility the object, and self-interest the guide, of action, treated virtue and vice as lazy synonyms of prudence and miscalculation. Coleridge, on the other hand, contended that enlightened self-interest is not virtue, nor duty regard to personal consequences; but that moral goodness is more than prudence, and religion higher than morality.

The distinction between reason and understanding underlies his argument. Understanding is "the faculty of judging according to sense." In its highest form of experience it "remains commensurate with the experimental notices of the senses from which it is generalised. Reason, on the other hand, either predetermines experience, or avails itself of a past experience to supersede its necessity in all future time; and affirms truths, which no sense could perceive, nor experiment verify, nor experience confirm." This distinction Coleridge had borrowed from Kant, and in the process of borrowing he altered its purpose. With Kant the distinction between reason and understanding has a restrictive purpose. Reason has a regulative or suggestive function in the ordering of knowledge. Understanding, going hand in hand with sensible intuition, possesses the sole title to the discovery of truth. Naturally such a distinction can lead to agnostic conclusions. Instead of separating the spheres of the two faculties, as Kant does, Coleridge unites them. He allows to the one an apparently unlimited power of re-affirming what the other had found it necessary to deny. Carlyle indeed thought that Coleridge had discovered "the sublime secret of believing by the reason what the understanding had been obliged to fling out as incredible." Yet it may well be that for Coleridge reason formed an instrument of apprehension to a deeper degree than Carlyle dreamed. There is a spiritual experience for Coleridge, and it can be referred to an objective basis on which it rests. Certainly Kant leaves us face to face with agnosticism, while Coleridge leaves us face to face with a faith which can be reasonably justified. We all know his aphorism that every man is born either a Platonist or an Aristotelian, and he was undoubtedly born a Platonist. It is the philosophical statement of the political position laid down by Gilbert:

> Then let's rejoice, with Loud Fal la,
>   That Nature wisely does contrive
> That every boy and every gal
>   That's born into the world alive
> Is either a little Liberal
> Or else a little Conservative.

The political presuppositions for the moment we leave to the one side. The philosophical ones we cannot. The distinction between reason and understanding is of importance. But as Coleridge does not distinguish religion from morality, no systematic treatise is to be expected. His one object is to vindicate the spiritual side of man, and his responsibility to higher laws than those of nature. The ideal of prudence may be the carefully calculated love of one's self, while the ideal of morality is a pure life on pure principles. Though prudence implies self-sacrifice, it is essentially selfish. Its dictates and those of morality may correspond, but on different grounds. Prudence is the animal instinct, appealing to the senses and understanding, ignoring motives, regarding only results. Morality appeals to the heart and the conscience; it distinguishes good from evil unconditionally; it commands not only our duty but our reverence. Few men can by their own strength live under the iron rule of duty, or warm the cold purity of the moral law into a vital principle. The dynamic force of morality lies, according to Coleridge, in reason, religion, and will; in reason, the representative of divine reason, the source through which the moral law is revealed; in religion, which, contracts universal rules into universal duties; in will, which coerces our conduct. The three powers are legislative, executive, and ministerial. The highest life is that of a man whose will is subjugated to the universal will, so that he wills the will of God. Of this harmony conscience is the witness.

Coleridge's theology was based on the great divines of the Tudor and Stuart periods. Hooker, Field, Donne, Taylor, Andrewes, Bull, Jackson, Smith, Cudworth, and More—the last three Cambridge Platonists even yet have not come into their own—were among his favourite authors. From eighteenth century authors he derived little satisfaction. Leighton's commentary on St. Peter he placed next to the inspired Scriptures. Equally with Leighton he valued Luther, as the man whose grasp on spiritual truths was firmest, and whose writings contained the "very marrow of divinity"; he could not "separate his name from that of St. Paul." He respected St. Augustine because of his Pauline affinities, but despised the rest of the Fathers, with one or two exceptions, as credulous and ignorant. Luther, Melanchthon, and Calvin he considered to be "worth a whole brigade of the Cyprians, Firmilians, and the like." In the grave controversies of the Reformation era he leaned rather to the Arminians than the Calvinists; though he protested equally against the gloomy tyranny of the latter, which crushed the joyous freedom of life, and the apologies for Christianity offered by the former, "pleadings fitter for an Old Bailey thieves' counsellor than for Christian divines." He held the Bible to be the best of all books, but a book after all. His posthumous letters on inspiration were highly valued by Arnold of Rugby. The mechanical theology which he combated was the counterpart of sensational metaphysics and Utilitarian ethics. In his *Aids to Reflection*, 1825, he emphasises the proposition that "Christianity is not a theory, or a learned speculation, but a life." Nor does he forget to remind us that "He who begins by loving Christianity better than Truth, will proceed by loving his own sect or Church better than Christianity, and end by loving himself better than all."

Coleridge's *Constitution of Church and State*, 1830, gathers views which have to be supplemented by hints scattered profusely throughout his writings. He "begs he may not be suspected of predilection for any particular sect or party; for wherever he looks, in religion or politics, he seems to see a world of power and talent wasted on the support of half-truths." The men of the Oxford Movement read this book, and it is hard to resist the conclusion that Disraeli also must have done so.

Speaking broadly, Church and State had been regarded as the same body under different aspects, or as two independent powers in alliance. Each theory admits various modifications, but with none of them does Coleridge wholly agree. With Hooker he held that the visible Church of Christ included all professing Christians, but denied that Church and State are one body in different aspects. Distinguishing, with Warburton, Church from State, he repudiated his theory of a convention between the two societies. His own theory is an application to constitutional law of his characteristic principles. Religion stands to law in the same relation which it bears to morality and philosophy. As it is their basis, it inspires law; it is the positive, the guiding element, as law is the negative, restraining element. Religion and law, Church and State, are not separate but distinct; they are harmonious not hostile, neither to be confounded nor opposed. The duties of the nation, he says, comprise both the outward functions, which every one attributes to civil government, and the inward work of education and civilisation. Yet these distinct kinds of action cannot be carried on by the same machinery and officers, or each will tend perpetually to destroy the other. Absolutely independent of all civil governments, there is also an universal Christian Church, having its own officers performing certain specially religious duties, and constituting an integral part of Christianity, without which Christianity is "vanity and dissolution." In Christian countries, where the same persons are both citizens and churchmen, the nation accomplishes its own purposes best by employing as its educative officers the existing officers of the Christian Church. This would of course be impossible or extremely inconvenient to both parties, if there were any real clashing between the two functions thus assigned to the same persons; but, on the one hand, the most complete education to make men good citizens is that which they will receive from such a body as the Christian clergy; and, on the other, the Christian clergy can never do their own proper religious duty to their congregations except in educating them to become good citizens. Education is to be on the Miltonic pattern, and it is to "form and train up the people of the country to be obedient, free, useful, organisable subjects, citizens and patriots, living for the benefit of the State, and prepared to die for its defence."

Coleridge distinguishes the Church in England from the Church of England, the localised Church of Christ from the National Church. Of his attachment to the Church of England there can be no doubt, but with this attachment he combined candour of judgment and freedom from sectarian prejudice. Politically speaking, his reverence for the Church in the abstract, as an integral portion of the State, was a ruling principle in his scheme of social government. In his view the revenues of the Church are neither more nor less than a portion of the public property set apart for the mental and physical benefit of all, especially of the poor. The mode of their application is in principle uncontrolled by any other law than the absolute good of the community. All educated men whose branch of study is such as to render their services available for the public benefit, including the whole body of the learned, are, in fact, the Clerisy, as he called them, to whose disposal these means are fitly entrusted. "There have been three silent revolutions in England,—first, when the professions fell from the Church; secondly, when literature fell off from the professions; and thirdly, when the press fell off from literature."

He is careful to insist that the proposition that the State had national possessions which it could resume at any time is one of those "half-truths, the most dangerous of errors (as those of the poor visionaries called Spenceans)," who aimed at the nationalisation of land. Still, property in land was a trust to be exercised on behalf of the weal of the people. Formerly this had been so, but since the Napoleonic Wars the relationship between landlord and tenant was commercial, replacing the old moral bond. This is disastrous. For the State must take care of its most precious property, "its own inalienable and untransferable property—I mean the health, strength, honesty, and filial love of its children."

There is to Coleridge an Idea of our Constitution just as there is an Idea of the Church. This Idea corresponds to the vital force which moulds the structure of the social organism. It often works sub-consciously, and Coleridge would not have been taken aback had he been informed that the controllers of the Idea were not altogether aware of it. Of the Idea of the State he writes: "Because our whole history, from Alfred onwards, demonstrates the continued influence of such an idea, or ultimate aim, in the minds of our forefathers, in their characters and functions as public men, alike in what they resisted and what they claimed; in the institutions and forms of polity which they established, and with regard to those against which they more or less successfully contended; and because the result has been a progressive, though not always a direct or equable, advance in the gradual realisation of the idea; and because it is actually, though (even because it is an idea), not adequately, represented in a correspondent scheme of means really existing; we speak, and have a right to speak, of the idea itself as actually existing, that is, as a principle existing in the only way in which a principle can exist—in the minds and consciences of the persons whose duties it prescribes, and whose rights it determines." He was in the true line of succession to Burke in laying stress on the Idea in the State as well as the Church.

It is significant that he agrees with James Mill in thinking that the "social bond" was originally formed to protect property, not to protect life. Yet he is not content to fall down and worship the abstraction called the State. As he hated abstractions, how could he? Your Ricardos may so fall down, but he, for his part, is utterly unable. Indignantly he demands, "What is this Society, this Whole, this State? Is it anything else but a word of convenience, to express at once the aggregate of confederated individuals living in a certain district?" He might listen to Kant on the moral law, but he undoubtedly refused to listen to Hegel and Fichte when they created that omnipotent power, der Staat. His, however, is no mere police State merely caring for property. "Let us suppose," he writes, "the negative ends of a State already attained, namely, its own safety by means of its own strength, and the protection of persons and property for all its members; there will then remain the positive ends:—1. To make the means of subsistence more easy to each individual; 2. To secure to each of its members the hope of bettering his own condition or that of his children; 3. The development of his own faculties which are essential to his humanity, that is, to this rational and moral being."

Every nation provides separate machinery for the performance of the external duties of government and for the moral government of the people. England entrusts these latter duties to the officers of the Christian Church, and allots to them for these services a portion of the national land. Thus the National Church is established by the State as the trustee of a national fund on fixed terms. As public servants the national clergy receive revenues, and are amenable to State laws. Still the union of the two functions in the same persons does not make them any the less members of the Universal Church; they do not merge their position as Churchmen in their citizenship; in each capacity their claim, their duties, and their obligations are distinct. Independent of civil government, having officers appointed for special duties of religion, is the universal Church of Christ, a theocratic institution, a spiritual society divinely incorporated, exercising that general spiritual authority, which is of the very Idea of Christianity. Coleridge condemned Laud's ecclesiastical policy because, as he conceived, the Archbishop limited the Church of Christ to the hierarchy. This is an instance of the working of the principles of our philosopher. Similarly he denied that dissenters could, by voluntary secession, exonerate themselves from the obligation of supporting the National Church. He admitted that the bishops of the Church of Christ have no vocation to interfere in legislation, while he at the same time asserted their sacred duty as national prelates to take part in national councils. He opposed the emancipation of the Roman Catholics, because their allegiance to a foreign power disqualified them from their proper education of citizens. When the Church of Ireland was attacked, he raised the cry of "the Church in danger," not because of the peril to her endowments, but as a breach of the idea of the Universal Church. However much he disliked the Tractarian deference to the authority of the early Fathers, he warmly sympathised with the revival of the idea of the Church as a co-ordinate and living power by right of Christ's constitution and promise. It is enough to recall the title of his book, the *Constitution of Church and State*.

A letter he wrote to Daniel Stuart on October 30th, 1814, is helpful towards a grasp of the Coleridgean position: "The view which our laws take of robbery, and even murder, not as GUILT of which God alone is presumed to be the Judge, but as CRIMES depriving the *King* of one of *his* subjects, rendering dangerous and abating the value of the King's Highways, etc., may suggest some notion of my meaning. Jack, Tom, and Harry have no existence in the eye of the law, except as included in some form of the PERMANENT PROPERTY of the realm. Just as, on the other hand, Religion has nothing to do with Ranks, Estates, or Offices; but exerts itself wholly on what is PERSONAL, viz., our souls, consciences, and the MORALITY of our actions, as opposed to mere legality. Ranks, Estates, Offices, etc., were *made* for *persons*! exclaims Major Cartwright and his partisans. Yes, I reply, as far as the DIVINE administration is concerned, but *human* jurisprudence, wisely aware of its own weakness, and sensible how incommensurate its powers are with so vast an object as the well-being of individuals, as individuals, reverses the position, and knows nothing of persons, other than as properties, officiaries, subjects. The preambles of our old statutes concerning aliens (as foreign merchants), and Jews, are all so many illustrations of my principle; the strongest instance of opposition to which, and therefore characteristic of the present age, was the attempt to legislate for animals by Lord Erskine; that is, not merely interfering with persons as persons; or what is called by moralists the imperfect duties (a very obscure phrase for obligations of conscience, not capable of being realised (perfecta) by legal penalties), but extending PERSONALITY to *things*."

He retained his faith in the Idea of things to the end, and it certainly affected his attitude to parliamentary reform in the thirties. In his *Table Talk*, on July 24th, 1832, he announces: "I have no faith in act of parliament reform. All the great—the permanently great—things that have been achieved in the world, have been achieved by individuals working from the instinct of genius or of goodness. The rage now-a-days is all the other way; the individual is supposed to be capable of nothing; there must be organisation, classification, machinery, etc., as if the capital of national morality could be increased by making a joint stock of it." Coleridge, who lived in the reigns of George IV and William IV, hazarded an opinion that foreshadowed the prestige Queen Victoria was to restore to the Crown, and he deserves credit for his long view in saying on April 9th, 1833: "I have a deep, though paradoxical conviction, that most of the European nations are more or less on their way, unconsciously indeed, to pure monarchy,—that is, to a government in which, under circumstances of complicated and subtle control, the reason of the people shall become efficient in the apparent will of the King. As it seems to me, the wise and good in every country will in all likelihood become every day more and more disgusted with the representative form of government, brutalised as it is and will be by the predominance of democracy in England, France, and Belgium. The statesmen of antiquity, we know, doubted the possibility of the effective and permanent combination of the three elementary forms of government, and perhaps they had more reason than we have been accustomed to think.

You see how this House of Commons has begun to verify all the ill prophecies that were made of it,—low, vulgar, meddling with everything, assuming universal competency, flattering every base passion, and sneering at everything noble and refined, and truly national. The direct and personal despotism will come on by and by, after the multitude shall have been gratified with the spoil and the ruin of the old institutions of the land."

The appeal to history is plain, yet we must be careful to note his position. "Of all the men I ever knew, Wordsworth himself not excepted," Coleridge writes, "I have the faintest pleasure in things contingent and transitory . . . Nay, it goes to a disease with me. As I was gazing at a wall in Carnarvon Castle, I wished the guide fifty miles off that was telling me, in this chamber the Black Prince was born—or whoever it was." Now we frankly admit that the historic instinct was not so strong in him as it was in Scott and Byron. At the same time his attachment to the reformers and the Jacobean and Caroline divines attests how deeply he cared for the past in which he took an interest, not in all the past but in his past. In sorrow J. S. Mill penned the words: "No one can calculate what struggles, which the cause of improvement has yet to undergo, might have been spared if the philosophers of the eighteenth century had done anything like justice to the Past." Coleridge was one of them who did justice to the past. He held, like Bacon, that knowledge of current speculative opinions affords the sole ground for political prophecy. He appealed to history to prove that all epoch-making revolutions coincided with the rise or fall of metaphysical systems. Before his day, history, studied not for the explanation of facts, but for the facts themselves, possessed for the most part only a biographical or antiquarian interest. Coleridge, like Lessing or Herder, recognised that the succession of historical events was capable of scientific treatment. He regarded history as the progressive unfolding of the capabilities of man, and claimed for its facts a meaning and a place in the evolution of humanity. He tested every organism of society; but there was nothing subversive in a criticism which endeavoured to justify the permanence of institutions by bringing to light the principles they embodied. His mind revolted from the unimaginative utilitarianism of the reformers of his day. In politics, himself an idealist of the Platonic pattern, he believed that laws underlay every form of social organisation. The existence of an institution or the prevalence of an opinion raised the presumption that each satisfied some want or represented some experience of the human mind; each had an aim and a meaning. The good for which each existed must be discovered before its obsoleteness or utility could be determined. Without regard to principles no reform should be attempted. Ruling Ideas might be deduced from history; to realise them in abstract perfection was impossible, though they should form the standard of legislative change. The rough-and-ready school of politics —then or to-day—regarded nothing but practical anomalies, advocated remedies worse than the disease, and destroyed eternal verities to cure casual disorders. Coleridge preached the value of the transcendental side of politics to an eminently practical generation. Nevertheless, his work was not valueless. He cherished institutions and surrounded hereditary beliefs with new lines of defence, and dignified contests, which often appear petty squabbles about the adjustment of temporary means to ephemeral ends, with the serene atmosphere of the eternal.

The lectures at Bristol, *The Friend*, the newspaper articles, the *Lay Sermons*, and the *Constitution of Church and State* attest his pride in citizenship as well as his glory in patriotism. After the attack of the French on Switzerland his cosmopolitanism is replaced by a gradually glowing patriotism. Country comes before corporation: national interests yield no place to corporative ones. "If I met a man who should deny that an *imperium in imperio* was in itself an evil," Coleridge holds, "I would not attempt to reason with him; he is too ignorant." What a hold England had upon him is evident from an article in *The Friend*, written during the height of the war against Napoleon. The lover of his country "knows that patriotism is a necessary link in the golden chain of our affections and virtues, and turns away with indignant scorn from the false philosophy or mistaken religion, which would persuade him that cosmopolitanism is nobler than nationality, and the human race a sublimer object of love than a people. . . Here, where the royal crown is loved and worshipped as a glory round the sainted head of freedom! Where the rustic at his plough whistles with equal enthusiasm 'God save the King' and 'Britons never shall be slaves'; or perhaps leaves one thistle unweeded in his garden, because it is the symbol of his dear native land! Here, from within this circle, defined as light by shade, or rather as light within light, by its intensity, here alone, and only within these magic circles, rise up the awful spirits, whose words are oracles for mankind, whose love embraces all countries, and whose voice sounds through all ages." The writer's descent from Burke is unmistakable.

The connection between the patriotism of Coleridge and his interpretation of Shakespeare is not obscure. Chatham learnt his history and his patriotism from the dramatist. It is to the eternal credit of Coleridge that he revolutionised once and for all the English attitude towards the greatest of Englishmen. All through the eighteenth century Shakespeare had been more and more acted, studied, edited; but till Coleridge came he had not escaped the indignity of being apologised for and even corrected. The impatience of Coleridge with the eighteenth century is more explicable if we bear in mind the attitude of its critics to Shakespeare. Nor do we think we wander far from the truth when we ascribe the revolution Coleridge created in the mind of our forefathers to Shakespeare some of the patriotism which enabled them to carry on the struggle against Napoleon for two-and-twenty dreary years. This achievement of Coleridge is really only part of the other achievement by which he made us see in all poetry no toy, no mere art even, but a vision of the truth. The key to that lies, of course, in a philosophy which aimed at covering life as well as literature. It lies, in a word, in Coleridge's doctrine of the imagination. He wanted to unite his poetic and philosophic faith, and the word by which he did was his imagination. For him imagination was always seeing the Idea, the reality behind the symbol, truth behind fact, God behind nature. This greatest of human faculties, "a dim analogue of creation, not all that we can believe, but all that we can conceive of creation," is seen at its highest in the poet. From this flows all the rest. Poetry is no longer an amusement for the drawing-room, or a contest of wits; it is a revelation of the deepest and profoundest of truths. It is the interpretation of nature which consists not in copying the external form, but in revealing that which is active through form and figure and discourses to us by symbols. To Croce "the judicial activity which criticises and recognises the beautiful is identical with the artistic activity which produces it." To Coleridge these two activities are also one.

The life of Coleridge is a unity, though a scattered one. He is not a specially systematic thinker, as compared with some others; he did not weld his speculations together with the iron bonds of Spinoza or Kant; and in appearance he is even more unsystematic than he is in reality. There is, however, a true sequence in all that he writes; he had formed to himself a full, broad, and not inharmonious conception of the world in which we live, and our duties in it, though, no doubt, he might have worked it out more clearly in detail, and expressed it in a much more convincing manner than he did.

His formal writings on Church or State might alone seem to come within our purview. Yet the essence of his political doctrine is the Idea lying behind every institution, and this Idea derives as much force from his criticism of Shakespeare and from his transformation of poetry as from his political articles or books. The gulf between the criticism that springs from the Coleridgean doctrine of the worth of poetry, and the old criticism at its very best, is one that cannot be bridged, and, what is remarkable, one which no one now wishes to bridge. Wordsworth and Coleridge have conquered the world of poetry, at least in England. If people care at all for poetry now it is more or less from this point of view. At any rate, no English poet will ever again think of his art, as Pope, and even Scott, thought of theirs, as a kind of cultivated amusement for idle hours. People whose children show a turn for reading poetry are not likely now to follow Locke in being alarmed at their idle propensities; they are much more likely to suspect them of over-seriousness. For those who use poetry at all it has now definitely become the occupation of the higher moments of life, not of the lower. That is a fundamental change of attitude; and it is the measure of the greatness of Wordsworth and Coleridge that they achieved it. They had some help from Shelley, and perhaps a little from Keats, but none at all from Byron and Scott. It is a revolution in poetry, and a revolution in criticism; and with this latter the name of Coleridge will always be identified. The old criticism still has its uses, is still practised, must always be practised; but it can never again be thought of as anything but subordinate. Never again will any critic worthy of the name think, with the early writers in *The Edinburgh Review* and *The Quarterly Review*, he has done his duty when he has treated a poem as a schoolmaster treats a schoolboy's exercise. If that is all the poem deserves, it is best left alone; if that is all that the critic is capable of, he has mistaken his vocation. Poetry is no longer, as it once was, a thing that can be pronounced correct or incorrect. It is a thing which must be felt to be either great or small; and to feel that the critic must have some soul of greatness in him. It is not the least of the debts we owe Coleridge that since his day no mere learning by itself, no merely intellectual powers of any kind, have been enough to enable any critic of poetry to attain to a position of a master.

Merely as a political writer he stands in a high position, but unless we take his three great poems into account we cannot understand the eulogies passed on Coleridge by competent judges. They, for the most part, treat all his thought as a unity, and such indeed it is. Wordsworth owns that he had "seen men who had done wonderful things, but only one wonderful man, namely, Coleridge." "I am grieved," said, Southey, "that you never met Coleridge; all other men whom I have ever known are mere children to him, and yet all is palsied by a total want of moral strength." To Lamb he was "an archangel, a little damaged." "He is like a lump of coal," confessed Scott, "rich with gas, which lies expending itself in puffs and gleams, unless some shrewd body will clasp it into a cast-iron box, and compel the compressed element to do itself justice." "He is the only person I ever knew," acknowledged Hazlitt, "who answered to the idea of a man of genius; his genius had angelic wings and fed on manna. He talked on for ever, and you wished him to talk on for ever." In another mood Hazlitt added that "his talk was excellent if you let him start from no premises and come to no conclusion." "He is," according to De Quincey, "the largest and most spacious intellect, the subtlest, and most comprehensive, that has yet existed among men." "Impiety to Shakespeare," cried Landor, "treason to Milton! I give up all the rest,—even Bacon. Certainly since their day we have had nothing comparable to him. Byron and Scott were but as gun-flints to a granite mountain. Wordsworth has one angle of resemblance." Poetry had had the hero; Wordsworth would give her the peasant. She had had the rose: he would give her the daisy. Coleridge and he consecrated the commonplace and the common people as they had never been consecrated before. T. Arnold deemed Coleridge on the strength of the results of his thought, the ablest man in England, and this in spite of what he considered the unsteadiness of his thought. His son Matthew pointed out "that which will stand of Coleridge is this; the stimulus of his continual effort,—not a moral effort, for he had no morals,—but of his continual instinctive effort, crowned often with rich success, to get at and to lay bare the real truth of his matter, whether that matter were literary, or philosophical, or political, or religious; and this in a country where at that moment such an effort was almost unknown. . . . Coleridge's great action lay in his supplying in England, for many years and under critical circumstances, by the spectacle of this effort of his, a stimulus to all minds, in the generation which grew up round him, capable of profiting by it. His action will still be felt as long as the need for it continues. When, with the cessation of the need, the action too has ceased, Coleridge's memory, in spite of the disesteem, —nay, repugnance—which his character may and must inspire, will yet forever remain invested with that interest and gratitude which invests the memory of founders." So

Matthew Arnold, poet, preacher, and critic, appraised S. T. Coleridge, poet, preacher, and critic.

The many-sided J. S. Mill bracketed Bentham and Coleridge together as "the two great seminal minds of England in their age." In his remarkable essay on the latter, J. S. Mill holds that "the name of Coleridge is one of the few English names in our time which are likely to be oftener pronounced, and to become symbolical of more important things, in proportion as the inward workings of the age manifest themselves more and more in outward facts. Bentham excepted, no Englishman of recent date has left his impress so deeply in the opinions and mental tendencies of those among us who attempt to enlighten their practice by philosophical meditation. . . . The influence of Coleridge, like that of Bentham, extends far beyond those who share in the peculiarities of his religious or philosophical creed. He has been a great awakener in this country of the spirit of philosophy, within the bounds of traditional opinions." Carlyle strikes a distinctly lower note. "Coleridge sat," we learn, "on the brow of Highgate Hill, in those years, looking down on London and its smoke-tumult, like a sage escaped from the inanity of life's battle; attracting towards him the thoughts of innumerable brave souls still engaged there. . . The good man, he was now getting old, sixty perhaps; and gave you the idea of a life that had been full of sufferings; a life heavy-laden, half-vanquished, still swimming painfully in seas of manifold physical and other bewilderment. . . . I still recollect his 'object' and 'subject,' terms of continual recurrence in the Kantian province; and how he sang and snuffled them into 'om-m-mject' and 'sum-m-mject,' with a kind of solemn shake or quaver, as he rolled along. No talk, in his century, or in any other, could be more surprising." The personal private character of Coleridge's talk was peculiarly calculated to irritate Carlyle. Not only was the bitter Scotsman antagonistic to Coleridge in mind and temper, but he had special reasons of his own for sneering. A rival talker, he listened "for two stricken hours" to Coleridge's "theosophico-metaphysical monotony." If he expected a short answer to a terse question, Coleridge would accumulate "formidable apparatus for setting out," and approach the subject as circuitously as possible. Carlyle suspected him of claiming, as Schelling claimed, an exclusive faculty of spiritual perception; he believed that his influence on John Sterling was disastrous; he wrote Sterling's life as an answer to Hare, who deemed Coleridge "a true sovereign of English thought." Even where no special cause appears for ill-feeling, estimates of contemporaries from Carlyle's pen must necessarily be distrusted. But, in his portrait of Coleridge, Carlyle has gratified not only his sarcastic spleen, but his private dislike. Yet, if Coleridge's philosophy was an empty bubble, he was that rainbow which Carlyle refused to see in anything. Both grappled with perplexing problems of life: Carlyle, vanquished by the inscrutable riddle, sank into morbid despondency, Coleridge never lost faith in humanity. Reduced to practice, Coleridge's philosophy succeeded while Carlyle's failed; at the close of their days the light on Coleridge's face is the expanding glow of sunrise, that on the face of Carlyle is the fading flush of sunset.

Coleridge was a revealer of truth and beauty in poetry and its interpretation: he was also a revealer of truth and beauty in politics and its interpretation. Nor is it possible to separate the revelation in politics from the revelation in poetry. He gave a reasoned and reasonable basis for truth in religion, and such a basis was sorely required in his day. The Evangelicals, to their infinite loss, were not interested in the problems set by reason, and from Paley's mode of meeting them Coleridge turned away in frank disgust. "Evidences of Christianity! I am weary of the word. Make a man feel the want of it; rouse him if you can to the self-knowledge of his need of it; and you may safely trust it to his own evidence." He contributed powerfully to the rise of the Broad Church School. T. Arnold, F. D. Maurice, and F. W. Robertson of Brighton were shaped by his attitude to the Bible, his free acceptance of it as a book to be analysed, his attitude to history, revealing the hand of God, and his utter desire to reach the leading Ideas in Christianity. If he contributed to the rise of the Broad Church School, he also contributed to the rise of the Oxford Movement. He was a Romantic, and Romanticism played no mean part in altering the attitude of men to the past, the very groundwork of the appeal enforced by Keble, Newman, and Pusey. What Scott had done one way, in spite of his poetry, Coleridge did another way. When, however, Newman claimed Coleridge as a philosophical initiator of Anglo-Catholic opinion, he admits that he "indulged a liberty of speculation which no Christian can tolerate, and advocated conclusions which were often heathen rather than Christian." Coleridge's learned daughter acutely wrote: "My own belief is that although an unripe High Church theology is all that some readers have found or valued in my father's writings, it is by no means what is there: and that he who thinks he has gone a little way with Coleridge, and then proceeded with Romanising teachers further still, has never gone with Coleridge at all."

"He builded better than he knew," so runs the old saw. It requires alteration, for "He builded *other* than he knew." The immediate followers of Coleridge in the Broad Church and the High Church Schools he could have understood in 1829, but what about their descendants in 1929? Would he have shown much sympathy with the Christian Socialism which has issued from the Broad Church School? Would he have shown any sympathy with the extreme ritualism which has issued from the High Church School? The foundations are those he laid, but is the superstructure in either case? And if it is, with what qualifications are we to take it? Nor can we doubt that the man who taught that permanence and progress were among the soundest elements in Church and State would have looked approvingly at the immense growth which the doctrine of development has received at the hands of Maine and the vigorous Historical School. The comparative point of view had been Coleridge's, and his attitude to history prepared the way for the "Ancient Law" and its numerous descendants. F. W. Maitland saw his debt to the labour of his great Cambridge predecessor. When Lord Acton said he had learnt little from Carlyle because he had read Coleridge first, he expressed in an epigram the deep debt which modern speculation owes to our philosopher, a debt Döllinger freely acknowledged. There are in Coleridge's writings hints of "a state of nature, or the Ourang-outang theology of the origin of the human race, substituted for the first ten chapters of the Book of Genesis." We do not like to say on the strength of a stray passage like this that Coleridge entertained a belief in evolution: that would be absurd. Still in his attitude to the doctrine of development which he brought back from Germany, it is possible to say that dimly he was groping his way towards it. There are germs in Coleridge, and these germs assume all sorts of forms. He was in truth, what J. S. Mill termed him, a great seminal mind.

The root idea of *Coningsby* is to be found in Coleridge's view that "Commerce has enriched thousands, it has been the cause of the spread of knowledge and of science, but has it added one particle of happiness or of moral improvement? Has it given a truer insight into our duties, or tended to revive and sustain in us the better feelings of our nature? No! When I consider the whole districts of men, who could otherwise have slumbered on in comparatively happy ignorance are now little less than brutes in their lives and something worse than brutes in their instincts, I could almost wish that the manufacturing districts were swallowed up as Sodom and Gomorrah." Lord Morley has told us how startled he was to read in J. S. Mill's *Principles of Political Economy* the sentences: "Hitherto (1848) it is questionable if all the mechanical inventions yet made have lightened the day's toil of any human being. They have enabled a greater population to live the same life of drudgery and imprisonment, and an increased number of manufacturers and others to make fortunes. They have increased the comforts of the middle classes. But they have not yet begun to effect those great changes in human destiny, which it is in their nature and in their futurity to accomplish." There is a ring about these sentences which thrills one, but Coleridge had already thrilled an earlier generation. He had fed on honey dew and drunk the milk of Paradise. He had woven moonlight enchantments and been beloved of the gods; and perhaps he should have died when he lost command of the spells which the gods only grant to youth. If ever we are inclined to feel with Carlyle and M. Arnold contempt for his shiftless, aimless middle age we should remember that men have to pay a price for genius which is as unimaginable to the rest of mankind as genius itself; and, as Coleridge's genius was the most incalculable that ever was, so surely was the price he had to pay for it. The man who was born to delight the world with his three great poems was not born to be an example of industry and consistency, a writer who practised philosophic Conservatism. He would have been if he could; with the critical part of his mind he understood the laws of life, political and other, but his creative powers belonged to another world and could not obey them. He confessed his faults often and piteously; and it is not for us, who understand no more of his temptations than of the powers of mind which produced the *Ancient Mariner*, to condemn him.

There is a close relationship between the political thought of Burke and Coleridge. Whole-heartedly would the latter have subscribed to the view of Burke when he laid down that "*Idem sentire de republica* was with them a principal ground of friendship and attachment; nor do I know any other capable of forming firmer, dearer, more pleasing, more honourable, and more virtuous habitudes." The French Revolution affected them both to the very depths of their natures, though we do well to remember that in 1789 Burke was an old man of sixty, Coleridge a boy of seventeen. Both were conservative in the deepest sense of this term, giving it a meaning in the past and a prestige in the present it never had before. Fixed institutions there must be, and it is the object of the statesman to divine the leading Idea of every one of them, though Coleridge was willing to pay more attention to this Idea than Burke. Nor is Coleridge by any means blind to the defects of Burke's versatility of principle. For he points out that "If his opponents are theorists, *then* everything is to be founded on prudence, on mere calculations of expediency; and every man is to be represented as acting according to the state of his own immediate self-interest. Are his opponents calculators? *Then* calculation itself is represented as a sort of crime. God has given us feelings, and we are to obey them, and the most absurd prejudices become venerable, to which these feelings have given consecration." Coleridge had distinguished between reason and understanding, and in his view reason was the cause of the fatal turn given to the French Revolution. The levelling effects due to fraternity were as abhorrent to him as they were to Burke. He indeed might have uttered the passionate words, "It is the science of cosmopolitism without country, of philanthropy without neighbourliness or consanguinity—in short, of all the impostures of that philosophy of the French Revolution, which would sacrifice each to the shadowy idol of all."

Burke and Coleridge believed in order and progress, yet their belief was tinged with differences. The former laid more stress on order, the latter on progress. This difference in the last resort, depends on their natures. Coleridge was an idealist; he was more dreamy and more subtly spiritual than Burke; and he had an esoteric side—an aspect that breaks out from his later letters in strange and unexpected lights. Both ever realised that power is from the heights. Burke was weightier, more positive; Coleridge, larger, finer, more interpretative. To both, the State rested upon aristocracy, classes, interests and property, and the aims represented by them did not always agree. To Coleridge, as to Burke, the State is "a body politic having the principle of its unity within itself," turning upon "equipoise and interdependency." There is to be an equilibrium of the opposing elements, a conception dear to the heart of Burke. To Coleridge "there is no unity for a people, but in a representation of national interests—a delegation from the passions or wishes of the individuals themselves is a rope of sand." Permanence and progression have each its allotted position. With Burke he believes that permanence rests on land and all that it means in the life of the nation. The professional, mercantile, and distributing classes stand for progression. Coleridge, however, is clearly of opinion that the permanent interests had dwarfed the progressive. Equilibrium must be renewed. "The organised powers," according to Coleridge, "brought within containing channels," which property represents, must be kept up with due regard to the "free and permeative life and energy of the nation." Each thinker was anxious that the classes should understand and respect one another, and that men and women of high standing should be imbued with the ideal of high responsibility. The two thinkers may have been Tories, but they were progressive ones, conservatives before Croker invented the term. They believed in liberty, but they also believed that liberty was embodied in the institutions of their country. The spirit of the Constitution required revival, but not the Constitution itself. For Coleridge will not allow us to forget that political liberty is not an end in itself, "though desirable, even for its own sake, it yet derived its main value as the means of calling forth and securing other advantages and excellences, the activities of industry, the security of life and property, the peaceful energies of genius and manifold talent, the development of the moral virtues."

The Utilitarians had placed a ban upon history, and it fell to Burke and Coleridge to restore it to its true place. Both were anxious to see the men, to see the things, to take the circumstances into consideration. Both men were the products of circumstance, governing their conduct by the distinguishing colour, the discriminating effect time gave to the event. Both paid due regard to the impulses of honour and glory, the tenacity with which our fancy clings to old customs, the respect for rank as an antidote to the worship of the golden calf, the apostolic descent of the Anglican episcopacy, and the long pedigree of the noblemen. Such regard ensured, in their eyes, a distrust of innovation and a trust in the established order. If you retain Conservative institutions, it means you retain Conservative instincts, for can you retain them with Radical instincts? To Coleridge, at any rate, it is clear that "a fancied superiority to their ancestors' intellects must not be speedily followed, in the popular mind, by disrespect for their ancestors' institutions." Under some circumstances stagnation might ensue, yet Burke and Coleridge were passionately working for the welfare of their country. In the judgment of the latter "nothing great was ever achieved without enthusiasm," and it was every whit as true of the former.

Burke and Coleridge blended in an exceptional degree the mystic with the practical, the spiritual with the intellectual. They were profoundly convinced that Church and State had their foundations in religious faith, and that they could not survive its disintegration. To them there was no question of the relationship between Church and State. Such relationship presupposed that they were two bodies in their nature distinct and independent, whereas to Burke "in a Christian commonwealth, the Church and the State are one and the same thing, being different integral parts of the same whole." Plato declared that it is vain to expect any man to be a great statesman unless he cares for the deepest matter in human nature, the life of the soul. Burke and Coleridge were then great statesmen, for they cared for the deepest matter in human nature, the life of the soul. Religion was for Coleridge "the centre of gravity," and Christianity was not only "a blessed accident, a providential boon," but it was what marked us off from the brute. It was for the National Church "to preserve the stores and to guard the treasures of past civilisation, and thus to bind the present with the past; to perfect and add to the same, and thus to connect the present with the future; but especially to diffuse through the whole community, and to every native entitled to its laws and rights, that quantity and quality of knowledge which was indispensable both for the understanding of those rights and for the performance of those duties correspondent." The mysticism of Coleridge is as apparent as that of Burke. For Burke also holds that the State is a divine institution. According to him, "without society man could not by any possibility arrive at the perfection of which his nature is capable, nor even make a remote and faint approach to it. He, the Divine Author, gave us our nature to be perfected by our virtue. He must therefore have willed the means of its perfection. He must therefore have willed the State, and He willed its connection with Himself, the source of all perfection." It is in truth a conception as old as Cicero, and as recent as Hegel and the powerful school founded by Fichte and himself. Society is a partnership, and association for the greater purposes of our being, for the promotion of science, art, virtue, which constitutes the task of the clerisy. "It is," Burke holds with all the fervour of his nature, "not a partnership in things subservient only to the gross animal existence of a temporary and perishable nature. It is a partnership in all science; a partnership in all art; a partnership in every virtue and in all perfection. As the ends of such a partnership cannot be obtained in many generations, it becomes a partnership not only between those who are living, but between those who are living, those who are dead, and those who are yet to be born."

Burke and Coleridge were familiar with the slow process of the discipline of nature as it operates through the centuries. The former knew "how many a weary step is to be taken before they (i.e. the people) can form themselves into a mass which has a truly politic personality." They were afraid of the stability of Church and State. Red revolution may remove from these institutions the results of the ages. They dreaded the spread of Jacobinism among the multitude, and this dread warped their judgment. The spread of the views of the rights of man and the sovereignty of the populace forced them to realise that the position of equilibrium they desired might prove unstable. Coleridge shares the apprehensions of Burke in his attitude to the multitude. He draws an Erasmian distinction between the people and the populace, the former to be trusted, the latter to be distrusted. "Oh!" cried Coleridge in 1807, "the profanation of the sacred word, the *People*! Every brutal mob, assembled on some drunken St. Monday of faction, is the People, forsooth!" His ideal is that of Burke, a government of the propertied classes, imposing itself upon the rest of the community from above. In *The Friend* he writes: "I appeal to history... What does it contain, but accounts of noble structures raised by the wisdom of the few, and gradually undermined by the ignorance and the profligacy of the many?" It is the task of the statesman, according to Burke and Coleridge, to awaken the rich and powerful to a sense of their duty. Long before Drummond, Coleridge insisted that property has its duties as well as its rights. Moral right is the foundation of society within the State, the security of all just dealings without between State and State. No mere mechanism of government departments will suffice. Burke and Coleridge understood the limits as well as the benefits of compromise; both were the champions of a sound, as opposed to a sentimental, tolerance; both remained adherents to forms which they wished to inspire.

Devout faith and reverent rationalism, shrewd wit and shrewder simplicity, are characteristics of each.

It is curious to observe the care with which Burke avoids the metaphor of the organism. The State is a "venerable" castle; it is the keep of Windsor, looking proudly over the plain beneath. He quotes Dryden to tell us

> 'Tis not the hasty product of a day
> But the well-ripened fruit of wise delay.

It is a vessel requiring to be cunningly balanced. He draws his imagery from the works of nature, eschewing botany and zoology in favour of inorganic—not organic—chemistry and physics. The art in his selection of illustration is perhaps subconscious, for obviously he perceives an analogy between the life of the State and the life of a plant, he must allow for change, be it ever so slowly. And this is precisely what he refuses to allow, and what Coleridge allows. Nevertheless, he admits in all but formal words that the State is an organism. Its essence, from this angle, lies in his statement that "Constitutions grow and are not made." Coleridge almost acknowledges in formal words that the State is an organism. In his *Table Talk* he affirms that "A State is an intermediate idea between an inorganic and an organic body—the whole being the result from, and not only a mere total of, the parts, and yet not so merging the constituent parts in the result, but that the individual exists integrally within it." He advances beyond Burke in laying stress on the consent of the people, a position as old as St. Augustine. "If there be any difference between a Government and a band of robbers, an act of consent must be supposed on the part of the people governed." Man is a free agent, and can exercise his free will. When Rousseau emphasises the general will, and its purity, he is, in Coleridge's eyes, expounding what is merely a matter of probability. Besides, this theory confounds the moral or religious with political claims. It "confounds the sufficiency of the conscience to make every person a moral and amenable being, with the sufficiency of judgment and experience requisite to the exercise of political right." The identity of reason would validate only one form of the constitution, a conclusion as repugnant to Burke as to Coleridge. He reaches the verdict that "a constitution equally suitable to China and America, or to Russia and Great Britain, must, surely, be equally unfit for both." Such an appeal to history would have satisfied Burke, and he would have agreed with the Coleridgean view that by a system, like that of Bentham and J. Mill, "the observation of times, places, relative bearings, national customs and character, is rendered superfluous; and by the magic oracles of certain axioms and definitions it is revealed how the world with all its concerns should be mechanised; and then let go of itself."

REFERENCES

ALLSOP, T. *Letters, Conversations and Recollections of S. T. Coleridge.* (London, 1864.)
ANSON, H. I'A. *S. T. Coleridge.* (London, 1926.)
AYNARD, J. *La vie d'un poète.* (Coleridge.) (Paris, 1907.)
BENN, A. W. *The History of English Rationalism in the Nineteenth Century.* Vol. I. (London, 1906.)
BRANDL, A. *Samuel Taylor Coleridge and the English Romantic School.* (London, 1887.)
BRINTON, C. *The Political Ideas of the English Romanticists.* (Oxford, 1926.)
BROOKE, S. A. *Theology in the English Poets.* (London, 1874.)
CAINE, T. H. *Life of Samuel Taylor Coleridge.* (London, 1881.)
CAMPBELL, J. D. *S. T. Coleridge.* (London, 1896.)
CARLYLE, T. *The Life of John Sterling.* (London, 1851.)
CESTRE, C. *Les Poètes anglais et la Révolution française.* (Paris, 1906.)
COTTLE, J. *Early Recollections of S. T. Coleridge.* (Bristol, 1839.)
COTTLE, J. *Reminiscences of S. T. Coleridge and Robert Southey.* (London, 1848.)
GILLMAN, J. *The Life of Samuel Taylor Coleridge.* (London, 1838.)
GREEN, J. H. *Spiritual Philosophy.* (London, 1865.)
HANEY, J. L. *The German Influence on S. T. Coleridge.* (Philadelphia, 1902.)
HAZLITT, W. *Works.* (London, 1902.)
HORT, F. J. A. *Cambridge Essays.* (London, 1856.)
LEGOUIS, E. *La Jeunesse de William Wordsworth.* (Paris, 1896.)
LOWES, J. L. *The Road to Xanadu.* (London, 1927.)
LUCAS, E. V. *Charles Lamb and the Lloyds.* (London, 1898.)
MAITLAND, F. W. *Collected Papers.* Vol. I. (Cambridge, 1911.)
MILL, J. S. *Dissertations and Discussions.* (London, 1859–75.)

SCHANK, N. *Die sozialpolitischen Anschaunngen Coleridges u. sein Einfluss auf Carlyle.* (Berlin, 1924.)
STEPHEN, Sir L. *Hours in a Library.* Vol. III. (London, 1892.)
STORR, V. F. *The Development of English Theology in the Nineteenth Century.* (London, 1913.)
TRAILL, H. D. *Coleridge.* (London, 1884.)
TULLOCH, J. *Movements of Religious Thought.* (London, 1885.)
WATSON, L. E. *Coleridge at Highgate.* (London, 1925.)
WINGFIELD-STRATFORD, E. *The History of English Patriotism.* (London, 1913.)

Chapter VI.
DISRAELI THE NOVELIST-STATESMAN

Disraeli was as real a man of letters as Coleridge, for was he not born, according to himself, in a library? His novels are an amazing mixture of the tawdry and the cynical, the mysterious and the mundane. Some of them are dead beyond hope of any resurrection. Yet his political stories and his life of Lord George Bentinck must always interest and amuse politicians of every degree. He had a marvellous power of self-effacement, of turning aside and looking at the struggles in which he was himself engaged as though he were a mere spectator. He once confessed in the House of Commons that his views on the question of Jewish disabilities were shared by no other human being. This isolation was by no means confined to a single topic. He did not think like the men around him: his mind was working on different lines. That was why he understood them better than they understood themselves, and why *Coningsby* or *Lothair* is so much more instructive than most treatises on the British Constitution. Of all English Ministers, if he was an English Minister, Disraeli had the literary temperament in the amplest measure. He knew it and was proud of it. "I am a knight of the Press," he once said in his strange style, "and have no other escutcheon."

Benjamin Disraeli (1804–81) was the son of Isaac, whose *Curiosities of Literature* still lingers with the reader. The past haunted the Jewish father and his son, and in its glories they contrived to escape from the degradation of the present. The lad always assigned a foremost place to his father among the few from whose wisdom he never failed to draw profit. His affection for his sister Sarah was romantic. Four great men of the nineteenth century have alike been distinguished for their lover-like devotion to a sister—Byron, Macaulay, Mendelssohn, and Heine. Disraeli like Pitt, Macaulay, Samuel Wilberforce, Cobden, Bright, and Cecil Rhodes, was never at a public school. As he was never at a university, he made no pretence to classical scholarship, although he was better acquainted with the classical writers than some who had been to both a public school and a university, and he was thoroughly imbued with their spirit. Whether the absence of a public school and university education is to be regretted in his case is open to question. His character and disposition unfitted him for the training which it affords, but was it the training he required? Men of the peculiar genius of Disraeli are perhaps better left to educate and form themselves. Disraeli, for good or for evil, made himself what he was to a larger degree than most men.

"To enter high society," runs one of Disraeli's *obiter dicta*, "a man must have either blood, millions, or a genius!" and he clearly relied on the last. Nor did it ever fail, and in *Vivian Grey*, published in 1826, he was to afford a fruit of it. It was the inevitable explosion of a highly-charged intellect. He was a youth of two-and-twenty. At his father's house he had met and conversed with men distinguished in literature and concerned with public affairs; with Rogers, with John Murray, with Crofton Croker. He was not ignorant of the world; his knowledge of life was distinctly precocious. To be a great man he was determined, and that right speedily. What was his immediate ambition is not obvious perhaps even to himself. A snob in the ordinary sense he never was. He revered the aristocracy as an institution; and, as his writings attest, he believed in its immense power in the State. He sought the society of the great because they represented action, and therefore power. He had the oriental love of colour and sumptuous living. Later in life he moved in the stateliest society in England; but he never ranked its members with children of his own race. Literary success undoubtedly attracted him: witness his appreciation of Byron's fame in *Venetia*. To make life vivid, to be "in the movement"—this was his desire. If, at the outset, he plunged into peerages and palaces, it was in search of interest, not by reason of vulgar social aspiration. Nor is it amiss to remark that his love of a gathering of our aristocracy had not a little to do with his eventually gaining its goodwill. He wooed our aristocracy, and at last he won its heart. In all his writings he told its members that no country could prosper under a democratic constitution without an aristocracy with great duties as well as great privileges. This aristocracy was to furnish leaders of the people, and these leaders were to be examples of manliness and nobility of character. Disraeli's themes concerned England, but they concerned England not as an island but as part, the heart, of an Empire. Here he was to stand out in contrast to his two great rivals, Peel and Gladstone. To them west and east meant Cheshire or Lancashire and Lincolnshire whereas to Disraeli it always meant the Old World and the New. He was an Englishman, if he was an Englishman, who was always a cosmopolitan. Government to him was divine or it was nothing but "a mere affair of the taxgatherer, of the guardroom." In the general preface to his novels, written in 1870, he reaffirms this doctrine: "The divine right of Kings may have been a plea for feeble tyrants, but the divine right of Government is the keystone of human progress, and without it government sinks into politics, and a nation is degraded into a mob."

In 1828 the Utilitarians were influencing public opinion, and Disraeli satirised them in *The Voyage of Captain Popanilla*. The satire of Swift is unpleasant and inspired by ill-humour: the satire of Disraeli, though on a lower literary level, is pleasant and inspired by good-humour. The pathometer our satirist applies—if he could apply one at all—is not one that nicely calculates the balance of pleasure and pain, but one which judges the present by the past. Instinct with historical imagination and the mystery of life, as mystical in some ways as Coleridge himself, can he help caricaturing the soulless conceptions of the Benthamite school? It is easy work, all the easier because there is no attempt to do justice to the innate humanitarianism of Bentham and his followers. Nor is it surprising to read ridicule of the Corn Laws and the Colonial system of the twenties. John Bright admired *Popanilla*, and we can well believe that this great representative of the Manchester school, as Disraeli came to term it, should have enjoyed the attack on the Corn Laws and nascent Imperialism by one who was in the future to be a defender of both.

The reputation which he had acquired by *Vivian Grey*, his travels in the East, where Jerusalem aroused in his breast those thoughts and emotions he afterwards embodied in *Tancred*, and his calculated eccentricities of dress and manner, now opened the doors of society to him; and we find him intimate with Edward Bulwer, Count d'Orsay, Lady Blessington, and most of the leaders of fashion who appreciated his genius and encouraged his foppishness. A novel of society life he gave the public in *The Young Duke*, which appeared in 1831. The feeling for tradition, the reverence for the past, the devotion to religion, the instinct for order—all four qualities are already visible to the reader of *The Young Duke*. True, the novelist declares himself a Gallio in his allegiance to party, yet for a young man such a declaration is by no means blameworthy.

A panegyric on patriotism—and Disraeli was a fervent patriot—did not commend *The Young Duke* to the Utilitarians, and we feel no surprise in learning that the *Westminster Review* assailed his book. In 1833 he wrote: "The Utilitarians in politics are like the Unitarians in religion; both omit imagination in their systems, and imagination governs mankind." He instinctively dreaded the effects of Utilitarianism which he perceived fraught with the predominance of the middle class after 1832, a class he disliked as much as James Mill liked it. Nor did he fail to note the ultimate democracy latent in it. If every one was to count for one, how could you stop short, in 1832 or any other year, of that democracy which he considered as a tool in the hand of ambitious tribunes? He believed in the system of estates on which Coleridge laid stress, and democracy was inconsistent with this system. He cared for the happiness of the people just as much as Bentham himself, but it seemed to him that this happiness was often marred by Mill to whom the Utilitarian leader in his old age lent more countenance than Disraeli at all admired. Nor must we overlook the fact that the two great parties, the Tories and the Whigs, did not display popular sympathies in the thirties. The

Whigs dreaded Radicalism just as much as the Tories. The middle class tone of the Whigs and the aristocratic tone of the Tories blinded them both to the possibilities of enlisting the people on their respective sides. It is not the least of Disraeli's merits that he discerned this possibility, and his task was to graft new ideas of freedom on the Tory tree of order. Democracy was to be natural and national, led by the aristocracy. It was a bold conception in the thirties, a conception that was wholly Disraeli's own. "To be wise before the event," he urged more than once, "is statesmanship of the highest order," and it is plain that he possessed it.

The problem as Disraeli envisaged it in 1833 was to give the wage-earning class a share, perhaps a large one, in political power without giving them the whole. In 1833 he already saw that this whole share was the tendency of Utilitarianism and of the Reform Act of 1832 which embodied it. Nor can we shut our eyes to the fact that then William IV was on the throne, and that his predecessor had been George IV, one of the greatest blackguards who ever wore a crown. Yet Disraeli has prescience enough to feel that the monarchy will not always be so. There is to be an orderly succession of estates, holding their interests in due subordination to the common weal, and at the top of this social pyramid we are to behold the aristocracy with a sovereign worthy of the respect of all the estates. Queen Victoria was to realise some of this dream, and the magician who was to stand at her side was the visionary of 1833.

In 1832 Disraeli stood as a candidate for High Wycombe, and it is significant that he did not enter the House of Commons till after the dissolution of 1837 consequent on the death of William IV. The new member's career in it was to last without a break for nearly forty years. In 1832, as in 1833, he had been revolving in his mind a political programme, and he had also been revolving it in *Contarini Fleming*, which appeared in the former year. Despite disclaimer, Contarini Fleming is Benjamin Disraeli. His doctrines on race and destiny are now given in outline. The view that all is race peeps out in Contarini's meditations amid the ruins of Athens. It is well to remember that

Buckle did not publish his history of civilisation in England till 1853 and that Treitschke did not deliver his lectures in the University of Berlin till 1876. Nothing is outside the novelist's ken. "I think that, ere long, science will again become imaginative, and that as we are become more profound, we may become also more credulous." The increasing mysticism of science has been revealed to our own day, for men like Sir J. J. Thomson or Sir E. Rutherford are as mystical or as imaginative as the soul of the novelist could desire. There were no signs of this mysticism in Disraeli's day, and indeed science had to pass through the materialism advocated by Tyndall, Huxley, and the dominant scientific school of the eighties. This is really an instance of the astonishing insight of the man of imagination.

Although much absorbed in politics, and engaged in fresh negotiations for obtaining a seat in Parliament, he worked, to use his own expression, "like a tiger" to finish a romance which he had contemplated during his eastern travels. He chose for his theme a romantic tale founded upon the tradition existing among the Jews of the Captivity, that they were to find among the descendants of David a prince of the House of Judah, who was to restore them to their native land, and to establish them once more as a great and independent nation. In *The Wondrous Tale of Alroy*, Disraeli revealed in 1833 more than in any other writing the degree to which Judaism had tinctured the whole of his nature. With the background of the twelfth century Alroy appears before us as another Judas Maccabæus. Can he not win back the independence of Israel? Can he not restore her ancient glory?

A short pamphlet *What is He?* was to explain to the average man what the politics of its author were in 1833. The future of the Jewish race, no matter how glorious, was not in the least likely to provide any effective appeal to him. Accordingly we hear little about race and destiny, though they lie in the very texture of Disraelian thought. Even in ordinary politics, his thoughts were not those of the Tory or the Whig. He sought for a National Party, and he was not in the least willing to give up to either party what he meant for the whole of English mankind. The political pyramid he had erected is still in his mind, and he eagerly seeks to set before others the splendid vision of a united country. The pamphlet is far more anxious to witness the growth of this National Party than to recommend such measures as the repeal of the Septennial Act, election by ballot, and the immediate dissolution of Parliament. Disraeli's first speech in Parliament proved a failure, yet he was not in the least daunted by this. He confidently announced, "I sit down, but the time will come when you will hear me." In 1834, Melbourne, anxious to advance him, inquired what his object in life was. "To be Prime Minister," was the reply which startled Melbourne, who set to work to prove how impossible this ambition was. The years came and went, and Disraeli continued steadfast to his purpose. Moved by this, Melbourne at last exclaimed, "By God, he will do it yet!" Gladstone was destined to be his rival, and there is little in common between the two statesmen. Each was a Prime Minister, an author, and an affectionate husband, but this is very like saying that each had a pair of eyes, a mouth, and a voice. Gladstone was worshipped for his goodness and Disraeli for his genius, and people rallied to the one leader or the other according to their predilection for character or intellect respectively. To say this is not of course to reflect either on Gladstone's intellect or Disraeli's character, but merely to point out what were the qualities in the two men that fired the popular imagination. The feeling for Gladstone among his admirers was almost a religious feeling. His outbursts of moral indignation were particularly relished. Conventional himself, he essentially appealed to the higher nature of the average church- or chapel-goer, especially to the latter, who felt that to support him was almost an act of religious worship. There never was any feeling of that sort towards Disraeli, who did not lay himself out to win it, and who would have disconcerted it by his flippancy if it had been entertained. By their practice both evinced how scanty was their real respect for consistency, though they paid lip service to this doctrine. Disraeli's admirers really were of two classes—those who were dazzled by the magnificence of his personal triumph, and those who were dazzled by his foreign policy as by a splendid pageant. It was probably in the former aspect that he fascinated so many clever young men. They admired him as the French —or some of them—admire Napoleon. That is to say, admiration of the man of genius came first, dragging admiration of his achievements after it. They saw him come from nowhere and impose new poetical conceptions on the prosaic craft of statesmanship. They did not pause to ask themselves whether he was, like Gladstone, a great moral force; for clever young men do not as a rule spend much of their time in looking out for moral forces. What they did see in him was first of all the successful adventurer —and clever young men are as naturally drawn to adventurers as Tory squires are opposed to them; and, secondly, the great political artist, who made Toryism interesting in the same sense in which the Tractarians made the Church of England interesting, by relating it to those great poetical and historical ideas which fascinate the imagination.

Mr. Monypenny advances the view that there is a certain ambiguity about the party affiliations of nearly all our greater statesmen, and he instances Chatham, Pitt, Burke, Canning, Peel, Palmerston, Disraeli, and Gladstone. There is of course the consideration urged by Newman: "In a higher world it may be different, but here below to live is to change and to be perfect is to have changed often." From this angle we can contemplate the two great rivals, Disraeli and Gladstone, as struggling by their changes to attain perfection. "Never complain and Never explain" was the motto of our novelist-statesman. It is, however, a defence which the average voter receives with repugnance, and there is no offence he dislikes more than that of inconsistency. We verily believe that Hansard is published not so much for the mere sake of recording speeches as for the sake of granting an opponent an opportunity of proving that his rival has been grossly inconsistent! After the manner of Burke, Disraeli pleaded in 1834: "The truth is, gentlemen, a statesman is a creature of his age, the child of circumstances, the creation of his times. A statesman is essentially a practical character; and when he is called upon to take office, he is not to inquire what his opinion might or might not have been upon this or that subject; he is only to ascertain the needful and the beneficial, and the most feasible measures to be carried on. The fact is, the conduct and the opinions of public men at different periods of their career must not be too curiously contrasted in a free and aspiring country. . . . I laugh, therefore, at the objection against a man, that at a former period of his career he advocated a policy different to his present one. All I seek to ascertain is whether his present policy be just, necessary, expedient; whether at the present moment he is prepared to serve the country according to its present necessities."

The genius of Toryism lies in the escape from theory to history, and Disraeli embodied this genius which he inherited from Harley as well as from Burke. Our novelist-statesman followed in the steps of the latter in bringing about that consciousness of history which had sorely been lacking in the abstract speculations of the eighteenth century. The distrust of the abstract, the trust in history, the insistence upon its continuity, the employment of the imagination in politics, the emphasis upon political institutions as things that cannot be made, but must grow, the faith in the national character of England, and the conviction that a nation is not a collection of equal atoms but an organic structure composed of parts with different powers and functions are *de fide* to Disraeli as to Burke.

Disraeli saw in 1835 that after the shock to Toryism in 1832 there was urgent need of a *Vindication of the English Constitution, in a letter to a noble and learned Lord*, who was Lord Lyndhurst. This treatise contains a sketch of Bolingbroke, which is evidently intended to represent what he aspired to be and his National Party aspired to be. The influence of Burke is as discernible in the *Vindication* as is that of Bolingbroke. The "smugglers of adulterated metaphysics" were as hateful to Burke as the Utilitarians were to Disraeli. "The metaphysical knights of the sorrowful countenance" were odious to the two thinkers. Burke would have heartily subscribed to Disraeli's view that "nations have characters as well as individuals, and national character is precisely the quality which the new sect of statesmen in their schemes and speculations either deny or overlook." To our pamphleteer "This respect for precedent, this clinging to prescription, this reverence for antiquity, which are often ridiculed by conceited and superficial minds appear to me to have their origin in a profound knowledge of human nature."

The *Vindication* re-asserts the Coleridgean principle of the representation of the separate estates of the realm in Parliament and of the dependence of the balance of the constitution on the maintenance of their respective rights. If Radicals like O'Connell plead on behalf of the conception of the people, he pleads on behalf of the conception of the nation as a living organism. Why should the House of Commons be looked on as all-important? Was it not "only an estate of the realm, a privileged and limited order of the nation, in numbers a fraction of the mass?" On the other hand, "The House of Lords represents the Church in the Lord Bishops, the law in the Lord Chancellor, and often in the Lord Chief Justice, the counties in the Lord Lieutenants, the boroughs in their noble recorders. This estate, from the character of the property of its members is also essentially the representative chamber of the land; and, as the hereditary leaders of the nation, especially of the cultivators of the land, the genuine and permanent population of England, its peasantry." Let the future attest the possibilities of this conception. If Lord Shaftesbury is a pioneer in social legislation in England, so is Baron von Kettler in Germany, and so are Vicomte de Villeneuve-Bargemont, Comte de Coux, and the Marquis de la Tour du Pin in France.

Responsibility characterised the Upper House just as much as the Lower. Besides, the hereditary principle is of the last importance. A sovereign may call three hundred men together, and may dignify them by the august title of a senate. He may create peers, but can he create a House of Lords? Not in the least. For "the order of men, of whom such an assembly is formed, is the creation of the ages." There is no nobility cut to European pattern in our country: the caste system of other lands does not prevail with us. Civil equality forms the basis of our social fabric, preserving the democratic nature of our peerage. The members of both Houses are linked together by ties of birth and blood. Surely his political pyramid stands secure against the attacks of all comers, the Utilitarians like James Mill and the Radicals like O'Connell. Disraeli defends our throne and our nobility as stoutly as Bismarck defended the Prussian throne and its nobility.

The interpretation of the past of parties provides a clue to the present. The Whigs have of course, in his opinion, invariably been the anti-national party since their first formation in the latter part of the seventeenth century. Some peers, animated by a hostility of the monarchy, and some Puritans, animated by a hatred of the Church of England, combined in 1688. The outcome was that the House of Russell took Venice for its model, and the Puritans took Geneva. A Venetian oligarchy, in the name of civil and religious liberty, aimed at the destruction of the Monarchy and the Church. The Tory party, the true national one, opposed this combination of Peer and Puritan, safeguarding true democratic interests. The man who stood forth as the gifted exponent of Tory views was that amazing genius, Bolingbroke. Accordingly, the *Vindication* adumbrates the true character of a statesman second to none in the intuitive knowledge of his race, a comprehensive experience of human affairs, and all the wisdom derivable from literature.

That there is an element of paradox in this reading of the past is obvious, yet it is not quite so strong as is sometimes imagined. Since the days of Walpole there have been four periods during which either individual ministers or ministries closely allied in political opinion have held office. They were the periods from 1715 to 1742, from 1782 to 1829, from 1846 to 1867, and from 1886 to 1906. In every instance, though the Administrations were sometimes Whig and sometimes Tory, they were fundamentally conservative. Walpole came into office by the fear of a Jacobite revolution, and he continued in office partly by corruption and partly by the dread of the only alternative to his policy which was that of the far-reaching and adventurous Bolingbroke, the first and most brilliant of Tory

Democrats. True, Walpole brought forward an excise, but the moment opposition turned serious he dropped it. He refused to remove the grievances of his political friends, the Dissenters, because he would not rekindle the fires of a dangerous controversy.

The younger Pitt displayed a similar spirit when he opposed the political revolution threatened by Fox's India Bill. He employed his victory to carry legislation on essentially conservative lines. In fact, the lines were too conservative. He committed in 1785 the mistake of 1692 in refusing to permit reform and a redistribution of seats which would have delivered the Tories and the country from the selfish and unrepresentative rule of borough-mongers who were dominant all through the Hanoverian period. If Pitt's measures excited determined opposition, he quietly dropped them. True, he departed from this attitude when he passed the Union with Ireland. This is the only instance of his departure, and the necessity in which he conceived his country to be placed forced his hand. Nor is it insignificant that the Union led indirectly to his resignation and the interlude of the Addington Administration. It is remarkable to note that the Tories developed free trade principles. In 1787 Pitt promulgated a system of reciprocity while Fox and the Whigs straitly stood for the old system of restriction. The fear of the French Revolution combined with the folly and the lack of patriotism shown by Fox and his friends left Pitt again supreme. He was in truth the only possible ruler of the country. The few months during which the Ministry of All the Talents held sway attests the accuracy of this proposition. Canning no doubt was the greatest Foreign Secretary we ever possessed, but after 1820 he led his party gradually to depart from the path of Conservatism. For these departures there is much to be said, yet they deeply offended conservative sentiment. Here is an instance. The Roman Catholic Emancipation measure of 1829 ought to have been passed. When those who constantly resisted it at length passed it, this shook for many a day the confidence of conservatives in the Conservatism of their leaders. The proof of this is quite apparent in 1832. Then the men who were conservative forces in the country steadily refused to exert themselves in moderating and moulding the changes Lord Grey carried out. The result was the practical annihilation of the Tories, and this annihilation was due to conservative apathy.

From 1841 to 1846 Peel governed the country with remarkable success on true conservative lines. Public weal weighed with him so much that he forced himself to break with the past, but he forgot that he who breaks with the past loses control of the future. In 1846 he became honestly convinced that the repeal of the Corn Law was essential to the prosperity of the whole country. His conviction led him to carry this repeal by the votes of the Whig opposition against the majority of his own party. It was the story of 1829 over again, with results not less calamitous to his party than on that occasion. The Conservative party was shattered, and the Whigs came into power, which they retained to 1874. Peel in truth never grasped the significance of a great historic party as an organ of government neither lightly created not lightly destroyed. In 1829 he sacrificed consistency and character to the public duty of averting a revolution, and in 1846 he sacrificed them again to the needs of Ireland.

The Whig domination of twenty-eight years may be divided into the two periods from 1846 to 1865 and from 1865 to 1874. During the first period the dominating personalities among the Whigs were Lord John Russell and Lord Palmerston. The former proved an opportunist in politics, and never enjoyed a large following in England. Had he been in sole command, he would probably have allowed the Radical wing of the party led by Bright and Cobden to dictate the party policy; and the Conservative reaction of 1874 might have been antedated by twenty years with *inter alia* the gravest influence on Disraeli's destiny. But until 1865 the chief direction fell to Palmerston, who belonged to a very different school of thought. Nominally a Whig, he was really a typical Conservative. His main anxiety was to safeguard the security and therefore the credit and confidence of the country; and he believed that his object could best be attained by making

Great Britain respected abroad and peaceful at home. Vigorous and energetic in his foreign policy to a fault, in domestic matters he did his best to avoid all acute controversy. For the most part he was successful, though from time to time the Radical elements in the Government insisted on some anti-conservative measures, chiefly of a financial nature.

Excursions into Radicalism provided opportunities for the Conservative Opposition which they failed to utilise for two reasons. One was that the events of 1846 continued to hamper them. Peel carried off with him almost the whole of the intellect of his party; and of these that were left very few believed in Protection. Disraeli himself never did. His announcement in 1852 that Protection was not only dead but damned, represented not less his own judgment than his reading of the signs of the times. He could not propose import duties as a means of revenue, for 1846 had settled them quite effectively. If he suggested an increase of indirect taxation, he was no match for the financial genius of Gladstone. The second reason is that neither Derby nor Disraeli offered any reasoned convictions on domestic policy. It seemingly did not strike them that to win the confidence of the country Conservative leaders must attest their genuine belief in Conservatism. Occasionally they defeated the Government in the House only to encounter the distrust of the Radical electors in the polling booths. The presence of Palmerston with the opposite party prevented a sufficient transfer of conservative votes from the Whigs to the Tories to give the latter a majority.

The death of Palmerston in 1865 gave the command of the Whigs to Gladstone, and for the first time the Whigs were led by a Radical. Our history presents two very different types of statesmanship, one of which is more likely to fit in to the Cabinet system, which fundamentally rests on the existence of two parties, than the other. One, of which Gladstone and Peel are the most conspicuous illustrations, is that of men who are, as the latter said of himself, "greatly absorbed in working the institutions of their country." The other, which is not less conspicuously illustrated by Chatham and Canning, is that of men who are absorbed by high aims but are much less patient of traditions and conventions which interfere with their pursuit. It is one of the ironies of history, however, that while Chatham never bowed the knee to party, and Canning yielded it an intermittent and not very willing allegiance, yet Gladstone and Peel both shattered their parties.

Gladstone revived the controversy of 1832, and introduced an advanced Reform Bill. No doubt the Reform Bill of 1855 was Russell's decision, though Gladstone bore the larger burden. The Cave of Adullam led by Lowe defeated it. Disraeli and Derby took office and, misled by the fallacy which has so often been fatal to the Tory party, attempted to "dish the Whigs" by stealing their policy. They forsook conservative principles in the hope of saving Conservatism, and inevitably they failed. By an overwhelming majority at the polls the electors declared that they would have none of it.

Disraeli was defeated, and he learnt his lesson. Never again would he play with Radicalism. During six years one of the ablest Governments that ever held office in this country, under Gladstone's inspiring leadership, carried out a programme of comprehensive reform. The Irish Church, Irish land, Education, Ballot, Licensing, Trades Unions, and many other subjects, came under review. The friends of progress in the press and on the platform applauded the passing of measure after measure, yet their passing alienated section after section of the electorate. In 1874 the dissolution came, and the Tories were triumphantly returned. For the first time since 1846 they were in power as well as in office; and they were there because the newly-enfranchised electors, like every other electorate that has existed, wearied very rapidly of legislative change and turned to any party that would afford them security and repose. The very adventurous foreign policy of Disraeli obscures the issues in 1880, as the very unadventurous foreign policy of Gladstone obscures them in 1885. The disasters in Egypt coupled with the surrender after Majuba are the cause of the Liberal failure at the polls as much as any dislike of Radical legislation.

With the election of 1886 dates a period of Tory ascendancy

due to the conservative sentiment of the voter. The resistance to Home Rule placed the Unionists in power. The success of the Liberals from 1892 to 1895 was as much attributable to conservative discontent with such measures as the Irish Land Act of 1887, the Local Government Bill of 1888, and the Free Education Act as to any content with Radical remedies. The attack on the Welsh Church and the renewal of the Home Rule outcry overthrew the Radicals in 1895 and kept them out of office for ten years. Nor is this interpretation of the history amiss in the electoral landslide of 1906. For the resentment aroused by Chinese labour in South Africa, the Education Act of 1902, and the fair trade policy were all at bottom conservative. The fear of change, the desire to leave well, or even moderately ill, alone weighed with the voters, as it weighed with Disraeli.

In 1836, Disraeli analysed *The Spirit of Whiggism*, contending that revolutions were generally effected by a faction and a small one at that. The reference to 1688 and 1832 is plainly indicated. The nation is reminded that a revolutionary party is not necessarily a liberal one, if liberal is spelt with a capital letter or without one, and that a republic is not indispensably a democracy. Let the nation ask the question, What preserves its rights and liberties? The answer is to be found in the institutions of the past.

In his speech in the House in 1839 he evinced a decided sympathy with the Chartists, if not with Chartism. The series of bad harvests which began in 1837 gave rise to it. The Poor Law of 1834, in Disraeli's eyes, treated the pauper as a criminal, whereas he was then often simply an unfortunate wretch. Besides, it abolished the old parochial constitution, and by its centralising tendency violated the traditional principles of local government. "Great duties could alone confer great station," and some of these duties had been taken from those in great station. It is noteworthy that the Chartists neither attacked the aristocracy nor the Corn Laws. Benthamism implicitly attacked both, and when Benthamism was taken over by Manchester, we have the Manchester School and all that it meant under the skilful leadership of Cobden and Bright, a matchless combination. Did the manufacturer who slept in the bosom of Peel prevent his seeing that the agricultural labourers might rally to his side? Not a little of Cobden's power arose from the fact that Peel was at bottom on the side of the Manchester School, and this deprived Peel of his influence over his own party. Had he possessed a tithe of the political insight or the popular sympathy of Disraeli, it is possible that the Manchester School might have perished at its birth. "There," Wellington crushingly remarked of Peel, "is a gentleman who never sees the end of a campaign."

The Tories were not absolutely committed to high import duties. Had not Pitt in 1787 set forth a system of reciprocity? The nationalism of the Tories is as apparent as the internationalism of the Whigs. Disraeli in 1843 read List's book, and his reading of the author of the Bible of modern protection confirmed him in his nationalism. Considerations of mere £. s. d. weighed as little with him as they did with Coleridge. The stability of the country was what really mattered, and this stability depended far more on the landed interest than on the commercial. The mechanisation of England was as abhorrent to him as to the Lake poet. He loathed "a sort of spinning-jenny, machine kind of nation." Like Goldsmith, he stoutly continued to believe that a bold peasantry formed their country's pride. At any rate, the tall chimneys and the black smoke of the factories of the North appealed to him with nothing like the force of his own rural Buckinghamshire. Free trade had won, but its victory was due not so much to the statesmanship of Peel as to the development of steam and railways in the forties, supported by the gold discoveries of California and Australia. This unparalleled prosperity strengthened the free trade forces and no less decidedly weakened the Chartist cause. Protection was dead and damned beyond any hope of a resurrection then. Circumstances proved Peel right in his change of front, but did he—could he?—divine the rise of these circumstances? Was it not a leap in the dark which happened to be justified?

The romanticism of Disraeli is very apparent. He was the contemporary of the great romantics, of Victor Hugo and Dumas, of Georges Sand and Balzac, and of Alfred de

Musset. His writings, notably his novels, are great English examples of the work of the Romantic movement. It led him to dislike the preponderance of the middle class which Peel had enthroned in power. In its place he sought to instal peers with privileges exercised on behalf of the people. The Young England movement with such members as Lord John Manners, whose notorious couplet exposed it to ridicule, and George Smythe, whose *Historic Fancies* still deserves reading, stood behind Disraeli. Faith in the genius of Toryism and scepticism in Whiggery and the middle-class Liberalism with which it was blending supplied the motive power of this short-lived movement. Faber was a friend of Manners and Smythe, and he introduced the influence of the Oxford Movement. Little as he realised it, Newman was fighting the battle against Liberalism every whit as much as Carlyle or Disraeli. On the surface perhaps no three men could be more unlike, yet at bottom they were contending for the defeat of the foe common to all of them. The romantic temperament stirred them to entertain the same deep reverence for the past which creates conservatism and destroys liberalism. The Oxford Movement swept men along till they came face to face with the Church of the Fathers. Disraeli swept them along till they came face to face with Bolingbroke. The Young England movement swept them along till they came face to face with the martyr who died for the Church of England, Charles I. True, the Erastianism of the Whigs could be effectively contrasted with the Jacobitism of the Tories, yet this Jacobitism could be transmuted to give the Church that high position it always occupied in the thought of Disraeli. He held that there are few great things left, "and the Church is one," just as he held in his *Runnymede Letters* she forms "a main obstacle to oligarchical power."

Of the spiritual mission of the Church he entertains the loftiest conception, a conception tinged with a political outlook. In *Tancred* we learn that "the equality of man can only be accomplished by the sovereignty of God." The Church of England stands rooted in the parish, a source of life and leading to its inhabitants, a security for local government, the educator of the people, the defender of their liberties which her spiritual authority assures, and the hallower of civil power by the religious sanction. The Church stands for a great conservative force with a splendid historical tradition: she also stands to him as a continuer of the conception of his own race, a living witness on behalf of the unseen. He was emphatically on the side of the angels. He could not bear the ritualists, in spite of the developments of the Oxford Movement, any more than he could bear the Broad Church. Did he not remind A. P. Stanley, "Pray remember, Mr. Dean, no dogma, no dean"? Nor did he fail to remind the English people that "the notes on the gamut of their feeling are few, but deep. Industry, Liberty, Religion, form the solemn scale. Industry, Liberty, Religion,—that *is* the history of England." In 1869 he proclaimed that "it is because there is an Established Church that we have achieved religious liberty and enjoy religious toleration; and without the union of the Church with the State, I do not see what security there would be either for religious liberty or toleration." He plainly testified, "I worship in a Church where I believe God dwells, and dwells for my guidance and my good."

The ideals of the Young England movement found a statement in *Coningsby* which appeared in 1844. Its subtitle was "the new Generation." There was the new generation indeed, the creation of the Industrial Revolution. The members of the aristocracy had, despite the self-indulgent, done their duty. God, however, fulfils Himself in many ways lest one good—not bad—custom should corrupt the world. The aristocracy must adapt itself to the needs of the altered generation. The purpose of the novel was "to vindicate the just claims of the Tory party to be the popular confederation of the country," and to demonstrate that "Toryism was not a phrase but a fact." Coningsby expounds the pure doctrine of Young Englandism when he sets forth "the idea of a free monarchy, established on fundamental laws, itself the apex of a vast pile of municipal and local government, ruling an educated people, represented by a free and intellectual press." He is filled with contempt for the attitude Peel took in 1829 and was destined to take up in 1846. "A sound Conservative government ... I understand: Tory men and Whig measures," a policy that has invariably brought destruction to the conservatives. "What is the cause of our glorious institutions?" inquired Coningsby. "A Crown robbed of its prerogatives"—in 1832—"a Church controlled by a commission; and an Aristocracy that does not lead." The novelist had his remedy. All national interests of importance should find adequate representation in the house, and no class, certainly not the middle class, should be placed in a predominant position.

The condition of England is duly set forth in 1844 in *Coningsby*, and it is no less duly set forth in 1845 in *Sybil*, the deepest novel he ever wrote. He portrays the plight of the poor with a realism akin to that of *Alton Locke* or *Les Misérables*. *Coningsby* discusses the two parties, *Sybil* the two nations, the rich and the poor. Their author had visited the north in the autumns of 1843 and 1844, and he had been horrified by the sights he had witnessed. The reports of the Children's Employment Commission, the debates on the Factory Bill in 1844, and the grievances of the Chartists aroused his active attention. The novel of purpose, nevertheless, is not his invention. Richardson and Godwin begin it, though literature for literature's sake appealed more to Fielding, Jane Austen, and Scott. Lytton continues the novel of purpose, and of course it is conspicuous in Disraeli. Dickens assails the Poor Law in *Oliver Twist*, the school system in *Nicholas Nickleby*, and political economy in *Hard Times*. Charles Reade exposes prison discipline in *It is Never too Late to Mend*, lunatic asylums in *Hard Cash*, and trade unions in *Put Yourself in his Place*. Christian Socialism appears in Kingsley's *Yeast* and *Alton Locke*. In *Hypatia* he illustrates the Protestant point of view just as Newman illustrates the Roman Catholic one in *Callista* and *Loss and Gain*. Mrs. Gaskell's *Mary Barton* sketches Manchester in the age of machinery, limning the unforgettable portrait of Carson the hard-hearted employer. Charlotte Brontë's *Shirley* details Yorkshire life with an imagination that fires one's blood. The novel of purpose is not at all confined to England, for French literature also attests its presence.

Victor Hugo, as a novelist, hurled vague thunderbolts at social injustice: Eugène Sue did the same, though in a more blunt and obvious manner; Flaubert used the terrible weapon of minutely accurate description to expose the lives of the *petite bourgeoisie*; Dumas the younger deliberately handled themes relating to the status of the illegitimate and the unclassed; Balzac tried to give a picture of the whole of life as it was; and Zola, when he died, was engaged upon a canvas of the whole of life as he conceived it ought to be.

Sybil presents us with satire and sympathy in a remarkable succession of scenes: the satire is for the rich, the sympathy for the poor. Nor is the satire undiscriminating. If there are mill-owners like Shuffle and Screw, there is also Trafford. If there is the tyrant Lord Marney, there is his brother Charles Egremont. The aristocracy, the manufacturers, and the Church are obviously all arousing themselves to cope with the unprecedented situation. The philosophy of history in *Sybil* is the same as that in *Coningsby*. We glean that in 1845, as in 1844, there has been a Venetian constitution since 1688, the work of the Whig oligarchs who governed England from 1715 to 1832. William III was not a pliant instrument in their hands, but George I and George II were: these two monarchs were in fact Doges. George III tried to shake off the oligarchy, but could not rid himself sufficiently of the Venetian constitution to assume the rôle of a "Patriot King." Bolingbroke, Shelburne, and the younger Pitt struggled against Venetian politics, Dutch finance, and hostility to France, the triple result of the 1688 Revolution

In the Disraelian philosophy of history Burke and Pitt find their due place. The former effected "for the Whigs what Bolingbroke in a preceding age had done for the Tories: he restored the moral existence of the party." Once more Disraeli reinforces with Burke the truth that property possesses duties as well as rights, and that in fact it has rights simply because it has duties. The labours of Lord Shaftesbury witness how strongly men like him realised their responsibility. Religion combined with humanitarianism was his guiding motive, and we must not

forget the fact that he was as stout a Tory as Southey and
Coleridge, Oastler and Sadler, the men who guided the
movement for the passing of the Factory Acts. No single
man did more to ameliorate the condition of the working
classes than Lord Shaftesbury. Nor is it without significance
that Lord Melbourne introduced him to Queen Victoria as
"the greatest Jacobin in Your Majesty's dominions." It
was not at all easy to be a reformer, and Disraeli's novels
smoothed the path for the Tory reformer. His novels
sound vague to the reader who wants a cut-and-dried
plan: such a plan is nowhere to be found in them. The
impulse to pursue such a plan is everywhere to be found
in them. He drove home to the minds of the budding
Shaftesburys that privileges mean payment in public service
to one's country, and he drove it home with incomparable
force. In the general preface to his novels, written in 1870,
he sums up the creed of Toryism. "The feudal system may
have worn out, but its main principle—that the tenure of
property should be the fulfilment of duty—is the essence
of good government." For a similar message let the reader
turn to the novels of Maurice Barrès. The sense of the
immutability of the race, in which the individual is but a
moment, scarcely a separate existence, the love of tradition
and hierarchy, the aristocratic individualism, the tendency
to decentralise and feudalise—all of them have passed
into the message of this great Nationalist leader.

The glory of race is never long absent in the novels, and
it is conspicuously present in *Tancred* which insists in 1847
on the outstanding qualities of the Jew. It is the essential
and unalienable prerogative of the Jewish race to be at once
the moral ruler and the political master of humanity.
These are the real sentiments of the novelist, though it is
strange that when he was Prime Minister he did not elevate
a single member of his own race to Cabinet rank. In the
trilogy *Coningsby* and *Sybil* as clearly possess an ethico-
political purpose as *Tancred* does a racial one.

There are many matters in *Tancred* as well as race. There
is a criticism of the Church of England, and there is an
assault on materialism. The creed of the Church must
possess its old authority before the diseases of society can

be healed. Disraeli was saying in his fashion what Newman had been saying in his. As Newman anticipated the theory of evolution in his essay upon development, so Disraeli anticipated it. In *Tancred* he hints that "what is most interesting, is the way in which man has been developed. You know, it is all development. The principle is perpetually going on. First there was nothing, then there was something; then, I forget the next, I think there were shells, then fishes; then we came: let me see, did we come next? Never mind that; we came at last. And the next change there will be something very superior to us, something with wings. Ah! that's it: we were fishes, and I believe we shall be crows."

Evolution is an issue in the background of *Tancred*, yet religion is never long absent from the foreground. There are clues to his attitude to it. The famous saying that "all great men are of the same religion" is one of those clues. The constant reference to dissent as a phenomenon purely political is another. The third and surest is to be found in the general preface prefixed to the Hughenden edition of *Lothair*, where Disraeli discusses the secession of Newman from the Church of England. "That extraordinary event has been 'apologised for,' but has never been explained. It was a mistake and a misfortune. The tradition of the Anglican Church was powerful. Resting on the Church of Jerusalem, modified by the divine school of Galilee, it would have found that rock of truth which Providence, by the instrumentality of the Semitic race, had promised to Saint Peter. Instead of that, the seceders sought refuge in mediaeval superstitions, which are generally only the embodiments of pagan ceremonies and creeds." The implications here, both positive and negative, can be disengaged without great difficulty. The first implication is an absolute unconcern as to the truth of any specific dogma of any Christian creed or the authority of any Christian Church. The second is a profound sense of the importance of religion—and of organised religions—to human society. A world without God would be a terrible thing, and theocratic institutions are needed to avert that evil. That is the *raison d'être* of a national Church; and to quit the

National Church for another upon mere doctrinal grounds is to show a false sense of proportion, and even to misapprehend the true purpose of religion. For religion, in its essence, is a "feeling about the infinite" which impels men to moral conduct and inspires them with high ideals, originating in the East, and finding its loftiest expression in Hebraic literature. All religion, in fact, is a kind of Judaism which has ceased to be exclusive; and provided that, by means of institutions, we make it an organic part of national life, it does not much matter whether we adopt it in the form of Puseyism or in some other shape. The Church of Rome is nothing since the Church of Jerusalem overshadows it; and what we have to seek is not the truest religion, but the most spiritual. The most spiritual is the truest.

This is the essence of the religious ideas conveyed in *Tancred* and in Young Englandism generally in so far as Disraeli was its interpreter; though the greater number of his followers did not climb to this lofty altitude. For them, as one gathers from Lord John Manners's poems, Puseyism was the essential, and the rest was more or less fantastic embroidery. Nevertheless Disraeli, though deeply religious in his vague fashion, entertained no illusions about the religions that particularised on the dogmatic side. He looked through them, and saw beyond them to the first principles of which they seemed to him to be secondary manifestations. One can even picture him saying with Gibbon that all religions were equally true and equally false and equally useful. He would not have said it with a solemn sneer. He would have said it with the profoundest reverence, and would have limited his generalisations to religions of Judaic origin.

There are a hundred-and-one issues in *Tancred*, but the main one is the all-importance of race, a point which is every whit as much emphasised in the famous chapter on the Jews in his biography of *Lord George Bentinck*, published in 1851. "All is race—there is no other truth," so Sidonia states. Nor did he ever forsake this doctrine, for it appears in *Endymion*, the novel that appeared in 1880. The old statesman and the young author are at least consistent in this. Civilisation, if it means anything, means the superiority of race. Material civilisation fills him with contempt as he contemplates the spiritual destinies of man. Language and religion do not make a race: only one thing makes it, and that is blood. Such is the teaching of *Endymion*. In *Lord George Bentinck* he dwells on the intimate tie between religion and race. God has only spoken to one race, the Jewish; His full revelation was made by a Divine Jew, Jesus; the Apostles, the preachers of the true religion to the world, were all Jews. Beyond question "The Jews represent the Semitic principle; all that is spiritual in our nature. They are the trustees of tradition, find the conservators of the religious element. They are the living and the most striking evidence of the falsity of that pernicious doctrine of modern times, the natural equality of man. The political equality of a particular race is a matter of municipal arrangement, and depends entirely on political considerations and circumstances; but the natural equality of man now in vogue, and taking the form of cosmopolitan fraternity, is a principle which, were it possible to act on it, would deteriorate the great races and destroy all the genius of the world." Obviously he approaches political questions less as a politician than as an artist to whom it is given to see events through a temperament, and by so doing to puzzle the unimaginative of both parties in the State.

There was an air of newness in the doctrine of race in the forties and fifties which accounts in part for the eager reception of *Tancred*, but one's pleasure in perusing it to-day is dimmed by the price the world paid since 1914 for another doctrine of race. Gobineau crossed the t's and dotted the i's of the message Disraeli had proclaimed half a century before. Chamberlain's *Foundations of the Nineteenth Century* flung in the face of Germany the creed which Gobineau had taken up. Like Disraeli, Chamberlain discusses the Aryan, the Assyrian, the Egyptian, the Greek, the Roman, and the Jew, though, unlike Disraeli, he violently attacks the last. Like Disraeli, he holds that no influence has exercised the same power on civilisation as Christianity. The Jew is the central figure in Disraeli's canvas, the

Germane, the Teuton, in Chamberlain's. The Teuton is "one of the greatest, if not the greatest, power in the history of mankind." Under his leadership European Kultur was to flourish under the *pax Germanica* and move from strength to strength in German literature, German art, and German science, which embody all that is best in the literature, art and science of all other countries. It is a perilous doctrine at all times, in *Tancred* as in *The Foundations of the Nineteenth Century*. For it breeds what the Greeks dreaded, and that is *hubris*, the insatiable desire for power which drives a race or a nation headlong to destruction. For despite Disraeli and Chamberlain there is no such thing as Jewish or German science. Truth in any field of knowledge recognises no national limitations. Catholicity is of the essence of truth. Scholars, whether Jewish or German, win knowledge not for themselves or for their race but for the whole world.

Disraeli was scornful in 1848 of "this modern, new-fangled, sentimental principle of nationality." To him nationality is a mere matter of locality: race depends on blood. A Jew is a Jew first and then an Englishman. His doctrine of race led him to regard German nationality as "dreamy and dangerous nonsense," yet he never perceived the place of nationality in effecting the unity of Germany and Italy. Neither of these events, when they occurred, converted him to sympathy with the conception of nationality. He was in fact obsessed by the notion that his idea explains history through the periodical preponderance of certain races in a nation, and provides the essential clue to men and their movements.

In spite of a single petulant outburst in 1852 he was always an imperialist, anxious to consolidate the empire by evoking the sympathies of the colonies for the Mother Country. His view was that "you can only act upon the opinion of Eastern nations through their imagination," and in spite of opposition he added in 1876 to the Queen's titles that of Empress of India. Let the Delhi Durbar of 1911 and the World War attest the prescience of the novelist. *Imperium et Libertas* was the ideal he succeeded in popularising, and it is one of his outstanding feats.

"A real Throne" was a matter much in his mind, and all the more so because his personal relationship with Queen Victoria was of the most intimate nature. He successfully induced her to forsake her retreat in order to discharge her ceremonial duties, for he divined that the people fervently desired to see their sovereign. Her length of days combined with her high position elevated her to the status of an institution. Till Disraeli persuaded her to be seen of her subjects, she had been a private institution, not a public one. The unattractive characters of George IV and William IV had been replaced by the attractive one of the young Queen. Her personal prestige and her popularity steadily grew with her people at large. If her son was to become *l'oncle de l'Europe*, she was undoubtedly the general grandmother of the Emperors and Kings. As a constitutional sovereign her position could have been second to none. But she really aimed at the old Tory position, and in so aiming partly missed her mark. Her letters reveal how repeatedly she opposed her ministers. She opposed Gladstone on Egypt and Home Rule, and she even opposed Disraeli because he would not face Russia with what she judged to be adequate firmness. Yet in spite of this opposition, she never pushed matters to extremes, allowing the Cabinet in the last resort to decide the large issues of policy. She toiled as painfully with her communications to her Cabinets as Raleigh ever toiled, and yet the toil seems for nothing. She so busied herself with her boxes of letters that till Disraeli's day she seldom found time for opening or proroguing Parliament. Elizabeth made her royal "progresses" and they helped to win her popularity. Victoria refused to make her royal "progresses" and this refusal delayed her widespread popularity to the Jubilees of 1887 and 1897. The share taken by imagination and pageantry she never saw as our novelist saw. Failure and success blend in her life, failure in securing control of the Cabinet, success in securing control—the loyalty—of her people. Her throne proved a real bond, not merely between the inhabitants of the British Islands but throughout the length and breadth of the British Empire. To her coloured subjects she was no distant sovereign: she was the "Great White Mother." To all, at home and abroad, she symbolised the link that joined them together. In 1830 or 1837 the death of George IV or of William IV meant but little to our island, and less outside it. In 1901 the death of the Queen meant much to our island and perhaps even more outside it. She represented the whole Empire, and she represented it all the more worthily for the myth and mystery that during her long reign of over sixty years gradually clustered around her personality.

The imperialism of the sixties did not attain the dimensions of that of the eighties and nineties. There is a price to be paid for it, and in the sixties the imperial and foreign policy of Disraeli was deemed too adventurous. On the opposition benches he secured some leisure, and in 1870 appeared *Lothair*, a novel with a thesis every whit as much as the trilogy of *Coningsby*, *Sybil* and *Tancred*. The new novel discusses such old topics as the Church of Rome and her claims and methods, the conflict between science and theology, and the secret societies of the day with their international energies. On the last our author at all times laid intense stress, and we, knowing how powerfully they contributed to the downfall of the Tsarist *régime* at one extreme of Europe and of English rule in Ireland at the other extreme, may well conclude that Disraeli spoke of what he knew with an intimacy denied to most. In his own day he realised the machinations of these societies in Italy, Ireland, recognising the dangers from Irish-American Fenianism, and France, where the workings of the International Society in the Paris Commune demonstrated the realities of what many regarded as the fictions of the novelist's brain. "It is the Church against the secret societies. They are the only two strong things in Europe, and will survive kings, emperors, or parliaments." Manning and Samuel Wilberforce figured in the novel, and Goldwin Smith certainly thought that he did. For the soul of Lothair the contending Churches fight. Disgusted with the narrow Protestantism, seduced by broad Roman Catholicism, Lothair at length experiences an intelligent Christianity thanks to the traditionary influences and divine associations of the Holy Land. If we note the dignity and the gravity of the Church of Rome, we also note her tricks and artifices. The old gospel of race re-appears.

Lothair himself is full of philanthropy, much more like Egremont than Lord Marney, ready to spend thousands on cottages for the labourers on his estates. The dukes and duchesses whom he so plentifully meets care for the welfare of others as well as for their own. We feel the presence of the nation of the rich, and we also feel the presence of the nation of the poor. "It seems to me," according to Lothair, "that pauperism is not an affair so much of wages as of dwellings. If the working classes were properly lodged, at their present rate of wages, they would be richer. They would be healthier and happier at the same cost." Here we meet the originator of the Artisans' Dwellings Acts. The brain of the writer is in *Lothair*; so too is the brain of the statesman, for the moment out of office though not out of power. We pay to *Lothair* an attention not unlike what we pay to the sayings of Napoleon at St. Helena, and our interest is alike. For the view of the novel and the sayings of Napoleon were to take parts, very unequal, we grant, in the making of history. The old topics were in the new novel but not in the old fashion. In his trilogy he delivered his message, and then he was silent for a quarter of a century. The period of silence was one of political activity, and when it was broken all the conditions had been changed. The world had progressed, though by no means on Young England lines, and the novelist was twenty-five years older. It is no longer the dreamer who writes, impelled to tell the world what he has dreamt and to persuade it to dream with him. It is the man of action and experience who finds himself at last with leisure to re-shape his message. The Manchester School could be successfully fought, if not with feudalism, at least with Factory Acts in which something of the paternal spirit of feudalism might be embodied.

In 1874 Disraeli returned to office as well as to power, able at last to realise some of the programme he had laid down in his writings. With Young England in the shades of opposition he had supported Shaftesbury and other

Tories in their heroic struggle for the Ten Hours' Bill in 1847. The Manchester School in the shape of Bright and Cobden stood out against it. Hear the indignant words of Shaftesbury, recorded in his private diary. "I had to break every political connection, to encounter a most formidable array of capitalists, millowners, doctrinaires, and men who, by natural impulse, hate all 'humanity-mongers.' They easily influence the ignorant, the timid, and the indifferent; and my strength lay at first . . . among the Radicals, the Irishmen, and a few sincere Whigs and Conservatives. Peel was hostile, though, in his cunning, he concealed the full extent of his hostility until he took the reins of office, and then he opposed me, not with decision only, but malevolence, threatening, he and Graham, to break up his administration, and 'retire into private life' unless the House of Commons rescinded the vote it had given in favour of my Ten Hours' Bill. The Tory country gentlemen reversed their votes; but in 1847, indignant with Peel on the ground of the corn law repeal, they returned to the cause of the factory children. . . .

"In very few instances did any mill-owner appear on the platform with me; in still fewer the ministers of any religious denomination. . . .

"O'Connell was a sneering and bitter opponent. Gladstone ever voted in resistance to my efforts; and Brougham played the doctrinaire in the House of Lords. Bright was ever my most malignant opponent. Cobden, though bitterly hostile, was better than Bright. He abstained from opposition on the Collieries Bill, and gave positive support on the Calico Print-works Bill.

"Gladstone is on a level with the rest; he gave no support to the Ten Hours' Bill; he voted with Sir R. Peel to rescind the famous division in favour of it. He was the only member who endeavoured to delay the Bill which delivered women and children from mines and pits; and never did he say a word on behalf of the factory children, until, *when defending slavery in the West Indies,* he taunted Buxton with indifference to the slavery in England.

"Lord Brougham was among my most heated opponents He spoke strongly against the Bill in 1847.

"Miss Martineau also gave her voice and strength in resistance to the measure."

There is no reason to charge the Manchester School with lack of humanity. Its members were thorough-going individualists who believed in *laissez-faire*, and *laissez-faire* suffered its first great defeat in factory legislation. Melbourne called Shaftesbury a Jacobin, and herein he was at least as far-sighted as Bright and his colleagues.

"*Sanitas sanitatum, omnia sanitas,*" in the broadest sense, was the motto of the new Prime Minister on assuming office in 1874. There had been a Vaccination Act in 1867. The Public Health Act of 1875 was supplemented by many subsequent measures. The Sale of Food and Drugs Act dated from 1875, and in 1879 and 1899 received extensions. The Artisans' Dwelling Acts of 1875 and 1879 were completed by the Working Classes Act of 1890, crowned by the Chamberlain Act of 1923. In 1867 a Conservative Act had regulated work-shops. In 1875 employers and employed stood equal before the law in labour contracts. Before that date a breach of contract by the employed was a crime, by the employer simply a civil offence. Now both were declared only liable in the civil courts. Conspiracy in trade disputes in 1875 was no longer constituted a crime except when it was done for the purpose of committing what would be a crime if done by a single person. In 1875 tenants obtained compensation for unexhausted improvements in land. For Disraeli thought that "the palace is not safe when the cottage is not happy." In 1876 a measure prevented any further enclosure save where it would be a public as well as a private benefit, and promoted free access to commons and their use as public playgrounds. In 1878 the factory laws were improved and codified by a Consolidation Act which moved Shaftesbury to express his liveliest satisfaction. He said that he was lost in wonder at the amount of toil, of close investigation, and of perseverance involved in its preparation; two millions of people in this country would bless the day when Cross was appointed Home Secretary. The Miners' Act of 1878 was described by Thomas Burt, the miners' leader, as "the greatest measure of its kind yet passed by a British Government."

What Disraeli was carrying out in the seventies, Lord Balfour continued in the great consolidating and amending Factory and Workshops Act of 1901. In 1876 the Cabinet passed a measure widely extending the benefit of elementary education. In 1877 a statutory commission reformed the Universities of Oxford and Cambridge. Primary, secondary, and university education alike received attention, and in the process the Prime Minister did not forget the education of his party. He passed a bill in 1878 for the extension of the episcopate. Tait, the Liberal Archbishop of Canterbury, declared in the House of Lords, that it was the greatest ecclesiastical reform since the Reformation. Increased spirituality in the Church of England, better homes and happier minds for the people—these were some of the ideas of the novels, and at last Disraeli was able in some measure to carry them out. "Nothing," he announced, "is so expensive as a vicious population." In 1879 Alexander Macdonald, speaking as an artisan, declared: "The Conservative party have done more for the working classes in five years than the Liberals have in fifty." The years when the Liberals were in power, between 1846 and Gladstone's death in 1898, show scarcely a measure of social reform.

The electorate in 1880 saw social reform at home and increased reputation abroad. At the same time it also witnessed disasters in the Asian and African policy of the Conservative Cabinet, the series of bad harvests, and the prolonged depression in trade. In his Midlothian campaign Gladstone pressed home the truth that no matter how Disraeli had safeguarded British interests, yet morally his policy had been wanting. The outcome was that Disraeli suffered an overwhelming defeat at the polls. Many of his followers realised the sharp shock of chagrin he suffered. He retired to silence and betook himself to Hughenden as quietly as Cincinnatus to his Sabine farm, acting on the principle he once enunciated in the House of Commons, "I make it a point never to complain." Nor did he nurse in solitude his wound, severe as it was. He was writing his last novel, *Endymion*, which appeared in 1880. A similar tale is told of Fox. After playing at Almack's for twenty-two hours without intermission, he rose from the table a loser to the tune of £11,000. The fashionable gamblers of that negligent time were accustomed to find themselves occasionally on the side supposed to be agreeable to Cato; and to all of them in turn, as they staggered homewards in the dawn with empty pockets, might have been applied the line in the *Fasti* :

Inde domum redeunt, sub prima crepuscula maesti.

But the losses of Fox had been so enormous on this occasion that his friends feared lest he should be prompted to some desperate act. Accordingly, they betook themselves to his house, and, unseasonable as was the hour, brushed the servants aside, and insisted on forcing their way into his presence. They found him prone upon the hearth-rug, leaning upon his elbow, reading a chapter in Herodotus. Like the great historian, who was visited and consoled in the hour of defeat, not by the Queen of Gain, the Queen of Power, or the Queen of Pleasure, though these wayward sprites had by no means neglected him, but by One, "the last, the mightiest, and the best," the author of *Endymion* might listen to her alluring voice:—

>Yes, darling, let them go; so ran the strain,
> Yes; let them go, gain, fashion, pleasure, power;
>And all the busy elves to whose domain
> Belongs the nether sphere, the fleeting hour.
>
>Without one envious sigh, one anxious scheme,
> The nether sphere, the fleeting hour resign;
>Mine is the world of thought, the world of dream,
> Mine all the past, and all the future mine.
>
>Fortune that lays in sport the mighty low,
> Age that to penance turns the joys of youth,
>Shall leave untouched the gifts which I bestow,
> The sense of beauty and the thirst of truth.

The man is born under the happiest star who most effectually combines the energy of active life with the repose of contemplation. Disraeli lived a life of successful contention; he wielded the highest power in the State; he won all the honours that the favour of his sovereign could confer. Beyond these gifts of fortune he possessed the habit of thought and observation, which he bore with him alike in society and in retirement, the power of giving his opinions a literary coinage, which passes current in all the languages and all the civilised communities of the world. The reason the Hebrew and the Hellene were by far the most powerful races in history is, according to him, that they had a literature. What is true of the race is true of the statesman. Does any oratory, any diplomacy, any legislative ingenuity confer so lasting an influence on a ruler of men as that which he derives from a combination of literary excellence with political power? Here at least Disraeli stands on an eminence Gladstone cannot approach. From an angle like this we can ask questions from a consideration of past unliterary Prime Ministers. Who was Lord Wilmington? Who was Perceval? Who was Lord Goderich?

The leading idea of *Endymion* is the decisive share taken by woman in directing the career of man, notably of political man. In the novelist's own life, his sister Sarah's sympathy, Mrs. Austen's encouragement, his wife's devotion, the friendship of Lady Blessington and Lady Londonderry, Mrs. Brydges Willyams's benevolence, his intimacy with Lady Bradford and her sister Lady Chesterfield, and the extreme graciousness of Queen Victoria towards him had all tended to make him give as exalted a position to woman as J. S. Mill. "I owe everything to woman," so Disraeli declared, and declared with sincerity. Nevertheless, it was no more true of him than it was of Mill, the man he characteristically looked on as the political finishing governess. As a test of Disraeli's attitude to women, take his novels. They all lack emotion. No reader ever believes in the passion of Coningsby for Edith or of Egremont for Sybil. Statements are offered on these subjects; yet the actual passions are not conveyed to the reader because they are not realised by the writer. This is the price Disraeli pays for realising other sentiments too vividly. Overweening ambition to succeed in the world and the doctrine that the world is well lost for love are incompatibles. A man must choose between them, although it will be an unconscious choice determined by his temperament; and the choice will be reflected in his writings. So with Disraeli. It was through the eyes of ambition—a magnificent and grandiose ambition—that he regarded the world he was to interpret as a novelist. Endymion owed everything to woman, and it is significant that Disraeli's last hero was a man who, thanks to the crafts of three of the sex, became at the age of forty Prime Minister of England. Myra is the most inspiring genius of the three. She reads with a glance the high destinies of Prince Florestan, with whom her own life is at last so strangely united; and she alone supplies the resources and the energy which raises her brother Endymion in the world. In the mystical verses which conclude the second part of *Faust*, the German poet hears the voices of the angels singing that:

> Das Ewig-Weibliche
> Zieht uns hinan.

It means that the feminine principle in life drives us through the spheres. Such is the belief Disraeli avows. The feminine principle is the spring not only of society, but of politics, forecasting the feminist movement of our day.

If there is a new feminist philosophy, there is the old philosophy of history and of party re-appearing. "The cause for which Hampden died," for instance, "on the field, and Sidney on the scaffold" is identified with the Whig government of England, not with the life and liberty of the subject. Napoleon III and his deadly foe, Bismarck, also appear. The forecasts of the future include more than feminism. "My books," he confided in Lady Bradford, "are the history of my life. I don't mean a vulgar photographs of incidents, but the psychological development of my character. Self-inspiration may be egotistical, but it is generally true." They are remarkable enough in the realm of literature as they developed the political novel as it had never been developed before, and they are no less remarkable in the realm of politics for they often foreshadowed the dreams the statesman turned into realities. There are prophecies in his novels, but is there a shrewder one than in *Endymion*? There he foretells that in the fullness of time Labour will throw off the Whigs. Nor does he confine himself to a vague hint. The movement of revolt will originate in the industrial west of Scotland in the neighbourhood of Glasgow rather than in Glasgow itself. Such was the declaration of 1880.

Keir Hardie, the future founder of the Labour Party, came from the Airdrie district, an unknown man of twenty-four when *Endymion* appeared. In 1887 he delivered his soul on the attitude of the Liberals towards Labour, for he was smarting at the rejection of his candidature the preceding year by the North Ayrshire Liberals. There was a vacancy in 1888, and Keir Hardie asked the Liberal Association to accept him as a lifelong member of the party. This Association was committed to Captain Sinclair, afterwards Lord Pentland. Keir Hardie took up the position: "Better split the party now, if there is to be a split, than at the General Election, and if the Labour Party only make their power felt now, terms will not be wanting when the General Election comes." As a split was serious, Henry Drummond, the once well-known author of *Natural Law in the Spiritual World*, Lady Aberdeen, Captain Sinclair, and Mr. Cunningham Graham intervened. Captain Sinclair withdrew, and when the way seemed clear for Keir Hardie a young Welsh barrister, Phillips, the future Lord St. Davids, swept the negotiators off their feet with his persuasive powers. Keir Hardie was not nominated. Behind his back a deal was arranged by Mr. Schnadhorst, the Liberal party manager, Sir George Trevelyan, and Mr. Conybeare. Keir Hardie naturally refused to meet Mr. Schnadhorst, but he met Sir George Trevelyan, though even he failed to abate Keir Hardie's wrath at his treatment. He rejected the offer of a seat at the General Election and a salary out of the party funds as "offensive."

Mr. Phillips beat Keir Hardie badly at the General Election, though he beat him by the Irish, not by the mining vote. Keir Hardie polled less than 700 votes, merely 20 per cent. of the Liberal side. What was a small amount like this? Still, had the Liberal leaders been wise they would have noticed that the political sky was clouded by the hand of a justly angry man. The enfranchisement measure of 1885 was not tending to the weal of the workers, who "are being used for selfish purposes by those who are more intelligent than themselves." Labour was entitled to at least a share in Parliamentary representation. In 1889 he attended the Second International in Paris, and he attended it as a Socialist with war in his heart against Liberalism. In 1892 he entered the House of Commons for a London, not a Scots, constituency. The cap he wore and the two-horse charabanc in which he drove to St. Stephen's with a bugler on the box advertised the fact to all and sundry that there was actually a real live Labour member in existence. He had preached social salvation to his brother Scots. Why should he not preach it to the English? In 1893 the Independent Labour Party was born at Bradford. Keir Hardie was not only its parent, but he was its sole representative in Parliament, and he was the editor of its official organ *The Labour Leader*. As chairman of the party for the first seven years of its existence he settled its policy to no mean degree, and that policy was the preaching of the gospel of Socialism in general and relentless criticism of Liberalism in particular. Yes, the man of Airdrie fulfilled his destiny in the evolution of the party system on which our novelist had often pondered. In 1880 he had foreseen the advent of the Keir Hardie type. What did his shade think of it in the years from 1893 to 1900?

Disraeli's inspiring advent saved Toryism from the fate that now threatens Liberalism. In the main he rendered service to his country, as well as to his party, by looking at great questions from a point of view which was not that of party politics. Without him Toryism might easily have been stereotyped not only as the stupid, but also as the selfish, party. What he hated above all things was an oligarchy that was not also a natural aristocracy and was hostile to genius. He, looking before and after, saw that Toryism always had represented, and might always represent something more than the stubborn defence of obsolescent privileges. On the one side, it represented the continuity of our institutions, and, on the other, not the obstruction of the inevitable stream of democracy, but its proper guidance under its natural leaders for the greater glory of the country. He recognised the real necessity of employing all the popular elements in the Constitution in support of the monarchy. Hence Tory Democracy—which at first seemed like the vain conception of a poet or a novelist, but which was proved in the event to be the only sort of Toryism that was possible under modern conditions.

REFERENCES

BAILEY, J. *Some Political Ideas and Persons.* (London, 1921.)
BLEASE, W. L. *A Short History of English Liberalism.* (London, 1913.)
BRANDES, G. *Lord Beaconsfield.* (London, 1880.)
BUTLER, Sir G. G. *The Tory Tradition.* (London, 1914.)
CAZAMIAN, L. *Le roman social en Angleterre.* (Paris, 1904.)
CLARKE, Sir E. *Benjamin Disraeli: the romance of a great career.* (London, 1926.)
COURCELLE, M. *Disraeli.* (Paris, 1922.)
CUCHEVAL-CLARIGNY. *Lord Beaconsfield et son Temps.* (Paris, 1890.)
EWALD, A. E. *The Rt. Hon. Benjamin Disraeli, Earl of Beaconsfield, and his times.* (London, 1881.)
FRASER, Sir W. *Disraeli and his Day.* (London, 1891.)
FROUDE, J. A. *Lord Beaconsfield.* (London, 1905.)
GORST, H. E. *The Earl of Beaconsfield.* (London, 1900.)
HARRIS, W. *The Radical Party in Parliament.* (London, 1885.)
HILL, R. L. *Toryism and the People, 1832–1846.* (London, 1929.)
KEBBEL, T. E. *A History of Toryism, 1783–1881.* (London, 1886.)
KEBBEL, T. E. *Life of Lord Beaconsfield.* (London, 1888.)
KEBBEL, T. E. *Lord Beaconsfield and other Tory Memoirs.* (London, 1917.)
MACKNIGHT, T. *The Rt. Hon. Benjamin Disraeli, M.P.: a literary and political biography.* (London, 1854.)
MAUROIS, A. *Vie de Disraeli.* 16th ed. (Paris, 1927.)
MEYNELL, W. *Benjamin Disraeli. An unconventional biography.* (London, 1903.)
MEYNELL, W. *The man Disraeli* (a revised edition of the above). (London, 1907.)
MONYPENNY, W. F. and BUCKLE, G. E. *Life of Disraeli.* (London, 1910–20.)
MURRAY, D. L. *Disraeli.* (London, 1927.)
RAYMOND, E. T. *Disraeli: the alien patriot.* (London, 1925.)
RUGGIERO, G. de. *The History of European Liberalism.* (Oxford, 1927.)
SCHMITZ, O. A. H. *Die Kunst d. Politik* (On Disraeli). (Berlin, 1911.)
SICHEL, W. *Bolingbroke and his Times.* (London, 1901–02.)
SICHEL, W. *Disraeli: a study in personality and ideas.* (London, 1904.)
SOMERVELL, D. C. *Disraeli and Gladstone: a duo-biographical sketch.* (London, 1922.)
SPEARE, M. E. *The Political Novel in England and America.* (New York, 1924.)
STEPHEN, Sir L. *Hours in a Library.* Vol. II. (London, 1892.)
WHIBLEY, C. *Political Portraits.* Second Series. (London, 1923.)
WHIBLEY, C. *Lord John Manners and his Friends.* (London, 1925.
WOODS, M. *A History of the Tory Party.* (London, 1924.)

Chapter VII.

THE OXFORD MOVEMENT AND THE SCOTS DISRUPTION

As age, an epoch, slips away from us, and grows distinct, even as it shows itself detached, in its receding, we see in all its parts, however different, a certain resemblance, a family likeness which proclaims their relationship. The Augustan Age, the Age of Chivalry, the Elizabethan Age, le Siècle de Louis XIV, the Age of Byron, are recognisable entities, each standing separate in our imagination, and each arrayed or enveloped (as in a shining veil or Iris-like scarf) in its own ideal. Our own times are so close to us that we do not see them in their due perspective, in the true character of their attitude, in all the bloom of their peculiar perfection. The critics, the interpreters, if you will, in analysing and recomposing the past, are all too anxious to find some stable origin for the fluctuating movements of life; reason and logic lead them astray; pre-occupied with the problems of cause and effect, they forget just that Something New— that unforeseen and imprevisible quality—which is the creation and the character of an epoch. The most essential aspect of all sometimes escapes them; so that we are inclined to echo the profound and ironical sentence of M. Bergson: "L'intelligence est caracterisée par une incompréhension naturelle de la vie." For logic does not seize the finer shades, and its formulas are too simple to be true. Some of our critics are all too anxious to prove something; they are not content to perceive and receive; they have never fed their minds in a wise passiveness, nor feared lest

> our meddling intellect
> Mis-shape the beauteous forms of things.

The interpreters anxiously explore the origins of movements, and trace them to one particular source. This is perhaps especially true of the interpreters of Romanticism. What is a Romantic? A lover of nature? A worshipper of passion? A believer in impulse, spontaneity, free-will? A man who prefers the individual to the society? A planner of progress?

A dreamer of dreams? Obviously Rousseau is the parent of this movement. It was, however, a child with more than one father. Its origins are not to be sought exclusively in France. The emigrés returned to their mother country charged with new ideas, as bees heavy with pollen return to their hive. Chateaubriand in exile (as his memoirs assure us) composed his "Atala" and "René" as he strolled and mused through the shady walks and green open spaces of Hyde Park; Rousseau was Swiss; and so were Madame de Stael and Benjamin Constant. The author of *Werther* was German, and the author of *Ossian* Scots. The Romantic Movement, like every other great literary revival—like the period of Chaucer in England or like the Renaissance in Italy—was due to the germinating of ideas brought from without and fallen on a fertile soil. Like to like is all very well, but unlike with unlike are the true begetters of greatness.

The central principle of the change that literature has undergone since Pope and Voltaire were its high-priests is the revolution wrought in its attitude to the Middle Ages. It was in the third quarter of the eighteenth century that the cultivated mind which had been divorced from the Middle Ages ever since the Reformation first began to coquet with this subject again. The incipient stages of the new fashion afford a good deal of entertainment to the observer. It began with a rage for chivalry, plate armour, and lancet windows; then came old ballads, antique poetry, Percy, Gray, Warton, Ossian, Walpole, Chatterton, Shakespeare, Chaucer, Vortigern, Mrs. Radcliffe and Mallet's *Northern Antiquities*. The *Great Cham* conceived a contempt for the new propaganda which he was at no pains to dissemble. Yet the stone which Johnson rejected was very soon to become the head of the corner.

Many curiosities which had been termed crazes converged in Sir Walter Scott, and, coalescing in a mind of such creative vigour and fertility as his, made an impact upon the mind of Europe. Scott was not altogether the *homme moyen* age of whom Gautier dreamed, for he had a sense of humour and a sense of humanity at large too great to be circumscribed even by the centuries; but he had a generous love of the remote past and its records, and his knowledge was linked with a power of story-telling which enabled him to popularise romance as nobody else could have done. History became a subject read by every thinking man. True, history had been studied during the eighteenth century, but consider the attitude of the historians to their subject. Voltaire explored the past, but he never concealed his contempt for the "learned lumber" of the antiquary. Gibbon explored the past, but he never concealed his contempt for the record of the crimes, follies, and misfortunes of mankind it exposed. The romantic glow and the romantic simplicity were lacking in the pages of both, though they are to be found in the pages of Burke. The poems and novels of Scott supplied these qualities, and supplied them with a strong pure feeling running through them. The Middle Ages were not the scufflings of kites and crows that historians had represented them to be. Scott painted the kings and the peasants, the queens and the peasant-women of the Middle Ages, as if they were as much creatures of flesh and blood as those of the circle at Abbotsford. His Richard I and Saladin, his Louis XI and Charles the Bold, his Margaret of Anjou and René of Provence are all alive, influencing the present—this is the crucial point—as well as the past. Scott, in truth, taught the continuity of history as it had never been taught before, and he convinced the average man and woman that the past counted. His poems and his novels are great literature—at any rate, the Waverley novels are—and they were read on all sides. Disraeli's Young Englanders swept their followers past the eighteenth century to the age of Charles I and Laud, but they stopped short of the Reformation. Scott swept his readers past the sixteenth century to the Middle Ages, and the transition to the earliest centuries *Anno Domini* was perfectly easy. The imagination of the Churchman resorted to the ages when the Church was one, no division by a Reformation, no division into Eastern and Western Churches by views on the procession of the Holy Ghost. The prose and the poetry of Scott did their work and we can well understand that Keble and Newman offered prayers for the soul of the minstrel of Scotland. Rousseau is a father of Romanticism: Scott is another, and for readers in these islands of inestimably more importance than the Swiss.

The influence of the Lake School of Poets cannot be ignored. Wordsworth, Coleridge, and Southey are among the influences that transformed poetry, and in the transformation of poetry the past was involved. In our chapter on Coleridge we have drawn attention to this point which is occasionally missed. Wordsworth consecrated the commonplace, and in the second book of the Prelude he shows us how he became conscious of "affinities In objects where no brotherhood exists To passive minds." Was anyone ever less like Rousseau? Yet he could take up Rousseau's rhetorical gospel of the life according to nature and give it body and soul: he gave it spirituality as well as actuality. He sang of the present as Scott sang of the past. In May, 1802, a few months before his marriage, Wordsworth's sister Dorothy read to him Milton's sonnets. He "took fire" at once, and he wrote immediately the sonnet "I grieved for Buonaparte." That summer the Peace of Amiens made it possible for them to go to France, and on his return he was struck by the wealth and luxury of England contrasted with the "quiet and desolation" of the Calais which rejoiced so soberly over Napoleon's new rank as Consul for life; and he wrote the famous apology to his country, the lines which include the much-quoted "Plain living and high thinking" and "Pure religion breathing household laws," the sonnet to Milton, and another which will appear valuably characteristic of his thought:

> Great men have been among us; hands that penned
> And tongues that uttered wisdom-better none:
> The later Sidney, Marvel, Harrington,
> Young Vane, and others who called Milton friend,
> These moralists could act and comprehend:
> They knew how genuine glory was put on;
> Taught us rightfully a nation shone
> In splendour: what strength was, that would not bend
> But in magnanimous meekness. France, 'tis strange,
> Hath brought forth no such souls as we had then.
> Perpetual emptiness! unceasing change!
> No single volume paramount, no code,
> No master spirit, no determined road;
> But equally a want of books and men!

Wordsworth was no more a renegade than Coleridge. His passion, like Milton's was for that liberty in order which is the result of the justice of God and the laws which free man makes for himself. Napoleon, in his opinion, acted in defiance of both, and after 1793, still more after 1802, Wordsworth could be nothing but anti-Bonapartist. Napoleon, to the Lake Poet, was always the Tyrant; and that phrase "no master spirit" is the keynote of his view of Consul and Emperor. "It was a high satisfaction," so he writes in his pamphlet on the Convention of Cintra," to behold demonstrated . . . to what a narrow domain of knowledge the intellect of a Tyrant must be confined . . . To the eyes of the very peasant in the field, this sublime truth was laid open—not only that a Tyrant's domain of knowledge is narrow, but melancholy as narrow; inasmuch as—from all that is lovely, dignified, or exhilarating in the prospect of human nature—he is inexorably cut off; and therefore he is inwardly helpless and forlorn."

Twenty years later he seems to include Napoleon in the pity he evidently felt for Trajan, as he looked upon the Pillar in Rome. Nevertheless he followed his career with intense interest, and the suppressed excitement characteristic of him found vent in a series of sonnets that commemorate nearly every event in the story.

As we look back over the body of his patriotic poetry, it is easy to see the qualities which give it permanence, its value and its beauty. There is no insularity, no mere "Rule Britannia!" about his patriotism. The very rarity of this note of satisfaction is one of the explanations of his supremacy among our patriotic poets. The youth who had been ready to hate his England when she had appeared to him an enemy of liberty and justice, was ready to love her in so far as she lived up to his ideals, and was ready to admonish her severely and warn her gravely even while she followed the path he held to be right. He loved nothing English merely because it was English and he was English; he loved what was English because, being English, it held a part in the glory which England in the past and present had won for herself:

It cannot be that England's social frame,
The glorious work of time and Providence,

Before a flying season's rash pretence,
Should fall; that She, whose virtue put to shame,
When Europe prostrate lay, the Conqueror's aim,
Should perish, self-subverted. Black and dense
The cloud is; but brings *that* a day of doom
To Liberty? Her sun is up the while,
That orb whose beams round Saxon Alfred shone;
Then laugh, ye innocent Vales! ye streams, sweep on,
Nor let one billow of our heaven-blest Isle
Toss in the fanning wind a humbler plume.

With the deaths of Coleridge and Scott, Keats and Byron, there certainly came an ebb in the Romantic flood. Keats was, however, in many respects, a close precursor of the pre-Raphaelites, among whom mediaevalism was no longer so much a tendency as a militant creed. Toleration, always the stumbling-block of the neophyte, was to them, not a virtue, but a vice. Like the group of young men in France who fought the battle of "Hernani," who wore Merovingian beards and sought to replace the old cry of "*à bas* Shakespeare" with the new cry "*à bas* Racine," so the full-blooded Romantics in England drew up their Index Expurgatorius and endeavoured to efface the twin monsters of Renaissance and Reformation, but, above all, to blot from remembrance "the Slough of Despond which we call the eighteenth century." The tables were indeed turned since the days of *Ecrasez l'Infâme*. The Infâme was now the contracted vocabulary, the calculated wit, the transparent clearness, and the common-sense urbanity of the ages of Addison and Walpole.

The extravagances of the new cult were numerous, and Romanticism was seen to run riot in much of the propaganda of Rossetti and Morris, Ruskin and Swinburne. Rossetti, who placed Chatterton upon a pedestal in the immediate neighbourhood of Shakespeare, devoted his whole mind for weeks to the exact reproduction of a brick wall; but, with all his skill in depicting landscape panels for the oriels of his damosels and the harness of his love-crazed knights who kissed the long wet grass, he could not represent to us the open air of Heaven; and all his nature is, as it were, double-distilled. Pugin declined to believe that a man such as W. G. Ward could live in a room without mullions, and, when asked to dinner, stipulated for Gothic puddings for which he enclosed designs. One tendency of all this mediaevalism, which saw everything through stained-glass windows, was the disposition of men's minds to Catholicism. It was so with W. G. Ward and his friend, Newman. It was clearly an appreciation of this danger which led George Borrow into that ferocious antagonism to all Catholic and mediaeval ideas by which his work is disfigured. He was justified to the extent that a considerable number of converts were, in Ruskin's contemptuous phrase, "piped into a new creed by the squeak of an organ pipe."

It is noticeable that the greatest pioneers of English Romanticism, with Scott at their head, notwithstanding their fondness for antiquarianism and the feudal past and their picturesque Jacobitism, were all the time stout Erastians and Protestants, strong Tories and devoted subjects of George IV. With all his enthusiastic love for the past, Scott's practical instinct informed him that the common sense of the eighteenth century formed the best rule of modern life. The Romantic leaders of the second generation were far less content with conventional ideals. In spite, however, of all extravagances, the net gain from the Romantic Movement, and the widening both of the range of knowledge and of the scope of emotion which have resulted from it, can hardly be overrated. The advances made in our accurate knowledge of the Middle Ages, advances due in part to the stimulus of Romanticism, can be gauged by anyone who compares the historical methods of Thierry, Maitland, and Freeman, with those of Voltaire, Robertson, and Hume. Gibbon stands in solitary pre-eminence. Innumerable bye-ways in mediaeval thought and manners have been explored. We are in many ways far nearer to Chaucer and his time than the eighteenth century was. No other English poet has probably come so near to Chaucer as William Morris.

In the matter of taste, as in every other species of human activity, the operation of the pendulum is very clearly to be traced as soon as ever a vantage-ground of detachment can be attained. In literature, as in everything else, *tout casse, tout passe, tout lasse.* The age of Romanticism culminates and declines, and public interest veers from a history of Romanticism to an inquiry into the beginnings of such a Counter-Reformation as the Oxford Movement. It is not easy to discern any radical alteration in the conditions of life, or any term to the process by which during the eighteenth century active minds became increasingly immured in towns and suburbs, and from which in large measure sprang the love of mountains, of nature, of solitude, and of all that is wonderful and mysterious and distant in the Romantic Movement. Heine had groaned at the ubiquity in time and place which goes to form the essence of the literature of those cavaliers that hack and hew at one another in knightly tournaments, those gentle squires and virtuous dames of high degree, the glorification of the feudal system and the baronial hall, the knight-errantry of those far-off days which the Romanticists brought so near. The leaders of the Oxford Movement consciously and unconsciously had rejoiced at the existence of the monks and nuns in their quiet monasteries and convents, their devotions in their chapels, the ages of faith when the Church counted and when the State executed her orders.

A deeper seriousness had been breathed into the minds of men not only in England by the French Revolution and the Romantic Movement. In Germany there was the manifestation of such men as Görres on the Roman Catholic side and of Schleiermacher on the Protestant. In France it appeared in Madame de Staël and Chateaubriand, as well as in Bonald, Lamennais, and De Maistre. Religion for Bonald as for the early Lamennais formed the basis of the State. Lamennais proceeds by successive steps. "*Point de pape, point d'Eglise.*" Then "*point d'Eglise, point de christianisme.*" The conclusion is, "*point de christianisme, point de religion . . . et par conséquent point de société.*" For De Maistre the steps are, "*plus de pape, plus de souveraineté; plus de souveraineté, plus de unité; plus de unité, plus d'autorité; plus d'autorité, plus de foi.*" In England it revealed itself in the enterprise of the Abolitionists and in Wilberforce's *Practical Christianity* as well as in the Oxford Movement. In Scotland it was manifested in four writers, if of unequal fame, yet all in their several ways representing the enlarged relations of the human mind to literature and to religion—Sir Walter Scott, first and foremost, and following upon him the most eloquent statesman of that time, Thomas Chalmers, the most eloquent preacher then, Edward Irving, and the sombre genius of Thomas Carlyle.

These converging streams of spiritual life had already begun to produce a steady increase of all the more practical elements of religious activity in the early years of the nineteenth century. The first Oriel School, of which Thomas Arnold was the chief representative, the admirable combination of piety and literature in Reginald Heber, the acute and powerful mind of Whately, the devouring industry and the wide liberality of Milman belong to this stage of the English revival. The pastoral energy and the intellectual research stimulated by these and like examples illuminated the course of many a worker in country parish and crowded city. The clergy that appear in the novels of Disraeli and of George Eliot are instances of the unaffected piety and good sense which adorned the pastoral ministrations of the period. The characters of the Bishop in *Venetia*, and of Irwine in *Adam Bede*, show what two acute observers noted. The Evangelical clergy, chiefly in the University of Cambridge, had produced a visible effect in stirring the hearts of the undergraduates, and in throwing something of their own cherished dogmatic phraseology over the spirit of the age. The work of the Evangelical Clapham Sect was of the most far-reaching order. In the humanitarian world as in the world of religion the labours of such members of it as William Wilberforce and Granville Sharpe, of Zachary Macaulay and Thomas Clarkson, are known of all men. Newman declared that the Evangelical Thomas Scott the commentator was "the writer who made a deeper impression on my mind than any other, and to whom (humanly speaking) I almost owe my soul." His earliest pilgrimage was to Aston Sanford where Scott had ministered. The Evangelicals, however, had created no literature and attracted no men of genius; they despised philosophy and degraded art, had barely tolerated scholarship and satisfied scarcely any intellectual want.

Alongside the Oriel School, the precursor of the Broad Church School, and the Evangelical School, there is the

Oxford Movement in 1833, deriving some of its most persuasive elements from the Romantic School in general and from Sir Walter Scott in particular. As a separate school of thought, it sprang into existence, not as a religious or historical tendency, but as a political reaction against the panic which the Reform Bill of 1832 created, which shook so robust a mind as that of the historian Hallam, so practical a statesman as Lord Derby and so romantic a one as Lord Beaconsfield. Its thoroughly political origin may be inferred from the circumstances that the day Cardinal Newman long observed as the birthday of the Movement was Sunday, July 14th, 1833, the anniversary of the fall of the Bastille, on which day Keble preached his Assize sermon before the University of Oxford directed against the suppression of ten bishoprics of the Church of Ireland. "It was published," records Newman in his *Apologia*, "under the title of 'National Apostasy.' I have ever considered and kept the day, as the start of the religious movement of 1833." This political antagonism, combined with determined antipathy to the Liberals in every form and to Nonconformists of every denomination, formed the prevailing colour of the earliest *Tracts for the Times.* "I had fierce thought against the Liberals" was a guiding idea of Newman and his followers.

The triumvirs of the Oxford Movement were Keble, Pusey, and Newman, and yet we cannot overlook the influence of Hurrell Froude and W. G. Ward. Hurrell Froude was one of the authors of this Movement—perhaps, in a sense, he was its "only begetter," for he was the link which first bound Keble and Newman together. In his *Remains*, this saying is preserved: "Do you know the story of the murderer who had done one good thing in his life? Well; if I was ever asked what good deed I had ever done, I should say that I had brought Keble and Newman to understand each other." No young man of those days, with the possible exception of Arthur Hallam, seems to have made a deeper and more lasting impression on his friends and contemporaries. To him, as to Holbein's labourer in the field, the summons came to lie down beside the uncompleted furrow. "It's a long field," says Death, "but we'll get to the end of it to-day—you and I." Froude was the eldest of three famous brothers, and men who knew them all would declare that he was the greatest genius of the three. Newman speaks glowingly of his high and many-sided gifts, "of the gentleness and tenderness of nature, the playfulness, the free elastic force and graceful versatility of mind, and the patient winning considerateness of discussion which endeared him to those to whom he opened his heart," of his intellect as being "as critical and logical as it was speculative and bold."

For ten or fifteen years after 1825, the influence of the Utilitarians proved powerful in the University of Cambridge in the persons of the two Austins, Charles Buller, and others, yet in the University of Oxford there was scarcely a single follower save W. G. Ward. Nor must we forget that J. S. Mill described his father's two great "objects of detestation as an aristocracy and an established Church, the great depravers of religion and opponents of the progress of the human mind." Like the Utilitarians, Ward evinced an absolute dislike of history. He owned that he was "*deplorably* ignorant of facts," and usually, when strictly cross-examined, would answer, "Newman told me so." Ward disliked the English Church in the present and naturally knew nothing of her past. He was, as Newman has told us, "Never a Tractarian, never a Puseyite, never a Newmanite; he was one of a small party of eager, acute resolute minds, who had heard much of Rome, and cut into the original movement at an angle, and then set about turning it in a new direction." The remarkable men of this party were Ward himself, Father Faber, and, in a less degree, Father Dalgairns. In spite of the Cardinal's disclaimer, Ward confessed, "My creed is very short. *Credo in Newmannum.*" "You catholics," he once owned, "know what it is to have a Pope. Well, Newman is my Pope. Without his sanction I cannot move." Of course there may be resistant and contradictory facts to this short creed, but so much the worse for the facts. The area of vision is narrowed: the eye-plate of prepossession (so easy to adjust, so difficult to get rid of) is affixed to the telescope: every star which does not come within the immediate field of vision is declared to be nameless or even non-existent.

Ward's influence over Newman was far larger than is sometimes imagined, and it was not for nothing he was called the "Goad" of the Oxford Movement. His relations to his leader resemble those of Carlstadt to Luther. Ward was as logical as Carlstadt: Newman was as illogical as his own countrymen. Ward constantly asked Newman, "If you think so and so, surely you must also say something more." Newman was thus obliged to make each conclusion Ward drew the basis of a fresh set of premises. The result was that the chief leader of the Oxford Movement advanced, like Luther in this respect, "at a pace much more rapid than his natural one. When a thinker is in a state of doubt a questioner such as Ward not only forces him to resolve, but also by the persistence of his interrogatories raises additional difficulties. "There is no doubt," remarks Dean Church, "that Mr. Newman felt the annoyance and unfairness of this perpetual question for the benefit of Mr. Ward's theories, and there can be little doubt that, in effect, it drove him onwards and cut short his time of waiting. Engineers tell us that, in the case of a ship rolling in a sea-way, when the periodic times of the ship's roll coincide with those of the undulations of the waves, a condition of things arise highly dangerous to the ship's stability. So the agitations of Mr. Newman's mind were reinforced by the impulses of Mr. Ward's."

John Keble was ten years senior in university standing to Newman, and twelve to Pusey; and ten or twelve years at Oxford count for more than twenty elsewhere. Though only forty in 1833, Keble was yet reckoned a senior in Oxford; and, he was, as Newman says, more than once, the foremost man in the university, though seldom seen there, when the other Oxford leaders graduated. He had taken a double first-class when that distinction had only been achieved by one other man, Sir Robert Peel. All unconsciously on his part, he had acquired a reputation for holiness which made his lightest word to be received almost as a message from another sphere, and his retirement to Hursley invested him with a halo which belonged to no other man. His steady, clear conviction is apparent in the last words of his Assize sermon: "He is calmly, soberly demonstrably *sure* that, sooner or later, *his will be the winning side*, and that the victory will be complete, universal, eternal." His edition of Hooker and his life of Bishop Wilson are models of painstaking labour which probably he would have hardly cared in later years to expend on the author of the *Ecclesiastical Polity*, had he come into contact with his Erastian leanings, or had he been alive to the homely style of the Bishop's *Maxims*, which he never once mentions, but which his famous godson Matthew Arnold exalts to a high place among English moralists. He declared with extraordinary vehemence that most of the men who had difficulties respecting the mechanical view of Biblical inspiration were too wicked to be reasoned with. He maintained to the end a rigid adherence to ecclesiastical tradition, and, with a sagacity which was not altogether misplaced, he was one of those who to the last adhered to Gladstone, declaring that after all he was "only a clergyman in a blue coat." Keble was as unbending a Tory in politics as Gladstone was in religion.

Keble and Isaac Williams contributed to the *Tracts for the Times*, No. 89, "On the Mysticism attributed to the Early Fathers of the Church," and No. 80, "On Reserve in Communicating Religious Knowledge" respectively, and no tracts, save No. 90, gave more offence. It was bruited abroad that these two authors were keeping something back, a dark mystery, a secret meaning, a disciplina arcani—things to be abhorred by all plain straightforward Englishmen. They were involved in a storm of controversy uncongenial to the natures of both poets.

Keble's ideas were intuitional and instinctive rather than the product of intellectual reasoning. They were the visions of a poet, not the proofs of a logician. Over Newman he exercised a moderating influence. In his relations with him Newman compared himself to a pane of glass, which transmitted heat, being cold itself. Even in 1833, he felt he was only developing Keble's convictions, interpreting them to the outside world by the force of his own rhetorical gifts. His intimacy with Keble began in 1828. The *Christian Year* had appeared the preceding year, and in it Newman found the expression of two principles which he firmly, but less articulately, held. One was the unreality of material phenomena.

Reinforced and illustrated by Keble's poetical vision from every department of nature, it naturally led to the sacramental view, which treats the world of sense as a veil and curtain of God's presence. The poems confirmed him in his acceptance of his second principle, which is Butler's, that "probability is the only guide of life." It brought home to him with new force the cogency of faith and its dependence on the moral attitude of the believer. These two principles showed him that certainty in matters of religion is less due to the inherent probabilities which commend it than to the reverence and love by which it is accepted. These feelings of the heart lend probability a new assurance, and impart to it the inherent weight of internal conviction. Moral truth could not, he thought, be proved. Logically it may often be refuted. None the less it is attainable by the perception of formed and disciplined minds. With Pascal it is true that "*le coeur a ses raisons que la raison ne connoît point.*"

We are the fools of fancy still, and fondly believe that causes are advanced by argument and that men are swayed by reason. This is the misfortune of the few, the fortune of the many. The bulk of men are appealed to through imagination and aroused through their emotions. Disraeli was right. It was not reason that besieged Troy or produced any of the great events of history. Man is irresistible when he appeals to the imagination, if to the poetic imagination so much the better. The *Christian Year* appealed to the imagination of the members of the Church of England, and the appeal met with instant success. When the copyright expired seventy-five years ago it had reached nearly a hundred editions, and how many has it reached since? The society around Keble, full alike of tragic memories and new aspirations, was on the eve, so many thought, of kindling into revolution. To all this the poet is absolutely indifferent, and indeed the indifference of the Fathers of the Oxford Movement to the social question is quite remarkable. With the real world, its passionate questionings, its humours, its perplexities, its despair, its hope uncovenanted, its love undisciplined, there is no sign of sympathy in the *Christian Year*. Beyond the garden wall of his country vicarage; the poet sees but a "loud stunning tide of human care and crime"; and his only wisdom is to withdraw from the tumult into an inner shrine of pious meditation, disturbed only by anxiety for the fate of the Church.

As a nature poet Keble has been justly praised. He reverenced and learnt much from Wordsworth, though that poet proposed to revise the *Christian Year* in order to correct its English. His nature-symbolism is part of the sacramentalism—the assertion of mystery and inner significance in life and nature—which inspired the Tractarians in their defiance of the cold materialism of the times. It has little relation to the old Celtic sense of the strange powers behind the veil, and almost as little with Wordsworth's large recognition of the divine in nature. What it does sometimes remind one of is the fantastic parallelisms of the school which Johnson has dubbed "metaphysical." When the spontaneous emotion of a poet in the presence of nature is regulated by the traditions of the primitive Church he is at a disadvantage among singers of freer utterance. Both in its view of nature and in its general acknowledged aim—to bring men's "thoughts and feelings into more entire unison" with the Prayer-book—the *Christian Year* is primarily a book of edification; and it is Keble's chief merit that he so often merged the teacher in the poet. A man brought up in another communion, Thomas Erskine of Linlathen, owned, "I have Keble lying open before me. The hymns for the Holy Week are beautiful: Monday is exquisite. I think I like it best of them all. The use made of Andromache's farewell is quite filling to the heart, and the theology of the fourth stanza, 'Thou art as much his care,' etc., is worth, to my mind, the whole Shorter and Longer Catechisms together." Keble's Evening Hymn has been sung by multitudes, and has consoled with better hopes and inspired with fresh courage the hearts of thousands journeying towards the sundown. The *Christian Year* sang the doctrines of the Tractarians every whit as effectively as the hymns of Luther sang the doctrines of the Reformation. Keble's special audience is, of course, an Anglican one. The country rectory has been the nursery of much that is best in modern England, and its atmosphere breathes through every line of Keble. The "kneeling hamlet" at the altar-rail in the silent summer dawn; the garden quiet with the hush of Sunday; the evening hymn of rest and self-surrender sung in the gathering twilight—these have a subtle poetic fragrance of their own, and for thousands they still recall the poetry of Keble, and stir boyhood memories of its refining and chastening influence. Its true secret and virtue were best understood, with a touch of rare sentiment, by a novelist and a man of the world writing seventy-five years ago: "The *Christian Year* was a book which appeared about that time. The son and the mother whispered it to each other with awe. Faint, very faint, and seldom in after life Pendennis heard that solemn church music; but he always loved the remembrance of it and of the times when it struck on his heart and he walked over the fields full of hope and void of doubt, as the church bells rang on Sunday morning."

The second member of the triumvirate was Pusey, whose adherence in 1835 strengthened Newman's position. As a Canon of Christ Church and Regius Professor of Hebrew, he conferred a university standing which was distinctly desirable. The merit of Pusey was that he was a theologian, and the Movement was a theological one or it was nothing. The *Tracts* were no longer leaflets, but ponderous treatises of a hundred or four hundred pages. Their author was deeply read in the Fathers and the Anglican divines and owned—what was very rare in those days—a wide knowledge of the theological speculations of Germany. "What a difference it would have made," once exclaimed Dean Stanley, "if Newman had known German!" The answer, not to the remark, but to what the remark implied, is, "But Dr. Pusey *did* know German." "I can remember," Pusey said in 1878, "the room in Göttingen in which I was sitting when the real condition of religious thought in Germany flashed upon me. I said to myself, 'This will all come upon us in England, and how utterly unprepared for it we are!'"

In 1828 the choice for the vacant provostship of Oriel lay between Hawkins and Keble, and it is amazing to relate that Pusey and Newman both voted against Keble. "The whole of the later history of our Church," Pusey said, in the sermon preached at the dedication of Keble College, "might have been changed had we been wiser.... To us it became the sorrow of our lives." Keble as Provost of Oriel would have made a difference to the Oxford Movement. Pusey replied in 1830, to what he conceived to be the attacks of Rose on the state of religious thought in Germany and in particular the German attitude to inspiration. Later he wrote, "As the subject has been revived I am glad of an opportunity of expressing regret of having ever spoken at all upon the subject of minute discrepancies in Holy Scripture. ... I ever believed the plenary inspiration of the Bible and every sentence in it, as far as any doctrine or practice can be elicited from it." In ritual his position was : "We have too much to do to keep sound doctrine and the privileges of the Church to be able to afford to go into the question about dresses." Keble and he were averse from anything likely to give rise to scandal or inflict pain. When celebrating Holy Communion in Christ Church Cathedral Pusey stood to the last at the north end. "Our own plain dresses are more in keeping with the state of our Church, which is one of humiliation." There was no incense, no water mixed with wine, no shortened surplice. The Holy Communion was administered almost in Presbyterian form to the worshippers who knelt, not at the table, but encircled the whole of the chancel of St. Mary's in a form which had probably descended from the time of the Puritans. The parish clerk and the black gown were also at St. Mary's. In ritual the attitude of Pusey and Newman was alike: in authority it was unlike. The former records: "I remember Newman saying, 'Oh Pusey! we have leant on the Bishops and they have broken down under us!' ... I thought to myself, 'At least I never leant on the Bishops: I leant on the Church of England.'"

Whatever of pathos or romance belongs to the Tractarian Movement centres round the picturesque figure of Newman. The deeply furrowed, austerely outlined face, its clear cut Dantesque features, its air of habitual command, and its expression of wistful melancholy have become hauntingly familiar to us. His strong family feeling, the affection and the pride which his own people, especially his mother, had in him come out in his letters. As a boy he was an omnivorous reader. Scott was his favourite author, and no student of his writings needs to be reminded how abundant is his command of appropriate illustrations from the great novelist, whom he regarded as the literary precursor of the Tractarian Movement. His life at Trinity College, Oxford, is the story of a young man, nursed in the lap of Evangelicalism, meeting the thoughtful, and finding that the system would not bear the strain of the wider and deeper, the ampler view of life, presented to him there. He worked too hard and only gained a second class at his degree. His failure in the schools and the gradual deepening of his religious convictions led to his decision in 1821 of taking orders. Like Ward and unlike Pusey, he inclined to Liberal views after his election as a Fellow of Oriel. His success is evident. At 23 he was invited to join the Athenaeum and preach a University sermon, and at 27 he was appointed Preacher at Whitehall. Froude altered his political views, and he infected Keble and Newman with a hatred of Liberalism which was non-juring in its ferocity. "How Whigery," wrote Froude, "has by degrees taken up all the filth that has been secreted in the fermentation of human thought! Puritanism, Latitudinarianism, Popery, Infidelity; they have it all now, and good luck to them!"

Newman was a lovable man, whose emotions were strong. He loved poetry, and was no mean poet. He wrote prose of incomparable force and subtlety. He loved music, and was no mean player of the violin. The beauties of nature appealed to him as they did to Wordsworth. His religion blended with the glories of the country. Whately had first taught him to think rightly of the Church as a spiritual society. He imbued him with the idea of the Church as a Divine appointment, independent of the State, endowed with rights, powers, and prerogatives of her own. Under the influence of Froude and Keble, he passed into a different field of thought from that in which he moved with Whately. He embraced the idea that antiquity was the true exponent of Christian doctrine, the true basis of the Church of England. He began to read the Fathers chronologically. Towards the Alexandrian school he felt powerfully attracted. Here he found worked out in infinite detail his own sacramental theories. The golden age of the Church, or several golden ages, lay, in the first three centuries, in the time of Edward the Confessor, or in the seventeenth century. He was quite sure that the sixteenth century was composed of baser material. The classics he read, but did he read them altogether in the spirit of Erasmus? "Of the world of wisdom," remarks Mark Pattison, "and sentiment—of poetry and philosophy, of social and political experience, contained in the Latin and Greek classics, and of the true relation of the degenerate and semi-barbarous Christian writers of the fourth century to that of the world—Oxford, in 1830, had never dreamt."

In Sicily in 1833 Newman, recovering from a fever, burst into tears and sat on his bed repeating the words, "I have a work to do in England." After his recovery, and while becalmed in the Straits of Bonifacio on his way home from Palermo to Marseilles, he wrote the hymn "Lead Kindly Light." The familiar lines epitomise the conviction which had been growing upon him during the last three years, the struggle which he had made against it, and his self-dedication to his appointed task. They breathe the spirit of absolute submission to the leadings of the "Pillar of Cloud," his complete devotion to his divine mission, his readiness to obey the heavenly impulse implicitly without asking to look forward to the distant consequences of his actions.

The *Tracts* and Newman's four o'clock sermons at St. Mary's begin the general Oxford Movement. Newman could not only write; he could preach differently from anyone else. Dean Church thinks that the famous four o'clock sermons were even more effective agents than the *Tracts* in the early Movement. Lord Coleridge writes: "There was scarcely a man of note in the University, old or young, who did not during the last two or three years of Newman's incumbency habitually attend the services and listen to the sermons." Their exquisite descriptive passages, their insight into the waywardness of the human heart, their severe austerity, their passages of tenderness, and their lofty bursts of indignant fervour impressed the undergraduates. And yet when we come to read these sermons dispassionately, it seems clear that they contemplate truth as a fixed quantity.

The world in fact is a similar series of fixed quantities; it forms stereotyped notions, corresponding to sterotyped objects of thought. Hard and fast distinctions are perfectly possible, and the preacher contrasts the religious and the secular, the supernatural and the natural, the Church and the world. But are not these distinctions dualistic? Is there no unity of experience? Is there no movement in both thought and things? Statisticians speak of hard facts, but is there anything so fluid as fact? Is there a single fixed quantity in nature? Is there, accordingly, a fixed notion in thought? Surely for the thoughtful the world is a process, a thing becoming, not a thing become. Newman shrank from such ideas; they were part of the Liberalism in thought that was breaking up ancient institutions in Church and State. Clericalism was not the enemy; Liberalism was. From 1833 to 1839, he regarded the Church of Rome with no less horror. The Papacy was Antichrist. But what if his confidence in Anglicanism were shaken? Was there any refuge for him save Rome?

The man as well as the leader requires understanding. His temperament always counted for much: it led him to Tractarianism, it led him to Rome, and it led him to anti-Vaticanism. It incapacitated him from taking the historical view of the issue between the Church of England and the Church of Rome. It induced him to treat the Anglican Church as an instrument for saving his own soul; and it led him to the discovery that though it might be a true Church to others, she could never be so to him. "Where shall I be most *safe*?" is an argument he employs repeatedly, but does he ask, "Where shall I find most truth?" He tended to substitute personal for general principles, individual for collective relations. True, as Bremond reminds us, he rarely uses "I" and "me" in his writings, but does he not always reveal and describe himself? He rests in "the thought of two, and two only, absolute and luminously, self-evident beings—myself and my Creator."

Wordsworth, daring Platonist that he was, speaks of reason with hardly more respect than Newman as:

> The inferior faculty that moulds
> With her minute and speculative pains
> Opinion, ever changing.

Coleridge's distinction between understanding and reason might have saved these great writers from the appearance of blaspheming against the highest and most divine faculty of human nature. For the reason is something higher than logic-chopping; it can provide, from its own resources, a remedy for the intellectual error which is just now miscalled intellectualism; it is the activity of the whole personality under the guidance of the highest part; and because there is a real unification of our disordered nature, it can bring us into real contact with the higher world of Spirit. Newman's scepticism was not of course about matters of faith; it was a wholly unjustifiable contempt and distrust for the unaided activity of the human mind. Tradition came to him to mean more than testimony. "A fact is not disproved because the testimony is confused and insufficient." "As if evidence were the test of truth!" "Faith does not regard degrees of evidence." "The more you set yourself to argue and prove, in order to discover truth, the less likely you are to reason correctly." Yet between his metaphysical views of religious judgments and those of Coleridge there are remarkable coincidences. Both claimed for faith the first condition of spiritual knowledge. Both vindicated the maxim *Credo ut intelligam*. Both recognised the religious character of morality. Both traced the germ of devout belief to the experiences of conscience.

Newman, in his Anglican days, was a born leader of men, a fearless fighter, confident in his own powers. Late in life he owned that he had "generally got on well with juniors, but not with superiors"—a sign of leadership. He was, according to Shairp, "the centre and soul" of the Movement, the rest, according to Froude, were comparatively "ciphers." "My ἔργον," wrote Newman in 1845, "seems to be the direction or oversight of young men." Even in childhood the same quality was evident. After a struggle for the mastery between his mother and himself, his mother said to him, "You see, John, you did not get your own way." "No," came the reply, "but I tried very hard." Throughout his Anglican life he tried hard, and generally succeeded, though he found it by no means easy to work with his equals. During the height of the Movement he confesses, "I have learnt to throw myself on myself . . . God intends me to be lonely; He has so framed my mind that I am in great measure beyond the sympathies of others and thrown upon Himself." He laments a year later, "I am very cold and reserved to people, but I cannot realise to myself that any one loves me; . . . or I dare not realise it." A leader is alone and necessarily alone. Once Provost Copleston met him walking by himself. He bowed to Newman with the words, "*Nunquam minus solus quam cum solus.*" The leader must travel in strange seas of thought alone by the very fact that it falls to him to guide others. It is more singular to note that when he had a large following of devoted men he could write: "I do not think that you enter into my situation, nor can any one. I have for several years been working against all sorts of opposition, and with hardly a friendly voice. Consider how few persons have said a word in favour of me." In 1845 he complains that "no one has spoken well of me"; in 1859 that "all through my life I have been plucked"; and these complaints are not based on fact. Yet from this mistrust of others as well as from mistrust of himself came his secession to the Church of Rome.

The leaders of the Tractarians are before us, and it is time to consider the condition of the Church. The repeal of the Test and Corporation Act in 1828, the Act of Roman Catholic Emancipation in 1829, and the Reform Act in 1832 were viewed as successive blows against the Established Church. Men without the Church were ready to destroy her: her anomalies were paraded in public; and her resources were declared to be vast and useless. Men within the Church confessed that reforms were needed and that she should adapt herself to changing circumstances. In 1833 the Government proposed the suppression of two archbishoprics and ten bishoprics in Ireland. Indignant surprise was felt in many quarters. Churchmen realised that their alarms were abundantly justified. Was this the fruit of Liberalism? Profane hands had been laid on the ark, not to protect, but to destroy. This policy was not one of hostility alone: it was a policy of intrusion. It was the sin of Uzzah aggravated by the apostasy of Julian. The Whigs had been guilty of this thing. All the Tory feeling took flame:

religious indignation made common cause with political indignation. Toryism cried out against so wholesale an attack upon national institutions. Churchmen asked whether the State had a right to do this thing. "Half the candlesticks of the Irish Church were extinguished without *ecclesiastical sanction.*" A petition to Archbishop Howley was signed by 7,000 of the clergy and a similar address "for the preservation of this our national Church in the integrity of her rights and privileges, and in her alliance with the State" obtained 230,000 signatures from laymen—heads of families alone signing—and was presented to the Archbishop of Canterbury in May, 1834.

In 1832 Arnold wrote, "The Church, as it now stands, no human power can save." His conception of the Church, the darling dream and almost the dying prayer of his life, was one of identity of Church and State. This result he believed to have been intended by Henry VIII and Cranmer by investing the State with power to combine all communions into a miscellaneous mass, a view not altogether unlike that entertained by Coleridge.

Now if the Church were realising her functions, the State was also realising hers. Bentham had developed a view of sovereignty which is substantially that put forward by John Austin in 1832 in his *Province of Jurisprudence determined*. He teaches that a law is a command enforcing a course of conduct. It is an intimation by a stronger to a weaker rational being, that if the weaker does or forbears to do some act the stronger will injure him. God sets laws to men, and of these some are revealed and others unrevealed. The test by which the purport of the unrevealed laws may be discovered is the test of Utility. Men set laws to one another; those who set them are called sovereigns, and those to whom they set them are subjects. In every independent political society there is a sovereign and there are subjects. The tests by which an independent political society may be known are, first, that the bulk of the given society are in a habit of obedience to a determinate and common superior; let that common superior be an individual or an aggregate of individuals. Secondly, this common superior must not be in a habit of obedience to a determinate human superior.

The Austinian conception of sovereignty coloured the legislation to which Churchmen took objection, and accordingly we proceed to illustrate it. Whenever people associate together for political purposes some one or more of them possess a power of publishing and enforcing commands which is not controlled by any other power of the same kind. True, it is restrained by positive moral rules which have in point of fact been established by the common sentiment of the community, including under that head the conception they have formed of the Divine law. Those who possess this power form individually, or collectively, as it may happen, the sovereign of society, and sovereign authority is always from its nature absolute. Accordingly it is a mistake to classify governments as despotic or free; at least such classifications do not point to the extent of their power, but to the use they make of it. From this it follows that sovereigns and subjects have neither legal rights nor duties, nor is a sovereign power capable of legal limitation. It may commit iniquity, not injustice. The deduction is, on Austinian principles, that a law is a command enforced by a common superior, and if the sovereign had any superior he would not be sovereign. The sovereign may, however, be under moral or religious obligations, because such obligations are enforced either by God or by those whose common sentiment establishes moral rule. Churchmen could ponder such rules.

These opinions may appear to some minds favourable to tyranny; but a perusal of the *Province of Jurisprudence determined* will dispel this idea. Austin proceeds to illustrate his conception of the bodies which possess sovereign power. In our own country, for instance, he says that sovereignty, which it must be remembered means the power of making and enforcing the laws, resides in the King, the House of Lords, and the constituencies by whom the House of Commons are chosen, jointly. The share of the constituencies in the sovereignty is delegated by them unreservedly to their representatives with the single exception of the power of choosing the representatives. It may easily be seen how exactly the tests of sovereignty apply to this body. The King must be a member of the Church of England; the House of Lords may not amend money bills; the House of Commons cannot legislate by a simple resolution. The constituencies were remodelled by the Reform Bill, but attempts to bind the sovereign are simply futile. For example, by the articles of the Union between England and Scotland the preservation of the Church of England and the Kirk of Scotland is declared to be a fundamental condition of the Union, yet no one can doubt that the existing Parliament of Great Britain could, if it pleased, abolish both or either; and such an abolition would be legal in the strictest sense of the word. It is equally true that, against a sovereign so defined, no one had legal rights. If the King can do no wrong, this sovereign can do no legal wrong. A man's right not to be put to death is the most important and most beneficial of all rights, yet a bill of attainder—an act of parliament for cutting off the head of a person convicted of no crime—is as good a law as any other bill whatever, and executions done under its provisions would not only be legal, but to neglect to do it would be a crime.

Leaders of the Oxford Movement, if ever they perused the *Province of Jurisprudence determined*, must have had qualms. A sovereign power capable of committing iniquity but not injustice—how monstrous! Here was the State developing an authority which promised to crush that of the Church. The Church must state her pretensions in the sight of all men, and she proceeded to do so. Despite the teachings of men like Austin the leaders of the Oxford Movement determined in 1833 to issue the *Tracts for the Times*. According to the Rev. W. Palmer, "We thought it necessary to teach people that the duty of adhering to the Church of England rested on a basis somewhat higher than mere Acts of Parliament, or the patronage of the State, or individual fancy. We were anxious to impress on them that the Church was more than a merely human institution—that it had privileges, sacraments, a ministry ordained of Christ; that it was a matter of the highest obligation to remain united to the Church." In the first tract, published in 1833, Keble writes: "A notion has gone abroad that the people can take away your power. They think they have given it and can take it away. They have been deluded into a notion that present palpable usefulness, produceable results, acceptableness to your flocks—that these and suchlike are the tests of your Divine commission. Enlighten them on this matter. Exalt our holy fathers the Bishops, as the representatives of the Apostles, and the Angels of the Churches, and magnify your office, as being ordained by them to take part in their ministry."

A brotherhood was formed to defend the Church, and it included Newman, Mansell, the Kebles, Froude, Bowden, Copeland, and Isaac Williams, who were in touch with Rose, Hook, Perceval, and Palmer. At first its efforts were political, and the efforts of Newman and the brotherhood were directed to meet the inroads of Liberalism. Peel was denounced after his appearance on the public scene in the character of a Conservative-Liberal, partly in Whitehall Chapel as Pontius Pilate, partly by Newman himself in a series of sarcastic letters addressed to *The Times*. It was clearly of the last importance to set forth a worthy conception of the Church. She was a visible body, maintaining the apostolical succession among her ministers, offering divine grace through the channels of her sacraments, possessing in tradition, of which she was the depository, the means of ascertaining the truths of Christianity. Her true notes were recited in the Creed: she was One, Holy, Catholic, and Apostolic. The success achieved by the new Movement was wonderful. The idea of a Divine society has been and is the inspiration of thousands of ardent workers in the Anglican Church. If we ask on what grounds men like Newman chose to prefer the authority of the Church to other authorities, such as natural science or philosophy, we are driven to lay great stress on the almost political necessity which he felt that such a Divine society should exist.

Austin drew no line of demarcation between the *jus publicum* and the *jus sacrum*: the Tractarians drew such a line. Against the pretensions of the State, urged in the name of Utility, they assumed a Guelfic attitude. Their attitude was essentially mediaevalist. John of Paris and Gregory of Heimberg, Wyclif and Hus, had urged on behalf of the State all that they vigorously denied. In 1833 Lord John Russell took for granted that the State was perfectly entitled to legislate for the Church, whether she was in

Ireland or England. The Whig assumption was that the Church was a department of the State, the position taken up by Marsiglio of Padua. Against this Whig assumption the Tractarians passionately pleaded with St. Thomas Aquinas that the Church was a State. They were willing to render to Caesar the things that are Caesar's, but they were unwilling to render to Caesar the things that are God's.

The progress of the Movement 1833 and 1845 was almost entirely in the direction of teaching the clergy to "magnify their office." The other part of the scheme, the combat against Liberalism, theological and political, fell quite into the background. The main reason for this was that during these years the theologians so completely dominated Oxford that Liberalism could hardly raise its head, and was despised as well as hated. If Newman could have foreseen the victory of his party, would he have remained? We cannot tell. His influence was disturbing and subtly disintegrating to every cause for which he laboured. Anglo-Catholicism and Modernism are among his bequests to the Church of England and the Church of Rome respectively.

The culminating point of success of the Tractarians was in the year 1836, before its members had lost the confidence of the Conservative party of which they had been the ecclesiastical representatives, and when they bent their whole power in opposing the nomination of Dr. Hampden by a Liberal ministry to the Regius Professorship of Divinity at Oxford. Then Arnold stood forth, and attacked them with all his usual vigour and more than his usual vehemence for an attempt to crush in its progress the beginnings of a Liberal theology at Oxford. Archbishop Alexander's poem, *Oxford in 1845*, set forth the view of the time:

> Let Newman mould the Church and Gladstone stamp the State.

The future Liberal Prime Minister set down in 1838 in his *State in its relations with the Church*, the case for Establishment based upon two fundamental principles; the first of which is that the State has a conscience, "representing the result of the general belief of the people." As all government implies moral responsibility, which is not only that of the individual governors, but belongs to the nation as a whole, the establishment of religion, upon which moral responsibility rests as its only sure ground, becomes a natural and legitimate consequence of the fact of government. Given the acceptance of this principle, Gladstone has no difficulty in showing the advantages that a religious establishment confers upon a nation. It brings the sanction of a ruling institution to the principles of Christianity. It makes possible to give a universal application to religious influences by a territorial division of the country into manageable districts like parishes. In his account of the "sustaining, correcting and befriending" offices of the Church, he falls back on Coleridge, whose argument he characterises as "alike beautiful and profound." In spite of its profundity, Macaulay pertinently asked the question, "Did Gladstone wish to revive the Test Act, repealed ten years before?"

The second fundamental principle is that, by virtue of its conscience, the State can take cognisance of religious truth and error, is indeed bound to do so, and accordingly must encourage religious truth and discourage religious error to the best of her power. Here we discern Tractarian influence and political considerations. It is hard to resist the suspicion that this idea appears as a defence of the Establishment in Ireland. Thirty years later he was disestablishing this very Church, and in *A Chapter of Autobiography*, Gladstone referred to his old book: "My doctrine was that the Church, as established by law, was to be maintained for its truth; that this was the only principle on which it could be properly and permanently upheld; that this principle, if good in England, was good also for Ireland; that truth is of all possessions the most precious to the soul of man; and that to remove, as I then erroneously thought we should remove, this priceless treasure from the view and the reach of the Irish people, would be meanly to purchase their momentary favour at the expense of their permanent interests, and would be a high offence against our own sacred obligations."

There were awkward facts in 1838. One was that the Church established in Scotland was Presbyterian, and the other was that a grant was regularly made from the

Exchequer to the Roman Catholic College at Maynooth. These awkward facts he sets aside as anomalies. Still, "many persons of sincere piety do not object to consider themselves as members both of the English and the Scottish Church, according as they happen to reside, at different seasons of the year, south or north of the border. And no man can think that the personality of the State is more stringent, or entails stricter obligations, than that of the individual." With Scots blood in his veins, this is his attitude in Scotland. In Ireland it is different. He pronounces the Maynooth grant to be vicious, and advises its continuance. But already he faces the surrender of his principle as a possible alternative. "Unless (the State) is bound in conscience to maintain the national Church as God's appointed vehicle of religious truth, it should adopt as its rule the numbers and the needs of the several classes of religionists; and in either aspect the claim of the Roman Catholics is infinitely the strongest. In amount the grant is niggardly and unworthy."

The Toryism of Gladstone in 1838 is manifest. With the growth of democratic ideas and the increase of popular representation, it seemed as if the function of government was to be reduced to that of "the index of a clock worked by a pendulum." In a letter to Newman he then denied that the popular State owned a conscience. The next thirty years witnessed another alteration in his outlook. In his *Gleanings* he announces: "During those years, what may be called the dogmatic allegiance of the State to religion has been greatly relaxed; but its consciousness of moral duty has been not less notably quickened and enhanced. I do not say this in depreciation of Christian dogma. But we are still a Christian people." In his latest opinion the alliance between Church and State must be maintained mainly because of its beneficent effects on our social life. "It is," so he remarks, "by a practical rather than a theoretic test that our Establishments of religion should be tried. . . . An Establishment that does its work in much, and has the likelihood of doing it in more; an Establishment that has a broad and living way open to it, into the hearts of the people; an Establishment that can command the services of the present by the recollections and traditions of a far-reaching past . . . such an Establishment should surely be maintained."

The early attitude of Gladstone to the alliance between Church and State, Newman would have approved: the late one he would have disapproved, even though here below to live is to change. Still, in the thirties the Tractarians were making decided progress. The publication of Froude's *Remains* in 1841 gave the first shock to this halcyon state of affairs. "The special charm of the book," wrote Ward to Pusey, "is his hatred of our present system and of the reformers, and his sympathy with the rest of Christendom." Not a few Churchmen began to feel suspicious of the Rome-ward trend of the Movement. It was no longer a unity. Newmanites like Ward evinced their sympathy with Roman formularies and practices and their antipathy to Cranmer and Jewel. "Restoration of active communion with the Roman Church," Ward wrote in 1841, "is the most enchanting earthly prospect on which my imagination can dwell." From active leadership, Newman withdrew to Littlemore in 1842, eating out his heart in his retirement. "The heads of the Church," he complained, "had thought fit to condemn and silence him, and they would now have to deal with younger men whom it was not in his power to restrain."

The Bishops had been upset by the fashion in which Newman undertook to explain the Thirty-nine Articles in 1841. "The great stumbling-block," so he perceived, "lay in the Thirty-nine Articles. It was urged that here was a positive note *against* Anglicanism: Anglicanism claimed to hold that the Church of England was nothing else than a continuation in this country (as the Church of Rome might be in France or Spain), of that one Church of which in old time Athanasius and Augustine were members. But, if so, the doctrine must be the same; the doctrine of the old Church must live and speak in Anglican formularies, in the Thirty-nine Articles. Did it? Yes, it did; that is what I maintained; it did in substance, in a true sense. Man had done his worst to disfigure, to mutilate, the old Catholic Truth, but there it was in spite of them, in the Articles still. . . . It was a matter of life and death to show it."

Tract 90 was to show it. Newman's interpretation was no new one. For in 1634 Christopher Davidson, known after his secession to Rome as Franciscus a Sancta Clara, had anticipated it in an anonymous treatise dedicated to Charles I. What was new was the open advocacy of this mode of interpretation by a leading Oxford divine. His arguments led him to maintain that as the Articles had been framed before the publication of the Tridentine decrees, they could not have been intended to attack them. The question inevitably arose whether the Roman view of the Mass, of Purgatory, of the Invocation of the Saints, and the like were tenable in the Church of England. The upshot of this Tract was, as Stanley remarked, that "all Roman doctrine might be held within the limits of the English Church." To the dismay of friends of the Movement and the joy of its enemies, Pusey, Palmer, and Hook wrote warmly in favour of Tract 90. Four Oxford tutors, of whom Tait was one, addressed to the Board of the Heads of Houses a resolution that this Tract "evaded rather than explained the Articles, and was inconsistent with the observance of the Statutes." The Heads of Houses and the Bishops assumed an attitude of open hostility. Privately neither Pusey nor Keble was satisfied. Pusey represented to Newman that "the Tract might be understood to imply that the Articles had no definite meaning, but might mean anything." "Did not the Trent Fathers," asked Keble, "whom Newman would exculpate from the censure of Article XXII. mean the Schoolmen's Purgatory? And was that different from the Homily, and therefore by implication, what the Article thought of?" A few of the senior Liberals instigated the attack on Newman, but the mass of this party, men like Tait and Maurice, stood studiously aloof from it. Yet Newman wrote: "The Liberals drove me from Oxford; it was they who gained a second benefit if I went on to retire from the Anglican Church."

The State again interfered with the Church. On the part of the King of Prussia, incited by Chevalier Bunsen, there came a proposal for a bishopric at Jerusalem, to be jointly supplied by Prussia and England, and to ordain clergy for both nations who should minister at Jerusalem. This, in effect, was to combine the Church of England with the "Evangelical" Prussian Establishment, which stood lower in theology than Lutheranism. What, asked the Tractarians, was the place of Apostolical succession in the ordination of such ministers? None. Newman was wavering in his allegiance, and he records, "it was one of the blows which broke me." In 1843, there was yet another blow. Pusey's sermon on the Eucharist was condemned by the Oxford Board of Six Doctors, and the preacher was condemned unheard. In 1843, Newman formally resigned St. Mary's. His feeling was expressed in his words: "This is no longer any place for us; let us go hence."

In the summer of 1844 appeared Ward's *Ideal of a Christian Church*, written with the avowed object of showing the superiority of the Roman over the English Church. Gladstone criticised it, pointing out that its author was "never struck by the fact that a nation, which is by universal confession one of the most powerful and distinguished in the world, is nevertheless in civil and social, as well as religious matters of practice, one of the least systematic: it trusts more to personal character and less to external law." Precisely, but what are you to say to a man who trusts to external law? And Ward was such a man. The Heads of the Houses proposed to Convocation to condemn Ward and to pass a strict test intended specially to hit No. 90, declaring that henceforth the Articles must be accepted and signed in the sense of their writers. At once the Conservative High Church party and the Liberals united in Ward's favour. Among the latter was Stanley, who had opposed his friend Tait's assault on No. 90, and J. S. Mill. "I always hailed Puseyism," owned Mill, "and expected that thought would sympathise with thought." Maurice expressed himself with the generosity characteristic of him, and stood out against the action of the Heads. Tait opposed any test, "which would narrow the limits of the Church of England." Ward spoke admirably in English, plainly avowing his position: "O most joyful! O most wonderful! O most unexpected sight! We find the whole cycle of Roman doctrine gradually possessing numbers of English Churchmen!" Ward was not unnaturally condemned, but the

Proctors interposed their veto on the censure of Tract 90. In spite of his assaults on Liberalism, the members of this party befriended Newman. His life was one long crusade against the outlook over the world which he knew as Liberalism, and yet on his secession from the Church of England in 1845 he discerned the beginning of the ultimate triumph of Liberalism along the whole line. "Now it is scarcely a party," so he confesses in his *Apologia*, "it is the educated lay world."

Newman's secession marks a stage in the history of the Oxford Movement of which the end is not yet. Its centre ceased to be in the university town, because it extended its area to cover the Church of England. Some just preceded, some followed him to Rome; some underwent a violent reaction and became ultra-Liberals; but the vast majority remained firm to the Church of their baptism. A party which still retained such men as Pusey, the Kebles, Isaac Williams, Copeland, Marriott, Mozley, Moberly, Palmer, Hook, and Church, had no reason to despair. Yet Anglicanism of the ecclesiastical type owes Newman much: more than any other man he was its creator. Roman Catholicism owes him more: he restored its prestige and its poetry. He will live in history, not as the recluse of Littlemore or Edgbaston, not as the wearer of the Cardinal's hat which fell to his lot, almost too late to save the credit of the Vatican, but as the real founder and leader of nineteenth century Anglo-Catholicism, the movement which he created and then tried to destroy. Yet he drove a wedge into the Church of England by his creation just as he drove a wedge into the Church of Rome by his Modernism. Surely he was a great man, and more surely he was an unhappy one. He stirred movements which still agitate the two communions of which he was a member, and the end of these movements is not yet in sight. With the same grace of style and the same keen perception of things, Renan was not unlike Newman. It is a remarkable coincidence that he practically left the Roman Church on October 9th, 1845, the very day on which Newman was received into it. Men may be divided into two classes, according as they face onwards or backwards. And the tragedy of Newman's life, with his splendid gifts and unsurpassed powers, is that he was the father of them that look back. "O liberty, what crimes have been committed in thy name," ejaculated Madame Roland. "O Romanticism, what crimes have been committed in thy name," we may well ejaculate.

The attitude of Church to State wore one form in England at the hands of the Tractarians, and it wore a not dissimilar one in Scotland at the hands of the leaders in the Disruption Movement of 1843. In a sense the English movement begins in 1833, and ends in 1845, while the Scots movement begins in 1834 with the abolition by the General Assembly of lay patronage, and ends in 1843 with the secession of those who refused to accept the terms of the State. Each repelled the efforts of the State to control the Church by legislation, for each recognised the Austinian theory of sovereignty as the foe. This was as plain to Gladstone as it was to Chalmers. Neither the English Movement nor the Scots one allowed complete liberty of investigation in thought. The Tractarians and the Disruptionists worked out a comprehensive theory of the Church as a society demanding the whole-hearted allegiance of its members. Parliament resisted the English conception as the Courts resisted the Scots. This is simply an historical accident, for essentially both conceptions ran contrary to that put forward by the State. Singularly enough, the occasion of each Movement was the question of the appointment of Church officers, in the one case the appointment of ministers and in the other the appointment of Bishops. The leaders of both movements are such outstanding personalities as John Henry Newman and Thomas Chalmers. Both have left as a legacy the memory of great figures and great forces. The world knows Newman: it is the Scots world that knows Chalmers. His stage was too small for the powers with which he was endowed. He was neither a writer nor a poet of the rank of Newman, yet Scots Evangelicalism, like English Tractarianism, was an outcome of Romanticism. He was no more an originator in philosophy or theology than was Newman. In influence on others he was as magnetic as his English contemporary. Out of a thousand ministers in the Established Church in 1843, no less than 453 followed his leadership. Had he lived in London he might have left one of the great names of history, and as it is he is the most outstanding minister since Knox. His oratorical powers were as fine as those of Newman, exercising the same magic spell over his hearers. With both men their will power was as conspicuous as that side of statesmanship which consists in ability to persuade others, and to carry through a definite policy against all opposition. In two respects Chalmers differed from the recluse. He was a statesman to his finger's tips, and he was a man intensely concerned with the welfare of the poor. As a leader, he was less effective than Newman, for his outlook was too broad. The devotion of the two men to their common Master is striking, and both made the great sacrifice for His sake. As Newman forsook the Church of his baptism, so Chalmers forsook his. Just as Newman believed that he was joining the true Catholic Church, so Chalmers believed that he was joining the true Church with its presbyterian form. They had tried to purify the Establishment, and they had tried, as they conceived, in vain, and on the failure of their attempt they felt bound to leave. The parting cost both no common pain. Let anyone turn to Newman's last sermon as an Anglican, "The Parting of Friends," if he wishes in some measure to see what that great heart suffered. Chalmers "went out" in 1843 with a heart as heavy as Newman's. It is under this pathetic aspect that the story whether of the Anglican or Scotsman reveals a tragic solemnity, and redeems them from the pettiness incidental to arguments about jurisdiction, courts of appeal, or the significance of ceremonies. By their religion of the heart they have the sure touch of greatness.

The Church of Scotland claimed that she has a life of her own controlled by her, and this of course is the Tractarian contention. She is no mere department of State dependent on officials outside her jurisdiction. Within her bosom were the Moderates and the Evangelicals. Moderatism was supposed to consist chiefly of "cauld morality," but how did such morality come to command the support of the strongest men in Scotland? It was no doubt an ethical reaction against the fierce dogmatism of the age of the Covenanters, and the stress on conduct as compared with creed is intelligible to all who know the annals of persecution in the North. It believed that its ministers were none the worse for being learned and that the whole of life was not necessarily bound by asceticism. The preaching of Blair attests that spirituality was present, and that hearers craved for it. Men like Principal Robertson attracted to the ministry men of whom the Kirk could be proud. The dangers of Moderatism were not so much on the ethical as on the rationalistic side, and the influence of Hume was present to a greater degree than is sometimes imagined. Witness the proposal in 1781 to get rid of the Westminster Confession of Faith.

The Evangelicals were conservative in their outlook on theology. They traced their pedigree back to the Evangelicalism of the Covenanters, to the "Marrow Men," and even the disciples of Dr. Webster. Among their outstanding men were Chalmers, Candlish, whose influence was second only to Chalmers's and James Roberston, the powerful minister of St. George's, Edinburgh. He impressed his own strongly conservative nature on his party, leading it more wholeheartedly than Chalmers. He died, however, in 1831, before there was a whisper of the Disruption Movement.

The Miltonic saying that new presbyter is but old priest writ large contains a deeper truth than is always perceived. There is a High Church Presbyterianism which combines with love of evangelical doctrine an assertion of the authority of the Church as lofty as that of the Ultramontane or the Tractarian. Its great exponent was Andrew Melville, the Scots Hildebrand; and the principles for which he fought are nowhere more clearly put than in his famous words: "There are two kings and two kingdoms in Scotland. There is King James, the head of this Commonwealth; and there is Christ Jesus, the King of the Church, whose subject James VI, is, and of whose kingdom he is not a king, nor a lord, nor a head, but a member." It is a position which commended itself to Newman.

The Act of 1712 gave back to patrons of livings the rights of which, during a season of political and religious confusion, they had been deprived. Patronage is not so congenial to the Church of Scotland as to the Church of

England. For Presbyterianism bases its system on trust in the people and asks them to exercise authority. Patronage worked badly in Scotland, and the records of the courts of the eighteenth century attest the number of disputes raging round it "The British legislature," Macaulay pointed out in a perfectly true indictment, "violated the Articles of Union and made a change in the constitution of the Church of Scotland. From that change has flowed almost all the dissent now existing in Scotland . . . year after year the General Assembly protested against the violation, but in vain; and from the Act of 1712 undoubtedly flowed every succession and schism that has taken place in the Church of Scotland."

The General Assembly contained members hostile to the repeal of the Test and Corporation Acts of 1828 and the Roman Catholic Emancipation Act of 1829, but Chalmers was able to overcome this hostility. He, like the members, offered stout opposition to the Reform Bill of 1832. The feelings of the Tractarians were those of the Presbyterians and for similar motives. The Veto Act of 1834 was an attempt to buttress patronage in the face of popular dissatisfaction with it. The stoutest defender of the rights of the Church saw a debatable land looming before him. The Church of course is to control her spiritual rights, but what about the temporal ones? Has Caesar no power over stipends and church buildings? Where property comes in, must not Caesar come in? Take the settlement of a minister. The Evangelicals offered what seemed their simple solution. Let the State confer the emoluments on the minister, but let it not dare to say who shall have control of souls. But is such a dualism really practicable? When pressed, the Evangelicals retreated behind vague statements, which seemed to say that it was for the Church to lay down the line of demarcation, a position which the Moderates characterised as pure popery. Chalmers told a London audience in 1838 that "In things ecclesiastical we decide all. Some of the things may be done wrong, but still they are our majorities which do it. They are not, they can not, be forced upon us from without. We own no head of the Church, but the Lord Jesus Christ. Whatever is done ecclesiastically is done by our ministers as acting in His name and in perfect submission to His authority . . . even the law of patronage, right or wrong, is in force, not by the power of the State, but by permission of the Church, and, with all its fancied omnipotence, has no other basis than that of our majorities to rest upon. It should never be forgotten that in things ecclesiastical, the highest power of our Church is amenable to no higher power on earth for its decisions. It can exclude; it can deprive; it can depose at pleasure. External force might make an obnoxious individual the holder of a benefice; it could never make him a minister of the Church of Scotland. There is not one thing which the State can do to our independent and indestructible Church, but strip her of her temporalities. *Nec tamen consumebatur*—she would remain a Church notwithstanding, as strong as ever in the props of her own moral and inherent greatness; although shrivelled in all her dimensions by the moral injury inflicted on many thousands of her families."

A few months after the passing of the Veto Act, the Earl of Kinnoull presented to the parish of Auchterarder, in Perthshire, Mr. Young, a licentiate, and therefore fully eligible for ordination. There was opposition on the part of the parishioners, and the Presbytery declined to sustain the call to Mr. Young. There was an appeal to the Synod of Perth and Stirling, and afterwards to the General Assembly which, in 1835, repelled the objections taken to the decision of the primary Court. The patron applied for redress to the Court of Session, which decided against the Presbytery, and the Presbytery falling back on the General Assembly for support, that body directed its law officer to carry the question into the House of Lords. The decision of the Lords fully maintained that of the Court of Session; and Lord Chancellor Brougham, in delivering his opinion, very distinctly stated that the Presbytery, which should persist in disobeying the decree of the Court of Session would expose itself to "the consequences, civil and other, of disobeying the positive and clear order of a statute." Austinianism was to be felt in Edinburgh as in London.

The Auchterarder case inevitably gave rise to others. In 1835 the Crown presented Mr. Clarke to the living of

Lethendy; the people vetoed the presentation, and the Presbytery rejected the presentee. A similar state of affairs arose at Marnoch in the Presbytery of Strathbogie. Sir James Graham and Sir Robert Peel agreed with the judgment of Brougham, yet the Church refused to give way. Candlish devised a great "Convocation" to be held in Edinburgh in November, 1842. Its outcome was that the 450 ministers present pledged themselves to vacate their livings if the Government persisted in supporting the claims of the patrons. Chalmers was the chairman, and passed this resolution: "That as the principle involved in these decisions—(of the Court of Session and the House of Lords)—and particularly in the recent Auchterarder judgment, is that of the supremacy of the civil courts over those of the Established Church in the exercise of their spiritual functions, so the members of the Convocation declare that no measure can in conscience be submitted to, which does not effectually protect the Church against the exercise of such jurisdiction of the civil courts in time to come." Chalmers and Candlish had crossed the Rubicon, little as they thought it. The parallelism with Puseyism is remarkable. As Evangelicals the two leaders manifested horror of Puseyism, yet the same general assumption pervades the speeches of Chalmers and Candlish. English Tractarian and Scots Evangelical are alike persuaded that in matters of faith and Church discipline the civil power has no right to interfere. There is this difference. Puseyism confined itself strictly to points of doctrine and ecclesiastical discipline, while the Free Kirk intermingled questions of temporal benefice and spiritual teaching very closely indeed.

"Convocation" sent its decision to the Cabinet. Graham took no notice of it, declaring that to yield to the demands of the Church would "lead directly to despotic power." The Commission of the General Assembly sent a petition to the House of Commons on March 7th, 1843, and Fox Maule, afterwards Lord Panmure, a steady ally of Chalmers, moved that the House should resolve itself into a Committee to consider the grievances of the Kirk. Sir James Graham spoke against this motion "because he was satisfied that such expectations (of the Church) could not be realised in any country in which law, or equity, or order, or common sense prevailed." Lord John Russell agreed with Graham; while Peel expressed his hope that "an attempt would not be made to establish a spiritual or ecclesiastical supremacy above the other tribunals of the country: and that, in conjunction with increased attention to the duties of religion, the laws of the country would be maintained." Maule lost his motion by a majority of 240 votes to 76. The handwriting on the wall was as plain for the Puseyites as for the Evangelicals of Edinburgh.

The General Assembly was to meet on May 18th, 1843. From as early as four o'clock, Edinburgh was astir; and, as the morning advanced, the grave countenances of all who met and conversed in the swarming streets showed that for no holiday—rather for a holy day—had they quitted their shops and offices. Towards noon the great gallery of Holyrood was thrown open, and the Marquis of Bute, the Lord Commissioner, received the most crowded levee which had been witnessed for years. Just as it was at its fullest, a portrait of William III which hung opposite to the spot where the King's representative stood, fell heavily to the floor. "There goes the Revolution settlement," exclaimed a voice from the throng; and the words were received as if a prophet had spoken.

At the close of the levee the Lord Commissioner proceeded to St. Giles's Church in state. According to custom the retiring Moderator, Dr. Welsh, preached a sermon, alluding to things past and things to come which fell like warning notes on the ears of his audience. The members of the Assembly then proceeded to their Hall where the Evangelicals found themselves in a minority. When the Lord Commissioner entered Moderator and members rose to greet him with respect. After prayer, Dr. Welsh announced that he and those who agreed with him were unable to continue in that house. The close of his memorable document is: "We protest that in the circumstances in which we are placed it is and shall be lawful for us, and such other Commissioners chosen to the Assembly appointed to have been this day held, as may concur with us, to withdraw to a separate place of meeting, for the purpose of taking steps, along with all who adhere to us—maintaining with us the Confession of Faith and standards of the Church of Scotland—for separating in an orderly way from the Establishment, and thereupon adopting such measures as may be competent to us, in humble dependence on God's grace and the aid of the Holy Spirit, for the advancement of His glory, the extension of the Gospel of our Lord and Saviour, and the administration of the affairs of Christ's house according to His holy Word; and we now withdraw accordingly—humbly and solemnly acknowledging the hand of the Lord in the things which have come upon us because of our manifold sins and the sins of the Church and nation; but, at the same time, with assured conviction that we are not responsible for any consequences that may follow from this our enforced separation from an Establishment which we loved and prized, through interference with conscience, the dishonour done to Christ's crown, and the rejection of His sole and supreme authority as King in His Church." The Melvillean view had been worked out to its last result.

Then came one of the great dramatic moments in modern history. The Moderator bowed to the Commissioner and left the building, followed by Chalmers and the whole of the Evangelical party. Ministers and elders marched three abreast to the hall at Canon-mills prepared for the occasion. A new Assembly was constituted, with the claim that it, not the remnant remaining with the Commissioner, was the true successor of former Assemblies. Chalmers was elected Moderator, and he gave out that moving psalm:

> O send Thy light forth and Thy truth;
>   Let them be guides to me;
> And bring me to Thine holy hill,
>   Even where Thy dwellings be.

The chronicler relates how the day had been overcast by a heavy thundercloud, which made the interior of the badly lighted hall so dark as to render it almost impossible to distinguish the faces of those present. As the familiar psalm rolled up from a thousand voices, the sun shone through a rift in the cloud, and a ray of dazzling light filled the hall. Men saw in it a manifest token of divine favour. Yet there were spectators like Sir William Hamilton who spoke something about men who were martyrs by mistake.

Chalmers and Candlish had won, but there is always a price to be paid for victory. The Free Kirk had the same theological standards as the Established Church, though its conservatism was apparent in the assaults of Candlish on the heresies of Maurice, whom he opposed as much as Pusey did, and of McCleod Campbell, who warmly sympathised with Maurice. The collapse of the Establishment was daily expected, but this collapse never came. Under the leadership of such men as James Robertson the Established Church refrained from railing and controversy. This is all the more creditable to the Moderates, as in the chief cities and the Highlands the Evangelicals won a resounding victory. A third of the churches were vacant; the foreign missionaries and the undergraduates joined the Free Kirk. It fell to Robertson of Ellon, Story of Roseneath, and Norman MacLeod to regain the unity of the broken Church, and right well they performed their onerous task. A roll of members which includes John Caird, John Tulloch, Robert Lee and Robert Wallace is one which stands in the line of succession to Principal William Robertson the historian.

By the adoption of Knox's Confession in 1560, and of the Westminster Confession, the Church of Scotland had declared its power to legislate in doctrinal matters. The latter was regarded as "a subordinate standard," which contained the admission that "all synods and councils," and accordingly its authors, "may err, and many of them have erred; therefore they are not to be made the rule of faith or practice, but to be used as a help in both." The Barrier Act of 1697 assumed the right of the Church to make changes in doctrine by providing, in order to prevent "sudden innovations in either doctrine, worship, or discipline," that all "overtures" on these subjects should first be submitted to the consideration of the presbyteries of the Church; and only then, "if the general opinion" be found to approve of them, should be passed as Acts of the Church. These precedents were in the mind of the Free Kirk leaders. In 1866 the Moderator of the Free Church, Dr. Wilson, Dr. Fairbairn, a distinguished theologian, and Dr. Gibson, a conservative ecclesiastic, claimed freedom to revise, or even, as Dr. Wilson asserted, to abolish the Westminster Confession. There was liberty in the Established Church as well as the Free, and accordingly in 1874 patronage was abolished, and the members of the Established Church are free to elect their ministers. In 1879 she passed a declaratory Act, relaxing the rigidity of the Westminster Confession, and this measure was compulsory.

The Free Church was orthodox, and boasted of her orthodoxy, yet one of the prices paid for orthodoxy is rigidity. The crust of this rigidity was broken, remarkably enough, by the revival mission of Moody and Sankey, taken up by that strange personality, Henry Drummond. From 1876 to 1881 occurred the trials of Robertson Smith, the eminent biblical critic, who was almost as orthodox as Candlish himself in his theology. By her conduct to him the Free Kirk behaved with a supposed moderation that put her in a false and indeed ridiculous position in the opinion of all who counted. The Privy Council, to the wrath of the Tractarian, sometimes sheltered the heretic in England, but in Scotland—since 1843—he was at the mercy of the General Assembly of the Free Kirk; but no Evangelical except perhaps Dr. Carnegie Simpson, has been able to draw anything but cold comfort from this circumstance. Principal Rainy assumed the rôle for which he was admirably fitted, the rôle of the ecclesiastical statesman, in this prolonged trial of Robertson Smith, and the critic—not the heretic—was at last ejected. Yet he inflicted on his Kirk a grievous loss of prestige from which she still suffers. It is noticeable that the great Biblical scholar, A. B. Davidson, never employed his vast influence on behalf of another scholar who was fighting his battle for the freedom of investigation.

The influence of the Robertson Smith case is evident in the Declaratory Act of 1892, which certainly seems to explain away beliefs dear to the Fathers of the Disruption. This Act was "Declaratory" of the Westminster Confession, and belongs to the same class of legislation as the 1869 measure in England. In spite of the Westminster Confession, the 1892 Act emphasises "as standing in the forefront of the revelation of Grace, the love of God . . . to sinners of Mankind," and declares that "all who hear the Gospel are warranted to believe to the saving of their souls," and that, if any reject God's call, the sin is their own. Nor is the Confession to be regarded as "teaching the foreordination of men to death irrespective of their own sin." It does not teach that any who die in infancy are lost, or that God may not extend His mercy to those who are beyond the means of grace. On the question of the Establishment principle, the Act disclaims "intolerant and persecuting principles"; and more generally declares the Church "does not consider her office-bearers in subscribing the Confession of Faith committed to any principles inconsistent with liberty of conscience and the right of private judgment." At the same time "while diversity of opinion is recognised on such points in the Confession as do not enter the substance of the Reformed Faith therein set forth, the Church retains full authority to determine, in any case which may arise, what points fall within this description and thus to guard against any abuse of this liberty, to the detriment of sound doctrine, or to the injury of her unity and peace."

If words mean anything, this Act of 1892 modified—contradicted is perhaps too strong an expression—the doctrine of the Westminster Confession on predestination. The Free Kirk claimed in 1892 that she possessed power to determine what is and what is not "of the substance of the Reformed Faith." She implicitly asserted her continuity with the Church of 1843, and her members agreed with this assertion. True, a few of her members withdrew on this very point of change in doctrine, and formed "The Free Presbyterian Church of 1843." These appellants dissented from the Declaratory Act; but, as it did not involve questions of property, and as its provisions were made permissive, they remained within the Free Kirk.

Scotland was presented with the prospect of two great Churches agreed in doctrine, yet separated on the question of the Establishment principle. It is easy to understand that the question of reunion should be mooted almost from the very first after 1843. In 1896 the Free Kirk raised this question for union with the United Presbyterians or the Established Church; and, after three years of negotiations, a plan of union was prepared, and was adopted in 1900. The theological standards of the two Churches were the same. The 1879 Declaratory Act of the Established Church was compulsory, that of the Free Kirk permissive. Provision was therefore made in 1900 that "members of both Churches shall have full right to assert and maintain the views of truth and duty which they had liberty to maintain in the said Churches." Plainly, the members of the Free Kirk might hold their old views on the wrongfulness of the Establishment if they pleased.

Out of seventy-four presbyteries no less than seventy approved of the union of the two Churches, and it was passed as a uniting Act in the Assembly of May, 1900, by 593 to 29. This Assembly transmitted to the presbyteries the "overture" that the union now take place. Seventy-one presbyteries approved, and this was passed as an Act in the Assembly of October, 1900, by 643 to 27. The same Assembly decreed that the property held by the General Trustees should be conveyed to new trustees to be appointed by the United Free Church. The Free Kirk in 1900 consisted of over 1100 congregations. Her roll of communicants reached nearly 300,000; her Sunday Schools contained over 200,000 children; and practically she had a million people in her care at home. Abroad she had 200 missionaries, 1350 native agents, and nearly 12,000 communicants. A conservative estimate of her property placed it at four or five millions.

Thirty ministers with 4000 or 5000 communicants, who lived largely in the Highlands, appealed against this union. In 1901 Lord Low heard this appeal, and decreed in favour of the United Free Church. In 1902, the Lord Justice Clerk with Lords Trayner and Young confirmed the judgment of Lord Low. In 1903, the House of Lords, before six judges, and again in 1904, in consequence of Lord Shand's death, before seven judges heard the appeal of the "Wee Frees." The seven judges were the Lord Chancellor, Lord Loreburn, Lords Macnaghten, Davey, James of Hereford, Robertson, Lindley, and Alverstone. By five to two they reversed the decision of the Scots Courts, and gave the property to the Free Church minority.

Lord Low assumed in his decision that the 1697 Barrier Act implicitly bestowed the right of the General Assembly to decide non-essentials. As the Confession of Faith was capable of diverse interpretations, such a power was necessary to the Assembly. The Free Church had not defined the Establishment doctrine in her documents as essential or unalterable. Moreover, this doctrine was as capable of diverse interpretations as the Confession itself, and indeed some Free Kirk adherents had come to regard it as an open question. Accordingly, the union of the Free Kirk with the Established Church did not imply the surrender of her vital doctrines. The Lord Justice Clerk was prepared to decide the case on the sole ground that the existence at intervals of the Church of Scotland, even before 1843, in separation from the Establishment, and the experience of the Free Church of Voluntaryism after 1843, proved that the Establishment doctrine was "not vital to the existence of the Church." Besides, the Barrier Act of 1697 assumed the right of the Church to regard such a doctrine as an open question. Lord Young took the broad ground that there is no rule of law to prevent a dissenting Church from changing her creed. The only legal question which can arise about her property is whether this is held under a limited title—that is, whether it is expressly attached to specified doctrines. No such title appeared in this case. The property was vested in General Trustees who were appointed to hold it and use it as directed by the Assembly. In Lord Trayner's judgment the Free Church had by the Declaratory Act made no change in the essentials of the Confession. No doubt she had altered her attitude to the doctrine of the civil Establishment of religion, but this was not essential to her constitution, nor was it so defined in her documents. As for doctrine "it appears to me difficult to hold that a mere opinion as to what some third person was bound to do, which he might neglect or refuse to do, and which the Church could not compel him to do, could in any way be an essential part of the constitution of the Church." The practical voluntaryism of the Free Church had led her to treat the Establishment doctrine as "a dead letter." How could it be fundamental? From the first the Church, by the Barrier Act of 1697 and her

Deed of Demission of 1843, had powers to change her doctrines. Such were the judgments of Lord Low, the Lord Justice Clerk, Lord Young, and Lord Trayner respectively.

The four Scots judges were not prepared to define how far the powers of the Free Kirk extended. Lord Low held that the General Assembly could not repudiate either the Confession or Presbyterianism, apparently deeming that these were fundamental. Lord Trayner took the view that the Barrier Act covered Presbyterianism and the doctrine of the divinity of Christ. The main matter is that they recognised powers inherent in the constitution of the Church which enabled her to change her opinion on the Establishment. They also recognised that as the Confession and the Establishment doctrine were capable of different interpretations, it was natural and even necessary for the Assembly to possess powers of change. The four Scots judges agreed that the practical experience of the Free Kirk on the question of voluntaryism meant that she "naturally" modified her theories of Church and State.

In the House of Lords, Lord Macnaghten and Lord Lindley agreed with the four Scots judges in their view of the legislative powers of the Free Church, of the absence from her trust-deeds of specified titles, and of the "naturalness" of her modification of the Establishment doctrine. Lord Macnaghten complained that the Establishment doctrine had bulked too large in the argument, and defined the main question as that of the character of the Free Church as a whole. Had she come out in 1843 "with peculiar tenets cut and dried and defined in the precise language of a conveyancer," or had she come out with all the powers of a National Church? To him the "real and only question is" this, "Was the Free Church by the very condition of her existence, forced to cling to her Subordinate Standards with so desperate a grip that she has lost hold and touch of the Supreme Standards of her faith? Was she from birth incapable of all growth and development? Was she, in a word, a dead branch and not a living Church?" Such was the lofty issue which Lord Macnaghten placed before the House of Lords. In his view the Free Church gained, through her independence of the State, liberty to alter her formulae of subscription, for she was a living Church. No doubt the dislike of Establishment is to be found in her Confession, but her powers as a National Church covered also this. Had she not exhibited diversity of doctrine about it immediately after 1843? Dr. Candlish and other leaders had called it purely theoretical. As her voluntaryism grew the "natural tendency" was to think that the Church could exist not only without an Establishment but also without a profession of the Establishment principle. Acting upon the Confession of Faith, the Barrier Act, and the early documents of the Free Church, Lord Lindley came to the conclusion that she had powers—within limits, and only to be used bona fide—to alter or replace her Confession. These powers were in truth as fundamental to her constitution as any of the doctrines contained in the Confession. She had fulfilled her functions as a Church without State aid, and she had witnessed her failure to obtain this while repudiating State control. He pointed out that the Model Trust Deed affirmed the whole "power of the keys," which of course included control over doctrine, contemplated union with other bodies, and subjected the trustees to the direction of the General Assembly of the Free Church, or of any united body which she may enter.

It is obvious that Lord Macnaghten recognised that the Church was a corporation with powers of her own. In this respect he was quite consistent publicly and privately. For in the latter capacity he signed the Ulster Covenant. At the same time the five judges of the other way of thinking adopted the Austinian theory of sovereignty. The State could grow, and in the course of her growth she could issue commands which must be obeyed. She stood supreme, and all other bodies were subordinate to her.

In 1813, curiously enough in another Scots case, Craigdallie versus Aikman, Lord Eldon had laid down that if there was no provision for a schism in the title-deeds by which a congregation for religious worship held their property, the law would not execute the trust "at the expense of a forfeiture of their property by the cestui-que-trust, for adhering to the opinions and principles in which the congregation had originally united." In another case Lord Eldon had also laid down that it is not in the power of individuals who manage a religious institution at any time to alter the purposes for which it was founded. He decreed that "In such a case ... when a congregation become dissentient among themselves, the nature of the original institution must alone be looked to as the guide for the decision of the Court; and to refer to any other criterion, as to the sense of the existing majority, would be to make a new institution, which is altogether beyond the reach and inconsistent with the duties and character of this Court."

Taking their stand on the opinions of Lord Eldon, the five judges found in fact that the majority of the Free Church had abandoned tenets once professed by her as fundamental; that her documents nowhere conferred on them the power to do so; and that they had broken trust in conveying her property to another body. Out of the five only Lords Loreburn, Davey, and Robertson decided that the Declaratory Act was an illegitimate modification of the Confession of the Church. It is plain that the judgment of the House of Lords turned on the change in attitude of the Free Church to the question of Establishment. The five judges held that this was enough to disinherit her. The law of trusts binds a religious association in respect of its property by its principles of union. The question at issue was whether the United Free Church in altering certain ecclesiastical and doctrinal tenets had forfeited endowments, through the law of trusts, which had been given her while these tenets were held in their unchanged form. There is the historical argument and there is the philosophical one. The historical argument is, Has not a Scots Church, with her traditions behind her, the right to change her tenets within certain broad limits and to retain her endowments, unless the instruments creating such endowments contained specific words to the contrary? The philosophical argument is, Does not identity only exist through change and difference? On the one hand, Lord Loreburn held that "the identity of a religious community described as a Church must consist in the unity of its doctrines." On the other hand, Lord Macnaghten held that "I cannot form a conception of the National Church, untrammelled and unfettered by connexion with the State, which does not at least possess the powers of revising and amending the formula of subscription required of its own office-bearers, and the power of pronouncing authoritatively that some latitude of opinion is permissible to its members in regard to matters which, according to the common apprehension of mankind, are not matters of faith."

The judgment of the House of Lords naturally raised an outcry on the part of all who favoured the union of the Churches, and in deference to that outcry the State stultified itself by passing a measure giving back to the United Churches some of the property the Free Church formerly owned. In spite of the decision of the House of Lords the Established Church and the Free Church have always been at one, and inner unity was at last symbolised by outward. The truth is that though there have been differences in the present and in the past, Moderatism and Evangelicalism are children of one parent.

Consciously or unconsciously, Lord Macnaghten was influenced by the Melville two-Kingdom theory which won a great triumph in a measure which is surely unique in the history of British legislation. For in 1921 was passed "An Act to declare the lawfulness of certain Articles declaratory of the Constitution of the Church of Scotland in matters spiritual prepared with the authority of the General Assembly of the Church" or, in short, the Church of Scotland Act. These Articles declare the Church of Scotland to be a part of the Holy Catholic Church: it must be Trinitarian and Reformed. Though "This Church acknowledges the divine appointment and authority of the civil magistrate within his own sphere," yet the Church owns "the right and power subject to no civil authority to legislate, and to adjudicate finally, in all matters of doctrine, worship, government, and discipline in the Church," a provision that would have forced John Austin to gasp with absolute astonishment at such a two-Kingdom theory. In 1925 a measure transferred Churches and manses from the heritors to the General Assembly, but such a proceeding is in no wise comparable to the unique Act of 1921, whose implications are of the most far-reaching nature.

With the full sanction of Parliament, willingly given,

the Established Church has secured entire control over its faith and doctrine and over its finances, and the way is now opened for the Free Church to enter. Recent changes in Scots life and character have undoubtedly impressed upon religious leaders the growing necessity for bringing Christian forces together in a common effort for the welfare of the country. The rapid movement of the rural population to the industrial areas has created an over supply of Churches in some parts with a deficiency in others. The result has been the growth of a large class outside the influence of the Church. Once the most potent force in national life, the Church has been steadily losing ground. A United Church will be able to face these and similar problems with greater energy and confidence, and it will be then not only in name, but in fact a National Church. In the United Free Church there is still a small, but persistent minority; and it remains to be seen whether they will remain outside the United Church and form yet another of those small religious groups of which there have been so many in Scotland. While all respect is due to those who fight for principles against heavy odds and who for conscience' sake struggle on in a losing battle, the world is coming more and more to realise that the work of no Church can prosper through negations and bickerings and narrowness of view. The future power and efficacy of the Church must lie rather in an ever-expanding comprehensiveness and a wide and all embracing charity.

References

ABBOTT, E. A. *The Anglican Career of Cardinal Newman.* 2 vols. (London, 1892.)
BARRY, W. *Newman.* (London, 1904.)
BLENNERHASSET (C. J.) Lady. *John Henry Kardinal Newman.* (Berlin, 1904.)
BREMOND, H. *The Mystery of Newman.* (London, 1907.)
BRILIOTH, Y. *The Anglican Revival.* (London, 1925.) He gives a careful bibliography in App. 2, pp. 334–42.
BROWNE, E. G. K. *Tractarian Movement, 1842–60.* (London, 1868.)
BRYCE, J. *Ten Years of the Church of Scotland.* (Edinburgh, 1850.)
BUCHANAN, R. *Ten Years' Conflict.* (Glasgow, 1849.)

REFERENCES

CAMBRIDGE HISTORY OF ENGLISH LITERATURE. Vol. 12. (Cambridge, 1915.) Canon Ollard gives an exhaustive bibliography on pp. 453-63.
CECIL, A. *Six Oxford Thinkers*. (London, 1909.)
CHARTERIS, A. H. *A Faithful Churchman: Memoir of John Robertson*. (London, 1897.)
CHURCH, R. W. *The Oxford Movement*. (London, 1892.)
COLERIDGE, Sir J. T. *Memoir of the Rev. John Keble*. (London, 1869.)
CRAIK, Sir H. *A Century of Scottish History*. (Edinburgh, 1901.)
DIMNET, E. *La Pensée Catholique dans l'Angleterre Contemporaine*. (Paris, 1906.)
FAURE, L. F. *Newman, sa vie et ses oeuvres*. (Paris, 1901.)
FIGGIS, J. N. *Churches in the Modern State*. (London, 1913.)
GLADSTONE, W. E. *The State in its Relations with the Church*. (London, 1838.)
GLADSTONE, W. E. *Gleanings*. Vols. V and VI. (London, 1879.)
HANNA, W. *Memoirs of Thomas Chalmers*. (Edinburgh, 1878.)
HATSCHEK, J. *Englisches Staatsrecht*. Vol I (on the 1905 Scots Judgment). (Tübingen, 1905.)
HUTTON, A. W. *Cardinal Manning*. (London, 1884.)
HUTTON, R. H. *Cardinal Newman*. (London, 1891.)
LASKI, H. J. *The Problem of Sovereignty*. (Yale, 1917.)
LATHBURY, D. C. *Mr. Gladstone*. (London, 1910.)
LATHBURY, D. C., Ed. *The Correspondence of William Ewart Gladstone*. (London, 1910.)
LIDDON, H. P., JOHNSTON, J. O., WILSON, R. J. *The Life of Edward Bouverie Pusey*. (London, 1893 ff.)
MACPHERSON, H. *Scotland's Battles for Spiritual Independence*. (Edinburgh, 1905.)
MALLET, Sir C. E. *History of the University of Oxford*. Vol. III. (London, 1927.)
MATHIESON, W. L. *English Church Reform, 1815–1840*. (London, 1923.)
MORLEY, Lord. *The Life of William Ewart Gladstone*. (London, 1903.)
MOZLEY, A. *Letters and Correspondence of John Henry Newman during his Life in the English Church*. (London, 1891.)
NEWMAN, F. W. *The Early History of Cardinal Newman*. (London, 1891.)
NEWMAN, J. H. *Apologia pro Vita sua*. (London, 1890.)
PURCELL, E. S. *Life of Cardinal Manning*. (London, 1895.)
RIGG, J. H. *Oxford High Anglicanism*. (London, 1895.)
THUREAU-DANGIN, P. *La Renaissance Catholique en Angleterre*. (Paris, 1905–06.)
THUREAU-DANGIN, P. *Newman Catholique d'après des documents nouveaux*. (Paris, 1912.)

WARD, W. *Wilfrid George Ward and the Oxford Movement.* (London, 1889.)
WARD, W. *Wilfrid George Ward and the Catholic Revival.* (London, 1893.)
WARD, W. *The Life of John Henry Cardinal Newman.* (London, 1913.)
WEBB, C. C. J. *Religious Thought in the Oxford Movement.* (London, 1928.)
WHITE, N. J. D. *John Henry Newman.* (London, 1925.)
WILSON, W. *Memorial of Robert Smith Candlish.* (Edinburgh, 1880.)

Chapter VIII.

CARLYLE THE ROMANTIC RADICAL

ROMANTICISM affects all sorts and conditions of men, and affects them in widely different fashions. It affects Coleridge in one way, Newman in another, and Carlyle in yet another. It appears in Byron as it appears in Carlyle. Both were poets, though Carlyle was a prose poet. Both were self-centred to an unusual degree. Carlyle felt the immeasurable longing for happiness which Byron felt; and, like Byron, he rejoiced in the beauty and delight of external things. Both attacked the individualism of the ages in which they lived, protesting against its disappearance. Byron, like Carlyle, denounced the restraints of the time, notably the social restraints which the Scotsman also found irksome. The hot heart, the big brain, and the store of winged words they lavished on the shams of the day are common to both. A pessimistic vein ran in each, and in relief of this pessimism, in the true Romantic spirit, each sought relief in the past. The present was detestable, and was becoming more so: the past could be gilded by the rays of their genius. Both implicitly believed that unless our literature were crossed by another of different breed, it would tend to sterility. Goethe counted for much in their outlook on the world of thought. Of set purpose they cultivated an intercourse with the literature of Europe, and are as much European forces as English or Scots.

Thomas Carlyle (1795–1881) was born at Ecclefechan in Annandale. His father James was a Scots Adam Bede, and set so lofty a standard of workmanship that his son judged—and for the most part condemned—other workmen by their attainment or non-attainment of it. James was a stern Scots Calvinist, and if he bequeathed to his son little worldly gear he undoubtedly bequeathed to him that Calvinism which so deeply coloured his thought. To Calvin the first idea in his theology was the greatness of God. The innumerable and inexplicable things of life are simply the whirling wheel on which the clay is changed and shaped till the potter's design is finally accomplished. Eastern nations realise the sovereignty of God: Western nations do not. In this respect the Carlyles were markedly Eastern in their mental affinities. To them the independence and the restlessness of the Westerner were utterly abhorrent. God is great, and it is not in our power to resist His decrees. God knows all, and, in spite of the saying of Alfonso of Castile, it is not in our capacity to criticise. We are His creatures, and are at His disposal. Has He sent good? Blessed be God. Has He sent evil? Still, Blessed be God. We are the clay and He is the potter.

Belief in the sovereignty of God creates a majestic view of God, and this lies at the root of reverent religion. It also lies at the root of the making of strong men. There was only one thing the Calvinist feared, and that was sin. The Calvinist feared God with all his soul, and this exhausted his capacity for fear. The face of man he did not fear. What was man, even though he be a king, compared with the King of Kings? Everything is *sub specie aeternitatis*. Nor does the power of God mean the powerlessness of man. If Luther could say, "*Credo, ergo sum,*" Calvin could say, "*Ago, ergo credo.*" The belief in predestination formed the school of vigorous political and ecclesiastical life. God is active and energetic, and therefore His servant, man, must also be active and energetic. Order and obedience, gravity and chastity, temperance in life and sobriety in thought are qualities every whit as valuable for the State as for the Church. Economy and industry lead on to property, and this in turn leads on to prosperity in the State as much as in the Church. The sovereignty of God might seem at first sight as if it would lean to absolutism in politics, whereas it does nothing of the kind. The fear of God takes away the fear of man. As no power comes from man, and as all power comes from God, all in His sight, king and subject alike, are equal. There is a halo around the heavenly King: there is none around the earthly king. The Calvinist ecclesiastical system acknowledges no head with right divine. There are simply representatives chosen by the people. The ecclesiastical republic in time leads on to a political republic. For when men have learned in ecclesiastical affairs to govern themselves through their elected representatives, the stage to representative government in the State is but a short one. James I was never more right than when he uttered the words, "No bishop, no king."

In the atmosphere of Calvinism Thomas Carlyle grew up, and it left a lasting impression on his mode of thought even when he seemed to depart from it most widely. For repulsion as well as attraction modifies a man's thought. To his mother Janet he was always passionately devoted, and she mitigated the sternness of the creed in which he was brought up. His father belonged to the strict sect of the Burghers, and his son furnishes us with a description which conveys the permanent impress left on him: "Very venerable are those old Seceder clergy to me now when I look back. ... Most figures of them in my time were hoary old men; men so like evangelists in modern vesture and poor scholars and gentlemen of Christ I have nowhere met with among Protestant or Papal clergy in any country in the world. ... Strangely vivid are some twelve or twenty of those old faces whom I used to see every Sunday, whose names, employments or precise dwelling-places I never knew, but whose portraits are yet clear to me as in a mirror. Their heavy-laden, patient, ever-attentive faces, fallen solitary most of them, children all away, wife away for ever, or, it might be, wife still there and constant like a shadow and grown very like the old man, the thrifty cleanly poverty of these good people, their well-saved coarse old clothes, tailed waistcoats down to mid-thigh—all this I occasionally see as with eyes sixty or sixty-five years off, and hear the very voice of my mother upon it, whom sometimes I would be questioning about these persons of the drama and endeavouring to describe and identify them." What the sovereignty of God meant to them is apparent in the story Carlyle told of old David Hope, the farmer who refused to postpone family worship in order to save his grain during a storm. David was putting on his spectacles when a man rushed in with the words, "Such a raging wind risen will drive the stooks into the sea if let alone." "Wind!" answered David, "wind canna get ae straw that has been appointed mine. Sit down and let us worship God."

James Carlyle influenced his son, but Janet even more. She taught him reading, and at five his father taught him arithmetic. As the village schoolmaster was incompetent, Johnstone, the Burgher minister, taught the lad with his son, an Edinburgh undergraduate. In 1805 Carlyle attended Annan grammar school. As his temper was violent, his mother made him promise not to return a blow. The result was that he suffered much cruelty till he turned against a bully. *Sartor Resartus* reflects the wretchedness of his school days, and he counted the two years he spent there among the most miserable of his life. As his abilities were already manifest, his father determined to send him to Edinburgh University with a view to the ministry. His passion for books was most decided, and he devoured all he could by any means secure. He walked the hundred miles to Edinburgh in November, 1809, and went through the usual course. He acquired some Greek and Latin, and was as pleased with Leslie in mathematics as he was displeased with Brown and the association philosophy. If history does not repeat itself, biography does. Carlyle was as little satisfied with his university as Milton and Locke, Gibbon and Adam Smith were with theirs. Teufelsdröckh announces that "the university where I was educated still stands vivid enough in my remembrance, and I know its name well, which name, however, I from tenderness to existing interests shall in no wise divulge. It is my painful duty to say that out of England and Spain ours was the worst of all hitherto discovered universities." This may account for the view he set down in his *Lectures on Heroes* that "the true university of our days is a collection of books," a position that ignores the personality of a great professor. His Rectorial address of 1866 represented a more balanced view. "What I found the university did for me is that it taught me to read in various languages, in various sciences, so that I go into the books which treated of these things, and gradually penetrate into any department I wanted to make myself master of, as I found it suit me."

"Everyone has two educations: one which he receives from others, and one, the more important, which he gives himself." So taught Gibbon, and so believed Carlyle. Yet Carlyle as little escaped from the compelling influences, the wonderful charm of Edinburgh University as Gibbon from those of Oxford University. All unconsciously, he was absorbing that spirit of the past which he was to impart to his generation. His desire to enter the ministry was waning, for he was convinced that "no church or speaking entity whatever can do without formulas, but it must *believe* them first if it would be honest." The difficulty with him—and it was a grave one—was to reconcile advancing knowledge with the retreating theology of the Burghers. Robertson's preliminary dissertation to his Charles V delighted and amazed him, opening "new worlds of knowledge, vistas in all directions." Gibbon's history was "of all the books the most impressive on me in my then stage of investigation and state of mind. His winged sarcasms, so quiet and yet so conclusively transpiercing and killing dead, were often admirable, potent, and illustrative to me." He met Chalmers, who explained to him "some new scheme for proving the truth of Christianity," "all written in us already *in sympathetic ink* ; Bible awakens it, and you can read." In 1847 he was to have a flying visit from Jeffrey, the sometime editor of the *Edinburgh Review*. Carlyle says: "A much more interesting visitor than Jeffrey was old Dr. Chalmers, who came down to us also last week, whom I had not seen before for, I think, five-and-twenty years. It was a pathetic meeting. The old man is grown white-headed, but is otherwise wonderfully little altered—grave, deliberate, very gentle in his deportment, but with plenty, too, of soft energy; full of interest still for all serious things, full of real kindliness, and sensible even to honest mirth in a fair measure. He sate with us an hour and a half, went away with our blessings and affections. It is long since I have spoken to so *good* and really pious-hearted and beautiful old man." In a week or two Chalmers was suddenly called away. "I believe," wrote Carlyle to his mother, "there is not in all Scotland, or all Europe, any such Christian priest left. It will long be memorable to us, the little visit we had from him."

The Decline and Fall of the Roman Empire sapped the faith of Carlyle. If it unsettled his opinions in one direction, it settled them in another, for it convinced the romanticist that history is a great subject, demanding all one's powers. In 1814 he was mathematical tutor at Annan. With characteristic Scots thrift he saved from his salary of £60 or £70 a year. The next year he met Edward Irving who directly and indirectly left a marked impression on him. In 1835 he uttered his lament over him: "Edward Irving's warfare has been closed; if not in victory, yet in invincibility, and faithful endurance to the end. . . . The voice of our 'son of thunder,' with its deep tone of wisdom, has gone silent so soon. . . . The large heart, with its large bounty, where wretchedness found solacement, and they that were wandering in darkness, the light as of a home, has paused. The strong man can no more: beaten on from without, undermined from within, he must sink overwearied, as at nightfall, when it was yet but the midseason of the day. Scotland sent him forth a Herculean man; our mad Babylon wore him, and wasted him, with all her engines; and it took him twelve years. He sleeps with his fathers, in that loved birth-land: Babylon with its deafening inanity rages on; to him henceforth innocuous, unheeded—for ever."

"One who knew him well, and may with good cause love him, has said: 'But for Irving, I had never known what the communion of man with man means. His was the freest, brotherliest, bravest human soul mine ever came in contact with: I call him, on the whole, the best man I have ever (after trial enough) found in this world, or now hope to find.'" Obviously, Carlyle is speaking of himself: he is the one who knew Irving well. Carlyle continues: "The first time I saw Irving was six and twenty years ago, in his native town, Annan. He was fresh from Edinburgh, with college prizes, high character, and promise. . . . We heard of famed professors of high matters classical, mathematical, a whole Wonderland of knowledge: nothing but joy, health, hopefulness without end, looked out from the blooming young man.

"The last time I saw him was three months ago, in London. Friendliness still beamed from his eyes, but now from amid unquiet fire; his face was flaccid, wasted, unsound; hoary as with extreme age: he was trembling on the brink of the grave. Adieu, thou first Friend; adieu, while this confused twilight of existence lasts! Might we meet where Twilight has become Day!"

Irving entered the life of Carlyle when he was only nineteen, a critical period. They walked and they talked together; they toured together in holidays through the Highlands; and they became inseparable mental comrades. Carlyle read Irving's books, and in his *Recollections* Carlyle confesses that he owed them "something of his poor affectations" in style. Irving "received me with open arms, and was a brother to me and a friend there and elsewhere afterwards—such friend as I never had again or before in this world, at heart constant till he died."

Teaching mathematics was singularly distasteful to Carlyle, and he came to hate schoolmastering. He had not a friend save Irving. He saw little society, but was attracted by Margaret Gordon, an ex-pupil of Irving's, probably the original of "Blumine" in *Sartor Resartus*. An aunt with whom Miss Gordon lived checked the intimacy with Carlyle who resolved to return to Edinburgh. In September, 1818, he told his father that he had saved £90, and with this and a few mathematical pupils he could support himself in Edinburgh till he could qualify for the bar. In December, 1819, with his lifelong friend Irving, he set out for the city of his old university. He also set out with his lifelong enemy, dyspepsia. In these years it assumed its most torturing form, like "a rat gnawing at the pit of his stomach." The irritability of Carlyle is deplorable, yet we must allow for his acute sufferings. His mother had described him as "gey ill to deal wi'," and dyspepsia rendered him intolerably irritable. Coleridge and De Quincey had taken to opium but Carlyle resorted to tobacco, which he was informed was the occasion of the whole mischief. "Gave it up, and found I might as well have poured my sorrows into the long hairy ear of the first jackass I came upon as of this select medical man." He endured incessant agony aggravated to desperation by the wretchedness he was already undergoing from "eating of the heart, misgivings as to whether there shall be presently anything else to eat, disappointment of the nearest and dearest as to the hoped-for entrance on the ministry, and steadily growing disappointment of self—above all, wanderings through mazes of doubt, perpetual questionings unanswered."

Carlyle's was a troubled mind. He saw things through the medium of his own dark vision and not as they were. He was utterly destitute of self-control and guidance, and expressed himself with a degree of violence, bordering on ferocity in speaking or writing of the outer world, of the order and progress of society, and even of those who had befriended him. In fact, his own language does him considerable injustice, for he was a man of kindlier feelings and wider sympathies than he would allow the world to believe. He might have risen to a higher and nobler standard if he could have shaken off the incurable habit of referring all things to himself. Nothing did he reprobate more than self-consciousness; yet he was the most self-conscious of men. Rarely could he write five pages without reference to himself. "Sauerteig," "Teufelsdröckh," "Gathercoal," "Crabbe," "Smelfungus," these, and many more, were all so many aliases of Thomas Carlyle. The reader could well dispense with some of these masquerading shapes, whose varying garbs ever give vent to one well-known hollow yet bitter voice, a compound of Heraclitus and Democritus, the weeping and the mocking philosopher in one.

The conflict of the old faith and the new knowledge gave rise to the crisis described "quite literally" in *Sartor Resartus*. After much mental agony, he one day in June 1821, after "three weeks of total sleeplessness," came to his "spiritual new birth," though he suffered keen labour-pangs for four years more. He was reading German, and Goethe gave him comfort. Carlyle quotes Père Bonhours's pregnant question: "*Si un Allemand peut avoir de l'esprit?*" and records his negative answer. Our sage's answer was emphatically a positive one.

In the moonlight of memory the shadows of one's youth are apt to take fantastic shapes, and truth, as Goethe in his old age proved, to become confused in it with poetry. Nevertheless it is clear that as the apostle of German literature, Carlyle mostly won such meed of recognition as he received in those days. This praise has been denied him. Madame de Stael, it is said, foreran him, and Coleridge, and Scott. But Madame de Stael's *Allemagne,* so highly praised by Richter, and acknowledged by Carlyle as the precursor of his own endeavours, cannot take from the Scots translator of *Wilhelm Meister* in 1824 the honour of spreading and strengthening that acquaintance. We think of Pusey in 1825, more intent upon sitting at the feet of Eichhorn than upon making a pilgrimage to Weimar. We open the correspondence of Carlyle and Pusey; and we feel with Swedenborg how many are the circles in our human world that do not intersect. Carlyle's life of Schiller appeared in 1825 and his literary impulses are evident in his translations of German romance which appeared in 1827. Neither Coleridge's magnificent version of *Wallenstein,* nor Scott's version of *Götz von Berlichingen* appealed widely to the English public. Hayward's translation of *Faust*—the best, Matthew Arnold has called it, in our language, "because the most straightforward"—and Mrs. Austin's *Goethe and his Contemporaries,* were not published till most of Carlyle's German work had been done. He had taken the field for three years before Taylor brought out his *Historic Survey of German Poetry.* Before he sounded his first note, the general English mind had mostly drawn its ideas on German literature from the witty parody in the *Anti-Jacobin,* a desperately bad translation of *Werther,* and the fustian of such writers as Mrs. Radcliffe, and "Monk" Lewis were accepted as true disciples of this new school of "Sturm und Drang."

This new school had not been much corrected in its ideas by the "old-established British critics," as Carlyle, with more than usual justice in his scorn, called the reviewers of the day. To read that Germany was "a vast tract of country, overrun with hussars and classical editors," where the adventurous traveller might see "a great tun at Heidelberg," and "be regaled with excellent old hock and Westphalia hams," did not suggest a likely nursing ground for the Romantic Movement. These mists of ignorance and prejudice Carlyle unquestionably did much to clear away, though the manner of his cloud-compelling was not always the wisest. Not all the people whom the apostle drew to him approved of the preaching. To some even of his first and staunchest followers it seemed that he praised these "nobles of German literature," even Goethe and Schiller, too highly; to Irving it seemed so, to Sterling and to Emerson, though the latter changed his tone after a while. And in truth he did not always praise them wisely. Goethe's prose, for instance, is "to be reckoned the most excellent that our modern world in any language can exhibit"; the second part of *Faust* is as good as the first; in "Helena" we are bidden to find a "Grecian spirit," a "classic dignity," in "the Tale" (*Das Mährchen*) a performance "in such a style of grandeur and celestial brilliancy and life, as the Western imagination has not elsewhere reached"—a judgment which, for sheer wrongheadedness, perhaps only Swinburne of modern critics has matched by praising Victor Hugo's *L'Homme qui rit* for the fulness of its "divine and passionate love."

Many gifts were bestowed upon Carlyle, but the critical faculty was not among them. He liked and disliked, fiercely always, often finely, but he never judged, and could not. For art as art he had the supremest scorn, as he had for all things he did not understand. When he read a book, its literary qualities mattered nothing to him; it was the man, not the work, he looked at, and if he could not find him, he fashioned himself a likeness, fair or foul, according as his own humour jumped with what he found, or fancied he had found, in the book. And when the image he had fashioned pleased him, he accepted the reality without reservation of any kind whatsoever. In nearly all his critical essays, he is really judging the man, and not his works, and often from a purely arbitrary point of view. The result is often striking and suggestive, but it is not always, nor even often, convincing.

In order to understand Carlyle's attitude to men, we must see how he understood man. Macaulay is supposed to be more sober-minded than our Scots author, yet a contrast of the attitude to Boswell leaves us wondering. Here are a few of Macaulay's sentences: "Servile and impertinent, shallow and pedantic, a bigot, and a sot, bloated with family pride, and eternally blustering about the dignity of a born gentleman, yet stooping to be a talebearer, an eavesdropper, a common butt in the taverns of London; . . . such was this man, and such he was content and proud to be. Everything which another man would have hidden, everything the publication of which would have made another man hang himself, was a matter of gay and clamorous exaltation to his weak and diseased mind. That such a man should have written one of the best books in the world is strange enough. But this is not all. Many persons who have conducted themselves foolishly in active life, and whose conversation has indicated no superior powers of mind, have left us valuable works. But these men attained literary eminence in spite of their weaknesses. Boswell attained it by reason of his weaknesses. If he had not been a great fool, he would never have been a great writer. Without all the qualities which made him the jest and the torment of those among whom he lived, without the officiousness, the inquisitiveness, the effrontery, the toad-eating, the insensibility to all reproof, he never could have produced so excellent a book. He has printed many of his own letters, and in these letters he is always ranting or twaddling. Logic, eloquence, wit, taste, all those things which are generally considered as making a book valuable were utterly wanting in him. He has, indeed, a quick observation and a retentive memory. These qualities, if he had been a man of sense and virtue, would scarcely of themselves have sufficed to make him conspicuous; but because he was a dunce, a parasite and a coxcomb, they have made him immortal."

From the paradox of Macaulay we turn to the perspicacity

of Carlyle: "Boswell was a person whose mean or bad qualities lay open to the general eye; visible, palpable to the dullest. His good qualities, again, belonged not to the time he lived in; were far from common then; indeed in such a degree were almost unexampled; not recognisable therefore by everyone; nay, apt even (so strange had they grown) to be confounded with the very vices they lay contiguous to, and had sprung out of. That he was a winebibber and gross liver; gluttonously fond of whatever would yield him a little solacement, were it only of a stomachic character, is undeniable enough. That he was vain, heedless, a babbler; had much of the sycophant, alternating with the braggadocio, curiously spiced with an all-pervading dash of the coxcomb; that he gloried much when the tailor, by a court-suit, had made a new man of him; that he appeared at the Shakespeare Jubilee with a ribbon, imprinted 'Corsica Boswell,' round his hat; and in short, if you will, lived no day of his life without saying and doing more than one portentous ineptitude; all this unhappily is evident as the sun at noon. . . . Unfortunately, on the other hand, what great and genuine good lay in him was nowise so self-evident. The man, once for all, had an 'open sense,' an open loving heart, which so few have: where excellence existed, he was compelled to acknowledge it; was drawn towards it, and could not but walk with it,— if not as superior, if not as equal, then as inferior and lackey, better so than not at all. It has been commonly said, the man's vulgar vanity was all that attached him to Johnson; he delighted to be seen near him, to be thought connected with him. Now let it be at once granted that no consideration springing out of vulgar vanity could well be absent from the mind of James Boswell, in this his intercourse with Johnson, or in any considerable transaction of his life. At the same time ask yourself: Whether such vanity, and nothing else, actuated him therein. . . . The man was, by nature and habit, vain; a sycophant-coxcomb, be it granted: but had there been nothing more than vanity in him, was Samuel Johnson the man of men to whom he must attach himself? At that date Johnson was a poor rusty-coated scholar, dwelling in Temple Lane, and indeed throughout their whole intercourse afterwards were there not chancellors and prime ministers enough; graceful gentlemen, the glass of fashion; honour-giving noblemen; dinner-giving rich men; any of whom bulked much larger in the world's eye than Johnson ever did? To any one of whom, by half that submissiveness and assiduity, our Bozzy might have recommended himself."

Browning justly thought "The little more, and how much it is," and this little more is evident in Carlyle's discriminating survey. The weaknesses of the immortal biographer are laid bare, and so is the strength. He liked the man, and he proceeded to like his work. He always insisted on seeing a portrait, if he possibly could, of any one whose character he was describing. His own soul was solitary, and on this account he could sympathise with another solitary soul like Dante. "To me it is a most touching face; perhaps of all faces that I know, the most so. Blank there, painted on vacancy, with the simple laurel wound round it; the deathless sorrow and pain, the known victory which is also deathless; significant of the whole history of Dante! I think it is the mournfullest face that ever was painted from reality; an altogether tragic, heart-affecting face. There is in it, as foundation of it, the softness, tenderness, gentle affection as of a child; but all this is as if congealed into sharp contradiction, into abnegation, isolation, proud hopeless pain. A soft ethereal soul looking out so stern, implacable, grim-trenchant, as from imprisonment of thick-ribbed ice! Withal it is a silent pain too, a silent scornful one: the lip is curled in a kind of godlike disdain of the thing that is eating out his heart,—as if it were withal a mean insignificant thing, as if he whom it had power to torture and strangle were greater than it. The face of one wholly in protest, and life-long unsurrendering battle, against the world, affection all converted into indignation: an implacable indignation; slow, equable, implacable, silent, like that of a god! The eye too, it looks as in a kind of surprise, a kind of inquiry, Why the world was of such a sort? This is Dante: so he looks, this 'voice of ten silent centuries,' and sings us 'his mystic unfathomable song'."

Carlyle's liking and sympathy are evident in his sketches of Boswell and Dante: his dislike and lack of sympathy are no less evident in his sketch of Coleridge. "His express contributions to poetry, philosophy, or any specific province or enlightenment, had been small and sadly intermittent; but he had, especially among young inquiring men, a higher than literary, a kind of prophetic or magician character. He was thought to hold, he alone in England, the key of German and other transcendentalisms; knew the sublime secret of believing by 'the reason' what 'the understanding' had been obliged to fling out as incredible; and could still, after Hume and Voltaire had done their best and worst with him, profess himself an orthodox Christian, and say and print to the Church of England, with its singular old rubrics and surplices at Allhallowtide, *Esto perpetua*. A sublime man; who, alone in those dark days had saved his crown of spiritual manhood; escaping from the black materialisms, and revolutionary deluges, with 'God, Freedom, Immortality' still his: a king of men. The practical intellects of the world did not much heed him, or carelessly reckoned him a metaphysical dreamer: but to the rising spirits of the young generation he had this dusky sublime character; and sat there as a kind of Magus, girt in mystery and enigma; his Dodona oak-grove . . . whispering strange things, uncertain whether oracles or jargon."

It would be perfectly possible from Carlyle's sketch to draw a parallel between Coleridge and himself. For "the constant gist of his discourse was lamentation over the sunk condition of the world; which he recognised to be given up to Atheism and Materialism, full of mere sordid misbeliefs, mispursuits and misresults. All Science had become mechanical; the science not of men, but of a kind of human beavers. Churches themselves had died away into a godless mechanical condition; and stood there as mere Cases of Articles, mere Forms of Churches; like the dried carcases of once swift camels, which you find left withering in the thirst of the universal desert,—ghastly portents for the present, beneficent ships of the desert no more. Men's souls were blinded, hebetated; sunk under the influence of Atheism and Materialism, and Hume and

Voltaire: the world for the present was an extinct world, deserted of God, and incapable of welldoing till it changed its heart and spirit. This, expressed I think with less indignation and with more of long-drawn querulousness, was always recognisable as the ground-tone."

Our Romantic radical was an unrivalled interpreter for a character or an epoch for which he felt sympathy: he was an unrivalled misinterpreter for a character or an epoch for which he felt none. Where his sympathy failed, his insight also failed. Not a few of the poets, he thought, were too concerned with "vocables." Byron, in spite of his likeness to him or perhaps on account of this likeness, was a noisy egotist. Keats "gets ever more horrible to me." To the Romantic School he is less than fair, yet he is a Romanticist to the core.

What are we to say of his verdict on the Father of Romanticism? "It is a damnable heresy in criticism to maintain either expressly or implicitly that the ultimate object of poetry is sensation. That of cookery is such, but not that of poetry. Sir Walter Scott is the great intellectual *restaurauteur* of Europe. He might have been numbered with the Conscript Fathers. He has chosen the worser part, and is only a huge Publicanus. What are his novels—any of them? A bout of champagne, claret, port, or even ale drinking. Are we wiser, better, holier, stronger? No. We have been amused." As the novelist was dying, we learn "Walter Scott left town yesterday on his way to Naples. He is to proceed to Plymouth in a frigate, which the Government have given him a place in. Much run after here, it seems; but he is old and sick, and cannot enjoy it; has had two shocks of palsy, and seems altogether in a precarious way. To me he is and has been, an object of very minor interest for many, many years. The novelwright of his time, its favourite child, and *therefore* an almost worthless one. Yet is there something in his deep recognition of the worth of the past, perhaps better than anything he has *expressed* about it, into which I do not yet fully see? Have never spoken with him (though I might sometimes without great effort), and now probably never shall."

The narrowness that we find in these early estimates of

authors is a tendency to disparage, not all successful men, but those whose success was based on qualities perfectly intelligible to the crowd, and who, therefore, had not to undergo the apparent failure Carlyle himself had to undergo down to the publication of his *French Revolution* in 1837. This is most apparent in the case of Scott. Scott, says Carlyle, had no inward struggles—no fervent aspirations after the highest good; and he contrasts him not favourably with the Hindoo Ram-dass, who "had lately set up for godhead," and who said he "had fire in his belly to consume the sins of the world." "Ram-dass," says Carlyle, with wit, "had a spice of sense in him." But Scott was by no means without that "spice of sense" as well; Scott knew perfectly that to reform the world was a much-needed, but he also knew that it was a most difficult, task. He knew that to reform the world you must not take the rest of the world to be fools and yourself the only wise man; on the contrary, as Carlyle himself has said, the best way of reforming the world was to be continually reforming yourself. There is, as Ruskin has shown, an undercurrent of sorrow and self-introspection in Scott's writings which it is touching to trace.

To our seer Lamb was a despicable sot. To Macaulay's *History* even "four hundred editions could not add any value, there being no depth of sense in it at all, and a very great quantity of rhetorical wind." George Eliot's *Adam Bede* he pronounced "simply dull." Newman had "not the intellect of a rabbit," and Keble was "some little ape." Mazzini fretted Carlyle by "incoherent Jacobinism, George Sandism, and other Rousseau fanaticisms." If the Italian prophet of the present did not please him, neither did the statesmen of the past. Pitt, his anticipator in Imperialism, was insignificant. For Castlereagh he bestows the customary sneer. Disraeli was a cynical charlatan.

For some of these harsh verdicts there is no defence really possible. We may say that their author suffered from dyspepsia of the body, and that is part of the truth. He also suffered from dyspepsia of mind, and that is another part of the truth. It would of course be quite easy to collect judgments from Hobbes and Byron as perverse as any of Carlyle's. Hobbes thought that Sir John Davenant's *Gondibert*, which few of us have read, "would last as long as the *Aeneid* or the *Iliad*." Byron thought Samuel Rogers a good poet, and he also thought Hayley's *Triumphs of Temper* an enduring work. Carlyle was no more infallible than either of these critics. Men will remember, we believe, Carlyle's appreciation of Dante and Shakespeare, of Diderot and Voltaire, of Johnson and Boswell, of Goethe and Burns when his depreciations of others have long been forgotten. On his German masters, Richter and Novalis as well as Goethe, he has written with penetrating insight.

The narrowness of the range of the impressions of the Romantic radical must not be forgotten. Music he disliked, painting he ignored save the portraits of the people he was describing. Fascinated by the grand figure of Michael Angelo, he announced his intention of writing his life. It was suggested to him that some preliminary knowledge of art might be requisite. "Pooh!" was his reply, "what can that signify?" His contempt of art was singularly characteristic of the intolerant spirit he displayed towards all things of which he had neither knowledge nor feeling. When John Sterling was at Rome, his letters were full of enthusiastic artistic admiration of all that he saw there. Carlyle treated this sentiment of his friend with immeasurable scorn. "It is expected in this nineteenth century that a man of culture shall understand and worship art. Among the windy Gospels addressed to our poor century there are few louder than this of art. . . . Certainly of all subjects this was the one I cared least to hear ever greater talk of; indeed it is a subject on which earnest men, abhorrent of hypocrisy and speech that has no meaning, are admonished to silence in this sad time."

An ex-mathematician might have been expected to speak respectfully of the claims of science, then advancing by leaps and bounds. Sir Humphry Davy and Edward Jenner, Michael Faraday and Sir Charles Lyell, were men of mark. Darwin was beginning that long list of discoveries which was to make him the uncrowned king of nineteenth century science. There was no lack of men of genius. There are, however, vacant niches in the Pantheon Carlyle was to create. He has no place for the Hero as Man of Science or Artist. Darwin was described as "evolving man's soul from frog spawn," adding, "I have no patience with these gorilla damnifications of humanity." His comment on the *Origin of Species* was: "Wondered to me, as indicating the capricious stupidity of mankind, never could read a page of it, or waste the least thought upon it." He attended Tyndall's lecture on Faraday's genius and merits, which Tyndall, to the disgust of one of his hearers, treated as quite heroic. "A full and somewhat distinguished audience, respectful, noiseless, attentive, but not fully sympathetic, I should say; such, at least, was my own case, feeling rather that the eulogy was perhaps overdone. As to myself, 'the grandeur of Faraday's discoveries,' etc., excited in me no real enthusiasm, nor was either his faculty or his history a matter I could reckon heroic in that high degree. In sad fact, I cared but little for these discoveries—reckoned them uncertain—to my dark mind, and not by any means the kind of 'discoveries' I wanted to be made at present. 'Can you really turn a ray of light on its axis by magnetism? and if you could, what should I care?' This is my feeling towards most of the scientific triumphs and unheard of progresses and miracles so trumpeted abroad in these days, and I sadly keep it secret, a sorrowful private possession of my own." The spirit of enquiry and investigation came to be to him but another name for a disease of the human mind. The truth is that his early life and education had deformed his mind. He possessed imagination, strength, and command of language, but his life was spent in despondency and doubt. His range of thought was contracted to his own conceptions and sensations. For a liberal survey of the ever-widening field and scope of nature and of man, his faculties failed him, and they failed largely through the limitations of his life at Ecclefechan and Edinburgh.

Glance at the cardinal matters in Carlyle's life. These are his birth in 1795; his introduction to Irving in 1815, and to German literature in 1820; in 1821 his "conversion" or "new birth," as he has called it in *Sartor Resartus*, when he fondly conceived himself to have been purged for ever of his spiritual ills; in the same year his first introduction to Jane Welsh; the appearance of his biography of Schiller in the *London Magazine* in 1823, followed in the next year by his translation of *Wilhelm Meister*; in 1824, his first visit to London, and his first letter from Goethe; his marriage in 1825, and his settlement at Comely Bank, in Edinburgh; in 1827, his introduction to Jeffrey, and the beginning of his work for the *Edinburgh Review*; in the same year, the receipt of a second letter from Goethe, full of cordial praise for his *Life of Schiller*, which had been translated into German under the great man's own supervision, and generally for his "calm clear sympathy with poetical literary activity in Germany"; his migration to Craigenputtock, "the dreariest spot in all the British dominions," in 1828, where he and his wife were to spend six years; his second visit to London, in 1831, to negotiate for the publication of *Sartor Resartus*, which after many disappointments and bickerings, was two years later to begin its printed existence in *Fraser's Magazine*; in 1833, another attempt to make a home and life in Edinburgh; and then, in 1834, the "burning of the ships" at Craigenputtock, the migration to London, and settlement at Cheyne Row for the rest of his life.

"Henceforward," writes his biographer, Froude, "his life was in his works." It always had been in them, and it is not a little singular that of personal relationships the only ones to penetrate into the heart of his life were a man and a woman, Edward Irving and Jane Welsh. What did he know of the world whose diseases he presumed to diagnose? It was his misfortune that he knew very little of the world or society outside what he had met at Ecclefechan and Edinburgh. Even in London he led the life of a recluse, mistaking for realities his own dyspeptic dreams. The frame of mind in which he contemplated his fellow creatures was honest, silent pity for one half and indignation for the other half. Charity and humility find no place in his creed: he is one of the Elect. He was nearly forty years of age before his genius and his attainments had won for him any recognition. With him hope deferred certainly made the heart sick. The most brilliant years of youth and early manhood were overshadowed to him by doubt as to his own vocation in life, by repugnance to the pursuits that lay before him, by dyspepsia that never left him, by despondency which seldom failed to haunt him, by penury which only relaxed its iron grasp in his later years, and by disappointments more frequent than success. His humour seldom failed him, but it was a grim humour, which, like the wit of Swift, seemed to take a fierce delight in the laceration and the misery of his own species. Yet, unlike Swift, he was capable of strong domestic affections and of friendship. From these two sources sprang twin influences which shed a beam of light across his sombre path, the one his strong friendship for Edward Irving, the other his passionate attachment to his wife, Jane Welsh. She was an admiring and devoted wife, whose buoyant and graceful nature threw over her husband's rugged and despondent existence whatever cheer and comfort he would allow to reach him; and for forty years she fulfilled this difficult task. There is no harder task than to watch over the daily wants, real and imaginary, of a man of genius cursed with a bad digestion, intolerant of the slightest noise, irritated by contradiction, and of an atrabilious temperament. All this she did and endured; and this is the true monument to her memory. She was not happy. How could she be? Late in the evening of her laborious life, she confessed, "I married for ambition. Carlyle has exceeded all that my wildest hopes ever imagined of him—and I am miserable." She once told a woman friend, "Marrying a man of genius is a mistake. I've had a hard time of it. But wait till I die, and see what an apotheosis I shall have." She has had her apotheosis, for after her death her husband realised all she had been to him. We know Swift's comment on a lock of Stella, "Only a woman's hair." We know Carlyle's wail for the loss of his wife, "Oh that I had you yet but for five minutes beside me, to tell you all." When she died he turned to Lockhart for comfort, and the latter sent him his own beautiful lines. These Carlyle used to repeat in his declining years:—

> It is an old belief
> That on some solemn shore
> Beyond the sphere of grief
> Dear friends shall meet once more—

> Beyond the sphere of Time
> And Sin and Fate's control,
> Serene in changeless prime
> Of Body and of Soul.
>
> That creed I fain would keep,
> This hope I'll not forego;
> Eternal be the Sleep
> Unless to waken so.

Sir Henry Taylor described Carlyle as a "Puritan who had lost his creed." Nothing could be more terse, more accurate, or more true. The most potent element in his nature was his intense Scots nationality. On this stock was originality engrafted the strict Covenanting creed. The creed vanished with the increasing doubts and soul-storm of later years, but the stern dogmatism of the Covenanter remained, drawing not only its language, but its spirit from the old prophets of Israel. The Old Testament was his, not the New with the humility, the resignation, the charity of the revelation of Christ. Of the three apostolic graces, faith declined, hope grew dim, but charity vanished altogether.

The mantle of the Covenanters fell upon Carlyle. His tone and his principles, his loves and his hatreds, even down to minute instances, bear no small affinity to those which marked that most stubborn and most intense of religious sects. And through the Covenanters he is not ambiguously connected with the old Hebrews. With these he feels himself at one. Rarely does he refer to the New Testament; rarely does he think of the saints and martyrs, the souls that died in patience, without anger, without honour, without even the effort for an outward victory. But the old prophets and judges, who assumed the rule, and led armies, and denounced the evil-doer, and punished the enemies of God, are ever in his thoughts. Consider the following passages from the *Latter-day Pamphlets*, whether as regards their reference or their character: "There is one valid reason, and only one, for either punishing a man or rewarding him in this world; one reason, which ancient piety could well define: That you may do the will and commandment of God with regard to him; that you may do justice to him. This is your one true aim in respect of him; aim thitherward, and not elsewhither at all."

"God Himself, we have always understood, hates sin, with a most authentic, celestial, and eternal hatred. A hatred, a hostility inexorable, unappeasable, which blasts the scoundrel, and all scoundrels ultimately, into black annihilation and disappearance from the sum of things. The path of it is the path of a flaming sword: he that has eyes may see it, walking inexorable, divinely beautiful and divinely terrible, through the chaotic gulf of Human History, and everywhere burning, as with unquenchable fire, the false and deathworthy from the true and lifeworthy; making all human history, and the biography of every man, a God's Cosmos, in place of a Devil's Chaos. So is it, in the end; even so, to every man who is a man, and not a mutinous beast, and has eyes to see."

"The saddest condition of human affairs, what ancient prophets denounced as 'the Throne of Iniquity,' where men 'decree injustice by a law': all this, with its thousandfold outer miseries, is still but a symptom; all this points to a far sadder disease which lies invisible within."

"Like the valley of Jehoshaphat, it lies round us, one nightmare wilderness, and wreck of dead men's bones, this false modern world; and no rapt Ezekiel in prophetic vision imaged to himself things sadder, more horrible and terrible, than the eyes of men, if they are awake, may now deliberately see."

The attitude of Carlyle to man is important in noting his solution of political problems: his attitude to God is no less important. In all his writings, in spite of their manifold contradictions, he clings to the belief that goodness and justice ultimately prevail, and he clings to this belief passionately. He comes close to the Browning creed that God's in His heaven, though alas! all's wrong with the world. God is immanent in the process of the world's history, and the Elect realise this right well. When he was eighty-three, he confessed to Allingham: "The evidence to me of God—and the only evidence—is the feeling I have deep down in the very bottom of my heart of right and truth and justice. I believe that all things are governed by Eternal Goodness and Wisdom, and not otherwise; but we cannot see and never shall see *how* it is all managed. . . . Whoever looks into himself must be aware that at the centre of things is a mysterious Demiurgus—who is *God*, and who cannot in the least be adequately spoken of in any human words." With all thoughtful men this belief occasionally wavers in the face of the facts of life. It wavered with Carlyle twenty years before this confession. The American Civil War had broken out—a righteous war if ever there was one—and Carlyle spoke to Froude with a cry of pain, "He does nothing." God was doing His work through the life of Abraham Lincoln, but the eyes of Carlyle were momentarily holden. We can admire the foresight of Goethe when he remarked to Eckermann on July 25, 1827, "Carlyle is a moral force of great importance. There is in him much for the future, and we cannot foresee what he will produce and effect."

The Calvinist connected faith and works, and so did the Covenanter Carlyle. The intensely active spirit is manifest in his writings. There is no patient waiting in them, no quiet sympathy. All is zeal for action, and this accounts for the ground-tone of Jeremiah in them when action does not follow on writing. And, be it observed, there is no reasoning in them. When Browning tries to represent St. John, he makes him argue—a most fundamental error; for not in the whole of the Old and New Testament, except in the Epistles of St. Paul, who had a Greek education, is there a single instance of argument, as we understand the word. Everywhere there is the most intense, the most undoubting of affirmation. And Carlyle has by nature this quality; by virtue of it, and by virtue of his zeal for action, he is Hebraic.

Do we blame Carlyle for thus urging men to action? Far from it; he does well and rightly in doing so. But we blame him for this, that in his zeal for this one element of political reform he has wholly lost sight of all the other elements of a noble character. For thought, for systematisation, except in so far as it is conducive to immediate brilliant action, he cares not. This is due primarily to his theology. For the imagination which apprehends the beauty of material things he cares not. For the germination of great thoughts and great desires out of nothingness into that incomplete and immature existence which is the lot of all things at first, he cares not. All these things, of which his early writings are full, are in his later writings unmentioned, discarded, forgotten. Action, and the intellect which immediately determines action, is all that he admires. There is the Carlyle we like, and he writes before 1850: there is the Carlyle we dislike, and he writes after that year.

His lack of appreciation of science did not blind him to the aspects of the world it revealed, and in *Sartor Resartus* he crudely anticipates the evolutionary conception of society. As some men label and parcel their thoughts, so, Carlyle feared, the scientists were labelling and parcelling the universe, and his soul revolted from this attitude. "System of Nature! To the wisest man, wide as is his vision, Nature remains of quite *infinite* depth, of quite infinite expansion; and all experience thereof limits itself to some few computed centuries and measured square-miles. The course of Nature's phases, on this our little fraction of a Planet, is partially known to us; but who knows what deeper courses these depend on: what infinitely larger Cycle (of causes) our little Epicycle revolves on? To the Minnow every cranny and pebble, and quality and accident, of its little native Creek may have become familiar: but does the Minnow understand the Ocean Tides and periodic Currents, the Trade-winds, and Monsoons, and Moon's eclipses; by all which the condition of its little Creek is regulated, and may, from time (*un*miraculously enough), be quite overset and reversed? Such a minnow is Man; his Creek this Planet Earth; his Ocean the immeasurable All; his Monsoons and periodic currents the mysterious Course of Providence through Aeons of Aeons. We speak of the Volume of Nature: and truly a Volume it is,— whose Author and Writer is God." Here he reveals the influence of Fichte who taught that the world of experience is but the appearance or vesture of the divine idea or life; and that he alone has true life who is willing to resign his personality in the service of humanity, and who strives incessantly to work out the ideal that lends nobility and grandeur to human effort.

Carlyle insists that the world of experience is the vesture of divine life. He is all on fire not merely to perceive this vesture but to transmute it into the world of experience. He ever refuses to confine himself to the office of theorist. He appeals to the age, to his country, to the men about him, in strong and urgent entreaty: "Do this; do not do that." When he treats of the men of his time, or of preceding times, he does not discuss merely whether they have held right opinions, but whether they have acted rightly. Voltaire, Diderot, Fichte—these, whom others carelessly think of as thinkers—Carlyle insists on dealing with as men. He knows what an effect a man's life has on his opinions; and hence he refuses to make any divorce between the two. In the midst of many changes that came over him, notably after 1850, this fundamental characteristic remained. Hence, too, the simple, obvious nature of most of his precepts; for truisms and platitudes, though the bane and abhorrence of the thinker, have often to be urged in practical life, from the proneness of men to neglect what is most evident. "Work, work"; "speak the truth"; "shun cant"; "have a clear understanding"; —maxims like these form no small part of Carlylean ethics.

Over the precepts most easy of comprehension he contrives to throw a mysterious splendour by reminding men of their universality. From eternity to eternity these remain the same; Nature herself has ordained them; in every time and in every place those prosper who obey them, those fall into ruin who disobey them. These are the eternities, the immensities, of which he speaks so much; nay, they are even the divine Silences, for the force and vigour of these truths lie not in their being spoken, but in their being acted upon. These are the "unwritten and sure laws of the gods, that were not born to-day or yesterday, but live for ever, and no man knows whence they came," of which Sophocles speaks. These are what Moses describes; "the commandment which I command thee this day . . . is not in heaven, that thou shouldest say, Who shall go up for us to heaven, and bring it unto us, that we may hear it, and do it? neither is it beyond the sea. . . . But the word is very nigh thee, in thy mouth, and in thy heart, that thou mayest do it." Taking these laws as his rule and standard, Carlyle throws himself into the broad life of his own age and of other ages; narrating, criticising, preaching, advising, with reverence or with scorn, with laughter or with anger; passing in review statesmen, soldiers, writers, even quacks and imposters. To none is he indifferent.

The style of the prophet is as formless as the heaving waves of the ocean. Nor did Jeffrey fail to remind him even in 1828 how through it he was misusing his talents. "I suppose," he said, "you will treat me as something worse than an ass when I say that I am firmly persuaded the great source of your extravagance, and of all that makes your writings intolerable to many and ridiculous to not a few, is not so much any real peculiarity of opinions, as an unlucky ambition to appear more original than you are, or the humbler and still more delusive hope of converting our English intellects to the creed of Germany and being the apostle of another Reformation." So might a contemporary have spoken to Jeremiah. Nor was his style his chief deficiency in gaining the ear of the reading public. For a Scots he was singularly devoid of mental method and logical power. Not only did he not reason, but as one wave of incoherent sentiment succeeded another, he contradicted in one page what he had just said before. So spake the prophets of old. The great currents swelling in his life and character alone gave coherence and uniformity to his opinions.

In the annals of the past he sought confirmation for the positions he adopted, and naturally he found them. In his *Historic Survey of German Poetry* he held that the best picture of the past of a nation would come from an adequate account of its poetry. For the poet reflects the spiritual temper of the age, its hopes and its fears, and he reflects it unconsciously. From such an attitude Shakespeare is a finer interpreter of the Elizabethan age than Froude. He noted in his 1830 essay *On History* the suspicious fact that all manner of theorists—including himself—appeal to history with equal confidence. Burke taught that all

THE CONDITION OF ENGLAND QUESTION

beginnings were obscure and Carlyle reinforces this truth. "Our clock strikes when there is a change from hour to hour; but no hammer in the Horloge of Time peals through the universe when there is a change from Era to Era." The growth of evidence for the last hundred years has been so enormous that we cannot see the wood for the trees. He remarks that while the *Acts of the Christian Apostles*, on which the world has rested for eighteen hundred years, can be read in one short hour, the *Acts of the French Philosophers*, whose importance is almost spent, lie recorded in whole acres of typography, and would furnish reading for a lifetime. Church history, he lays down, is the most important of all, but the church of his dreams is to be in things eternal what true kingship is in things temporal. The emergence of the great man is the cause of movement in history: the occasion of his appearance may be trivial. In his early writings, as in his *Chartism*, 1840, the condition of the people is never out of his mind. In his 1840 book he cried aloud to politicians that in their manifold concern with the West India question, the game laws, and the queen's bedchamber question, they might spare a few days for the condition-of-England question. How much the writer was before his time is clear in Gladstone's letter to Gaskell, penned in 1832. It sums up the matters of note for a young member of Parliament. The first is the relative merits of Pedro, Miguel, and Donna Maria for the throne of Portugal. The second is Poland, and the third the affairs of Lombardy. The last is Free Trade.

Economic causes assume an increasing prominence in the thought of historians. In theory Carlyle made this assumption, but in practice he departed far from it. He is essentially picturesque. His personages are alive, painted as old Crome would paint a Norfolk heath or a stone quarry. The picture is not in the object, but in his own genius. His scenes are admirably put on the stage, producing a dramatic effect. He is not a deep thinker but a great word-painter. He had an almost unlimited command of language, especially of a rich metaphorical nature. The cold impartiality of a Hallam has its value; it keeps alive the sense of justice, so much needed among men. Carlyle, on the other hand, apprehends with warm intelligence not merely the end of a man's life but the whole course of it. His was a more patiently inquiring mind set on probing the springs of character. Minute analysis was never one of his qualities. Yet if he never owned the power of philosophic analysis, he owned a breadth of feeling and a width of range, truly philosophic. It is the union of this coupled with picturesque and animated description that constitutes a signal evidence of his genius.

His historical creed was simple. "Biography is the only history. Political History as now written and hitherto, with its kings and changes of *tax-gatherers*, is little (very little) more than a mockery of our want. This I see more and more." More familiar is the declaration: "The history of what man has accomplished in this world is at bottom the history of the great men who have worked here." Contempt for Voltaire, Hume and Gibbon is naturally an article in his creed. In the world of experience they never discerned the vesture of divine life. They never lifted the veil, hiding it. They never pierced behind appearances to the mystical fabric whose pattern was being woven in the looms of God. Nevertheless, the great man was assisting in this weaving. "He is as lightning out of Heaven: the rest of men wait for him like fuel, and then they too will flame." Such a man he describes with force and with brilliancy. Such a one is alive to Carlyle, and he certainly contrives to make him alive to all his readers. The verdict of Lowell is just. "The figures of most historians seem like dolls stuffed with bran, whose whole substance runs through any hole that criticism may tear in them; but Carlyle's are so real in comparison, that, if you prick them, they bleed." He is an historian with a mission, and like all writers with a mission his art has suffered thereby. His philosophy teaches by experience, the experience of the past. He never surrenders himself, accordingly, to the interpretation of the past. What he does surrender himself to is the interpretation of the past in the light of the problems of his own day, a totally different matter, though he never perceived this difference. He is a political prophet by nature, an historian by grace.

Thiers testifies to the justice and the necessity of the French Revolution, Mignet to its character as the logical outcome of the past which gave birth to a new society, Michelet to the grandeur of the position of the people, Lamartine to its pre-eminence as a factor in human history, Louis Blanc to the working of the principle of fraternity, Sybel to its place in international history, Tocqueville to its antecedents in the *ancien régime*, Taine to its grim horror, Sorel to it as the inevitable result of the history of France and Europe, and Aulard to the sovereignty of the people and equality. The only one to see in it the vindication of the ways of God to man is Carlyle. In his *French Revolution*, published in 1837, he sets down: "So many centuries, say only from Hugh Capet downwards, had been adding together, century transmitting it with increase to century, the sum of Wickedness, of Falsehood, Oppression of man by man. Kings were sinners, and Priests were, and People. Open Scoundrels rode triumphant, bediamonded becoronetted, bemitred; or the still fataler species of Secret-Scoundrels, in their fair-sounding formulas, speciosities, respectabilities, hollow within: the race of Quacks was grown many as the sands of the sea. Till at length such a sum of Quackery had accumulated itself as, in brief, the Earth and the Heavens were weary of. Slow seemed the Day of Settlement; coming on, all imperceptible, across the bluster and fanfaronade of Courtierisms, Conquering-Heroisms, Most Christian *Grand Monarque*-isms, Well-beloved Pompadourisms: yet behold it was always coming; behold it has come, suddenly, unlooked for by any man! The harvest of long centuries was ripening and whitening so rapidly of late; and now it is grown *white*, and is reaped rapidly, as it were, in one day. Reaped, in this Reign of Terror; and carried home, to Hades and the Pit!—Unhappy Sons of Adam: it is ever so; and never do they know it, nor will they know it. With cheerfully smoothed countenances, day after day, and generation after generation, they, calling cheerfully to one another, Well-speed-ye, are at work, *sowing the wind*. And yet, as God lives, they *shall reap the whirlwind :* no other thing, we say, is possible,—since God is a Truth, and His World is a Truth." The noblesse had rights without duties, and they at last paid the price for their anomalous position. Schiller is right. *Die Weltgeschichte ist das Weltgericht.*

We all know that through an accident, the maid of Mrs. Taylor, Mill's friend, destroyed the manuscript of the *French Revolution*, the book written with "his heart's blood." After a natural period of despair he resumed his task, producing a version which that able critic, his wife, pronounced better than the first. As he gave her the manuscript to read, he said: "I know not whether this book is worth anything, nor what the world will do with it, or misdo, or entirely forbear to do, as is likeliest; but this I could tell the world: You have not had for a hundred years any book that comes more direct and flamingly from the heart of a living man." To the credit of the world it perceived its worth, and for the future the position of Carlyle in the world of literature—if not in the world of history—was assured.

The figures in the *French Revolution* are boldly drawn, yet, in spite of its author's historical creed, it exhibits no tendency—save perhaps in the case of Mirabeau—to exalt the place of the hero. Men are artistically grouped, and the grouping is carried out as if by the hand of an actor, for the whole book is of the essence of drama. Nor does Carlyle omit to link the beginnings of his splendid narrative not with the Fall of the Bastille but with the battle of Mollwitz. This first of the victories of Frederick the Great announced that "indeed a new hour had struck on the Time Horloge, that a new Epoch had arisen. Slumberous Europe, rotting amid its blind pedantries, its lazy hypocrisies, conscious and unconscious: this man is capable of shaking it a little out of its stupid refuges of lies and ignominious wrappages, and of intimating to it afar off that there is still a Veracity in Things, and a Mendacity in Sham Things." So he explicitly wrote in his *History of Frederick the Great*, and so he implicitly wrote in his *French Revolution*. There was a revolution in 1740 of which the full effects have not been felt yet, for if there had not been the emergence of Prussia then would we have had the World War? Be that as it may, Carlyle joins the

French Revolution and Frederick, detecting behind the appearances of history "both that Real Kingship is eternally indispensable, and also that the destruction of Sham Kingship (a frightful process) is occasionally so." The destructive aspect of both he saw more clearly than their constructive one.

The death of Louis XV, the storming of the Bastille, the wild march of the Menads on Versailles, the fête of the federation, the flight to Varennes, the trial and death of Louis XVI, the unforgettable evening sun of July, and, strangest and strongest of all, that grim midnight scene in the Tribune when Philippe Egalité votes for his kinsman's death —these are among the scenes lingering on the memory of the reader. The drama unrolls itself, scene by scene, act by act, and we witness the horror and the hope of the actors. As a piece of literature it is as unsurpassable as Michelet's. "It stands pretty fair in my head," Carlyle had written, "nor do I mean to investigate much more about it, but to splash down what I know in large masses of colour that it may look like a smoke and flame conflagration in the distance."

The critical reader notes that Carlyle never read the accessible Croker pamphlets in the British Museum, and that he never dreamt of reading the documents of the day. His accuracy is high, and Bryce ranks him for accuracy with Gibbon, Ranke, and Thirlwall, placing Grote, Green, Macaulay, and Milman below them. The historian reflects that Carlyle thrust constitutional principles to the one side, that he misunderstood the Girondins, that he ignored the provinces and the relations of France to Europe, that he views the Revolution rather as the death of feudalism than as the birth of democracy, and that it was constructive as well as destructive. Mazzini saw some of this when he wrote that "he has done no more than give us tableaux, wonderful in execution, without connection, without a bearing. His book is the French Revolution *illustrated*— illustrated by the hand of a master, we know, but one from whom we expected a different labour." The Italian prophet recognised his kinship to the Scots one, yet he recognised the omission of a conception ever dear to him, the conception of humanity. The defect in the book is that "he does not recognise in a people any collective life or collective aim. He recognises only individuals. For him, therefore, there is not and cannot be any intelligible chain of connection between cause and effect."

The criticism of Mazzini goes to the very root of the matter, but there were other lines taken. Wordsworth exclaimed that no Scotsman could write English. Hallam declared that its style was so detestable as to make it unreadable. Prescott thought its "form and fonds" contemptible. FitzGerald condemned its lack of repose and of equable movement, as if Carlyle were capable of either. Taine deemed that the author "saw nothing but evil in the French Revolution. He judges it as unjustly as he judges Voltaire, and for the same reasons. He understands our manner of acting no better than our manner of thinking. He looks for Puritan sentiment, and, as he does not find it, he condemns us." On the other hand, Jeffrey acknowledged its success. Sterling wrote warmly of it in the *Westminster Review*, pointing out how the book echoes on and on in the hearts of men. To Sterling the author had confided that it was a wild, savage book. "It has come hot out of my own soul, born in blackness, whirlwind and sorrow." Southey was so carried away by it that he read it six times. Arnold desired the acquaintance of its author who showed such an understanding of history. Dickens carried a copy wherever he went, and it inspired his *Tale of Two Cities*. Kingsley regarded it as the single epic of modern times. Newman thought it "a queer, tiresome, obscure, profound and original work. The writer has not very *clear* principles and views, I fear, but they are very deep." Thackeray reviewed it with infectious enthusiasm in *The Times*. With insight, J. S. Mill saw in it the world of realities which Shakespeare revealed. Froude declared it the most perfect of all his friend's writings. Emerson was filled with admiration and wonder at its many great qualities, though by no means blind to its defects. According to Acton it delivered our mind from the thraldom of Burke. True, governments are not made; they grow. Carlyle dared to assert that the form of polity is, in some measure at least, a matter of choice on the part of the people. There was much more in the Revolution than a cataclysm of all order and hope. A poor Paisley weaver thanked the dramatist for teaching that "man does not live by demonstration, but by faith." The prophecy of Goethe had come true. Carlyle was recognised as a new moral force in Europe which counted and was to count increasingly.

Sartor Resartus appeared in 1838. It is based upon an idea which is already in Swift, an author strikingly akin to Carlyle. He combines the bitter and baneful humour of the *Tale of a Tub* with the idealism of Fichte and the language of Richter. In *Sartor Resartus* we learn that "all visible things are emblems; what thou seest is not there on its own account; strictly taken, is not there at all: Matter exists only spiritually, and to represent some idea, and *body* it forth. On the other hand, all emblematic things are properly Clothes, thought-woven or hand-woven. Whatsoever sensibly exists, whatsoever represents Spirit to Spirit, is properly a Clothing, a suit of Raiment, put on for a season, and to be laid off. Thus in this one pregnant subject of Clothes, rightly understood, is included all that men had thought, dreamed, done and been: the whole External Universe and what it holds is but Clothing; and the essence of all Science lies in the Philosophy of Clothes."

The unknown author of the finest philosophy of history in the New Testament announces in the Epistle to the Hebrews: "As a vesture Thou shalt change them, and they shall be changed." Here lies the germ of the Carlylean idea which is extended from the heavens to the structure of human society. Goethe gives voice to it:—

> Ich sitz' an die säuselnde Webstuhl der Zeit,
> Und wirke des Gotten lebendiges Kleid.
> Thus at the roaring loom of Time I ply,
> And weave for God the robe thou seest Him by.

We are in fact "spirits in a prison, able only to make signals to each other, but with a world of things to think and say which our signals cannot describe at all." It is a favourite idea of our theologian, and he expressed it in words which have been characterised as "perhaps the most memorable utterances of our greatest poet" by Sir James Stephen:

"It is mysterious, it is awful to consider, that we not only carry each a future ghost within him, but are in very deed ghosts. These limbs, whence had we them? this stormy force, this life-blood with its burning passion? They are dust and shadow; a shadow-system gathered round our Me, wherein through some moment or years the Divine Essence is to be revealed in the flesh. That warrior on his strong war-horse, fire flashes through his eyes, force dwells in his arms and heart; but warrior and war-horse are a vision, a revealed force, nothing more. Stately they tread the earth, as if it were a firm substance. Fools! the earth is but a film; it cracks in twain, and warrior and warhorse sink beyond plummet's sounding. Plummet's? Fantasy herself will not follow them. A little while ago they were not; a little while and they are not, their very ashes are not.

"So has it been from the beginning, so will it be to the end. Generation after generation takes to itself the form of a body; and forth issuing from Cimmerian night on heaven's mission *appears*. What force and fire is in each, he expends. One grinding in the mill of industry, one hunter-like climbing the giddy Alpine heights of science, one madly dashed to pieces on the rocks of strife in war with his fellows, and then the heaven-sent is recalled, his earthly vesture falls away, and soon even to sense becomes a vanished shadow. Thus, like some wild flaming, wild thundering train of Heaven's artillery, does this mysterious mankind thunder and flame in long-drawn quick-succeeding grandeur through the unknown deep. Thus, like a god-created, fire-breathing spirit-host, we emerge from the inane, haste stormfully across the astonished earth, then plunge again into the inane. Earth's mountains are levelled, and her seas filled up in our passage. Can the earth, which is dead, and a vision, resist spirits which have reality and are alive? On the hardest adamant some footprint of us is stamped in. The last rear of the host will read traces of the earliest van. But whence? Oh, Heaven whither? Sense knows not, faith knows not, only that it is through mystery to mystery, from God and to God."

> We are such stuff
> As dreams are made of, and our little life
> Is rounded with a sleep.

Our prophet seeks an infinite and sure peace to set over against the infinite and unsure happiness which Nature gives us. His search was long and arduous, and at last he believed himself to have found what he sought. The passage in which he imparts his discovery is contained in the chapter in *Sartor Resartus*, entitled "The Everlasting Yea." It is necessary to quote it: "There is in man a higher than Love of Happiness: he can do without Happiness, and instead thereof find Blessedness! . . . Love not Pleasure; love God. This is the Everlasting Yea, wherein all contradiction is solved; wherein whoso walks and works, it is well with him. . .

"Most true is it, as a wise man teaches us, that 'Doubt of any sort cannot be removed except by Action.' On which ground too, let him who gropes painfully in darkness or uncertain light, and prays vehemently that the dawn may ripen into day, lay this other precept well to heart, which to me was of invaluable service: 'Do the Duty which lies nearest thee,' which thou knowest to be a Duty! Thy second Duty will already have become clearer.

"May we not say, however, that the love of Spiritual Enfranchisement is even this: when your Ideal World, wherein the whole man has been dimly struggling and inexpressibly languishing to work, becomes revealed, and thrown open. . . . The Situation that has not its Duty, its Ideal, was never yet occupied by man. Yes, here, in this poor, miserable, hampered, despicable Actual: work it out therefrom; and working, believe, live, be free.

"But it is with man's Soul as it was with Nature: the beginning of Creation is Light."

All his writing converges on this outstanding passage: from it everything which succeeds diverges. It is his version of the Biblical statement that "if any man will do His will, he shall know of the doctrine." The doubt of the study could be resolved by the action of life. A purely theoretical knowledge of virtue is no knowledge at all; the true knowledge of virtue is a flame that kindles energy. Such a flame was *Sartor Resartus* to the generation of the thirties.

The whole life of society is carried on by drudges who are fortunate if they have a great man to direct their labours.

Sartor Resartus teaches that "Great Men are the inspired (speaking and acting) Texts of that divine Book of Revelations, whereof a chapter is completed from epoch to epoch, and by some named History." In his *Hero-Worship*, 1841, as in his *Past and Present*, 1843, and in his *Latter-Day Pamphlets*, 1850, this idea is driven home. According to the last, "there is no Biography of a man, much less any History, or Biography of a Nation, but wraps in it a message out of Heaven." In his *Miscellanies* he thinks that "History is the essence of innumerable biographies." *Heroes and Hero-Worship* reinforces this idea with wonderful force, not to say vehemence.

All heroism had departed from our country, if not from the earth, with the last of the Puritans in the seventeenth century, though there was a trace of it in another country in the eighteenth. For Oliver Cromwell and Frederick the Great belong to this select band. Not all its members have been so carefully chosen: they were certainly not apostles of genuine liberty, unselfish duty, and a general love of man. In his discourses "On the Nature of a Scholar," Fichte had perceived the presence of the "divine idea" everywhere, but above all in the shining spirits of the race. By divine right the ruler can, in the judgment of Fichte, and must compel, and the rest yield obedience. In similar fashion Carlyle desires, first, that the action of the State should be resolute, and directed with clear purpose. But, next, he sees that it is impossible to have a perfectly clear purpose perfectly carried out, except under the guidance of one man, who both conceives and executes. Accordingly, he demands a head of the State in whose mind the full purpose of government, which by others is conceived imperfectly and inadequately, should represent itself perfectly and adequately. He demands that the effort of all persons should be to recognise this man, or the man who comes nearest to this ideal, to set him over them, obey him themselves, and provide him with sufficient force to put down those who, from their selfish and partial view, oppose themselves to his wiser plan. He is specially indignant with those who think that a nation can be guided infallibly into the right course by the machinery of Parliaments or

Congresses, or by any device which makes the final decision rest with the majority, simply because they are the majority, without any effort to obtain the judgment of those most competent to decide. He demands that there shall be in every case a clear and wise design; and he insists that the wisest design can in its full compass be only comprehended by the one Wisest Man, whom all other men must call to the helm of the State. More than this; he would have, in every portion of society, the inferior natures avowedly guided by the higher, as these would be guided by those higher than themselves, till the whole culminated in that single man whom all the rest adjudged to be most eminent among them.

Now it is no theory of mere despotism which our thinker puts before us. There is a vast difference between saying that all nations should use their utmost endeavours to gain a Governor, a Wisest Man, in whom they can trust and saying that every nation which is governed by a single strong despot has a government which approaches the true aim and object of the State. The theory does not even say that every nation should immediately choose for itself a single individual as its head; but only that this is the ideal condition of things. It is, besides, at the very farthest possible distance from any theory that would sanction castes, or the hereditary domination of an aristocratic class, or even the hereditary descent of a monarchy from a king or his descendants. The doctrine of *Heroes* must be combined with that of the *Latter-Day Pamphlets*. In the latter we read: "This question always rises as the alpha and omega of social questions, What methods the Society has of summoning aloft into the high places, for its help and governance, the wisdom that is born to it in all places, and of course is born chiefly in the more populous or lower places? For this, if you will consider it, expresses the ultimate available result, and net sum-total, of all the efforts and confused activities that go on in the Society; and determines whether they are true and wise efforts, certain to be victorious, or false and foolish, certain to be futile, and to fall captive and caitiff. How do men rise in your Society? In all Societies, Turkey included, and I suppose Dahomey included, men do rise; but the question of questions always is, What kind of men? Men of noble gifts, or men of ignoble?" Robert Burns himself could not lay more stress on the essential equality of rights in men, born in whatever rank.

The Hero will need the advice, information, and assistance of others who are inferior to him. Accordingly, Parliaments have their due place in his system; for, though he has written much against parliaments as they actually are, he has something to say for them as they might be. In his 1841 book this is not so obvious as it is in his 1850 one. Turn to the *Latter-Day Pamphlets* to read the following two passages. According to the first: "To King Rufus there could no more natural method present itself, of getting his affairs of sovereignty transacted, than this same. To assemble all his working Sub-kings about him; and gather in a human manner, by the aid of sad speech and of cheerful, what their real notions, opinions, and determinations were. No way of making a law, or of getting one executed when made, except by even such a General Consult in one form or another. Naturally too, as in all places where men meet, there established themselves modes of proceeding in this Christmas *Parliamentum*. . . . So likewise, in the time of the Edwards, when Parliament gradually split itself in Two Houses; and Borough Members and Knights of the Shire were summoned to answer, Whether they could stand such and such an impost? and took upon them to answer: 'Yes, your Majesty, but we have such and such grievances greatly in need of redress first'—nothing could be more natural and human than such a Parliament still was. And so, granting subsidies, stating grievances, and notably widening its field in that latter direction, accumulating new modes, and practices of Parliament greatly important in world-history, the old Parliament continued an eminently human, veracious, and indispensable entity, achieving real work in the centuries."

According to the second: "Votes of men are worth collecting, if convenient. True, their opinions are generally of little wisdom, and can on occasion reach to all conceivable and inconceivable degrees of folly; but their instincts, where these can be deciphered, are wide and human; these, hidden under the noisy utterance of what they call their opinions, are the unspoken sense of man's heart, and well deserve attending to. Know well what the people inarticulately feel, for the Law of Heaven itself is dimly written there; nay do not neglect, if you have the opportunity, to ascertain what they vote and say. One thing the stupidest multitude at a hustings can do, provided only it be sincere: Inform you how it likes this man or that, this proposed law or that. . . . Beyond doubt it will be useful, will be indispensable, for the King or Governor to know what the mass of men think upon public questions legislative and administrative; what they will assent to willingly, what unwillingly; what they will resist with superficial discontents and remonstrances, what with obstinate determination, with riot, perhaps with armed rebellion. To which end, Parliaments, free presses, and such like, are excellent; they keep the Governor fully aware of what the people, wisely or foolishly, think. Without in some way knowing it with moderate exactitude, he has not a possibility of governing at all. For example, the Chief Governor of Constantinople, having no Parliament to tell it him, knows it only by the frequency of incendiary fires in his capital, the frequency of bakers hanged at their shop lintels; a most inferior *ex-post facto* method."

In *Heroes* the author palliates the brutal buffoonery of Frederick William and the mendacity of Prussian ambition, as if he were utterly devoid of moral sense. If a man is in any wise a hero, he is tempted, sorely tempted, to ignore his faults. Nor can we quite admit that some of them are heroes. Henry V at Agincourt; Henry IV of France at Ivry addressing his captains, "If you lose sight of your banners, do not lose sight of my white plume; you will find it always on the road of honour"; Bayard dying with his cross-hilted sword held up before him at Pavia; Sir Philip Sidney in the memorable scene at Zutphen; Condé at Rocroi, or throwing his baton over the palisades at Friedland; Montrose on the battlefield or the scaffold; Wolfe on the heights of Abraham exclaiming with his expiring breath, "They run—then I die happy"; Henri de la Rochejacquelin telling the Vendéans, "If I advance, follow me; if I turn back, kill me; if I fall, avenge me"; Nelson giving his last signal—such men are heroes. Many who have done greater things, who have filled a larger share in the world's history, who have exercised a wider influence on thought or creation, are not. Bismarck, for instance, is a man after Carlyle's own heart. Indisputably one of the two or three greatest men of his generation, yet no one would dream of calling him a hero—save in mockery.

Who are Carlyle's heroes? They are Odin, Mahomet, Dante, Luther, Knox, Johnson, Rousseau, Burns, Cromwell, and Napoleon. His criterion is, Do they possess power and strength of will? How then came Rousseau and Burns to be admitted of the sacred band? If Rousseau and Burns be admitted, what test will exclude a writer in prose or poetry? Was Johnson a hero? The selection of Mahomet, Cromwell, and Napoleon is a distinct announcement that the proposed objects of worship may have been wanting in patriotism or philanthropy, or what is commonly understood by goodness or virtue of any kind. Moral obligations are not meant to be binding on such men. Only they must be sincere. Next to power and success, sincerity is of the very essence of heroism. Does sincerity mean truth, or truthfulness, or good faith? Not at all. The sincere man is one who believes in himself, even when no one else apparently believes in him. Mahomet and Cromwell were sincere because they believed that they had a mission from on High, though they occasionally resorted to mundane means, deceit and dissension, to forward it. Napoleon was sincere because he believed in his star, though falsehood was habitual to him. On these lines what are we to say to the claims of Ignatius Loyola, the Black Pope? He was undoubtedly sincere. What are we to say to the claims of the Papacy? Many popes have been sincere as Ignatius Loyola, yet Carlyle simply tells us that the founder of the Jesuits was "a poor creature called Ignatius." His defence of the Protector leaves us wondering. "With regard to Cromwell's 'lying' we will make one remark. This, I suppose, or something like this, to have been the motive of it. All parties found themselves deceived in him; each party understood him to mean *this*, heard him even say so, and behold he turns out to have been meaning *that*! He was, say they, the chief of liars. But now, intrinsically, is not all this the inevitable fortune, not of a false man in such times, but simply of a superior man?" This is of course the very doctrine inculcated by Machiavelli.

Carlyle was not content with setting up a brazen image. Mommsen set up his, and offered up the reputations of Cato and Cicero to Caesar. The shrine inevitably demanded a victim or victims to be immolated thereat. Carlyle tells us, for example, that he has tried his hardest to admire such characters as Hampden, Eliot, and Pym. "At bottom I found that it would not do. . . . What man's heart does in reality, break forth into any fire of brotherly love for these men? They are become dreadfully dull men! . . . One leaves all these Nobilities standing in their niches of honour! the rugged outcast Cromwell, he is the man of them all in whom one still finds human stuff." If he is unfair to the Puritan leaders, he is also unfair to the pioneers of progress and of the truly original thinkers and benefactors of mankind; of men like Adam Smith, Malthus, Bentham, Howard, Clarkson, and Wilberforce. He finds no human stuff in them because they did not make their way by force.

On its good side his hero-worship approaches the Deity: on its evil side it approaches the Devil. Nietzsche set up the Superman not unlike the bad aspect of the Carlylean ideal, though he hated to be compared to the Scots philosopher. "Noble" for him, as for Carlyle, meant practical power. Like Carlyle, he thought that "once spirit was God, then it became man, now it is becoming mob." Both discerned that the flat plain of utilitarianism dispensed with the outlook of the "noble." To compass a race of heroes was the ideal of both. They expressed contempt for public opinion—the conscience of societies. Strength, courage, and efficiency attracted them. Both were at heart self-sustained and intractable. In either the capacity for mental suffering, heightened by illness and introspection, gave a keen sense of what pleasure there might be in life, were health its normal condition. Both turned from metaphysics as a delusion and from dogma as a mistake—or worse, taking refuge in different forms of Stoicism. The awful arrogance of a tormented soul had enormous power in the two men. Though they believed in the use of history, their teaching conduced to its abuse. Each preached a doctrine of redemption and deliverance. A "new creature" is needed for the regeneration of Europe. We are to endure to the end in order to attain to fullness of life. A few men are fitted to be masters, the many to be slaves. Happy for the world that recognises the Ubermensch! Nietzsche, like Carlyle, is more prone to discern power as a terrific explosion than as quiet confidence, holding back till the moment its reserve strength is required. Nietzsche admired Caesar Borgia and Napoleon as Carlyle admired Mahomet and Napoleon. From their objects of admiration men deduced that ruthlessness and treachery were not unjustifiable—if only displayed by the strong. *Past and Present*, which appeared in 1843, was suggested by reading the chronicle of *Jocelin de Brakelond*. In it the condition of the poor occupies the author's attention, and the remedy is that prescribed in *Heroes*. Abbot Samson governed his monastery of St. Edmunds as a paternal despot, and Peel and Russell might do worse than borrow hints from him. *Laissez-faire* had not been a success since the industrial revolution had spread so widely in the north. A strong Governor was one of the urgent needs of the moment. The transition to his *Life and Letters of Oliver Cromwell*, issued in 1845, is comparatively easy.

The question of might and right lies in the background of Carlyle's labours in the forties. In order to grasp his position, on its better aspect, we must remember that his creed was, There is one God, and right will prevail—must prevail—in the end. True, it is not always easy to reconcile this position with the view that the hero as king is always the chosen instrument of Providence. Was Cromwell right because he cut off Charles's head? Was Frederick right because he made Prussia great? Was Napoleon right to 1815 and wrong after that date? Such a position leads us perilously close to saying that the test of the hero is his success. "At any moment," remarks Sir Leslie Stephen, "the test of success may be precarious, while that of justice is infallible." Might and right may be divergent at first and for long afterwards, but they must converge ultimately, for God really is in His heaven. Lecky once attacked our seer for taking might as the symbol of right. "I shall have to tell Lecky one day," was Carlyle's retort, "that quite the converse or *re*verse is 'the great and venerable author's' real opinion, viz. that right is the eternal symbol of might; as I hope one day (he) . . . will with amazement and real gratification discover; and that in fact he probably never met with a son of Adam more contemptuous of might except when it rests on the above origin." Still, for the sake of the strong man he pardoned much. Sir Henry Taylor in his *Autobiography* comments on the strangeness of what he believes to be the fact that Carlyle worshipped success, and adds this story. "Long before his life of Cromwell came out, I heard him insisting in conversation on the fact that Cromwell had been invariably successful; and having with much satisfaction traced the long line of his successes to the end, he added 'it is true they got him out of his grave at the Restoration, and they stuck his head up over the gate at Tyburn, but not till he had quite done with it.'"

The aim of his biography of Cromwell was kindred to that of the *French Revolution*. In the new pages we are called upon to witness "this grand Puritan Revolt, which we may define as an attempt to bring the Divine Law of the Bible into actual practice in men's affairs on the Earth." Of this impersonal process we hear something, but of the personal process of the Protector we hear far more, for here we have the Hero as a Statesman. Almost for the first time his features on the canvas of history stood forth as they had never stood forth before. To Clarendon he was "a brave, bad man." To Ludlow he was an apostate, who, from the most selfish motives, had aimed at the sovereignty throughout. To the Anabaptists he was a "grand impostor," a "loathsome hypocrite." To Baxter "he meant honestly in the main, and was pious and conscionable in the main course of his life," though "success corrupted him." Nor had the predecessors of Carlyle been more favourable. To Hume he was a "frantic enthusiast." To Hallam he "had sucked only the dregs of a besotted fanaticism." Macaulay had perceived the noble lineaments of the man, but it was reserved for Carlyle to restore them in their full integrity. The Covenanter in Carlyle gave him clue after clue to the character of his Hero, and he revealed him once for all. A hypocrite he never could be called again by any who approached him in the light of Carlyle's work. Cromwell's sincerity and his patriotism shine forth before the gaze of all. With his own right hand Carlyle reversed the judgment of our nation about the greatest prince who ever bore rule over it. He never realised that the autocracy of the Protector was a failure, and that had he lived longer the bankruptcy of his financial policy would have been evident to the world. S. R. Gardiner gave the devoted labours of a long life to a study of the Commonwealth, and he demonstrated that Carlyle had been as successful in investigating the character of the Protector as he had been unsuccessful in expounding his policy. Carlyle fondly believed that the annals of the troubled years from 1649 to 1658 bear cogent testimony to the failure of Parliament whereas the truth is that they bear cogent testimony to the failure of the Protector. The historian took one-sided views of Puritan leaders who did not see eye to eye with Cromwell, and was as contemptuous of Ludlow and Vane as Mommsen was of Cicero and Pompey. Carlyle exploded for ever the old fanatic-hypocrite myth, but set up another myth in its place. Forster struck the true note—sincerity; and S. R. Gardiner and Sir Charles Firth, though they do not always agree in their estimate of what Cromwell intended or what he expected, agree emphatically in this.

Carlyle calls upon us to admire the magnanimous impulses in the heart of Cromwell, and the strong intellect in his head, and of course we do admire them. The portrait presented bears in it neither meanness, nor cowardice, nor vice; it indicates a character genuine and straightforward. The biographer makes us proud of his subject's imperial patriotism, of his unhesitating bearing towards foreign powers. Yet something more than this has characterised the great statesmen of the earth—the Solons and the Caesars of the distant past, the Napoleons and the Bismarcks of the more immediate present. Much of their work remained when they themselves were dead, and was the basis of legislation for generation after generation. The positive work of Cromwell vanished into mist as soon as ever his strong hand was withdrawn, his negative work alone enduring. He instituted no system into which the spirit of the nation might flow, preserving itself by its own vigour; he accomplished no permanent labour; he stood above those he governed, and did not amalgamate himself with their efforts. Yet we cannot grant that he was the perfect saint and perfect ruler of Carlyle's imagination. Such a combination is unusual, and perhaps Marcus Aurelius and Louis IX are the only instances of it. The truth is that in Cromwell, as in Frederick, as in all his heroes, he looked not so much for the man as for what he wished to find in the man. He used him, as he used all his heroes, in demonstration of his favourite theories of the divine right of strength. Like so many heroes, Cromwell left no successor, for his son Richard was never able to fill the position his father occupied.

Cromwell's policy failed: nevertheless the man himself stood forth in all his great purpose of soul. J. B. Mozley and R. W. Church stood alone in their dissent from the great interpretation given of the character of Cromwell. The verdict of the former is: "We see a coarse, and not a high strength. We do not bow to it. The dragon of old romance is great in his way, but his scales repel us; we look in wonder at him, but we do not touch him; he is mighty, but he is unseemly; he is tremendous, but he is vile. Human nature stands disarmed and weak before him; but still feels that after all she is lofty and he is low; she is human and he is bestial." The verdict of the latter is: "We believe that he (i.e. Carlyle) meant to bring out a genuinely English idea of excellence, to portray a man of rude exterior and speech, doing great things in a commonplace and unromantic way. But he must match his ideal with something better than Cromwell's distorted and unreal character, his repulsive energy, his dreary and ferocious faith, his thinly veiled and mastering selfishness." The discerning public felt that the verdicts of Mozley and Church ran contrary to the weight of evidence adduced by the historian. Oliver Cromwell has been lifted out of the region of political and theological controversy, and he stands to-day in the Pantheon of Protestantism beside William the Silent, the Liberator of Holland, Gustavus Adolphus, the Liberator of Europe, and William III, the Liberator of England and of Europe. S. R. Gardiner devoted a life of more than seventy years to an investigation of Cromwell's career, and his verdict is that he was "the greatest because the most typical Englishmen of all time."

In all the writings appearing after 1850—with the signal exception of the altogether delightful life of John Sterling—the old merits and emphasised demerits appear. This is true of his history of Frederick the Great, issued from 1858 to 1865. It is more violent than the *French Revolution*, more violent than *Cromwell*, and it is, which the *French Revolution* is not, and *Cromwell* much more rarely, very tiresome. True, the Germans do not think so. Besides testifying in the warmest terms to its accuracy, they have translated it into their own language, and made it a textbook in their military schools, though some of our own military critics feel less confidence in its value as a history of military events. Moreover, the German General Staff has compiled its own survey of the Seven Years' War. We fear that all Carlyle's faults are here in this "unutterable book" at their worst. It was written against the grain, even more than was *Cromwell*; the labour of writing was terrible, and, long before the end came, as hateful as it was hard. He found little assistance from German historians. Preuss had gathered material and Ranke had outlined the work of Frederick II, but Koser had not written his masterly narrative. "I cannot find how to take up that miserable *Frederick*, or what on earth to do with it," those "horrid struggles of twelve years," "the dreary task," such expressions occur again and again in his letters and journals of the time. When all allowance is made for Carlyle's unrivalled capacity for making mountains out of molehills, it certainly seems as if no more stubborn work in literature was ever voluntarily imposed on himself by man, or more painfully carried to an end. But a work executed in this spirit can never afford much pleasure or satisfaction to the reader. The sense of weariness and depression is everywhere apparent. The method he found so convenient in *Cromwell* is here pushed to an extreme. Pages after pages of confused transcripts from note-books are flung pell-mell at the reader's head, as though the writer could not, or would not, be at the pains to arrange them and fit them into the current course of the narrative.

Nothing can be better, as a lucid summary of a long period of history, than Carlyle's account of the gradual amalgamation of the intensely complex elements out of which the Prussian monarchy was founded. Nor do we know many narratives in which battles and military campaigns are so adequately described, with such power of seizing the salient points and impressing them on the reader. No words of praise can be too high for his description of such battles as those of Leuthen and Torgau. Having once read them, it is impossible to forget them. Frederick William I plainly attracts him more than his son. The sketches of Voltaire and Pitt, of George II and Belleisle, of Maria Theresa and Catherine II, and of Frederick's dearly loved sister Wilhelmina, adorn a brilliant portrait gallery. Beyond all doubt it is the military surveys that stand out. And it is clear, from Carlyle's character, why he shows this power of method in his military narrations, and nowhere else. Conquests and victories are blazing matters, carrying their results on the face of them. The king's reign is only half over in 1763, but Carlyle dismisses the last twenty-three years in half a volume largely engrossed with foreign policy. The reform of the finances, the development of administration, the improvement of the law, the exploiting of the resources of agriculture, the planting of new industries—all this is ignored. There is little that is brilliant in this side of the work of the Hero. Here we enter the region of doubt, of obscurity, of under-currents of purpose and character, of slow, scarce-recognised growth. It is possible to apprehend battles completely, perfectly. It is impossible to apprehend the social order other than incompletely and imperfectly, yet this is the very order Carlyle undertook when he began his historical investigations. Political history is precisely the reverse of military: the historian, if he is to be just, cannot always be clear in his judgment. Many points are necessarily uncertain. A nation, unlike an army, contains throughout its extent large tracts of utter darkness, large tracts of what is still more difficult to analyse, the twilight of semi-obscurity. And this is what Carlyle will not tolerate, will scarcely recognise, and therefore utterly fails in dealing with it.

In *Frederick the Great*, Carlyle has to prove a point, and for a Scotsman he is singularly unconvincing with proofs. He has asserted that Frederick was a hero, a surpassingly great man; and he has to show reason why we should think so too. His failure is obvious. What he does show is that Frederick was a surpassingly great soldier, a very different proposition. To substitute one of these propositions for the other is justly deemed immoral, since it makes material force the test of greatness. And the very faint reprobation with which the historian visits that audacious act of Frederick's, the seizure of Silesia, increases the impression of the immorality of the book. Nevertheless, we believe that the idea which Carlyle in a dim manner had conceived as the central point of his history, was not immoral. Frederick the Great does differ much from such monarchs as Louis XIV and Gustavus Adolphus in this, that his victories had a real permanent result; they were the starting point of a nation; and whereas France was ruined by Louis XIV, Prussia must date her solid and splendid development from the time of Frederick. This fact certainly points to Carlyle's conclusion; but it only points to it; it by no means proves it. And indeed there is very much—since 1914—to be said on the other side. It might be argued that the spur and stimulus of victory, in the long run, were likely to teach the Prussian people that war is a short cut to the success of a nation.

Carlyle essayed the most difficult of all tasks when he sought to interpret the ways of God to man. Something approaching omniscience is required for finding clues in the interpretation of the past. He found one at least in the hero as the sword of God, in the splendour of outward action, ruling and chastising the nations. Bismarck was a nineteenth century Cromwell in his religious views as in his statesmanship. Some such vision inspired the letter he wrote to *The Times* on November 11, 1870, during the latter stage of the Franco-Prussian War: "It is probably an amiable trait of human nature, this cheap pity and newspaper lamentation over fallen and afflicted France; but it seems to me a very idle, dangerous, and misguided feeling, as applied to the cession of Alsace and Lorraine by France to her German conquerors; and argues, on the part of England, a most profound ignorance as to the mutual history of France and Germany, and the conduct of the French towards that Country, for long centuries back. The question for the Germans, in this crisis, is not one of 'magnanimity,' of 'Heroic pity and forgiveness to a fallen foe,' but of solid prudence, and practical consideration what the fallen foe will, in all likelihood, do when once on his feet again. Written on her memory, in a dismally instructive manner, Germany has an experience of 400 years on this point; of which on the English memory, if it ever was recorded there, there is now little or no trace." The misdeeds of Louis XI, Francis I, Richelieu, Louis XIV, Louis XV, and Napoleon are duly chronicled at considerable length. The writer continues: "Considerable misconception as to Herr von Bismarck is still prevalent in England. The English newspapers, nearly all of them, seem to me to be only getting towards a true knowledge of Bismarck, but not yet got to it. The standing likeness, circulating everywhere ten years ago, of demented Bismarck and his ditto King to Strafford and Charles I *versus* our Long Parliament (*as* like as Macedon to Monmouth, and not liker) has now vanished from the earth, no whisper of it ever to be heard more. That pathetic Niobe of Denmark, reft violently of her children (which were stolen children, and were dreadfully ill-nursed by Niobe Denmark), is also nearly gone; and will go altogether so soon as knowledge of the matter is had. Bismarck, as I read him, is not a person of 'Napoleonic' ideas, but of ideas quite superior to Napoleonic; shows no invincible 'lust of territory,' nor is tormented with 'vulgar ambition,' etc.; but has aims very far beyond that sphere; and in fact seems to me to be striving with strong faculty, by patient, grand and successful steps, towards an object beneficial to Germans and to all other men. That noble, patient, deep, pious and solid Germany should at length be welded together into a Nation, and become Queen of the Continent, instead of vapouring, vain-glorious, gesticulating, quarrelsome, restless and ever-sensitive France, seems to me the hopefullest public fact that has occurred in my time."

Henry Bulwer said that in 1870 Europe lost a mistress and found a master, and in keeping the master in his new position, Carlyle's letter helped materially in his own country. The influence of his labours on Frederick the Great is apparent in every line of this letter, and it was his position as an authority on German history that lent such weight to it on its appearance in *The Times*. Perhaps our eyesight in reading the history of the founder of Prussia has been sharpened by the events of the last generation. Carlyle certainly saw in him the general more than the governor of his fatherland, and we see this even more so. Emerson regarded Carlyle's history as "infinitely the wittiest book that ever was written—a book that one would think the English people would rise up in mass and thank the author for, by cordial acclamation, and signify, by crowning him with oak-leaves, their joy that such a head existed among them, and sympathising America would make a new treaty or send a Minister Extraordinary to offer congratulation of honoring delight to England, in acknowledgment of this donation." More deep-sighted, Lowell declared that "it is open to all manner of criticism, especially in the point of moral purpose and tendency," yet "we must admit with thankfulness, that it has the one prime merit of being the work of a man who has every quality of a great poet except that supreme one of rhythm which shapes both matter and manner to harmonious proportion, and that where it is good, it is as good as only genius knows how to be." Ruskin owned that "the book oftenest in my hand of late years is certainly Carlyle's *Frederick*." Stubbs writes in his *Seventeen Lectures* that

"Although in the prophetic sight of the writer that most remarkable book may, at the moment it was written, have borne a conscious reference to events which were still future, but have since most wonderfully illustrated its great theme, the world in general recognised nothing of the sort. The author, if he knew himself to be a *vox clamantis* at the time, must have been astonished at the rapidity with which his Gospel of Force triumphed as soon as it had its chance. Some of us shook our heads over it, one great man amongst us, whose place I am proud to occupy, I dare not say to fill, did not hesitate to speak words of summary condemnation; but the doctrine itself was esoteric, the words, like much else of Carlyle's, were Φωνᾶντα συνέτοιν, but συνέτοιν only; to the ears of the many they required the sacred interpreter."

The eighteenth century witnessed the rise of Frederick II; the twentieth century witnessed the fall of William II. We may sigh as we please for the Hero as statesman. The eighteenth century received a general of genius, but what did the twentieth century receive? An egotist who ruined his country. The politics of the *Occasional Discourse on the Nigger Question*, 1853, and of *Shooting Niagara: and after?*, 1867, might be termed mirage politics. Behind, in the far distance, their author sees a smiling oasis; immediately before and around him a barren desert or a treacherous swamp. Oh, for the ages which men foolishly call dark! Oh, for an hour of the Conqueror who would make a clean sweep of Downing Street! Oh, for an Abbot Samson whose beneficent rule would heal the diseases of the body politic! Oh, for a Plantagenet or a Tudor or a Hohenzollern to inaugurate a practical mode of transacting the real business of the nation. We cannot help speculating whether Carlyle had ever heard the reply of the Emperor Alexander to Madame de Stael, who favoured him with a declamation in praise of paternal despotism. "Yes, Madam, but it is only a happy accident."

If Carlyle divined the future of Germany, he also divined the future of Imperialism. The Utilitarians and the philosophical Radicals desired at the beginning of the nineteenth century the separation of the colonies from us. Such

Colonial reformers as Buller, Carlyle's pupil, and Durham, Wakefield and Molesworth checked the growth of this separatist ideal which was then the dominant one. On the other hand the adoption of protection by the colonies shook the power of these Colonial reformers. Carlyle came to reinforce it. The condition of the people had been almost more prominent in his early writings than the plight of any hero, and in order to improve this condition he tolerably steadily advocated the maintenance of our Colonial Empire.

In *Sartor Resartus*, 1838, he inquires, "Too crowded indeed! Meanwhile, what portion of this inconsiderable terraqueous globe have ye actually tilled and delved, till it will grow no more? How thick stands your population in the Pampas and Savannas of America?" Emigration is one remedy propounded in *Chartism*, 1840. There is to be another Völkerwanderung and *Chartism* ends with a vision of it. "Now once more, as at the end of the Roman Empire . . . the Teutonic countries find themselves too full. On a certain western rim of our small Europe, there are more men than were expected. Heaped up against the western shore there, and for a couple of hundred miles inward, the 'tide of population' swells too high, and confuses itself somewhat. Over-population? . . . For all this of the 'painless extinction', and the rest, is in a world where Canadian Forests stand unfelled, boundless Plains and Prairies unbroken with the plough."

If he anticipates Disraeli in his pride in the empire, he no less anticipates Kipling in his pride in the present rulers of the colonies. At home our governors are highly useless, but abroad they are highly useful, and of this curious contrast he provides no explanation. In *Heroes*, 1841, we meet the strong silent man. "Ah, yes. I will say it again: the great *silent* men! Looking round on the noisy inanity of the world, words with little meaning, actions with little worth, one loves to reflect on the great Empire of *Silence*. The noble, silent men, scattered here and there, each in his department; silently thinking, silently working. . . . I hope we English will long maintain our *grand talent pour silence*. Let others that cannot do without standing on a barrel-head, to spout and be seen of all the market-place, cultivate speech exclusively." In *Past and Present*, 1843, the same note is evident. "Of all the nations in the world at present, the English are the stupidest in speech, the wisest in action. . . . The 'talent of silence' is our fundamental one."

The maintenance of our Empire is perfectly possible. So *Past and Present* assures us. There is in 1843 a glimpse of Imperial Federation in the idea that "Mycale was the Pan-Ionian rendezvous of all the tribes of Ion, for old Greece: why should not London long continue the *All-Saxon-home*, rendezvous of all the 'Children of the Harz-Rock.' . . . What a Future: wide as the world, if we have the heart and herosim for it."

Political Economy, in all its ways and works, he hated, and he dubbed McCulloch M'Groudy. In one of the *Latter-Day Pamphlets*, 1850 termed "The New Downing Street," he writes: "An instinct deeper than the Gospel of M'Groudy teaches all men that Colonies are worth something to a country. That if, under the present Colonial Office, they are a vexation to us and themselves, some other Colonial Office can and must be contrived which shall render them a blessing: and that the remedy will be to contrive such a Colonial Office or method of administration and by no means to cut the colonies loose. Colonies are not to be picked up off the street every day; not a colony of them but has been bought dear, well purchased by the toil and blood of those we have the honour to be sons of; and we cannot just afford to cut them away because M'Groudy finds the present management of them cost money. The present management will indeed require to be cut away;—but as for the colonies, we purpose through Heaven's blessing to retain them a while yet! Shame on us for unworthy sons of brave fathers if we do not. Brave fathers, by valiant blood and sweat, purchased for us, from the bounty of Heaven, rich possessions in all zones; and we, wretched imbeciles, cannot do the function of administering them? And because the accounts do not stand well in the ledger, our remedy is, not to take shame of ourselves, and repent in sackcloth and ashes, and amend our beggarly imbecilities and insincerities in that as in other departments of our business, but to fling the business overboard, and declare the business itself to be bad. We are a hopeful set of heirs to a big fortune!"

If realism is plain in Carlyle's writings on the colonial question, idealism is no less plain. In *Chartism* he strikes the true imperial note, which with him was another form of Romanticism. In it he asks the question: "How many brawny arms generation after generation, sank down wearied; how many noble hearts, toiling while life lasted, and wise heads wore themselves dim with scanning and discerning, before this waste *Whitecliff*, Albion so-called, with its other Cassiterides *Tin Islands*, became a British Empire! The stream of World-History has altered its complexion; Romans are dead out, English are come in. The red broad mark of Romanhood, stamped ineffaceably on that Chart of Time, has disappeared from the present, and belongs only to the past. England plays its part; England too has a mark to leave, and we will hope none of the least significant. Of a truth, whosoever had, with the bodily eye, seen Hengst and Horsa mooring on the mud-beach of Thanet, on that spring morning of the Year 449; and then, with the spiritual eye, looking forward to New York, Calcutta, Sidney Cove, across the ages and the ocean; and thought what Wellingtons, Washingtons, Shakespeares, Miltons, Watts, Arkwrights, William Pitts and Davie Crocketts had to issue from that business, and do their several taskworks so—he would have said, those leatherboats of Hengst's had a cargo in them!" In *Past and Present* he muses: "Nature alone knows thee, acknowledges the bulk of thee, thy Epic, unsung in words, is written in huge characters on the face of this Planet,—sea-moles, cotton-trades, railways, fleets and cities, Indian Empires, Americas, New Hollands; legible throughout the Solar System!"

The English are indeed a chosen race, chosen to fulfil a great Imperial mission. In *The New Downing Street* we note that "Sugar Islands, Spice Islands, Indias, Canadas,—these, by the real decree of Heaven, were ours." In *Chartism* we also note our duty towards them. "To the English people in World History there have been, shall I prophesy, two grand tasks assigned? Huge—looming through the dim tumult of the always incommensurable Present Time, outlines of two tasks disclose themselves: the grand industrial task of conquering some half or more of this Terraqueous Planet for the use of man; then, secondly, the grand Constitutional task of sharing, in some pacific endurable manner, the fruit of the said conquest, and showing all people how it might be done." Contrast this teaching with that given by Sir G. C. Lewis in his *Government of Dependencies*, published in 1841. In true Utilitarian spirit he contemptuously dismisses the "glory which a country is supposed to derive from an extensive colonial empire." His conclusion is that "If a dominant country understood the true nature of the advantages arising from the relation of supremacy and dependence to the related communities, it would voluntarily recognise the legal independence of such of its own dependencies as were fit for independence; it would, by its political arrangements, study to prepare for independence those which were still unable to stand alone." As War Secretary in a speech in the House of Commons in 1862 he contemplated the ultimate independence of Canada, to which he looked forward "without apprehension and . . . without regret."

Poetic vision and prophetic ardour are qualities common to Thomas Carlyle and Jules Michelet. Both were poets and prophets as well as historians, exercising a deep moral influence over their contemporaries. Both of them were sons of the people who lacked measure and self-control. To each, early poverty was a source both of strength and weakness. They possessed the capacity of acquiring friends in all ranks of life, an invaluable trait in one who is an historian. Both were keen if not serene; both regarded conduct as three-fourths of life. Both, if we allow for altered conditions, were devotedly sensible of a "mission," and were constantly "improving the occasion." Their courage and their sleepless industry unite them; so do their single-minded straightforwardness, their impatience of affectation or of "big words for little things." They were resolute in their aim not to make the worst of both worlds. They were at bottom, Stoics, Carlyle an unamiable one,

Michelet an amiable one. The marriage of each was perhaps a success, but certainly a difficult success. If duty was the watchword of the Scotsman, it was also the watchword of the Frenchman though he spelt it *La Patrie*. Approaching the past in the Romantic spirit, neither of them believed for a moment that all had been for the best in the best possible of worlds. As the Covenanters impressed a one-sided view of Christianity on Carlyle, so the Revolutionaries impressed a similar view on Michelet. The extreme Protestantism of their writings is quite unmistakable. In their genius for morality, their paramount and universal application of the moral outlook, in their "natural piety" conjoined with "rational enquiry," in their common sense leavening, and leavened by speculation, their attitude is alike. Each believed, in the spirit of Goethe, in solitude. As Carlyle sojourned for a time at Craigenputtock, so Michelet sojourned at Lausanne. What Irving meant to the former, Quinet meant to the latter.

In the world of history, Michelet and Carlyle are akin, for Carlyle professes as much anxiety to understand the condition of the people as Michelet steadily shows. Michelet indeed enters more truly into the whole of the complex life of the time he describes, Carlyle, into its personal and military aspects. The former swept the field of history with a microscope, the latter with a telescope. The people coloured the glass of Michelet as the hero the glass of Carlyle. The Frenchman's passionate sympathy for the dim, neglected multitudes produced the most brilliant picture of the sensuous court of France against which he sets his face. The Scotsman's similar sympathy produced the most alluring description of all sorts of heroes. As the Scotsman blackens the Puritan leaders in order to illustrate the transcendent merits of Cromwell, so the Frenchman blackens Napoleon in order to illustrate the transcendent merits of the Directorate. Intuition plays a large part in the interpretations of the past these historians offer to us. Nor is it too much to say that the problems of their own day constantly dim the light they throw on the problems of past days. We can never forget that primarily they are prophets. The *French Revolution* of each effects a new departure. "Every history of the Revolution," according to Michelet, "up till now has been essentially monarchical. This has been the first republican history, the first which has broken the idols and the gods. From the first page to the last it has only had one hero, the people. . . . All the glory of the Mountain has been monopolised by the Committee, that of the Committee by Robespierre; that is to say, republican history has constantly been written in a monarchical sense." The supreme quality of each lies in the fact that their writing is the attempt of a powerful genius to evoke the spirit of a whole people from the tomb. Each succeeds in adding to his attempt that undefinable something which gives the abiding charm that mysterious gift of genius which, as Coleridge says, converts the passing into the permanent. The power of political judgment is conspicuously absent in the interpretation each gives of the events of 1789. At the same time, each contrives to furnish us with the impression that in some mysterious way he was contemporary with the events of the French Revolution. Michelet and Carlyle tend in their bold and brilliant painting of character to individualise everything. Their reflections are sometimes childish, their analysis deficient, their passion strained. Yet they bring us face to face with men and women who think, feel, and act. Vauvenargues declares that "great thoughts come from the heart." The heart of Michelet or Carlyle was large enough to bring forth sentiments of heroic mould, thoughts inspired by their genius.

REFERENCES

ALTHAUS, F. *Englische Charakterbilder.* Vol. I. (Berlin, 1869.)
ARNOLD, M. *Discourses in America.* (London, 1885.)
BARTHÉLEMY, E. *Thomas Carlyle: essai biographique et critique.* (Paris, 1899.)
BAUMGARTEN, O. *Carlyle u. Goethe. Lebensfragen.* Vol. XIII. (Tübingen, 1906.)
BODELSEN, C. A. *Studies in Mid-Victorian Imperialism.* (London, 1924.)
CAZAMIAN, L. *Carlyle.* (Paris, 1913.)
CHERBULIEZ, V. *Thomas Carlyle. Revue des deux Mondes.* (March, 1881.)
CONWAY, M. D. *Thomas Carlyle.* (London, 1881.)

CROZIER, J. B. *Carlyle's Politics: Civilisation and Progress.* (London, 1885.)
DAVEY, S. *Darwin, Carlyle, and Dickens; with other essays.* (London, 1876.)
DUFFY, Sir C. G. *Conversations with Carlyle.* (London, 1892.)
FISCHER, T. A. *Thomas Carlyle.* (Leipzig, 1881.)
FLÜGEL, E. *Thomas Carlyle: religiöse u. sittliche Entwicklung u. Weltanschauung.* (Leipzig, 1887.)
FROUDE, J. A. *Carlyle: History of the first forty years of his life (1795–1835).* (London, 1890.)
FROUDE, J. A. *Carlyle: History of his Life in London (1834–1881).* (London, 1884.)
GARNETT, R. *Life of Carlyle.* (London, 1887.)
GAZEAU, J. *L'Imperialisme anglais: son évolution. Carlyle, Seeley, Chamberlain.* (Paris, 1913.)
GOETHE, J. W. *Goethe's u. Carlyle's Briefwechsel.* (Berlin, 1887.)
GOOCH, G. P. *History and Historians in the Nineteenth Century.* (London, 1913.)
GREG, W. R. *Literary and Social Judgments. Kingsley and Carlyle.* (London, 1877.)
HAMILTON, M. A. *Thomas Carlyle.* (London, 1926.)
HAMLEY, E. B. *Thomas Carlyle. An Essay.* (Edinburgh, 1881.)
HENSEL, P. *Thomas Carlyle (Klassiker der Philosophie, XI).* (Stuttgart, 1901.)
HUTTON, R. H. *Thomas Carlyle. Good Words.* (April, 1881.)
KEBBEL, T. E. *Essays upon History and Politics.* (London, 1884.)
KRÄGER, H. *Carlyles Stellung zur deutschen Sprache u. Literatur.* (Anglia, Vol. XXII, 1899.)
LARKIN, H. *Carlyle and the open secret of his life.* (London, 1886.)
LEOPOLD, W. *Die religiöse Wurzel von Carlyles literärischer Wirksamkeit.* (Berlin, 1922.)
LOWELL, J. R. *My Study Windows.* (London, 1871.)
MACCUNN, J. *Six Radical Thinkers.* (London, 1907.)
MACPHERSON, H. *Carlyle.* (London, 1896.)
MARTINEAU, J. *Essays philosophical and theological.* (New York, 1879.)
MASSON, D. *Carlyle personally and in his Writings.* (London, 1895.)
MAZZINI, J. *Life and Writings.* Vol. IV. (London, 1864–70.)
MORLEY, Lord. *Miscellanies.* Vol. I. (London, 1871.)
NICOL, J. *Thomas Carlyle.* (London, 1892.)
OSWALD, E. *Carlyle, ein Lebensbild: u. Goldkörner aus seinen Werken.* (Leipzig, 1882.)
OSWALD, E. *Thomas Carlyle noch einnial.* (Leipzig, 1904.)
ROBERTSON, J. M. *Modern Humanists.* (London, 1895.)
ROBERTSON, J. M. *Modern Humanists Reconsidered.* (London, 1927.)
ROE, F. W. *The Social Philosophy of Carlyle and Ruskin.* (London, 1922.)

References

Saintsbury, G. *Corrected Impressions.* (London, 1895.)
Schmidt, J. *Portraits aus dem neunzehnten Jahrhundert.* (Berlin, 1878.)
Schmidt, W. *Der Kampf um den Sinn des Lebens.* (Berlin, 1907.)
Schulze-Gävernitz, G. von. *Thomas Carlyles Welt- u. Gesellschaftsanschauung Dresden,* 1893.
Schulze-Gävernitz, G. von. *Zum sozialen Frieden.* (Leipzig, 1890.)
Stephen, Sir J. F. *Essays.* (London, 1862.)
Stephen, Sir L. *Hours in a Library.* Vol. III. (London, 1892.)
Streuli, W. *Thomas Carlyle als Vermittler deutscher Literatur u. deutscher Geistes.* (Zürich, 1895.)
Ströle, A. *Thomas Carlyles Anschauung vom Fortschritt in der Geschichte.* (Berlin, 1909.)
Ströle, A. *Carlyles Sartor Resartus. Ein Beitrag zum Verständnis Carlyles.* (Tübingen, 1913.)
Taine, H. *L'Idealisme anglais: étude sur Carlyle.* (Paris, 1864.)
Vaughan, C. E. *Carlyle and his German Masters.* Essays and Studies by Members of the English Association. (Oxford, 1910.)
Wilhelmi, J. H. *Th. Carlyle u. F. Nietzsche: wie sie Gott suchten u. was für einen Gott sie fanden.* (Göttingen, 1897.)
Wilson, D. A. *Carlyle till Married* (1795–1826). (London, 1923.)
Wilson, D. A. *Carlyle to the French Revolution* (1826–1837). (London, 1924.)
Wilson, D. A. *Carlyle on Cromwell and Others* (1837–1848). (London, 1925.)
Wilson, D. A. *Carlyle at his Zenith* (1848–1853). (London, 1927.)
Wilson, D. A. *Carlyle to Threescore and Ten* (1853-1865). (London, 1929.)
Young, N. *Carlyle: His Rise and Fall.* (London, 1928.)

Chapter IX.

COBDEN AND FREE TRADE

CARLYLE was a northerner who did his work in the south whereas Richard Cobden (1804–65) was a southerner who did his work in the north. Both came from an ancient stock of farmers for centuries rooted in their respective districts. The lad Richard attended a school in Yorkshire worthy of the picture Dickens was to draw of Dotheboys Hall. In 1819 his uncle gave him a clerkship in his warehouse, and in due time he proceeded on his rounds as a commercial traveller. The romanticism of Carlyle was not foreign to his nature. His duties brought him to Shrewsbury in 1825 when he seized the opportunity of seeing the venerable walls and the beautiful glass of the Abbey. "Oh! that I had money," he confides in his brother, "to be deep skilled in the mysteries of mullions and architraves, in lieu of black and purple and pin grounds! How happy I should be."

In 1828 he set up in business on his own account. Two friends and he borrowed a thousand pounds, and a calico-firm in Lancashire entrusted them with the sale of their goods on commission in London. In 1831 the three partners leased an old factory near Burnley, and printed their own calicoes, and printed them with handsome profits to themselves. The following year Cobden resided at Manchester, and Disraeli was to bestow the name of the Manchester School on the system of economic thought with which he identified himself. It was essentially individualist in character as the man himself. Acting on the principles of Smiles's *Self Help*, he taught himself French, read English history, and began to write. His eager intelligence received stimulus from his first visit to the United States in 1835 and his six months' tour in the east during the winter of the following year.

He loved to confess himself "a practical man," and a practical man he became and remained. He displayed a patience with life and an impatience with theorisers on it worthy of Burke, and like the Irish statesman he laboured incessantly on behalf of the public weal. From kin to kind was the ideal that inspired his conduct. In 1835 he wrote the first of the many pamphlets that flowed from his pen, *England, Ireland, and America*, and the following year one on *Russia*. The first attested how deeply the boundless resources of the United States had affected him. Here was a country with a virgin soil and all its mineral sources untapped. It was free from the burden of an onerous national debt such as we carried, and in our inevitable competition with it we were heavily handicapped by our system of protection. From these arguments he deduced a new orientation of our foreign policy. Our onerous debt was due to intervention in Europe. Why intervene in its affairs? If protection hindered the expansion of our trade, why continue protection? Non-intervention and free trade were the twin pillars of the policy he proposed. Now this meant that he at once came into conflict with the upholders of the balance of power, a conception he never ceased to ridicule. At the same time we register the fact that at the close of the sixteenth century we fought against the preponderance of Philip II of Spain, at the close of the seventeenth against that of Louis XIV of France, and at the close of the eighteenth against that of Napoleon of France, and one of the main reasons for all these wars was certainly the maintenance of the balance of power. Nor was this motive absent from the World War of 1914–18. Cobden's arguments were that our government must always have its hands full in attending to our domestic business. It can seldom be sure which party is in the right in a foreign quarrel, and less seldom can it be sure that the constituencies will discern the true course to pursue. Lastly, the government which keeps most close to morality in its political dealings will find itself in the long run to have kept most close to the nature of things. He concludes that the balance of power has failed in the past. Why not in the future try commerce? Let governments have as little to do with one another as possible, and let peoples begin to have as much to do with one another as possible. Such was the message he persistently delivered. What he preached abroad he tried to practise at home, for he sought a solution of the Irish problem.

In 1837 he stood for Stockport at the general election, and only polled 412 votes. As a Liberal candidate the electors asked him for his views on the property qualification for members of parliament, primogeniture, the Poor Law Amendment Act, and the Factory Acts. His *laissez-faire* attitude merges in his opinion of the last. For plain physical reasons he thought that no child ought to be put to work in a cotton mill so early as the age of thirteen, yet if restrictions on the hours of labour were desirable, it was not the duty of the legislature to impose them. It was for the workmen to insist upon them, relying not upon Parliament, but upon their own action. A workman could save twenty pounds, a sum that would carry him across the Atlantic where he could make himself independent of his employer. Therein Cobden forgot two considerations. One was that the workman might care for his country, refusing to leave it. The other was that the growth of the employer class in New York was as certain as its growth in Manchester. His own business was fast developing, and in 1836 the net profit of his firm exceeded £23,000. Nor was he oblivious of his civic duties, becoming an alderman of Manchester in 1838 and remaining one till 1844 when wider claims demanded his earnest efforts.

The history of England as commonly narrated is, up to almost the beginning of the nineteenth century, the history of the south of England. The north when it appears, appears by fits and starts, but never for long. Once the Industrial Revolution gathers strength, the north assumes the pride of place of the south. The interests of the south were mainly agricultural, those of the north mainly industrial. The members of parliament were for the most part landed gentry, who naturally bestowed most of their time and thought upon the interests of their estates. Now when the bulk of the people was agricultural their interests and those of the bulk coincided. This, however, was no longer the case when the factories of the north belched forth their smoke in ever-increasing volume. The growth of population was at the rate of a thousand souls a day. How were they to be fed when the Corn Laws practically forbade the importation of grain till the price at home rose to a certain level? If we exported manufactures to foreign countries, surely we must in turn import their corn or their produce in some other form. Such ideas had occurred to Grote and Hume, Roebuck and Molesworth, and they had formed the Anti-Corn Law Association in 1836. Their reasoning was admirable and their logical penetration was sound, yet they effected few converts. In 1838 Cobden joined a new Anti-Corn Law Association formed at Manchester, for he was impressed by the urgency of the question. He faced the bitter opposition he encountered, and he faced it without flinching. He gave his audience admirable reasoning and logical penetration, and yet neither at first impressed them as they came to do afterwards. The agitator, like all agitators, was learning his business. Men like Villiers, Ashworth, and George Wilson were attracted by his obvious devotion to a cause to which they were pledged. From 1838 to 1846 the Corn Law League steadily gathered adherents, and the gifts of Cobden were largely responsible for this growth in membership. He was calm in counsel, energetic in debate, and the enthusiasm of his personality communicated itself to his hearers. Above all, he developed those gifts for organisation which secured followers who were prepared to give up much for what he taught them to believe was vital for the common weal. To the simple and untrained intelligences of the factory operatives he appealed with a force that was nothing short of amazing. In 1841 he entered parliament, and he confined himself to the necessity of the repeal of the Corn Laws.

In 1841 there occurred the meeting of John Bright and Richard Cobden, and the acquaintance of the two men ripened fast into a friendship that meant much to them and even more to the course of politics. "It was in September . . .," said Bright. "The sufferings throughout the country were fearful; and you who live now, but were not of an age to observe what was passing in the country then, can have no idea of the state of your country in that year . . . At that time I was at Leamington, and I was, on the day when Mr. Cobden called upon me—for he happened to be there at the time on a visit to some relatives—I was in the depths of grief, I might almost say of despair; for the light and sunshine of my house had been extinguished. All that was left on earth of my young wife, except the memory of a sainted life and of a too brief happiness, was lying still and cold in the chamber above us. Mr. Cobden called upon me as his friend, and addressed me, as you might suppose, with words of condolence. After a time he looked up and said, 'There are thousands of houses in England at this moment where wives, mothers, and children are dying of hunger. Now,' he said, 'when the first paroxysm of your grief is past, I would advise you to come with me, and we will never rest till the Corn Law is repealed.' I accepted his invitation. I knew that the description he had given me of the homes of thousands was not an exaggerated description. I felt in my conscience that there was a work which somebody must do, and therefore I accepted his invitation, and from that time we never ceased to labour hard on behalf of the resolution which we had made."

"For seven years," confesses Bright, "the discussion on that one question—whether it was good for a man to have half a loaf or a whole loaf—for seven years the discussion was maintained, I will not say with doubtful result, for the result was never doubtful, and never could be in such a cause; but for five years (1841-6) we devoted ourselves without stint; every working hour almost was given up to the discussion and to the movement in connexion with this question." Bright and Cobden each supplied the deficiencies in the other, and supplied them with a skill that was wholly admirable. Bright was a preacher of righteousness second to none. Cobden and he employed homely illustration and wealth of detail, and their homeliness of illustration and their wealth of detail drove home the points they made with the utmost vividness. They appealed to different parts of their crowded audiences. While Cobden moved the reason Bright moved the heart. The former persuaded men that his cause was sound and the latter that it was moral, and this combination of persuasiveness of reasoning with righteousness of repeal swept people off their feet. They appealed to the heart and the conscience, to the sense of a justice and a love which are not merely human, but divine. Both men were intensely in earnest with the strongest conviction that political issues were almost always issues of moral right and wrong, and it was in this lofty fashion they argued for the repeal of the Corn Laws. Cobden was a member of the Church of England and Bright a member of the Society of Friends, and this meant they captured the former as well as the latter.

Bright was probably the greatest man who ever addressed a political meeting, and his eloquence and the enthusiasm of his friend Cobden account in no scanty measure for the success of an agitation of far-reaching consequences. What they said on the platform was repeated by men like Ebenezer Elliott in his *Corn Law Rhymes*. True, he was not a poet, but he was a writer of verse that came home to starving men and women.

> Bread-taxed Weaver, all may see
> What that tax hath done for thee,
> And thy children vilely led,
> Singing hymns for shameful bread,
> Till the stones of every street
> Knew their little naked feet.

The lines of Elliott were always in the heart of Bright and Cobden and often on their lips:

> Child, is thy father dead?
> Father is gone!
> Why did they tax his bread?

At a meeting of the Corn Law League a farm labourer crystallised the case in a single sentence, "I be protected and I be starving."

On the whole England had been a corn-exporting country during the eighteenth century, and the Corn Law then assumed the form of a bounty on the export of corn. During the Napoleonic wars the price of wheat varied between 49 and 126 shillings a quarter, and this was an enormous increase when compared with the variation from 34 to 57 shillings a quarter from 1763 to 1792. This enormous increase was due in part to the Industrial Revolution and in greater part to the war. Napoleon conferred more benefits on the landlords, whose rents had doubled, than all the mills. The Duke of Wellington in 1828 introduced a measure by which when the price in the home market was 64 shillings, the duty was 23 shillings and 8 pence. The effects of this measure was to perpetuate the artificial conditions to which the long war had given rise. The utter artificiality of these conditions is clear from the reports on the state of trade. In Stockport 37 spinning firms had gone bankrupt since 1836, 3000 dwellings remained unlet, and over 70,000 were in receipt of poor law relief. In Manchester 116 mills were idle, 681 shops and offices unlet, 5492 dwellings unoccupied, and in one district 2000 families were without a bed. Nor were Stockport and Manchester untypical.

In the whole north of England misery was acute, and the burning words of Bright and the calm reasoning of Cobden fell on ears prepared to listen to them. The Corn Law League began in 1841 to stir people already predisposed by their condition to believe all that they heard at its meetings. The agitation swelled in volume to such an extent that the manufacturers besought Sir Robert Peel, the Prime Minister, to receive a deputation from the League. As he knew right well that such a deputation would press him for an immediate repeal of the Corn Laws, he refused to receive it. Then was seen a strange sight. Arm in arm five hundred manufacturers, each a man of mark in his own district, marched upon the House of Commons as if they had been so many Chartists. In the procession walked John Bright, full as angry with Peel's refusal as the rest of the deputation. On arrival at the Palace Yard they shouted their demand for "Total Repeal" and "Cheap Food." As they marched away near Downing Street they met Peel. As he, the manufacturer's son, heard those angry shouts from his fellow-manufacturers, he leaned back in his carriage pale and grave. He might well be so, for this procession signified that the public opinion of the middle class was exerting, for the first time on a large scale, its pressure on members of parliament.

The Budget of 1842 testified to the impression left on Peel by the plight of manufacturers. He abolished most of the remaining duties on manufactured goods, he removed the weight of the import duties on raw material and on manufactured articles, and he introduced the income tax. At the same time he took occasion to show that at least part of the industrial distress was due to over-investment of borrowed capital in manufactures, the displacement of handloom weaving by steam power, monetary difficulties with the United States and the consequent diminution of demand for our manufactures, the interruption of the China trade, and alarms of war in Europe. How could alteration of the Corn Law touch these undoubted sources of industrial depression? Nevertheless, he thought the 1828 measure capable of improvement, for it had proved injurious to the consumer, the revenue official, the agriculturist, and to the commercial man. It proved injurious to the consumer because it kept back corn until it was dearer. It proved injurious to the revenue official because of the forced reductions of duty. It proved injurious to the agriculturist because it withheld corn until it reached the highest price, which was then suddenly snatched from him by the operation of the sliding scale, and his protection rendered useless. It proved injurious to the man of commerce because it introduced paralysing uncertainty. Peel did not propose to change the sliding scale into a fixed duty, for how could such a duty bear the strain of a time of scarcity and distress? His proposal was the modification of the existing principle of a duty varying inversely with the price. On the whole it was fit that the price of wheat should range between 54 and 58 shillings.

On the principle that half a loaf is better than no bread, the Corn Law League ought to have rejoiced at the long step towards Free Trade taken by Peel, yet such rejoicing was far from their thoughts. Cobden was furious. "I ask the Right Honourable Baronet," he demanded, "whether, while he fixes his scale of prices to secure to the Landowners 56s. per Quarter for wheat, has he any sliding scale for wages? Will he give the people a law to keep up the rate of wages?" It is to the credit of the angry speaker that the sufferings of the artisans had so impressed—and obsessed—him, that he could not bear the idea that they should last a moment longer. Nor did he hesitate to avow that the income tax was such a burden on the manufacturer that it vastly outweighed all the benefits conferred by the rest of this remarkable Budget. In spite of the beam in his own eye, he could see with the utmost distinctness the mote in the landlord's eye. Obviously if Peel was to make any headway with his desire to improve the condition of the whole country, he must tax the manufacturer if he were to deprive the landlord of income. If Cobden and Bright remembered the rough rhymes of Elliott, they also remembered a couplet that young Lord John Manners, a member of the Young England party, produced:

> Let trade and commerce, laws and learning die,
> But leave us still our old nobility.

What Bright and Cobden were determined to leave—and to leave in political possession—was their own class, not the effete nobility. Cobden insisted that the low wages then prevalent were economically a mistake. He pressed, with the experience of a practical man, the conclusion that low wages were not at all synonymous with cheap labour, a point that helped to convert Peel to Free Trade. He preached the novel doctrine that his policy would raise wages. Bright prophesied that Free Trade, notably in corn, would raise wages and shorten hours of work, and his prophecy proved accurate in the highest degree. Men said of him that if he had not been a Quaker he would have been a prize-fighter, and a prize-fighter he undoubtedly was with the happiness of the toiler for his reward. His impassioned speeches moved his audiences enthusiastically. The plan of the pair was that Cobden should speak first, and he spoke with persuasion and with sympathy supported by facts next to impossible to explain away. When the audience had been brought to a sympathetic consideration of the evils of Protection, then Bright stood up, and with incomparable power raised those present to the liveliest state of moral indignation. The affectionate friendship of the two men meant much to themselves, but it meant everything to the cause they both held dear.

Feeling ran high, for Cobden and Bright detected the taint of blood on the rent the landlord received. Was it not paid with a price, and that price the starvation of men, women, and children who could have feasted on the corn which the law denied them? A mechanic from Glasgow, Daniel M'Naghton, shot Mr. Drummond, private secretary to the Prime Minister, in the hope that he was shooting Peel, and this murder shook Peel's nerves. After this incident Cobden spoke in February, 1843, and in the course of his speech he said, "You passed the (Corn) law, you refused to listen to the manufacturers, and I throw on you all the responsibility of your own measure. . . . It is his duty, he says, to judge independently, and act without reference to any pressure; and I must tell the right hon. Baronet that it is the duty of every honest and independent member to hold him individually responsible for the present position of the country. . . . I say there never has been violence, tumult, or confusion, except at periods when there has been an excessive want of employment, and a scarcity of the necessaries of life." Peel hotly resented this charge of personal responsibility, and he no less hotly resented the menace that accompanied it. Cobden was compelled to explain that by personal responsibility he meant ministerial responsibility.

Inside the House the cause of Free Trade continued to progress, and outside it this was far more apparent. Great meeting after great meeting was held all over England, and public opinion was turning to the side of the Corn Law League in 1843. Agitation was the order of the day. The Oxford Movement in England, the Free Church Movement in Scotland, and the Repeal Movement in Ireland were all in full blast. Newman, Chalmers, and O'Connell were alike advancing the causes for which they passionately pleaded. Remarkably enough, all the causes were destined to triumph, though we wonder what Newman would think of the tendencies of some Anglo-Catholics, Chalmers of the fusion of the body he founded with the body from which he departed, and O'Connell of the murders of the Sinn Feiners. The success of Chalmers and Cobden was swift while that of Newman and O'Connell was slow but sure. Nor is it devoid of significance that the swift success of the forties is being replaced by the failure in our own day. Has not

Protection once more raised its head though to-day we term it safeguarding, fair trade, and the like? Has not the reunion of the Churches in Scotland shed a curious light on the position that Chalmers advanced?

In 1844 the main current was flowing with renewed volume towards Free Trade. There were, however, cross currents swept by other winds. For one thing, the Budget of 1842 had given trade a sorely-needed recovery. For another, there had been a series of good harvests, bringing wheat down to an average of little more than 50 shillings a quarter. Prosperous trade never suits the agitator. Cobden was an agitator, and agitator in a fine cause, and like all agitators he envisaged matters largely from his own point of view. Bright was a manufacturer, fighting the cause of other manufacturers. On New Year's Day, 1845, it seemed to him that the Corn Law controversy had assumed the form of "the towns against the squires, and the towns will win."

In spite of the apparent prosperity the attitude of Peel was plainly altering. *Punch*, possibly the best single source for English history during the nineteenth century, summed the situation in April, 1845:

"BIGAMY.

"A man, named Peel, was yesterday brought before the magistrate, Mr. Bull at this office, charged with having intermarried with a female named Free Trade, his former wife Agriculture being still alive. Their Graces the Dukes of Buckingham and Richmond, and a gentleman, named Ferrand, proved the fact of the former marriage. A Mr. Cobden deposed that Peel had within the last two years contracted matrimony with Free Trade, a young lady to whom he was himself engaged. He complained bitterly of Peel as having stolen his sweetheart."

In March, 1845, Peel sat intently listening to Cobden's argument against the Corn Law, taking notes as the orator proceeded with his reasoned assault. At length he crumpled up the notes he had been taking. Turning to Sidney Herbert, he said, "*You* must answer this, for *I* cannot." It was a dramatic moment for Cobden and Bright, for had they not convinced the Prime Minister? Herbert replied as best he could while Peel listened in solemn silence. With the deepest bitterness Disraeli said that Peel's Government, which represented the Protectionist party, was "an organised hypocrisy." Nor was this the solitary instance when Peel had betrayed his own side. Protection, continued Disraeli, now stood in the same danger as Protestantism in 1828, and the Conservatives present, those who were so spelt with a capital C, or without one, recalled to mind how their party had been ruined by Peel before and was to be ruined a second time.

The private affairs of Newman, Chalmers, and O'Connell had not prospered while they were attending to public business. Cobden found himself in a similar plight, and in September, 1845, he announced to Bright that he had determined at once to retire from the Corn Law League and devote himself to his work as a manufacturer as the one means of saving himself and his family from ruin. As Burke's friends rallied to his support, as Huxley's friends rallied to his, so Cobden's friends rallied. They gave him enough money to tide over the emergency, and right well it was for the cause of the toiler that they did, for it was the eve of victory for Free Trade. In the meantime a season of rain had set in, and day by day the farmers watched the ruin of their standing crops. In Ireland disease fell on the potato, and a population of eight millions stood face to face with starvation. The good harvests had suddenly come to an end, and famine in Ireland, if not in England, was a certainty. With a modern population the Irish had a famine of mediaeval dimensions, and the prospect was appalling. Protection was dead and damned. "Rotten potatoes have done it all," exclaimed the Duke of Wellington, "they put Peel in his damned fright." At the same time the Irish factor was not the main one in forcing Peel to come to his decision of repealing the Corn Law. Cobden had done his work, and had done it right well. Peel belonged to the middle class, and he did not wish to see his class remain radical. Nor did he wish to see the working class turn revolutionary, and unless he decisively rejected Protection, this was the prospect that lay before him. The Houses of Parliament were of one way of thinking and the country was of another. "There is no institution of this country," declared Bright in 1843, "the Monarchy, the Aristocracy, the Church, or any other, whose fate, if attached to the Corn Laws, cannot be predicted." And this prediction was precisely true, and no one realised its truth better than Peel himself. Besides, the third French Revolution took place in 1848, two years later, and even the Chartists did not seriously disturb the calm of the course of our history. Why? Largely because Peel gave up to mankind what others had given up to party. His comment in 1848 on the fall of the French monarchy was, "This comes of trying to govern through a narrow representation in Parliament, without regarding the wishes of those outside."

Neither Peel nor Cobden nor Bright could see so clearly as we can see to-day the consequences that lay hidden behind the Corn Law agitation. There is a story told that, when all England was clamouring for the death of Byng, Pitt made a brave effort to save him. "The House of Commons," he pleaded, "seems inclined to mercy." "Sir," answered the King, "you have taught me to look for the sense of my people in other places than the House of Commons." This is precisely the task that Cobden and Bright all unwittingly discharged. They taught men to look for the sense of the people outside the House of Commons, and men have ever since been reading, marking, learning, and inwardly digesting the significance of the enormous change in politics they ushered in. When Cobden and Bright began their public career Parliament was an independent deliberative assembly which acted on its own judgment or in its own interest, agricultural or otherwise, and never, except on the greatest occasions, heeded or even heard the voice of the people. By the time they had vanished from the public scene it had almost openly abandoned the right of deciding great issues of policy by its own judgment, and had, for evil as well as for good, become nervously sensitive to every breath of public opinion, especially as expressed, and often artificially manufactured, by the Press and the great party organisations. Lord Northcliffe and Lord Beaverbrook, Lord Randolph Churchill and Mr. Schnadhorst, trace their curious pedigree straight back to Cobden and Bright, as well as to Newman, Chalmers, and O'Connell. The process begun by the Corn Law agitations has been carried a good deal further in the generation that has passed since the days of Cobden and Bright, and the consequence is seen in the fact that the House of Commons has so largely lost the respect which is generally, with or without dislike, paid to masters, but never, under any circumstances, to mere servants. The power which Parliament has lost and which a chaotic and variable public opinion cannot exercise directly has passed to the Cabinet, who, nervous as a Roman Emperor of their many-headed masters, are not afraid to dictate to the two Houses in a manner which yearly makes less distant approaches to that with which the Caesars treated the Senate.

For this constitutional change, which few can think for the better, no men have a greater responsibility than two of the most independent and noble-minded men who ever sat in the House of Commons. The political career of Cobden and Bright is one of a series of assaults upon Parliament made at the head of forces from outside; and it was inevitable that each victory so won was a nail in the coffin of the greatness of Parliament. Had they foreseen such an outcome, it is one from which Cobden and Bright would shudderingly have turned. Nevertheless, this was their work as well as the abolition of the Corn Law. To such a man as Burke, Bright's only rival as a preacher of righteousness to the House of Commons, it is probable that no cause, not even that of Ireland or India, would have seemed worth the sacrifice. He would have preferred to wait for the conversion of the House of Commons. But that would have involved the delay of a generation; and it is the essence of the case of Cobden and Bright that Free Trade and the franchise were immediate necessities. Between the two views lies the whole gulf that separates the Conservative from the Radical temperament.

In 1846 Peel declared the repeal of the Corn Law to be complete, though it was not to take place at once. The ports were not to be entirely open for three years. During this interval there was to be a sliding scale, with a maximum duty of ten shillings when the price of wheat should be under forty-eight shillings, and a minimum duty of four shillings when the price reached fifty-four shillings a quarter. Peel was beaten on the Irish Coercion Bill, and he resigned, and in his resignation he was magnanimous enough to state: "The name which ought to be, and which will be, associated with the success of these measures is the name of a man who, acting, I believe, from pure and disinterested motives, has advocated their cause with untiring energy, and by appeals to reason, expressed by an eloquence the more to be admired because it was unaffected and unadorned—the name of Richard Cobden." It was a fitting tribute to pay, and we desire to add to it. There was a time when the Prime Minister of England was *primus inter pares*, and that time was before the heyday of Cobden and Bright. There is a time when he towers above all the members of his Cabinet, and that time is since their heyday. We build better than we know—so runs the ancient saw. Alack! We build far differently from what we know, and often if we could see what use our posterity would make of our labours we should shrink from building at all.

Cobden, Bright and Peel looked back on the immediate results of their labours, and they looked back on them with a degree of satisfaction that is difficult to feel when we note far-reaching results not then perceived. In July, 1846, Cobden moved and Bright seconded the resolution that their League should dissolve. There had been a preserving revolution in 1832 and there was another in 1846, and the outcome was that there was no destroying revolution in 1848. Obviously, the Reform Bill of 1867 lay not far ahead, but what would Cobden and Bright have thought of the extension of the franchise which 1928 witnessed? These results were hidden from them, and Bright could declare: "We have taught the people of this country the value of a great principle. They have learned that there is nothing that can be held out to the intelligent people of this kingdom so calculated to stimulate them to action, and to great and persevering action, as a great and sacred principle like that which the League has espoused. They have learned that there is in public opinion a power much greater than that residing in any particular form of government; that although you have in this kingdom a system of government which is called 'popular' and 'representative'—a system which is somewhat clumsily contrived, and which works with many jars and joltings—that still, under the impulse of a great principle, with great labour and with great sacrifices, all those obstacles are overcome, so that out of a machine especially contrived for the contrary, justice and freedom are at length achieved for the nation; and the people have learned something beyond this—that is, that the way to freedom is henceforward not through violence and bloodshed." It was Peel's belief that "I shall leave a name execrated by every monopolist who maintains Protection for his own individual benefit; but it may be that I shall leave a name sometimes remembered with expressions of good will in the abodes of those whose lot is to labour, and to earn their daily bread by the sweat of their brows, when they shall recruit their exhausted strength with abundant and untaxed food, the sweeter because no longer leavened with a sense of injustice." Such a name he undoubtedly has left.

The immediate results of Free Trade were that it mitigated the famine in Ireland and the shortage of food in England. The gold discoveries and the Crimean War would have raised the price of wheat enormously had it not been for the free importation of food from abroad. Had it not been for Peel's legislation prices would have increased whereas they fell. Bread entered into the general consumption, and potatoes and turnips ceased to be the staple food of the working classes as a whole. Wages rose because trade expanded, and trade expanded because of Free Trade. For thirty years to come the tale was one of unbounded prosperity. In the seventies the development of transport combined with the immense increase in the production of wheat in the United States told quite a different tale. An old soil like ours could not compete with a new soil like that of America, and the outcome was the ruin of Ireland and of Irish agriculture and the impoverishment of English. In 1846 the population of Ireland exceeded eight millions and to-day it slightly exceeds four. Even in England the effects of Free Trade have been to turn district after district into pasturage with the inevitable outcome of the exodus of the population from the country to the town. The average price of wheat per quarter from 1836 to 1846 had been 57 shillings; the average price from 1886 to 1896 was 29 shillings. Yet in the meantime population had doubled and the consumption of wheat had increased by leaps and bounds. English history used to be mainly that of the south, not that of the north. English history now is mainly that of the north, not that of the south. For in a circle whose centre is in Manchester and whose radius is thirty miles there is a far larger population than in a circle whose centre is London and whose radius is identical. Had Protection continued the growth of cottonopolis and the north of England would have been absolutely impossible. Protection would have meant that other countries would have passed her in the commercial struggle, and her people would have remained in the degraded condition pictured by the Disraelis and the Gaskells.

In 1846 Cobden believed that "the speculative philosopher of 1000 years hence will date the greatest revolution that ever happened in the world's history from the triumph" of Free Trade. He was not afraid to undertake the rôle of the prophet. Did he not foresee that there was "no interest in the country that would receive so much benefit from the repeal of the Corn Laws as the farmer-tenant industry?" Did he not foresee that "the repeal of the Corn Laws would not throw an acre of land out of cultivation?" Did he not also foresee that the landlords would enjoy "as good rents without a Corn Law as with it"? The example of England would prove contagious. Did he not divine in 1846 that "there will not be a tariff in Europe which will not be changed in less than five years to follow your example?" Alack for poor human divination! Did he not declare that the principles of Free Trade were "eternal truths," applicable at all times and in all places? Are not such truths "the international law of the Almighty"? For he is not ashamed to unveil the secrets of the mind of the Deity. Free Trade is nothing short of the exemplification of the Golden Rule of Christianity. In fact, in 1846 he held with unfaltering conviction that "we have a principle established now which is eternal in its truth and universal in its application, and must be applied in all nations and throughout all times." He discerned in Free Trade "that which shall act as the principle of gravitation in the universe. . . . I believe that the desire and motive for large and mighty empires, for gigantic armies and great navies will die away." So he spoke in 1846. Bismarck, who was then thirty-one, was revolving schemes which did not quite fit in with the ideals of Cobden. Nor did they fit in with the ideals of Carlyle and Ruskin who both poured contempt on "a calico millennium."

Burke had constantly affirmed that nothing universal could be maintained in politics, a view that never commended itself to the members of the Manchester School. Like ourselves, the Irish philosopher lived in an age which, more than most others, loved universals and generalizations, preferred philosophy to history and custom, and supposed that social and political institutions which suit one man will suit another. Burke set his face as a flint against such an attitude. He, more than any man, taught the world what is, in some respects, the greatest political discovery made since the fall of the Ancient World—the discovery of the truth that there are no abstract rules nor general laws in politics; that everything is growth, everything gradual, everything dependent, not on laws and constitutions suddenly imposed upon a people, but upon the nature of man as modified by character, circumstance, and custom which the particular people have inherited. As Einstein is the discoverer of the truth of physical relativity, so Burke is the discoverer of the truth of political relativity, a truth that Cobden and Bright persistently ignored. This far-reaching doctrine Burke applied to all the problems, English, Irish, American, Indian, and French, with which he had to deal. He says to the English you are treating America as if it were England; it is not, and no law will make it so. So he says about Ireland and India; you are ignoring their genius, their religion, their past history. And he says the same things to the French. You cannot cut yourselves off from your past; to build upon a mere theory is to build upon sand. And in each of these cases he appealed to a thing still mightier—to justice, which is above history and custom but accepts, uses and purifies them, and has nothing whatever to do with theoretic equality, the economic man, or indeed any abstract rights of man whatsoever.

Herein lies the secret and the genius of Burke, a secret that Cobden and Bright never pierced. No doubt Burke used it sometime, as a genius will, in a passionate and one-sided way, ignoring corrections and qualifications. Nevertheless, it remains the greatest of all modern keys to political wisdom: and no age can stand more in need of its applications than an age of democracy, whose darling vice is a love of large generalisations. Democracy likes to ignore history and to suppose that all men are alike, a manufacturer from Manchester and a manufacturer from Maine. But they are not; and the democratic catastrophes which are written all over the map of Europe and Asia to-day are there to teach it—if it will yet learn and save itself—the great lessons of Edmund Burke.

REFERENCES

ASHWORTH, H.   *Recollections of Richard Cobden.*   (London, 1876.)
BALFOUR, A. J.   *Essays and Addresses.*   (Edinburgh, 1893.)
BASTIAT, F.   *Oeuvres complètes. Cobden et la Ligue.*   (Paris, 1883.)
BREWSTER, D.   *The Radical Party; its Principles, Objects, and Leaders.*   (Manchester, 1867.)
CUNNINGHAM, W.   *Richard Cobden and Adam Smith.*   (London, 1904.)
DAWSON, W. H.   *Richard Cobden and Foreign Policy.*   (London, 1926.)
DINO, C.   *Riccardo Cobden.*   (Firenze, 1865.)
DUMCKLEY, H.   *Richard Cobden and the Jubilee of Free Trade.*   (London, 1896.)
GARNIER, C. J.   *Richard Cobden, les ligueurs, et la Ligue.*   (Paris, 1846.)
GOWING, R.   *Cobden.*   (London, 1897.)
HERTZ, G. B.   *The Manchester Politician* (1750–1912).   (Manchester, 1912.)
HOBSON, J. A.   *Richard Cobden. The International Man.*   (London, 1918.)
HOLTZENDORFF, F. v.   *Richard Cobden . . . von F. von Holtzendorff. Virchow (R.) and Holtzendorff-Vietmansdorf (F. v.) Sammlung gemeinverständlicher Wissenschaftlicher Vorträge, herausgegeben von R. v. und F. v. Heltzendorff.*   (Berlin, 1866.) Series I, Heft 17.
HOLTZENDORFF, F. v.   *Richard Cobden: Vortrag.*   (Berlin, 1866.)

References

KRETZSCHMAR, A. *Richard Cobden, der Apostel der Handelsfreiheit und die jüngste staatsökonomische Revolution in Grossbritannien. Nach der besten englischen und französischen Quellen.* (Grimma, 1846.)

MACCUNN, J. *Six Radical Thinkers.* (London, 1910.)

M'GILCHRIST, J. *Cobden, a biography.* (London, 1865.)

MAITRE, C. *Richard Cobden, ou l'Esprit Anglais contre l'Esprit Francais à propos de la Liberté des Échanges.* (Paris, 1846.)

MALLET, Sir L. *The Political Opinions of Richard Cobden.* (London, 1869.)

MORLEY, J. *The Life of Richard Cobden.* (London, 1881–2.)

PROTIN, P. O. *Les Économistes Apprécies, ou Nécessité de la Protection. . . Cobden, Michel Chevalier, Carey, Du Mesnil, Marigny, etc.* (Paris, 1862–63.)

REYBAUD, M. K. L. *Économistes modernes. . .Richard Cobden, M. F. Bastiat, M. M. Chevalier, M. J. S. Mill, M. L. Faucher, M. P. Rossi, etc.* (Paris, 1862.)

ROGERS, J. E. T. *Cobden and Modern Political Opinion.* (London, 1873.)

SALIS SCHWABE, J. *Richard Cobden. Notes sur ses voyages.* (Paris, 1879.)

SALIS SCHWABE, J. *Reminiscences of Richard Cobden.* (London, 1895.)

SIMONSON, F. *Richard Cobden und die Antikornzolliga, sowie ihre Bedentung für die wirthschaftslichen Verhältnisse des deutschen Reiches.* (Berlin, 1863.)

TREVELYAN, G. M. *The Life of John Bright.* (London, 1913.)

WALCKER, C. *Richard Cobden's Volkswirthschaftliche und politische Aussichten auf Grund aelteren und neurer Quellen systematisch dargestellt.* (Hamburg, 1885.)

WATKIN, Sir E. W. *Alderman Cobden, of Manchester.* (London, 1891.)

Chapter X.

J. S. MILL, THE OPTIMISTIC DEMOCRAT

AMONG the great autobiographies of the world we include the *Life* of Benvenuto Cellini, *Les Confessions* of Rousseau, the *Autobiography* of Gibbon, the *Dichtung und Wahrheit* of Goethe, the *Apologia* of Newman, and the *Autobiography* of J. S. Mill. The great autobiographies are generally written by men of thought, not by men of action, just as the great biographies deal with men of thought, not men of action. Nor is this surprising. Great soldiers like Cromwell and Frederick the Great, great statesmen like Beaconsfield and Bismarck, are rather parts of history than individual men. The line between their biography and history is exceedingly difficult to draw: in fact, it is impossible to draw it. On the other hand, literary men are steadily amassing material during the whole of their lives. Not only are the autobiographies and biographies generally written by the literary and the artistic class, but they are generally written by men. Yet we must not forget the great autobiography that Miss Ethel Smyth, the musical composer, has given us in her *Impressions that Remained*. Unless we are grossly deceived, time will seal it with the stamp of approval.

There is no Froude to perform for John Stuart Mill (1806–73) what he performed for Thomas Carlyle, yet in his *Autobiography* Mill has left us a matchless narrative of the formative years of his thought, the years on which we feel strongly most stress deserves to be placed. His *Letters* afford but little light on these important years. More than two-thirds of them date during the last ten years of his life when he had assumed a commanding position over the thought of that generation. It is only after his fifty-fifth year that these *Letters* attain anything like adequacy in amount, and by that time his leading books had all been written. His *Autobiography* is accordingly of paramount worth. Its sincerity is as intense as that of the man himself.

As Bentham was the spiritual father of James Mill, so the latter was the spiritual father of his own son, John Stuart Mill. In 1812 his father wrote to Bentham: "Should I die, one thought that would pinch me most sorely would be leaving the poor boy's mind unmade." Therefore, "I take your offer quite seriously"—an offer apparently to be the boy's guardian—"and then we may perhaps leave him a successor worthy of both of us." The force employed by the father on the son was such that we may question whether the real J. S. Mill ever existed. As we turn over the pages of the *Autobiography* we cannot help wondering whether another type of father might not have turned the son into a Coleridgean instead of a Benthamite. He was brought up after "the most straitest sect" of the Benthamites—that is, he was received into a school systematically adverse to the powers that be, and confident in the creation of powers *to be* by philosophical fiat. He indeed seriously endeavoured in his manhood to shake himself free from the sectarian narrowness imposed on him by his father. Yet to have outgrown Benthamism—or indeed any -ism—was not to have purged the soul of all tincture from the doctrinal sources of his youth.

J. S. Mill was initiated into the Greek language at the age of three. Latin was deferred till he was seven. By that time he had read, and read thoroughly, if not always or perhaps often, with real comprehension, Aesop, the *Anabasis*, all Herodotus, the *Cyropaedia*, the *Memorabilia*, parts of Diogenes, of Lucian (selection was certainly desirable here), and of Isocrates, ending with the six dialogues of Plato, on one of which Mill candidly remarks that "it was totally impossible that I should understand it." To add to the difficulty, in these and later studies, it must be remembered that in 1810 a Greek lexicon was a ponderous thing, weighing nearly as much as the tiny student, and intellectually also requiring "a robust genius to grapple with," as the renderings never fell below the dignity of Latin. Hence the father, the son's only teacher, and "one of the most impatient of men," had constantly to supply the English equivalents—a task which, when one thinks of all Herodotus only, must have rivalled his simultaneous labour upon the history of British India.

This represents but a fraction of the child's work before his eighth birthday. In history he read, noted, and analysed by memory Robertson, Hume, Gibbon, Watson, Hooke, Langhorne's *Plutarch*, Burnet, the *Annual Register*, Millar, and Mosheim. Between the age of three and eight the lad perused biography and travels, represented by the life of Knox, the histories of the Quakers, Beaver's *Africa*, Collins's *New South Wales*, Anson's and Hawkesworth's voyages. Nor were "children's books" wholly absent, though "allowed very sparingly"; and indeed *Robinson Crusoe*, the *Arabian Nights*, and even the tales of Maria Edgeworth herself, must have hardly felt themselves entitled to recognition in the society of such advanced competitors.

The next stage lasts to fourteen—an age at which most of us can recall our own acquirements with perfect ease, and count them on our fingers. But Pico della Mirandola, that early and still remembered Florentine paragon of precocity, could hardly have shown a more appalling catalogue, whether in bulk or difficulty, than is printed in the *Autobiography*. Virgil, Horace, Phaedrus, Livy, Sallust, the *Metamorphoses*, Terence, Cicero, Homer, Thucydides, the *Hellenica*, Demosthenes, Aeschines, Lysias, Theocritus, Anacreon, Aristotle's *Rhetoric*—this time we omit books read only in selections—were mainly read through "from my eighth to my twelfth year"; Euclid, algebra, higher mathematics, Joyce's *Scientific Dialogues*, and various treatises on chemistry, coming in by the way; while the list of English books would go far towards forming the nucleus of a considerable lending library. A boy to whom books, in Wordsworth's phrase, were such a "substantial world," could not resist the impulse to add to the number, and Mill "successively composed a Roman History, an Abridgement of Universal History, a History of Holland, and a History of the Roman Government." Meanwhile the boy was assiduously practised in English verse, to which a less modest man might have assigned with more confidence his rare mastery over prose. But in Greek he never wrote at all, and but little in Latin—not through his father's theories on the subject—but "because there was really no time"—a confession which will not surprise the reader.

The last two years of regular training lay not in "the aids and appliances of thought, but the thoughts themselves." Logic was first studied in Aristotle's *Organon* and *Analytics*, Hobbes, and some scholastic writers; Political Economy in Adam Smith; Plato, Tacitus, Quintilian, and other ancient writers being mastered; while, beside these fertile sources of thought, Mill's filial gratitude assigns much to the *History of India*, which he read "for the press" for his father.

Human nature craves the relief of a smile at a glance over the vast catalogue which we have imperfectly transcribed. Only a mature man, of unusually finished education, can even fully appreciate the range and the difficulty of the task accomplished by this boy of thirteen. "*Non equidem invideo,—miror magis*," will be the comment of some readers. Poor lad! will come from others. And even though Mill assures us that this system "was not such as to prevent him from having a happy childhood," yet we wish that occasionally he had had a cricket bat in his hand. Yet we pity more those whose scorn is aroused by it. For, after all, and all deductions in reason made (nor will it be seen that we hold these deductions slight), it is no small thing to have lived the life or done the work of John Stuart Mill. And though no one is likely to accept his humble estimate of his own natural capacities, yet these results must, in a more than common degree, be assigned to his education.

Some faults in his father's instruction he candidly admits; some intellectual requirements were too severe; some physical advantages and practical readiness were sacrificed. One obvious danger to a lad so educated, the danger of conceit, he escaped. He also escaped the danger that so much study might result in mere cramming of his mind. That his father's wise and patient care averted this danger is proved by the son's writings. In fact, the serious criticism we offer against the boy's early education is that it was too successful. Whether he was correct in entertaining "always a humble opinion of my powers as an original thinker," or whether originality may have been stifled by his training, it is remarkable how closely his aims and opinions, to the end, kept the forms of the mould into which his father poured his youth. Within those limits he moved somewhat, as indeed a less able and observant man who lived on into the century must have moved; but did he seriously outgrow them? In Logic and Political Economy, in Ethics and Theology, in hatred of priestly and aristocratic systems, in preference of a life of more rigid and injurious exclusiveness than any fashionable "exclusive" ever dreamed of, in contempt for the common ways of Englishmen, James Mill is substantially reproduced in his son. Even his developments are in general not so much vigorous shoots from the original trunk, as those abnormal and morbidly active growths which are found when abundant vital energies, long exposed to restricted light and strong pressure, are stimulated, not by "the common sun, the air, the skies," but by the artificial and unwholesome atmosphere of the closest of all conceivable coteries.

Beside the positive elements, the father's educational system had a restrictive side, the effects of which were through life stamped upon his son. To the injurious effects of one negative element he became soon awake, and his efforts to supply what are wanting colour his later life with almost the only tint in which it deviated seriously from the father's pattern. It was often charged against Benthamism, while Benthamism appeared to be a living thing, that it waged war against all the charm of life, despised art and poetry, and treated feeling as an infirmity; and Benthamists were not slow in repudiating these charges. Yet the terrible frankness of Mill's autobiography established them against his father, so far as they could be true of any able and intelligent man. It was not that the father was wholly dead to poetry: he cared for a few of our poets, reserving "his highest admiration" for Milton; a judgment which surprises us more than to learn that he did not appreciate Shakespeare. Yet "for passionate emotions of all sorts, and for everything which has been said or written in exaltation of them, he professed the greatest contempt." It is hardly possible to avoid the inference that what he valued in poetry could not have been its poetical side, or that it could penetrate the dour nature of the grim ex-Calvinist. At any rate, when the too docile pupil came forth completely clad in Benthamism, he confesses, with the fearless candour which throws a singular and indescribable charm over the *Autobiography* and the autobiographer, that he was, for a considerable time, more or less blind to the claims of this side of humanity. "From this neglect both in theory and in practice of the cultivation of feeling, naturally resulted an underrating of poetry, and of imagination generally, as an element of human nature."

Mill was really a man of high, of even over-wrought, sensitiveness and passionate impulse; and when he reached full manhood, nature revenged herself strangely and sadly on a training which had all the inhuman harshness of asceticism without its hopes and horizons. The reaction against Puritanism, which had guided his father to complete religious disbelief, guided the son into an emotionalism which was ever ready to pass into extravagance; singular testimony to the stubborn power of a system apparently so antagonistic to natural human feeling! Sentiment, in the intensity of this reaction, asserted its rights with revolutionary violence; but the balance between heart and head could not thus be reached. Science tells us of two modes in which elements combine, the chemical and the mechanical; the chemical being a true and vital fusion between atoms, the other a simple bond of close juxtaposition. Mill unhappily lacked during the plastic period of childhood the simultaneous training of reason and sentiment which is received every day by thousands of children who will never hear of Bentham or James Mill; and, lacking this, the union between sentiment and reason in his nature remained to the end mechanical. This we regard as the key to his life. If he was too finely organised, too fearless and honest, to allow the head and heart consciously to contradict each other, their conclusions were sometimes not homogeneous; the framework is austere and logical, the contents are heated and sentimental.

"I am one of the very few examples in this country,"

J. S. Mill remarks, "of one who has not thrown off religious belief, but never had it"; and the reason is that "it would have been wholly inconsistent with my father's idea of duty, to allow me to acquire impressions contrary to his convictions and feelings respecting religion." Yet did not his Puritanical father thereby spoil his son's efforts to reach a truly philosophical position on this great subject? There are branches of human research to which a child might be trained to absolute scepticism, yet which, in later life, he might be able to examine unfetteredly, whether for rejection or acceptance. Pure mathematics affords an example. This is partly because its ground-principles lie within a small compass, and partly because they lie wholly beyond the bounds of the emotional side of our nature. No man will die for the conclusion that the three angles of any triangle are equal to two right angles, but will not a man die for his race or his religion? Where the conditions of study are not such subjects as pure mathematics, where indeed the conditions are reversed, no one upon whom throughout his whole period of growth and education the entire nothingness, even the entire wickedness, of any system of knowledge and practice had been enforced and reiterated, could have the slightest chance of effectually escaping from such early prepossessions, provided the pupil—through the rigour and ability of this system—could never emancipate himself from its general tenour. Had J. S. Mill been trained to disbelieve and hate poetry, for instance, would he have reached even the stunted growth of appreciation to which his father's indifference to poetry limited him? He hailed the poems of Reuben Elliott, the Corn Law rhymer, as among those that "will go down to posterity as one of the principal memorials of his age." Yet how far simpler is the subject here, how far less involved with those sentiments and ideas which—intuitive or not—still from first childhood necessarily invest any religion, and Christianity beyond any other!

Bentham had lived with a coterie, J. Mill lived with a coterie, and it is plain from the *Autobiography* that J. S. Mill lived—though not to the same degree—with a coterie. It may well be that the reaction from this existence in a set induced him in the days to come to plead powerfully on behalf of varieties of opinion to such an extent that he seemed to esteem an opinion simply because it was different from the prevailing one. He attacks English society just as Carlyle attacked it, and he was just as ignorant of it as Carlyle was. Even if we travel on to his parliamentary days, we shall find that he persistently lived with a few sympathetic friends, and it seems as if he dropped those who dissented from his views. Now obviously such a procedure saves time, but it also tends to turn into a mutual admiration society. Mill announced that "a person of high intellect should never go into unintellectual society unless he can enter it as an apostle; yet he is the only person with high objects who can safely enter it at all." It was this element in his character which induced Disraeli to call him, "Ah, the finishing governess!"

Mill lived in a set with narrow views which he mistook for those of the Goethe who sits detached from the common herd. This comes out in his steady appreciation of French society as compared with English. He lived for a few months with an English family in the south of France where he mixed with the natives. He dwells on the free and genial atmosphere, the elevated sentiment, the culture of the understanding through the feelings, of what he terms Continental life, compared with "the low moral tone of what, in England, is called society." Hence he tended to overvalue the French intellect—Saint Simon and Comte, for instance—and to undervalue such German metaphysicians as Hegel and Fichte.

Milton's lion at creation struggled to secure freedom. The soul of Mill was held in bondage to his father and to his father's set, and though he too struggled to secure freedom, we wonder to what extent he actually secured it. He became a journalist, for it was his duty to proclaim the truth of Benthamism, as his father had also proclaimed it. Like his father he was an official in the India House with sufficient leisure to write copiously in reviews and newspapers. He began at the early age of sixteen, but what age was he really then? He was never a child, and then he was doubtless a man in thought. What is the ideal of a journalist? Not to see the good in all sides, but to see all good in one; not to convince the mistaken, but to deepen the convictions of the convinced; not to give reason and emotion their due, but carefully distinguished, places in argument, but to impassion reason, and to dress feeling in the forms of logic; not to produce belief by exhaustive marshalling of facts, but by massing together leading facts, to give the electric shock of a moment. Now the journalising habit is, of all literary habits, the one which most deeply enters into a writer. Mill contracted it at sixteen, and the traces of it are clearly manifested in his writings. There is little of it in his *Logic*, there is more of it in his *Political Economy*, and there is most of it in his essays and occasional tracts which, in their form and substance, approach journalism. In reviewing Sedgwick or Whewell he all unconsciously assumes that the truth is all on one side, and that of course his side. The reviews are not consciously unfair—a quality foreign to the whole nature of Mill. He came to see some of the danger, for he expressed his apprehension that the new spiritual power of the press might prove as perilous to the pure cause of truth as ever had been the old spiritual power of the priesthood.

In time the influence of his father's education, of his father's set and his own, and of journalism was partly spent, and then his moulding was undertaken by the woman destined to become his wife, Mrs. Taylor. In the *Autobiography* he tells us that he used to compare her to Shelley, "but in thought and intellect, Shelley, so far as his powers were developed in his short life, was but a child to what she ultimately became." When he first met her she was married, and his friendship inevitably led to difficulties with his set. He could brook no criticism on this score. His breach with Carlyle, with Mrs. Grote and Mrs. Austin, with Miss Martineau and Lady Harriet Baring was in each case due to their allusions to this friendship which disdained the observance of external conventions. Mill was never able to shake himself free from a master or a mistress who controlled his thought. The repeated cry for originality in life and character came from one who never completely owned either, and because of this craved them with passionate iteration. The element of poetry, the element of emotion, asserted itself. His heart and his head were in conflict, and the logic of his later writings is by no means fused with their sentiment. Mrs. Taylor, her mark, is plainly discernible all over them. Their fusion is mechanical, not chemical. From his wife came that sentimentalism which never came from his father. He inherited the love of wisdom, but the wisdom of love never became one with the love of wisdom. He remains to the end a type of consistent inconsistency.

The passion for humanity and its highest interests is the one that inspired Mill's singularly influential life. The "fire truly celestial" that consumed Rousseau for ten years consumed him for the whole of his life, and we experience no surprise when Gladstone called him the saint of rationalism. Reuchlin said, "I reverence St. Jerome as an angel, I respect De Lyra as a master, but I adore truth as a God." Whatever Mill's attitude to St. Jerome and De Lyra may have been, he, too, adored truth as a God, and spent his whole life in its ardent pursuit. Ever a learner in spite of his father and his father's education, of journalism, and of his coterie and Mrs. Taylor, we know of no philosopher who avowed and disavowed so many views. Bentham was his master in ethics and politics, but, on discovering the narrow range of his outlook, he broke away from him so far as he was able. Coleridge succeeded to the vacant place until he was superseded by Herder, Michelet, Guizot, and, above all, Comte. Mill began by regarding Ricardo as the creator of Political Economy, and he ended by throwing over some of the most fundamental of the creator's theories, e.g. his naked individualism and his belief in competition. Under the sway of Robert Owen and Louis Blanc, Mill preached co-operation in production as well as in distribution. Had his prediction of its infinite worth proved correct, co-operation would have resulted in one of the greatest of revolutions, all the greater because it would have quietly superseded the capitalistic system. An individualist in his *Principles of Political Economy*, 1848, and a thoroughgoing individualist in his able tract *On Liberty*, 1859, he is a Socialist in his *Autobiography*. In the last book he candidly confesses: "I felt that he (i.e. Carlyle) was a poet, and that I was not; that he was a man of intuition, which I was not; and that as such, he not only saw many things long before me, which I could only when they were pointed out to me, hobble after and prove, but that it was highly probable he could see many things which were not visible to me even after they were pointed out. I knew that I could not see round him, and could never be certain that I saw over him; and I never presumed to judge him with any definiteness, until he was interpreted to me by one greatly the superior of us both—who was more a poet than he, and more a thinker than I—whose mind and nature included his, and infinitely more." There is a peculiar interest in studying the development of those minds which first, and with the mightiest throes, labour under the bondage of tradition, time-worn or otherwise. We follow the intellectual and imaginative emancipation of a Marlowe or a Bürger or an Alfred de Vigny or a Mill with even keener curiosity than we give to greater men who do not struggle against such difficulties.

Without original intuitions and with logical acuteness Mill gave the intellectuals that synthesis the times demanded. His mind was a lighthouse, revolving and casting different lights from the same central fire. Yet he obtained only glimpses when some of us might wish for a view. It is astonishing that a man should do and be so much, and yet never, in spite of aspirations, succeed in being more. As one studies his calm face, "oppressive with the mind," one receives the impression of an infinite reserve of force, of power of toil and endurance almost more than human; and the impression is well founded. Ever ardent, he was also sanguine, so sanguine that he looked for more than was possible, and expected it sooner than it was possible. Life gives much. Does it give all that the social reformer demands from it? Can human nature even take from life, in consequence of its limitations, all that it can give? One sees the real Mill struggling towards freedom, and yet there is the Mill which his father's relentless training from infancy, his journalistic work, his set, and Mrs. Taylor all impressed upon him.

As a believer in progress, Mill occupied himself in the attempt to discover its laws. In his *System of Logic*, 1843, by the aid of Comte and Coleridge, he seeks to expound its laws. Bagehot did not exaggerate a whit when he pronounced in 1873 that "the effect of the *Logic* has been enormous—half the minds of the younger generation of Englishmen have been greatly coloured by it, and would have been sensibly different if they had not been influenced by it; and there is no other book of English philosophy of which the same can be said, even with a pretext of truth." Sir Leslie Stephen testifies from personal observation that it became "a kind of sacred book for students who claimed to be genuine Liberals."

Mill believed that all social phenomena, as well as physical phenomena, were subject to natural laws, and that societies in their evolution—he anticipated Darwin, just as Newman anticipated him—were subject to natural laws of change, of growth and decay, just as living bodies were. Comte claimed to place such a conception on a solid basis by his discovery of the Law of the Three Stages. The human mind, in considering the phenomena of nature, has passed through three grand stages; in the first (which subdivides again into three), phenomena were conceived to be produced by fetiches and the like; then among the nations of antiquity by a number of different deities, national or tribal, or, as with the Greeks, by deities having different provinces of nature under their direction—the winds, the lightning, the sea, etc.; while with the Jews all these deities become merged into one supreme Deity. These three successive sub-stages are known as the Theological stage of human conceptions and of the explanation of things. The next stage, which comes in due course of time in all civilisations, is the Metaphysical, when a superior order of minds becomes dissatisfied with the best theological explanation, and tries to explain them by "entities" behind or within the phenomena. This stage, Comte thinks, was reached among the Greeks by the philosophers about the time of Aristotle, and in the Western World in the Middle Ages, when the nascent science was filled with vicious metaphysical and scholastic entities such as "vital force,"

"Nature's horror of a vacuum," and the like, mere fancies and abstractions turned into realities by the schoolmen and followers of Aristotle which clogged the efforts of genuine scientific inquiry. This state of things persisted till the Baconian reformation, when science became finally emancipated from crude metaphysics. The theological view of things, with its naive explanations, still continued, in Comte's judgment, outside science, which metaphysics was still endeavouring to soften and make less rude and anthropomorphic. At length appeared a philosopher (Hume), a metaphysician even, endowed with the Positive spirit, who boldly asserted that the notion of cause was itself fictitious and illegitimate, that what was said to be causation was mere invariable antecedence and succession. In the first stage, the mind invents; in the second, it abstracts; in the third, it submits itself to positive facts. The proof that any branch of knowledge has reached the third stage is the recognition of invariable natural laws. For a time the Law of the Three Stages satisfied Mill. Becoming dissatisfied with it, he fell back on the far profounder philosophy of Coleridge, who, like Burke, put a new spirit into the old conservatism by his attempt in his political writings to find a philosophical basis for doctrines previously supported by little else save prejudice.

In his aim of discovering general laws of progress, Mill naturally had to face the problem occasioned by the sudden appearance of the great man. His solution is that "such men may be indispensable links in the chain of causation by which even the general causes produce their effects." He proceeds to tell us: "I believe this to be the only tenable form of the theory. Without Mahomet no Averroes or Caliphs of Baghdad or Cordova; without Newton no Newtonian philosophy, at least until there had been another Newton or his equivalent. It might have been produced, perhaps, in successive steps by inferior men coming after him. But even the least of these steps requires a man of great intellectual superiority." The influence of a great man (or a good government), of a Confucius, Lycurgus, Themistocles, Julius Caesar, Luther, he allows, but he thinks their influence tends to become less as compared with the broadening stream of other forces, and with the result that historical science becomes less subject to the disturbing influence of great or revolutionary characters.

Logician as he was, Mill occasionally did not perceive the full extent of the application of his own principles. Take an instance in the pages of his eloquent book *On Liberty*. In it he declares that "despotism is a legitimate mode of government in dealing with barbarians, provided the end be their improvement, and the means justified by actually effecting that end. Liberty, as a principle, has no application to any state of things anterior to the time when mankind have become capable of being improved by free and equal discussion. Until then, there is nothing for them but implicit obedience to an Akbar or a Charlemagne, if they are so fortunate as to find one." Precisely so, but did not Mill see that the principle laid down here applies to every case where a government is far more intelligent than the governed? Such a concession cuts the ground from under his feet just as surely as the admission that "even the least of these steps requires a man of great intellectual superiority." The truth is that the genius differs so much from the rest of mankind that the difference is barely measurable. Is it possible to compute how many average F.R.S.'s would, combined in mind, produce the work of a Newton? Surely such a gigantic genius voyages in seas of strange thought alone, and he is never less alone than when alone.

Talk as loudly as we please about the science of history or political philosophy, the front presented by such subjects is broken by the existence of the great man. Clerk-Maxwell used to imagine the effects upon a law of science if pixies were present, and he deduced, granted this premiss, astonishing results. In the domain of history and political philosophy, if we grant the presence of pixies in the shape of genius, we, too, are face to face with equally astonishing results. Of course it is possible to term our subjects scientific, if we accept the remarkable version of the laws of science presented by such a man as Henri Poincaré. For he shows that in the normal world in which we live such laws are clever statistical averages which do not rigidly apply to the infinitely small world of the atom or to the infinitely large world of the planet.

It is no more possible to resolve Newton into a thousand F.R.S.'s than it is possible to resolve Mohammed into a thousand Arabs. Would any number of Arabs produce the monotheism he produced? To ask such a question is to answer it. There is a street in Florence on each side of which stand statues of the famous Florentines of the fourteenth and fifteenth centuries—Dante, Giotto, Petrarch, Boccaccio, Ghiberti, Machiavelli, Michael Angelo and others scarcely less illustrious, all natives of this little city which in their day had never a population of more than seventy thousand. No one, as Lord Bryce justly says, can walk between these rows of world-famous figures, matched by no other city of the modern world, without asking himself what cause determined so much of the highest genius to this one spot; why in Italy herself populous Milan and Naples and Venice have no such list to show. Nor is this the only question the problem of genius suggests. Why did England produce no first-rate poet in the two stirring centuries between Chaucer and Shakespeare, and again in the century and a half between Milton's birth and Wordsworth's? Why have epochs of comparative sterility more than once fallen upon France and Germany? Why has music sometimes reached its highest pitch of excellence when the other arts are languishing? Why does the sceptre of intellectual and artistic leadership pass now to one great nation, now to another, inconstant and unpredictable as are the shifting winds?

All we can say is that "the wind bloweth where it listeth." There are such surprises as a Newton from a Lincolnshire farm—or a Tennyson from a Lincolnshire rectory—or a Kelvin from the heart of busy Belfast. Nor is it a whit more true of literature or war or statesmanship. Literature has its surprise in a Shakespeare from Stratford-on-Avon, war its surprise in a Napoleon from Ajaccio, and statesmanship in a Lincoln from the backwoods of America. Environment, no doubt, in skilful hands will explain much, but will it explain the origin of a Newton or a Kelvin, of a Shakespeare or a Tennyson, of a Napoleon or a Lincoln?

Great men are original forces, made to some extent by their society. They are of their age: they would not be great men else. Yet they are not wholly fashioned by circumstances. On the contrary, their greatness lies in this, that they are not. They are conditioned doubtless by environment, by evolution, by temperament, by heredity. But they are something more than an aggregate of conditions. Their thoughts, their energy, their action, their solitude, their suffering work wonders beyond time and matter and the subtlest effects of mechanical force.

If the great man cannot be resolved into his environment, there is yet another mode of disposing of him. He is no longer wanted. If we take science, we are told that the labours of Laplace and Lagrange, Young and Joule, Faraday and Clerk-Maxwell are tolerably far finished, and that only the lesser labour remains to be carried out. Men like the late C. H. Pearson, in his striking book on *National Life and Character*, assure us that chemistry rests on the atomic theory—by the way, does it?—and that even if future investigation enables us to forecast with absolute precision what the result of combinations hitherto unattempted will, that discovery will hardly eclipse the merit of Dalton's contribution to science. Whether Darwin or some one else shall have disclosed the great mystery of the generation of life, it is none the less certain, according to Pearson, that all future triumphs will be insignificant by the side of the first luminous hypothesis. Every astronomer knows that there was only one secret of the universe to be discovered, and that when Newton told it to the world the supreme triumph of astronomy was achieved. Yet in our own day Einstein has announced in his theory of relativity one of the most far-reaching of conceptions. The work of such Cambridge scholars as Sir J. Larmor, Sir J. J. Thomson, Sir E. Rutherford, N. Bohr and Henry Moseley promises to revolutionise our whole conception of the atom. We wholly repudiate the idea that the great man of science is simply one who utilises the labours of a thousand predecessors. In this department of knowledge, as in all others, the genius is as much in demand as he ever was, and his opportunities are just as limitless.

There was a golden age of English literature in the days of Wordsworth and Byron, of Shelley and Keats. Then came the interregnum before the great Victorians appeared on the scene. During the generation after 1815 there was complaint after complaint in the *Edinburgh* and *Quarterly Reviews* that the sun of our literary glory had set. We were then told that certain kinds of poetry had become impossible, and that certain others were rapidly being exhausted. Yet the Victorian bead-roll of poets contains such names as Tennyson, R. Browning and E. B. Browning, Arnold, Clough and Thomson. On the bead-roll of novelists we have Thackeray, Dickens, Disraeli, Reade, Kingsley, Trollope, Meredith, Butler, Gissing, the Brontës, Mrs. Gaskell and George Eliot, who possessed the Shakespearean power of putting life into every touch. Nor is it true to say that the labours of the statesman are finished when a Cavour has unified Italy, when a Bismarck has unified Germany, and when a Lincoln has preserved the unity of the United States. The genius is always wanted, and the genius in statesmanship is at this moment more urgently wanted than ever. The world is hungering for statesmen of the first rank. The man with instinctive sympathy for the conditions under which his work is done, who knows what he wants and knows what he does not want, who is aware of the limitations under which his tasks must be executed—such a man is in as keen demand as he ever was. Instead of him we get at Peace Conferences, for instance, the man who takes the readiest, the most obvious way to gain his end, who barely stops to consider how he can do his work, from the angle of the future, most acceptably. The difference between the politician and the statesman is obvious. The politician keeps his eyes on the ground, like Bunyan's man with the muck-rake, listening to the voice of the mob. The statesman keeps his eyes on the ground and also on the hills, divining, if he can, the future. Such a man has Chatham's gift of inspiring others with the confidence he feels himself. He is master because he is entitled to be and because he is fit to be. Like the high-minded man in Aristotle's *Ethics*, he thinks himself equal to great things, and he is equal to them. No one—not even Mill—will persuade us either that the times do not demand such a man or that he will find no scope for his genius when he appears.

Mill's *Unsettled Questions of Political Economy* appeared in 1844 and his *Principles of Political Economy* in 1848. The half-century from Ricardo's death in 1823 to the publication of Marshall's *Economics of Industry* in 1879 marks the change that passed over this subject. In his book Mill brought to a close the line of development proceeding from Adam Smith and Ricardo, J. Mill and Malthus, and of these four, Ricardo proved the most potent in the working of his mind. True, his book bears traces that he never shook himself altogether free from the gloomy theories of the second decade of the century which his father held, and duly impressed on him. How could he? For when he was thirteen, in 1819, his father began instructing him "by a sort of lecture," which he delivered as they took their constitutional. About this time he fell under the direct personal influence of Ricardo. At sixteen he was defending Ricardo and his father against Torrens in the *Traveller*, and his essays on the *Laws of Interchange between Nations* and on *Profits and Interest* proceeded from conversations which took place in 1826, though they were not written till 1829 and 1830, and were not published till 1844. During this long interval between composition and publication the mind of Mill was active though in other directions. A publisher had declined his essays. When a man has been giving time and thought to a subject, he does not take rejected manuscripts which have been lying fourteen years in his drawer, and print them with "a few merely verbal alterations."

In the early twenties Mill had been haunting the thought of his father and McCulloch, Torrens and Senior. In the late sixties he had been haunting the thought of Thornton and Cliffe Leslie, Cairnes and Fawcett. "The new political economy" of the twenties had turned to "the doctrines of the old school" in the sixties, full liberation from which, according to Mill, would mark a veritable "emancipation of political economy." As Dupont de Nemours sat at the feet of Quesnay in his youth and also sat at the feet of

J. B. Say—though at a respectful distance—in his old age, so Mill performed a similar singular feat. Bagehot was able to boast that he was the last man of the pre-Mill period. A developer of classical economy, Mill prepared the way for its downfall. A Free Trader, he allowed protection for infant industries, thereby letting in Protection. An individualist, he turned to Socialism. A Radical, he proved as imperialist as Carlyle. An empiricist, he drifted towards idealism. An Utilitarian, he refuted it and then transformed it so greatly that Bentham could not have recognised it. Mill would have been astonished to hear that he had diminished the authority of political economy, but he undoubtedly did so. By his assaults on it, he altered its position. It spoke in the indicative mood, no longer in the imperative. As a result of this he all unconsciously promoted the growth of collectivism. For it has flourished from no other cause more than the disintegration—some would say the discredit—of the body of classical economical doctrines.

The Malthusian population principle forms the essential foundation of all sound economical doctrine that can be addressed, in their own interest, to the working classes. "The niggardliness of nature, not the injustice of society, is the cause of the penalty attached to over-population." The Wages-fund doctrine, in deference to Thornton's objections, he gave up, but he never gave up his adherence to Malthusianism. He considers the popular remedies for insufficient wages, such as public works, allowances and allotments, and dismissed them with merited contempt. His own remedies are the application of the Malthusian principle, an effective national education of the children of the labouring classes, the settling the waste lands of the nation with peasant proprietors, and a great national colonisation. Devoted as he was to *laissez-faire*, he never mentions the Factory Acts, and in his *Dissertations* he refers to them as belonging to the quack schemes of reform.

His attitude to our colonies resembles Carlyle's. Like the Scots seer, he regards them as a remedy for over-population. Besides, the maintenance of the tie of the colonies with the mother-country is "a step, as far as it goes, towards universal peace, and generally friendly co-operation among nations." It prevents them from becoming absorbed into foreign States, forming a source of additional aggressive strength to a hostile power. It forms a guarantee against the extension of Protection. Lastly, it "adds to the moral influence and weight in the councils of the world, of the Power which, of all in existence, best understands liberty." Like Carlyle he doubts the capacity of the Englishman at home, but he does not dream of doubting it abroad. He warmly praises Dilke's *Greater Britain*, and in his *Representative Government* he looks with kindly eyes on Imperial Federation, though he perceived the difficulties lying ahead. He is quite willing to shoulder the white man's burden of the care of the backward races. His devotion to the cause of progress moves him to approval of conquest. He asks, "The Romans were not the most clean-handed of conquerors, yet would it have been better for Gaul and Spain, Numidia and Dacia, never to have formed part of the Roman Empire?" In his *Representative Government* he lays down the far-reaching doctrine that "if the smaller nationality, supposed to be the more advanced in improvement, is able to overcome the greater, as the Macedonians, reinforced by the Greeks, did Asia, and the English India, there is often a gain to civilisation." The official of the India Office is plain in the vindication of the annexation of Oudh. "To characterise any conduct whatever towards a barbarous people as a violation of the law of nations, only shows that he who so speaks has never considered the subject." Nor is he slow to express his amazement at "the predisposition of English public opinion to look unfavourably upon every act by which territory or revenue are acquired from foreign State, and to take part with any Government, however unworthy, which can make out the merest semblance of a case of injustice against our own country."

Mill draws a sharp line between the laws of Production and those of Distribution. The laws of Distribution are "partly of human institution: since the manner in which wealth is distributed in any given society, depends on the statutes or usages therein obtaining. But though governments or nations have the power of deciding what institutions shall exist, they cannot arbitrarily determine how these institutions shall work. The conditions on which the power they possess over the distribution of wealth is dependent, and the manner in which the distribution is effected by the various modes of conduct which society may think fit to adopt, are as much a subject for scientific enquiry as any of the physical laws of nature." In 1848 he thought in his *Letters* that the Socialists are "the greatest element of improvement in the present state of mankind." His distinction between the laws of production and those of distribution leans in their direction.

The many transitions in Mill's thought marked how many milestones on the road he had passed since he had been a fervent individualist. As he gradually realised the weakness of the utilitarian theory, he approached a form of socialism that at bottom was inconsistent with his faith in popular government. "In (Mill's) case," writes Henry Sidgwick, "we have the remarkable phenomenon that the author of the book which became, for nearly a generation, by far the most popular and influential text-book of Political Economy in England, was actually—at any rate when he revised the third and later editions—completely Socialistic in his ideal of ultimate social improvement. 'I look forward,' he tells us in his *Autobiography*, 'to the time when the rule that they who do not work shall not eat, will be applied not to paupers only, but impartially to all; and when the division of the produce of labour, instead of depending, in so great a degree as it now does, on the accident of birth, *will be made by concert on an acknowledged principle of justice.*' Having this ideal, he 'regarded all existing institutions and social arrangements as merely provisional, and welcomed with the greatest pleasure and interest all Socialistic experiments by select individuals.' In short, the study planted by Adam Smith, and watered by Ricardo, had, in the third quarter of the nineteenth century, imbibed a full measure of the spirit of Saint-Simon and Owen—and that in England, the home of what the Germans call 'Manchesterthum.'

"I do not mean to suggest that those who learnt Political Economy from Mill's book during this period went so far as their teacher in the adoption of Socialistic aims. This, no doubt, was far from being the case. Indeed—if I may judge from my own experience—I should say that we were as much surprised as the 'general reader' to learn from Mill's *Autobiography* that our master, the author of the much-admired treatise *On Liberty*, had been all the while looking forward to a time when the division of the produce of labour should be made by concert."

Mill anticipates in 1848 an increase of rent, an increase of the amount of wages estimated in manufactured commodities, an increase of the cost of wages estimated in raw produce, and, occasioned by this increased cost of wages, a diminishing rate of profit; a diminution which, though checked from time to time by improvements in production, and by the destruction or exportation of capital, always tends to bring society to the stationary state in which profits are so low that the motive to further accumulation is suspended.

This stationary state has been the terror of economists from Adam Smith to McCulloch. Mill looks forward to it not only without apprehension but with pleasure. "There is room in the world no doubt, and even in old countries, for an immense increase of population, supposing the arts of life to go on improving, and capital to increase. But, although it may be innocuous, I confess I see very little reason for desiring it. The density of population necessary to enable mankind to obtain, in the greatest degree, all the advantages both of co-operation and of social intercourse, has, in all the more populous countries, been attained. A population may be too crowded, though all be amply supplied with food and raiment. It is not good for man to be kept perforce at all times in the presence of his species. A world from which solitude is extirpated, is a very poor ideal. Solitude, in the sense of being often alone, is essential to any depth of meditation or of character; and solitude, in the presence of natural beauty and grandeur, is the cradle of thoughts and aspirations which are not only good for the individual, but which society could ill do without. Nor is there much satisfaction in contemplating the world with nothing left to the spontaneous activity of nature; with every rood of land brought into cultivation which is capable of growing food for human beings; every flowery waste or natural pasture ploughed up; all quadrupeds or birds which are not domesticated for man's use exterminated as his rivals for food; every hedgerow or superfluous tree rooted out, and scarcely a place left where a wild shrub or flower could grow without being eradicated as a weed, in the name of improved agriculture. If the earth must lose that great portion of its pleasantness which it owes to things that the unlimited increase of wealth and population would extirpate from it, for the mere purpose of enabling it to support a larger, but not a better or a happier population, I sincerely hope, for the sake of posterity, that they will be content to be stationary, long before necessity compels them to it."

Of the born solitary we may take up Ruskin's position that "an artist should be fit for the best society, and should keep out of it." On the other hand many a hermit is really an outlaw. An imperious temper like Carlyle's or even like Mill's creates a solitude. The true solitary prefers no companion to an uncongenial one. His poet is Wordsworth:

> Now thanks to Heaven! that of his grace
> Hath led me to this lonely place.

Mill realised that individuality forms the true dividing line between the minority and the mass of mankind. The type seeks the sociable: the exception to the type seeks solitude. The original mind, by very virtue of its nature, finds antagonism to rules the type absolutely accepts. Here is the origin of isolation. If conventionality is the unavoidable expression of social averages, originality is the avoidable expression of social averages. Solitude is the haunt—nay, the home—of the strong.

Between the genius of solitude and the solitude of genius there is an intimate connexion. Schopenhauer draws attention to the fact that he describes a genius as one whose centre of gravity lies in himself. The solitude of genius is the inevitable outcome of its enforced submission to the unwritten laws of the genius of solitude. Yet the record of the solitary bears melancholy testimony to the cruel disabilities under which they have lived. In his *Dialogue between Nature and a Soul*, Leopardi compels the soul to refuse the offer of the highest gifts of genius on account of the inevitable suffering connected with them. Lassitude and desolate feelings appear in the lives of one another so unlike as Coleridge and J. S. Mill. Goethe exhibits this with insight:

> Who never ate his bread with tears,
> Nor through the sorrow-laden hours,
> Sat nightly face to face with fears,
> He knows you not, ye heavenly powers.

No doubt Dante was able to stand four-square to the world, but how many other men of genius have been able? The genius is generally alone, comforted by the Alone. Dante stood alone, pondering his poem in the sylvan solitudes of Fonte Avellena. St. Paul, after his experience on the road to Damascus, spent over a year in the solitudes near Mount Sinai, a spot hallowed by the retirement to it of Moses and Elijah. It is noteworthy that the profoundest book St. Paul wrote, the Epistle to the Ephesians, and the greatest book of uninspired religious genius, the *Pilgrim's Progress*, were written in jail. Mohammed meditated his message on the mount above Mecca, and Cervantes wrote the saddest book in the world in the seclusion of a prison.

Marcus Aurelius lived in self-denying holiness, with little conscious support save from his own lonely heart. St. Augustine felt that in the chamber of his friend Alypius, "I was alone even in his presence." It is of course possible to be alone in a crowd, for the crowd in fact to intensify the feeling of loneliness. Michael Angelo lived among the creations of his brain, heedless of the feet which passed his studio. The world approved of him, but what cared he for its approval? The silent toiler of genius never fails of his reward. This exceeding ecstasy is described by Keats:

> Then felt I like some watcher of the skies
> When a new planet swims into his ken.

The Newtons and the Newmans voyage alone, feeling as the world refuses to receive their message, "Which of the prophets have ye not persecuted?" That the highest should suffer most is intelligible when the sufferings are due to their own pangs. That the highest should suffer most when the sufferings are due to the pangs inflicted by others is unintelligible. The man of genius owns the sensitiveness which feels, and therefore bears, the heavy load of Weltschmerz. This is in the nature of the case. He also feels, and therefore bears, the heavy load of neglect and misunderstanding. This should not be in the nature of the case. Why should he not receive balm for his sorrow, comfort for his loneliness? Why will the world never forgive his sin, his failure to conform to type? And yet it is the price he has to pay for his genius. How much solitude went to the creations of the brain of Dante or Petrarch? "Man is what God made him," says Cervantes. Genius sometimes is what men make it. So Milton was destined to realise. Weber gave way to a fit of despair when Beethoven's *Fidelio* was received with indifference. He complained that the audience could not understand the greatest music, and that the music-hall would suit them better. He should have known this. Genius has been ahead and above contemporary applause. A friend of Turner's remarked of one of his pictures, "I never saw the Thames look like that." The painter doubted his friend's insight, not his own, and replied, "I do not suppose you ever did." Hegel complained that there was only one man who understood him, and he misunderstood him. Poets so different in their outlook as Cowper, Byron, and Shelley alike sought seclusion. The quality of the approval bestowed on them did not atone for the lack of quantity. At first Browning, like Hegel, lacked this support both in quality and quantity. When questioned on the meaning of a poem he had written, he replied that the Almighty and he knew what it meant when he wrote it, but now only the Almighty knew.

The Church teaches the communion of saints, and if the men of genius are lonely in the present there is companionship with their fellows who have undergone their bitter experience in the past. They find their sympathy in the unseen comradeship which is denied them on earth. It is the mystical brotherhood, of which Heine speaks, who "bow to each other" across the centuries. The reverence for great names is nothing else save the secular side of the ecclesiastical doctrine of the communion of saints. No man, genius or other, can stand alone. No man wishes to stand alone. He wishes to feel that the mantle of some prophet has fallen upon his shoulders, that he has a source of inspiration for his own efforts, and that he is engaged in a continuous work which will pass on to others who follow him. With Carlyle he needs heroes for the purpose of the particular field of truth to which he has devoted himself. This is notably true of the man of genius. The last words of Crome were, "Hobbema, my dear Hobbema! How I have loved you." What Crome felt inarticulately Gainsborough felt articulately when he uttered the words, "We are all going to Heaven, and Vandyke is of the company."

Mill seldom soars in his *Political Economy*, but he certainly soars as he contemplates a world in which everything is to find its utility measurable in terms of £ s. d. His teaching led, in some respects, to "Manchesterthum," led by such men as Cobden and Bright. Now it is worth while pointing out that the Manchester School was imperial in its outlook at the end of the eighteenth century. The West Indies, not the United States, then provided it with cotton. An empire-builder like Clive wrote: "If I should be so far blessed as to revisit my own country, but more especially Manchester, the centre of all my wishes, all that I could hope for would be presented before me in one view." Within the space of a generation there was a transformation. The Tories of 1793 were the fathers of the Whigs of 1832. Nor is the cause of this transformation in any wise obscure. Cottonopolis was growing very steadily, and the cotton required for its growth could not be bought in the West Indies. It could be bought in the United States. The imperialism and State interference of the eighteenth century was replaced by the cosmopolitanism and State non-interference of the nineteenth. The Manchester man saw in the Continental System the failure of paternalism abroad, and he felt determined to rid himself of it at home. This determination was inevitably strengthened by the circumstance that the Toryism of Eldon and Wellington paid insufficient attention to the industrial North.

Take the condition of trade. The best customers for the manufactured product of Lancashire were foreign nations: the best customer for raw materials from a foreign nation, the United States, was Lancashire. Surely it was obvious that what was sorely wanted was the letting alone of the men who were building the tall factories. What to them was the reform of Parliament? It was little save that it meant that after 1832 the manufacturer had power to shape legislation as the trade of the North required. Mere political reform interested him but little: commercial reform interested him with the vehemence of his whole nature. Restrictions must be swept away, and the colonies might very well be swept away with them. Nor did it ever seem to strike Bright and Cobden that they had mistaken the passing for the permanent. The fact that Manchester had been imperialist and protectionist in the eighteenth century seemingly conveyed no warning to them. It is curious to read Shrewsbury's *Christian Thoughts on Free Trade*, 1843, to see that "free trade is implied in the primeval benediction God pronounced on man," or to turn to Odgers's *Tendency of Free Trade*, 1846, to find out that Peel's commercial policy was traceable to the negotiations between Solomon and Hiram, King of Tyre.

The Manchester School would have none of the Factory Acts, and it is well to bear in mind that part of its opposition is due to the paternalism of the eighteenth century. The Corn Laws were a remnant of this paternalism, and must go. Indeed they raised the price of food, interfering with the cost of production of cotton. Bright argued in the House of Commons that it was essential if England was to continue her sale of yarn to Russia to lower the cost of production. In 1847 he informed the members of Parliament that the intervention between employer and employed violated "one of the greatest privileges and one of the dearest rights" of the workers. Cobden used to recommend the operatives to emigrate to the United States—if they found life too arduous here. What other good was there in the colonies save as a place of emigration? The United

States were better than the West Indies, for they produced cotton, and the emigrant by growing more was really benefiting the land he left as well as the land to which he had gone. Cobden was forced to admit in 1842 that "the colonial system, with all its dazzling appeals to the passions of the people, can never be got rid of except by the indirect process of free trade, which will gradually and imperceptibly loose the bonds which unite our colonies to us by a mistaken notion of self-interest." In 1861 Bright expressed satisfaction with the prospect of the incorporation of Canada with the United States in order that "the whole of that vast continent might become one great confederation of states." Nor was his pleasure in this prospect a whit dimmed in 1867 when the American Civil War had finished two years before. Nor was there any disagreement on the part of Cobden. In his opinion, "it is for the interest of both that we should as speedily as possible sever the political thread, by which we as communities are connected." By these utterances, typical of the Manchester School, we can measure the prescience of Thomas Carlyle.

George Eliot thought that of all forms of mistake prophecy was the most gratuitous. Yet we read that in 1846 Cobden believed that he saw in "the free trade principle that which shall act as the principle of gravitation in the universe.... I believe that the desire and motive for large and mighty empires, for gigantic armies and great navies will die away." Bismarck was then thirty-one and Cavour thirty-six. If Cobden assailed the landlords, he was just as ready to assail the workmen. Individualist to the core, he uttered with profound conviction the words, "I would rather live under a Dey of Algiers than a Trade Committee." Heaven helped those who helped themselves. The employed stood alone. Why should not the cotton operative stand alone? He might have co-operation in distribution, but he certainly should not have it, in spite of J. S. Mill, in production. Cheap food he must have, and cheap food meant the downfall of the Corn Laws and of the landlord class. Naturally this class looked after the welfare of the artisan. By a curious working of the party system the Tories benefited the artisan and the Whigs the labourer, and between the parties the interests of different sections of the community received real attention.

From 1820 to 1860 the Manchester School controlled the destinies of the industrial North. Bright's defeat at the polls in 1857 marked the turning of the tide. Cosmopolitanism and State non-interference had produced the abominable evils to which Disraeli had drawn attention in *Sybil*. On practical grounds Manchester had dropped Imperialism and State interference at the end of the eighteenth century. On practical grounds Manchester dropped cosmopolitanism and State non-interference in the sixties of the nineteenth. The teaching of *Sybil* was reinforced by Carlyle's *Past and Present*, by Mrs. Gaskell's *Mary Barton*, by Dickens's *Hard Times*, by Kingsley's *Alton Locke* and by Ruskin's *Unto this Last*. These writings compel us to reverse the familiar proverb and say that what England thinks to-day Lancashire will think to-morrow. Carlyle demanded in 1843, "Deliver me these rickety, perishing souls of infants, and let your cotton trade take its chance." Nor were men like the sage of Chelsea to be consoled by the evolutionary beatitude, Blessed are the strong, for they shall prey on the weak. The salvation of the worker by the Factory Acts shook faith in the leaders of the Manchester School. For even in 1884 Bright wrote, "I still hold the opinion that to limit by law the time during which adults may work is unwise, and in many cases oppressive." As the Factory Acts came largely from the Tories, the Reform Act of 1867 was to reveal the existence of a being scarcely suspected till then, the Conservative working man. *Laissez-faire* was fast becoming a superstition of a bygone age. Yet it was a superstition that had accomplished much. It had abolished the slave trade; it had ended negro slavery; it had repealed the Corn Laws, thereby removing the deep-seated bitterness of the poor to the rich landlord. If there is much to the discredit of Bright and Cobden, there is much to their credit, though they can claim no credit for the loyalty of our Dominions, which *laissez-faire* assured. They did foresee the wages the labourer might secure in our Dominions, and this is to be reckoned to them for righteousness.

In his *Principles of Political Economy* Mill remains on the whole an individualist. He exempts from the interference of the Government all that part of human conduct which concerns only the life, whether inward or outward, of the individual, and does not affect the interests of others, or affects them only through the moral influence of example. Even within its proper sphere, the conduct of individuals by which others are directly affected, he opposes to the action of the Government three objections. Firstly, every additional function assumed by the rulers of a country increases their direct authority and, what is more formidable, their influence. Secondly, every new public office is a fresh occupation imposed upon a body already overcharged with duties. Thirdly, there is the general inferiority of official agency. His strongest objection is that the extension of Government interference is its tendency to keep the people in leading strings, and to deprive them of the power to manage their own common affairs, by depriving them of the practice without which the arts of administration cannot be acquired.

At first sight it might seem as if he were a thoroughgoing advocate of *laissez-faire* till we come to the consideration of cases in which some of these objections are absent, and others are overruled by counter considerations of still greater importance. The first exception from the general rule of non-interference comprehends the cases in which the interest and judgment of the consumer are not a sufficient security for the goodness of the commodity. The example he gives is the far-reaching one of education. He next takes up the class of case where there is no person in the situation of a consumer, where the interest is to be directed and the judgment which is to be controlled are those of the agent, where, in short, the person protected is protected from himself. A lunatic, an infant, and a child belong to this category, and so then did a married woman. On behalf of all women he always exerted himself most strenuously. Another exception consists of the cases in which the magnitude of the concern makes individual agency impracticable, as in the cases of railways and gasworks. The extension of the joint stock company lets us see what a door Mill was flinging open. Yet another exception is that in which the interference of the law is required, not to overrule the judgment of individuals respecting their own interest, but to give effect to that judgment. For they are unable to give effect to it save by concert, and this concert again cannot be effectual unless it receives validity and sanction from the law. The observance of Sunday as a day of rest is an example. Poor Laws and colonisation constitute further exceptions to the rule of *laissez-faire*. It is pretty evident that the Manchester School had but little to hope from the principles Mill laid down. His exceptions practically breached the defences of the individualist. Mill was in touch with J. E. Cairnes, and in 1870 the latter delivered an attack on *laissez-faire* which completed the downfall of the authority of the classical school of Political Economy. Mill, however, had departed from the path of individualism more unconsciously than consciously, but that he had so departed was plain to all who read the concluding chapter of his treatise.

The *Logic* and the *Political Economy* are Mill's two substantial contributions to knowledge, the knowledge of power rather than that of imagination. In the rest of his writings the old influences are still present though waning before his utter passion for his wife. He of course was never able to free himself from the grip of his father and his system of education, of his coterie and of the mark that journalism impressed upon him. He met Mrs. Taylor in 1831 when he was twenty-six and she twenty-three. According to Mill's brother, she was "a clever and remarkable woman but nothing like what John took her for." Bain suggests that, in addition to the affinity which defies analysis, she attracted him intellectually by expressing ideas which she had really learnt from him. The thoughts he cherished came to him with the voice of the woman he loved, and he never realised that it was from him that she had first learnt them. Twenty years after their first meeting her husband died and Mill married her. "What I owe to her intellectually," he records in his *Autobiography*, "is in its detail almost infinite."

When after a few years of their union his wife died at Avignon, in 1858 Mill bought a cottage near her grave.

Her memory was ever tenderly cherished, and after her death she was an even more dominating power than during her life. "Since then," he sorrowfully adds, "I have sought such alleviation as my state admitted of, by the mode of life which most enabled me to feel her still near me. I bought a cottage as close as possible to the place where she is buried, and there her daughter (my fellow-sufferer and now my chief comfort) and I live constantly during a great portion of the year. My objects in life are solely those which were hers; my pursuits and occupations those in which she shared, or sympathised and which are indissolubly associated with her. Her memory is to me a religion, and her approbation the standard by which, summing up as it does all worthiness, I endeavour to regulate my life."

The inscription on her tomb at Avignon ends with these words: "Were there even a few hearts and intellects like hers this earth would already become the hoped-for heaven." The dedication of his tract on *Liberty* pathetically concludes: "Were I but capable of interpreting to the world one half the great thoughts and noble feelings which are buried in her grave, I should be the medium of a greater benefit to it, than is ever likely to arise from anything that I can write, unprompted and unassisted by her all but unrivalled wisdom." And yet there is no real reason for thinking that she seriously modified any contribution Mill ever made to political—or any other—science. When he gives us specimens of her writing there is nothing specially luminous in them. "Only John Mill's reputation," dryly remarked Grote, "could survive such displays" of his complete devotion to his wife.

No Knight of the Round Table ever sought the Holy Grail one whit more ardently than Mill sought for liberty of thought in general and the emancipation of women in particular. His noble plea *On Liberty*, 1859, and his passionate plea against *The Subjection of Women*, 1869, might have been composed by a literary knight errant. His romantic love for his wife inspired him to be the Perseus to set free the modern Andromeda. He could have written a book on "The Subjection of Men," or at any rate, the subjection of one man. *On Liberty* forms a not altogether consistent apologia on behalf of individualism and its principle of *laissez-faire*. In it Mill eloquently denounces not merely legal oppression, but social. He realised the extent to which the action of the individual could be hampered by social habits and conventions. The one object of wise law and sound policy is the protection of freedom. So much is this the case that he deplores the intervention of the State in any function that the individual can discharge. For instance readers of his *Political Economy* now learn with some surprise that he deprecates the direct assumption by the State of educational facilities, contending that it ought to do no more than compel parents to provide for the elementary education of their children. He was so staunchly convinced of the value to be attached to individual spontaneity that he treated the promotion of freedom as the most important task of the State. The tyranny of opinion he dreaded every whit as much as Lord Bryce dreaded the fatalism of the multitude.

Mill's main object was to elevate the life of the mass of mankind to higher conditions; and his doctrine of *Liberty* was to forbear from social discouragement of whatsoever "experiments in living" individuals might choose to try—howsoever eccentric such experiments might generally appear to be. With this object in view, he recommended society to restrain itself from putting down, even by the force of opinion, any "experiment in living" which should not take the shape of overt acts of war with legal authority. "That so few now dare to be eccentric," he wrote, "makes the chief danger of the time." If one turns to the writings of 1859 one is somewhat puzzled by this statement. Take one of them. Darwin had published his *Origin of Species*, and if ever a book was eccentric, in the literal sense, it was this book which lies at the basis of all modern speculation. It is fascinating to note how closely Mill approximated to some of Darwin's thought. He pleads that free play shall be allowed to differences of character provided these differences do not injure other men. He also pleads that as a condition of individual—and social—progress, a man's actions must be determined by his own character, not by tradition or custom or abstract rules. This of course anticipates Darwin's view and was to be corroborated by it. If we have in 1859 George Eliot's *Adam Bede* and Victor Hugo's *Légendes des Siècles*, we also have George Meredith's *Ordeal of Richard Feverel*, Fitzgerald's translation of Omar Khayyam and Gontcharof's realistic novel, *Oblomof*. The last three works afford evidence that some did dare to be eccentric in 1859.

The leavening power of his father is still evident in spite of his wife's influence. For we must never forget that even in his most socialist hours Mill allowed private property, private capital, inheritance, contract, and competition. In his *Political Economy* he lays down that "no one can foresee the time when it (i.e., competition) will not be indispensable to progress." Those who charge competition with the evils of existing society "forget that wherever competition is not, monopoly is, and that monopoly in all its forms is the taxation of the industrious for the support of indolence if not of plunder." Competition means that the individual is free in his efforts to better his own condition, and therefore the condition of society. He must possess the right to deliver his mind. "It is the opinions men entertain and the feelings they cherish," said Mill, "respecting those who disown the beliefs they deem important, which make this country not a place of mental freedom." He pushed this doctrine so far as to hold that society ought in no case to permit itself to offer any deterrent demonstrations, even though these should be unenforced by legal penalties, against anything any of its members might say, or write, or do—except for the single purpose of direct and immediate self-protection. The truth is that Mill is torn in two opposite directions. His old self is prepossessed with the Benthamite formula of the greatest happiness of the greatest number, solicitous, in Sir J. Stephen's expression, to see equal rations of happiness served out to all the world and his wife, notably his wife, determined that every one should count for one, and no one for more than one. His new self is fully alive to the importance and the difficulty of preserving somehow something of individual force and freedom from the Argus eyes and Briareus hands of a tyrant majority. "I regard utility," he still holds, "as the ultimate appeal on all ethical questions; but it must be utility in the largest sense, grounded on the permanent interests of man as a progressive being."

The possible decay of individuality sends a shudder through the whole mental frame of Mill. We look back to the age of the Victorians as an age comparable to the Elizabethans as possibly our grandchildren may look back to the Georgian age as one of the most crucial for a hundred years. Mill, who lived in the Victorian era, is fearful for the disappearance of the great man. In the past there were outstanding personalities, but where are they in the present? Every age asks this question, and every age, for the most part, denies their existence. What test are we to apply? Humboldt suggests that the first or most essential of all human virtues is energy; for the greater the vitality, the more rich and various the type which cultivation can evolve. Tried by this test, is Knox inferior in energy or endurance to Aristotle? Was Luther or Calvin inferior in this respect? Mill seems inclined to think that the tendency of the ages is to dwarf the importance of the individual. It is obvious that William the Conqueror occupies a larger position in history than say, William IV, but that is partly because the monarchy stands in a different class. Would there have been a unified Germany had it not been for the personal qualities of Bismarck? Would there have been a unified Italy had it not been for the union of the personal qualities of Victor Emmanuel and Garibaldi, of Cavour and Mazzini? True, there is the great occasion and there is the great man. It frequently happens that there is the great occasion without the great man. In our own day it is usual to say the World War was a time of great events but not of great men. Yet if we may anticipate the verdict of posterity it seems to us that Ludendorff and Lenin, Foch and Sir Henry Wilson will stand out as great men.

To Mill liberty is a matter of feeling rather than of specific fact. The sense of freedom is the sense of exemption from arbitrary authority; and its source, its indispensable condition, is individual consciousness of actual or potential participation in the governing power of the community. Yet the sense of such participation—actual or potential—is not necessarily dependent on any particular form of rule.

There might be kept alive in feudal servitude itself, as Burke reminds us, "the spirit of exalted freedom." The humblest clansman of the proudest Highland chief felt himself and his claymore essential constituents of the military power of the head of his clan, and, in contributing to maintain that power, might have the full feeling of liberty—that is to say, of spontaneous unconstrained action. The actual possession, or facility of attainment, of the elective franchise, gives the humblest voter a sense of political power which would not fail to make itself felt on any adequate provocation. On the other hand, the subject of a ruler in the fifties who made himself absolute by grace of bayonet and bullet, or of a foreign sovereignty, like that of Russia in Poland, so long as the native despotism lasts, cannot easily cheat himself into the notion that he himself has any share in the governing power. When England waged war with Russia in 1854, she did so on the impulse of her voting millions who hated the Czar for his iron rule in Poland and for his aid to Austria to maintain hers in Hungary. When the American North waged war with the South, she did so on the like popular impulse. Those wars were wars of national feeling in both countries, and therefore their vicissitudes endangered the governing power in neither country. On the other hand when Napoleon III waged war in Mexico, he acted on no impulse but his own, and had no voluntary national force on which to fall back. Liberty must exist, however unregarded in imperial calculation of forces, for its presence or absence to make all the difference in the degree of persistency with which external enterprises can be carried out in the teeth of reverses. This is particularly evident from 1914 to 1918. At first autocracy swept all before it, yet in the end the countries democratically governed won.

In his *Liberty, Equality, Fraternity*, Sir James Stephen, who was an ardent admirer of Hobbes, falls foul of Mill's views. As an orthodox Utilitarian, Stephen ably attacks one who was departing from the strait gate and the narrow way of Bentham and Austin. Mill lays down that mankind, individually or collectively, are not justified in interference with others except on one ground, that of self-protection, and he develops a fallacious argument based on the distinction between actions self-regarding and other-regarding. Stephen vehemently argues that Mill never proves that we ought not to punish self-regarding conduct. What he does is to adduce particular cases, and Stephen resents this lack of proof. His attitude is that any diminution of the strength of the social bond tends to enervate society whereas he—and Mill too—seeks to invigorate it. A strong government is Stephen's ideal and his Indian experiences confirmed his faith in this ideal. Such a government directed and disciplined the Germans before 1914, and under it they display their best qualities, but these qualities in our people are displayed to most advantage under a *régime* of liberty.

The differences between Mill and Stephen are largely temperamental. The latter, curiously enough, looked on Mill as a man "cold as ice," whose patriotism was satisfied with abstract conceptions, duly weighed in the scales of Utilitarianism. Stephen insists on the place of coercion in mediaeval as in modern civilisation, where Mill speaks of liberty. Coercion is always present: it may be transformed but never abolished. Lincoln and Moltke commanded a force which would have crushed Charlemagne and his paladins and his peers like so many eggshells. This emphasis of force, in the background of society, runs through the whole of Stephen's vigorous volume. Liberty is good, argues Mill, and is opposed to coercion not in general but in certain cases. He tries to lay down rules for the interference of Government, whose interference is to be only occasional. Stephen allows these rules if they are regarded simply as experimental, but his fear, which he does not disguise, is that Mill tends to regard them as ultimate truths, and Stephen will fight this idea to the death. Practically, there is not much to separate the two thinkers: theoretically, there is everything, and Stephen feels jealous for the orthodoxy of Mill who does not seem to realise his departure from the true faith of Bentham.

The State means as much to Stephen as to Hobbes, and Stephen is sorely afraid that Mill's attitude to liberty tends to unmoralise the State. The State, in Stephen's judgment, is to be strong, and it is to be an organ of the moral sense of the community. Mill's excessive regard for individuality, so Stephen holds, defeats the conception of the State. He accuses Mill, as Maine almost accuses Bentham, of having at once too high and too low an opinion of mankind. Mill has too low an estimate of the actual average Englishman, and too high an estimate of the ideal man who will be perfect when all restraints on the part of the Government and everyone else are removed. Accordingly, Stephen strenuously assaults Mill's estimate of women, and he attacks it for precisely the same reasons as he attacks his estimate of men.

In 1861 appeared Mill's striking *Considerations on Representative Government*. His *Logic* was filled with a boundless hope in the possibilities of progress: his *Considerations* is still filled with a boundless hope in its possibilities. Democracy is coming, but he feels the pessimism engendered by life. May not the labouring classes try short cuts to raise their material condition? May they not seize capital? There had been a Reform Bill in 1832, and there was to be another in 1867. While Mill notes the advance in the democratic direction, he clearly desires this advance to be accompanied by checks which he fancied would protect the rights of minorities. There is still faith in democracy, but it is distinctly chastened.

The views of Montesquieu and Burke in the past, and the labours of the great Victorian historians in the present, render Mill unable to accept some of the Utopian hopes of progress entertained by Bentham. He believed that laws could be passed without any thought on what Burke deemed of paramount point, the circumstances that were bound to colour every clause of them. He denies the position of Burke, who held that forms of government are not made, but grow. Carlyle has shaken this position, and Mill shook it more. For according to the latter the form of government is a matter of choice, of will and purpose, if three conditions are fulfilled. "The people for whom the form of government is intended must be willing to accept it; or at least not so unwilling as to oppose an insurmountable obstacle to its establishment. They must be willing and able to do what is necessary to keep it standing; and they must be willing and able to do what it requires of them to fulfil its purpose," the word "do" being used in a wide sense, including to "forbear" from doing anything opposed to these conditions. Yet a twentieth century Burke may be found arguing that because Germany to-day is a republic, it is not correct to argue that she will remain one, as all her traditions are monarchical. There are, in fact, races with deferential traditions and races with liberty-loving ones. Even if both sets of races complied with Mill's three conditions, is it not certain that representative institutions will be a failure with the former compared with the latter? The power of public opinion has been ably analysed by Mr. W. Lippmann and Mr. A. L. Lowell and Mr. A. V. Dicey, and it is a power which Mill never sufficiently took into account.

In his *Considerations* he raises the question of the criterion of good government. Is the criterion order? Is it progress? The criterion cannot be that it harmonises order and progress, as Comte says, or permanence and progress, as Coleridge puts it. For what do we mean by order? Is it obedience? Mill defines order as "the preservation of all kinds and amounts of good which already exist, and progress as consisting in the increase of them." Surely this means that the conditions of order and progress are not opposed, but are the same. The same qualities in the citizen, the same social arrangements, a sound police, good laws, a good judicature which promotes order, are conducive to order—and conducive to progress. Are we to say, then, that progress forms the sole end of government? Metaphysically, we may indeed say so. Mill then considers ends that a good government should propose to itself. Finally, he tells us that the best government is that which tends "to promote the general mental advancement of the community, including under that phrase advancement in intellect, in virtue, and in practical activity and efficiency"; and which best organises "the moral and intellectual and active work already existing, so as to operate with the greatest effect on public affairs. . . . Government is at once a great influence acting on the human mind, and a set of organised arrangements for public business; in the first capacity its beneficial action is chiefly indirect, but not therefore the less vital." The best government raises the mental stature of the individual, and employs the finest means for the public business of the State.

Carlyle thought that if a good despot were always available despotic government would be the best. To Mill, with his sanguine belief in the merits of representative government, such a belief undermined all the foundations of his political creed. The benevolent despot—and the malevolent despot—has played his part, and no doubt will play it again. During the eighteenth century such enlightened sovereigns as Joseph II, Catherine II, and Frederick II, governed their respective countries because, as Mill admitted, they were far more intelligent than their subjects. "I am but the first servant of the State," was the position of Frederick the Great. Thinkers like Diderot defended this attitude, an attitude that received support from other benevolent despots. Joseph II defended his absolutism on the ground that he exercised his power for the benefit of his subjects. Nor is it possible to deny the fact that a section of the people have grown tired of representative institutions, and it has installed, at the point of the bomb and the bayonet, those who represent their ideas. A minority of Bolsheviks in Russia, of Fascisti in Italy, and of Sinn Feiners in Ireland, give the lie to much that Mill lays down in praise of the wonder-working qualities of the vote and of representative institutions. You can do everything with bayonets except sit on them, remarked a Frenchman. When the Russians grow tired of sitting on the bayonets of the Bolsheviks, the Italians of those of the Facisti, and the Irish of those of the Sinn Feiners, we think that a higher value will be given to the qualities of popular government on which Mill laid such stress. He shows convincingly that despotism lowers the character of the people, and that free government raises and expands it. It is noteworthy that he repudiated universal suffrage, one of the six points of the Chartists, and he came to condemn the ballot. Not less noteworthy is his adherence to women suffrage and to minority representation in the shape of Hare's scheme which is now proportional representation.

In his *Autobiography* he gleefully refers to the fact that he gave the nickname of the "stupid party" to the Conservatives. When in the House of Commons he defended this nickname. "I never meant to say that Conservatives are generally stupid. I meant to say that stupid people are generally Conservatives." His own middle class prejudices were as strong against the typical John Bull of this party, as the prejudices of John Bull were against him. He seemed to take up the position that there are two sets of parties, one radically wrong, the other radically right. The Conservatives were radically wrong and the Liberals—at least the Radical section of them—were radically right. In his *Letters* he actually writes: "If there were but a few dozens of persons safe (whom you and I could select) to be missionaries of the great truths in which alone there is any well-being for mankind individually or collectively, I should not care though a revolution were to exterminate every person in Great Britain and Ireland who has £500 a year. Many very amiable persons would perish, but what is the world better for such amiable persons? But among the missionaries whom I would reserve, a large proportion would consist of speculative Tories: for it is an ideal Toryism, an ideal King, Lords, and Commons, that they venerate; it is old England as opposed to the new, but it is old England as she might be, not as she is. It seems to me that the Toryism of Wordsworth, of Coleridge (if he can be called a Tory), of Southey even, and of many others whom I could mention, is *tout bonnement* a reverence for *government* in the abstract: it means that they are duly sensible that it is good for man to be ruled; to submit both his body and mind to the guidance of a high intelligence and virtue. It is, therefore, the direct antithesis of Liberalism, which is for making every man his own guide and sovereign-master, and letting him think for himself, and do exactly as he judges best for himself, giving other men leave to persuade him if they can by evidence, forbidding him to give way to authority; and still less allowing them to constrain him more than the existence and tolerable necessity of every man's person and property renders indispensably necessary."

In his *Political Economy* he regarded arguments depending on race as a trace of vulgar prejudice. Since 1848 he had learnt much, and in his *Representative Government* he analyses the elements of nationality with his wonted lucidity. These elements are race, religion, language, geographical position, manners, history, laws, a common civilisation, and even a prolonged subjection to the same sovereign. Of course he assumes an attitude equally impossible to his father and to Bentham to whom one race was pretty much the same as another. Mill comes close to Renan who held, "*Ce qui fait que les hommes forment au peuple, c'est le souvenir des grandes choses qu'ils ont faites ensemble et la volonté d'en accomplir des nouvelles.*" Community of interest creates national feeling, and continuity of common interest creates national history.

To Aristotle the ideal State was one of 20,000 citizens, though the idea of nationality was breaking through the narrow limits of the city-State. To Claudian it was the proudest boast of Rome that her name, once that of a city, had become co-extensive with the world. At other times the corporate unit is the clan, the fief, the Empire. It all seems to depend on which unit makes most for efficiency. If that be so, then the gradual contraction of the world owing to the advance of science will tend towards a constant enlargement of the idea of nationality, until, like Claudian's Rome, it becomes co-extensive with the world. On the other hand, it must not be forgotten that, side by side with this extension of the unit of nationality, there exists a smaller local nationality which has its roots as deep in human nature as the primitive passions. The truth is that the most efficient corporate unit embraces the world for some purposes, half a continent for others, and for others may be no wider than a ward. The future will perhaps lie in some development of the Federal idea, of which the League of Nations is the rudimentary germ.

Since Woodrow Wilson's day we are apt to conceive nationality in terms of self-determination only. Yet such other elements as strategy, economic efficiency, natural frontiers, and the like all enter into it. This argument indeed forms the basis of the defence of the compromises that the Conference of Paris of 1919 had to make in drawing the boundaries of the new nationalities that it called into being. If only nationalities would distribute themselves conveniently and in accordance with the demands for a natural frontier and economic efficiency, the problems at Paris would have been easy. As it was the Conference was always coming across isolated nationalities. You could not give each isolated nationality its appropriate place; something of abstract justice had to be sacrificed to the caprices of past migration and the claims of economic efficiency. In fact, the members of the Conference were obliged to fall back on the theory that some distinct nationalities were nevertheless inevitable portions of a political unit with which they were out of sympathy. Vilna and Lemberg are but examples of a problem quite common in the Balkan States. The philosophical argument in defence of this becomes dangerously thin. Yet what are negotiators faced with such questions to do? The real truth is that all political arrangements are an unstable equilibrium between the claims of a number of sound principles. Nationality which is insulated, or an inevitable portion of a larger unit, strategic or economic, owes a duty to those among whom its lot is cast; on the other hand, the larger the unit becomes the more it must recognise that its power is not a possession but a trust to be exercised for the good of all the components. For the object of all political combination, as Aristotle pointed, is the happiness and welfare of its components; and this is the basis of the ideal of the League of Nations. It is an attempt to find means to reconcile the efficiency of the world with justice and the claims of sentiment. Alas! the trend of events is unfortunate for Mill's outlook. For it is setting in the direction of leaving out the claims of sentiment—with what results the future only can disclose.

Mill's *Utilitarianism* appeared in 1863, and in it he defines his attitude. His creed "which accepts as the foundation of morals, utility, holds that actions are right in proportion as they tend to produce happiness, wrong as they tend to produce the reverse of happiness. By happiness is intended pleasure, and the absence of pain: by unhappiness, pain, and the privation of pleasure." Here it is perfectly plain that the definition of the greatest happiness principle differs by worlds from that of Bentham. He deleted right and wrong, the very words Mill is careful to insert. For Mill is highly indignant with those who think that Utilitarianism bids men seek *their own* happiness. On the other hand, Bentham assumed the axiom that "it is impossible that any man can desire or aim at anything but his own happiness; whoever pretends to do otherwise is a fool or a liar." Mill shook himself away from some Benthamite chimeras, but he never quite shook himself away from the chimera of rationing out happiness. He entertained the idea that the problem is to be solved by social arrangements in making the rations, so far as may be, equal. Arrange, as you will, you will not arrange away human nature, of which inequality is, ever and everywhere, the most prominent and conspicuous character. Malthus saw this when he wrote, "It is probable that if the world were to last for any number of thousand years, systems of equality would be among those errors which, like the tunes of a barrel-organ, will never cease to return at certain intervals." That every one should be equal in the eyes of the law is no discovery of Bentham or Mill. That legislation should seek to make every one equal in condition by class legislation is a principle which will shatter to fragments any old social system. The point is, Can it permanently organise a new one?

Mill was always optimistic. He was optimistic when he wrote his *Logic* in 1843, and he was optimistic when he wrote his *Utilitarianism* in 1863. He was then a man in his fifty-seventh year, an age when the illusions of youth have long fled. His note is one of sustained hopefulness, and he writes in 1863: "No one whose opinion deserves a moment's consideration can doubt that most of the great positive evils of the world are in themselves removable, and will, if human affairs continue to improve, be in the end reduced to within narrow limits. Poverty, in any sense implying suffering, may be completely extinguished by the wisdom of society, combined with the good sense and providence of individuals. Even that most intractable of enemies, disease, may be indefinitely reduced in dimensions by good physical and moral education, and proper control of noxious influences; while the progress of science holds out a promise for the future of still more direct conquests over this detestable foe. And every advance in that direction relieves us from some, not only of the chances which cut short our own lives, but, what concerns us still more, which deprive us of those in whom our happiness is wrapt up. As for vicissitudes of fortune, and other disappointments connected with worldly circumstances, these are principally the effect either of gross imprudence, of ill-regulated desires, or of bad or imperfect social institutions. All the grand sources, in short, of human suffering are in a great degree, many of them almost entirely, conquerable by human care and effort; and though their removal is grievously slow—though a long succession of generations will perish in the breach before the conquest is completed, and this world becomes all that, if will and knowledge were not wanting, it might easily be made—yet every mind sufficiently intelligent and generous to bear a part, however small and inconspicuous, in the endeavour, will draw a noble enjoyment from the contest itself, which he would not for any bribe in the form of selfish indulgence consent to be without."

Throughout the *Utilitarianism* the *anima naturaliter Christiana* speaks, and we feel conscious of its author's attitude to religion. This attitude came out more fully in his posthumous *Three Essays on Religion* which appeared in 1873. It created consternation among such disciples as Sir Leslie Stephen and Lord Morley, Herbert Spencer and T. H. Huxley, and A. Bain. The attitude of J. Mill to religion, as described by his son, was Lucretian—one not of indifference but of hatred. He regarded the established forms of religion as the outstanding enemies both of progress and of morality. The paternal influence remained with the son until the death of his wife gave it a serious shaking. While the external evidences of Christianity appealed to him but slightly, its morality appealed to him increasingly. It was a time of religious change. Coleridge and Sterling, Froude and Clough, altered their views in religion. Maurice and Erskine of Linlathen were the pioneers of Broad

Churchism in England and Scotland respectively. Carlyle left the Calvinism of his youth. Martineau ceased to be an orthodox Unitarian. R. H. Hutton travelled from Unitarianism to the Church of England. Newman travelled from the Church of England to the Church of Rome.

Changes were in the air, and Mill was too much the child of his age not to experience them. In his *Liberty* he foreshadows some of them. In it he holds, "I believe that the sayings of Christ are irreconcilable with nothing which a comprehensive morality requires; that everything which is excellent in ethics may be brought within them." In his *Utilitarianism* he maintains: "In the golden rule of Jesus of Nazareth we read the complete spirit of the ethics of utility. To do as you would be done by, and to love your neighbour as yourself, constitute the ideal perfection of utilitarian morality." Two years after his wife's death he earnestly sought a form of Theism, writing in 1860: "It would be a great moral improvement to most persons, be they Christians, Deists or Atheists, if they firmly believed the world to be under the government of a Being, who, willing only good, leaves evil in the world solely in order to stimulate human faculties by an unremitting struggle against every form of it." With his growing belief in Theism he links the belief in immortality. "It appears to me that the indulgence of hope with regard to the government of the universe and the destiny of man after death, while we recognise as a clear truth that we have no more ground for more than a hope, is legitimate and philosophically defensible. The beneficial effect of such a hope is far from trifling. It makes life and human nature a far greater thing to the feelings, and gives greater strength as well as greater solemnity to all the sentiments which are awakened in us by our fellow-creatures and by mankind at large. It allays the sense of that irony of Nature which is so painfully felt when we see the exertions and sacrifices of a wise and noble mind, only to disappear from the world when the time has just arrived at which the world seems about to begin reaping the benefit of it." When Sterling lay in the shadow of death, he wrote: "I have never so much wished for another life as I do for the sake of meeting you in it. . . . I shall never think of you but as one of the noblest, and quite the most lovable of men I have known or ever look to know."

The passage on Christ as possibly "a man charged with a special express and unique message from God" is: "When this pre-eminent genius is combined with the qualities of probably the greatest moral reformer, and martyr to that mission, who ever existed upon earth, religion cannot be said to have made a bad choice in pitching on this man as the ideal representative and guide of humanity; nor, even now, would it be easy, even for an unbeliever, to find a better translation of the rule of virtue from the abstract into the concrete than to endeavour so to live that Christ would approve our life."

The *Subjection of Women*, 1869, was never far out of the thoughts of its author. In 1792 Mary Wollstonecraft had published her *Vindication of the Rights of Women*. According to Rousseau, "women are specially made to please men," and she wrote her book as a protest against this view. Marriage to her forms "the foundation of almost every social virtue," but she complains that in England women are taught to look on man alone for their maintenance and to marriage as the sole end of life; to regard as unfeminine all serious studies that strengthen the understanding, and to cultivate as the chief womanly charm an exaggerated sensibility and dependence, and a proficiency in arts and qualities that have their empire only in the transient period of youth and passion. She emphasises the outstanding importance of chastity and morality, and she also emphasises the domestic nature of the chief duties of women. Anxious as she is to assimilate in no scanty measure the tastes and studies of the two sexes, she expresses a strong dislike for any of her sex who dare indulge in field sports. Mill takes up the ever-old, the ever-new, question of the relations of the sexes. As he believed in the indefinite modifiability of character and in the power of outward circumstances to determine differences, he stood forth as the unqualified advocate of women's rights. The principle of destruction is the principle of life. It is your business, if you are bringing a new force into the world, to begin by killing, or at least wounding, a tradition, even if that tradition once owned all the virtues. There was never a dragon that Perseus or St. George killed which had not been a centre of conservatism and a moral support. Perseus or St. George, it has never been thoroughly understood, was only able to kill him because his day was over, and he was falling behind the times. Dragons in their old age grow weak, and their teeth drop out before the spear strikes through the roofs of their mouth. It is not always even so hard and heroic to put them to death as is generally supposed. But it is essential.

Mill contemplated an ideal, for the better realisation of which he looked to the future. His optimism remained invincible. He is entitled to all the honours which attended the funeral of that famous mediaeval Master-Singer, surnamed Frauenlob, whom the grateful woman subjects of his poetical panegyrics carried to the grave with their own arms, raining tears over the tomb in which they laid him with such sorrow. Before Mill tells us what reforms he hopes for, he sketches for us the actual state of woman. The subject woman is emphatically his heroine, and she has been held captive by the monster man. Mill sets her before us, laden not only with personal chains, but with the shadow of those fetters in which her mother and all her female ancestors have been bound. As he writes there rises up before us the enormous shade of a despotism vaster and more monstrous than any other ever conceived by the most malevolent of despots. We seem to see one half of the race turned into minute and scientific tyrants, and the other half into blind and servile slaves. So deeply has her bondage entered into the nature of woman, we learn, that after all these thousand years we are in no position to say what she can or cannot do. She has never had the remotest chance of fair play. She has been so held down, silenced, and oppressed, that we can scarcely form a right idea of what she wishes, for her faculties have been benumbed by the damp and chill of the prison-house in which she was born.

The element of exaggeration in this picture is at once obvious, yet we do well to remember the position of women towards property before the Married Woman's Property

Act of 1882. Take an actual case. In 1850 a woman possessed of a large fortune married, without a settlement, an adventurer, Mr. Bowes, who is the original of Thackeray's picture of Barry Lyndon's married life. The moment the word "amazement" in the marriage service had been pronounced, he became the actual owner of all the goods and money which actually belonged to his wife. With or without her consent he obtained her money at her bankers, and the payment of all debts due to her. He sold her leaseholds and pocketed the proceeds. He spent, in fact, as he pleased the whole of his wife's income. He turned out a confirmed gambler, and squandered all his wife's property, except the freehold estate, which he charged with the payment of all his debts. These are facts of which Mill was well aware, and they explain—in part—the heat with which he wrote his burning indictment of his own sex. Nobody believes—even in 1869—that the bride, when her husband leads her from the church, is the chattel of the man by her side—a thing transformed, lost to the world and the race, absorbed in him, with no further claim to personal existence. Yet the law then said as much in the plainest language, and Mill built upon it his dismal survey of the condition of women.

The earliest and the ablest champion of the rights of woman, Mary Wollstonecraft, admitted a superiority in physical, involving a certain superiority of mental, strength in men. This physical incapacity of woman to become the rival and competitor of man, however well fitted to be the partner and helpmate of man, no legislative assertion of the equality of the sexes can alter. Mill disputes this, and argues on behalf of the equality of the sexes. Do men and women stand upon precisely the same ground? Are they adapted to the same work? Are they framed on the same model? Are they qualified to perform the same functions in the world? It is difficult to answer these questions in the affirmative. Even if his theory of equality were true, yet the very fact that for so many centuries women have not realised this should move the philosopher to a keener sense of the infinite difficulties of the subject. He mixes up the main question—the official superiority of man in the economy of the world—with local laws of marriage and individual hardships resulting from the same; strangely conceiving the greater to be produced by the less, and not the less by the greater. And looking on the matter in this light, the remedy becomes easy enough. It is but to repeal the laws which subject women to the legal authority of their husbands, and to place the sexes on a footing of external equality. The disabilities of woman removed, the superstition of her different standing in the world abolished, her equality recognised, her rights guaranteed, a perfect level of position established between men and women—this is Mill's remedy for all her evils. It would almost seem as if he believed that woman is man in petticoats. It is not so; it never was so; and devoutly we trust that it never will be so. At the same time we must treat men and women equally in the eyes of the law. No act of Parliament will, however, change in one iota the laws or conditions of nature. The alteration will be simply external.

The drift of the *Subjection of Women* is to set forth the equality of men and women. When we come to marriage we must not overlook the fact that if the sexes are really equal, the tendency will be to regard the bond between the sexes as simply a contract. If it is a contract, the inference is that it is dissoluble at the will of the contracting parties. From the masculine angle, this is perhaps desirable, but is it equally desirable from the feminine angle? A woman loses the qualities which render her attractive to men much earlier than a man loses the qualities which render him attractive to women. Besides, when a man marries, he does so when he feels that he is established in a suitable position. When a woman marries, she renounces the suitable position she held. For her children stand in the way of professional success. Mill asserts that slavery is the basis of the law of marriage, and we concede that there is much in his contention. Still, it is a contract by which the master is legally bound to labour for the slave, and the slave for the master.

Mill pushed his doctrine to extremes, though we freely admit that the hardships women suffered from the lack of Property Laws safeguarding their interests gave justification for his fierce indictment. The drift of legislation induced not a few men to look upon women as devoid of rights, for the law gave them scarcely any. His protest bore fruit in 1882. Nor is it too much to say that the higher education of women, the increased opportunities now afforded on all sides for the exercise of their practical talents, the franchise they received in 1918 and 1928—these are due in no scanty measure to his unceasing efforts on their behalf. Among the praises lavished upon him to-day women feel that he opened sphere after sphere to them. There was with a certain type of man contempt for women shown in the past, and that type has been taught to feel that such contempt is entirely misplaced. The heroic exertions of women at the front and at the base from 1914 to 1918 attest what service they splendidly lavished upon their country. On our side much of our opposition to Germany sprang from our feeling of her misuse of her power. On Mill's side much of his opposition to men's treatment of women sprang from his feeling of their misuse of their power. Thanks to his lifelong efforts, this misuse has largely passed away.

Between the philosopher in his study and the man of common sense Mill served as an admirable interpreter. Nor did his retirement to Avignon diminish his power. His high moral character combined with the eminence of the recluse impressed the imagination of the people. His mastery of his material and the lucidity with which he invested it deepened this impression with the thoughtful. To justice and humanity he early gave his life, and he served both with utter and unselfish devotion. He aroused the rising interest in political problems to a higher degree, and he succeeded in gathering around him a band of disciples whom he stimulated. His moral enthusiasm constitutes his great title to honour. He inspired men by his moral energy: he animated them by sentiments both noble and benevolent. Nor did he leave them uninfluenced by the mystery of life which we feel for all that is unknown. His ethical writings discuss principles in a large-minded fashion, and the singular and unfailing candour he exhibited in them is not the least of the attractions of the man. His economical writings exercised a wider and deeper influence than any other author from Ricardo to Marshall. Behind his ethical and economical writings we are conscious of the ardour of their author: he was a volcano covered with snow. The volcano burst forth in the pamphlets he felt impelled to write from 1848 onwards.

The enormous extent of his power is attested by writer after writer. Out of them we select Cairnes and Sidgwick, Bagehot and Bain, Spencer and Taine. Cairnes, a thinker whose premature death men still deplore, points out: "The character of his intellectual, no less than of his moral nature, led him to strive to connect his thoughts, whatever was the branch of knowledge at which he laboured, with the previously existing body of speculation, to fit them into the same framework, and exhibit them as parts of the same scheme; so that it might be truly said of him that he was at more pains to conceal the originality and independent value of his contributions to the stock of knowledge than most writers are to set forth those qualities in their compositions. As a consequence of this, hasty readers of his works, while recognising the comprehensiveness of his mind, have sometimes denied its originality; and in political economy in particular he has been frequently represented as little more than an expositor and populariser of Ricardo. It cannot be denied that there is a show of truth in this representation; about as much as there would be in asserting that Laplace and Herschel were the expositors and popularisers of Newton, or that Faraday performed a like office for Sir Humphry Davy." Henry Sidgwick was not wont to bestow his praise lightly, yet he testified: "We have lost in John Stuart Mill the best philosophical writer—if not the greatest philosopher—whom England has produced since Hume; and perhaps the most influential teacher of thought, if we consider the variety as well as the intensity of his influence, that this country has ever seen. Originality of the highest kind he only showed in one department—the theory of method and evidence; but the unequalled mastery of method which his logical speculations developed, his patient tenacity and comprehensiveness of study, his rare gifts of exposition and discussion, and the controlled fervour of his intellectual and social enthusiasm enabled him to do in other departments work equally important in forming the minds of his contemporaries."

As a busy banker Bagehot was filled with admiration that Mill with his multifarious duties contrived time for authorship. He confesses that "to treatises such as Mr. Mill's *Logic* and his *Political Economy*, it is not easy to give important praise which no one will deny." He enlarges on the enormous extent to which the two generations after 1848 were impregnated with the luminous thought of these two books in particular. In Bain's view, "A multitude of small impressions may have the accumulated effect of a mighty whole. Who shall sum up Mill's collective influence as an instructor in politics, ethics, logic, and metaphysics? No calculus can integrate the innumerable little pulses of knowledge and of thought, that he has made to vibrate in the minds of his generation."

Herbert Spencer testifies "how entirely his public career has been determined by a pure and strong sympathy for his fellow men—how entirely this sympathy has subordinated all desires for personal advantage—how little even the fear of being injured in reputation or position has deterred him from taking the course which he thought equitable or generous." In a vivacious dialogue with an Oxford friend in the sixties Taine records his impressions: "What have you English got that is original? Stuart Mill. What is Stuart Mill? A publicist: his little book on *Liberty* is as good as your Rousseau's *Social Contract* is bad, for Mill concludes as strongly for the independence of the individual as Rousseau for the despotism of the State.—That is not enough to make a philosopher. What else? An economist, who goes beyond his science, and subordinates production to man, instead of subordinating man to production.— Still not enough to make a philosopher. What more? A logician.—of what school? His own. I told you he was an original.—Then who are his friends?—Locke and Comte in the front; then Hume and Newton.—Is he systematic? a speculative reformer?—Oh, he has far too much mind for that. He does not pose in the majesty of a restorer of science; he does not proclaim, like your Germans, that his book is going to open a new era for the human race.

He walks step by step, a little slowly, and often close to the ground, across a host of instance and example. He excels in giving precision to an idea, in disentangling a principle, in recovering it under a crowd of different cases, in refuting, in distinguishing, in arguing.—Has he arrived at any great conception of a Whole?—Yes.—Has he a personal and complete idea of nature and the human mind? —Yes."

When told that he was dying Mill simply said, "My work is done." It was done with such completeness and such success that for another generation he remained the almost unquestioned master of it. Then the inevitable reaction came. His three posthumous essays on religion unloosed the allegiance of his Agnostic friends, and when they questioned his teaching in one direction this naturally led to questionings in directions of which they never dreamt. The thought of Oxford in the sixties had been dominated by Mill who had stood aloof from German thought. He had on the whole despised Hegel and Fichte, and under the powerful influence of T. H. Green these two philosophers came into their own. The sun of Mill set as such a new luminary as Hegel rose high in the heavens. A day, however, seems to have dawned when such writings as *Liberty* and *Representative Government* may return to a tithe of their old power.

"There is hardly a more striking example of the worthlessness of posthumous reputation than the oblivion into which my father has fallen among the world at large." So wrote Mill in his diary in 1854; and so might have written any time the last thirty years those who recall the position which he once held, the pontifical authority of his opinions, and the reverence with which his character was regarded by many who differed from him in most matters. He and his works have passed into the shade. His disciples if a remnant of them survive, are silent, critical, faithless, or wavering. There are, however, signs of a revival of interest in one who to another generation counted for so much, and who has so much to teach to people of to-day. The noblest of the precious metals cannot be handled by the goldsmith till it has been mixed with some alloy. There was alloy, no doubt, in Mill's gold; but in spite of it, or because of it, his work is imperishable. The man was greater than his work, his character rarer than his intellect. His is the life of a searcher after truth, with the penalties attached thereto, one being that, as Biran says, if you pierce it, truth will pierce you. For Mill it is:

> Enough if something from our hands have power
> To live, and work, and serve the future hour.

Honestly to seek the truth, boldly to speak the truth, patiently to suffer, if need be, for the truth's sake, is the ideal of inquiry. It was the ideal of Mill's life. It was in loyal obedience to it that he fought his good fight against the rulers of the darkness of this world. And the victory which he won was a victory for us, our children, and our children's children; a conquest, never to be undone, of light for liberty. Not in the storm of theological controversy, not in the earthquake of political revolution, but in the still small voice of the philosopher urging the pleas of reason, do we discern the promise and the presage of the liberties of the modern world.

References

BAIN, A. *John Stuart Mill. A Criticism with personal recollections.* (London, 1863.)

BECKER, L. E. *Liberty, Equality, Fraternity. Reply to F. Stephen's Strictures on Mill's "Subjection of Women."* (London, 1874.)

BLAKESLEY, G. H. *A Review of Mr. Mill's Essay on Liberty.* (Cambridge, 1867.)

BRIDGES, J. H. *Unity of Comte's Life and Doctrine to Mill.* (London, 1910.)

BUCKLE, H. T. *Essays.* (London, 1880.)

CHADWICK, E. *University of London (Essays).* (London, 1867.)

CLOUGH, J. S. *On Mill's Position as a Moralist.* (Cambridge, 1884.)

COMTE, A. *Lettres à Mill* (1841–6). (Paris, 1877.)

COURTNEY, W. L. *Life of John Stuart Mill.* (London, 1889.)

DAVIDSON, W. L. *The Utilitarians.* (London, 1915.)

DICKSON, W. M. *Absolute Equality.* (London, 1868.)

DOUGLAS, C. *John Stuart Mill. A Study of his Philosophy.* (Edinburgh, 1895.)

DRYSDALE, C. R. *The Population Question according to Mill and Malthus.* (London, 1892.)

FOX, C. *Memorials of old Friends.* (London, 1882.)

References

GOMPERZ, T. *Mill.* (London, 1889.)
GRAHAM, W. *English Political Philosophy.* (London, 1914.)
GUYAU, M. *La Morale Anglaise Contemporaine.* (Paris, 1900.)
HARRISON, F. *Tennyson, Ruskin, Mill.* (London, 1889.)
HERTZ, G. B. *The Manchester Politician, 1750–1912.* (London, 1912.)
JENKS, E. *Thomas Carlyle and John Stuart Mill.* (Orpington, 1888.)
KEYNES, J. M. *The End of Laissez-faire.* (London, 1926.)
LANGE, F. A. *Mill's Ansichten u. d. sociale Frage.* (Berlin, 1866.)
LAURET, H. *Philosophie de Stuart Mill.* (Paris, 1886.)
LITTRÉ, E. *Comte et Mill.* (Paris, 1866.)
M'COSH, J. *An Examination of Mr. J. S. Mill's Philosophy. Being a defence of fundamental Truth.* (London, 1866.)
MACCUNN, J. *Six Radical Thinkers.* (London, 1900.)
MORLEY, Lord. *Miscellanies.* Vols. III and IV. (London, 1892 and 1908.)
RITCHIE, D. G. *State Interference.* (London, 1891.)
ROBERTSON, J. M. *Modern Humanists.* (London, 1895.)
SAENGER, J. S. *John Stuart Mill. Sein Leben u. Lebenswerk.* (Stuttgart, 1901.)
STEPHEN, Sir J. F. *Liberty, Equality, Fraternity.* (London, 1874.)
STEPHEN, Sir L. *Life of Sir James Fitzjames Stephen.* (London, 1895.)
STEPHEN, Sir L. *The English Utilitarians.* (London, 1900.)
TAINE, H. *English Positivism. A Study on J. S. Mill.* (London, 1870.)
TAYLOR, Sir H. *Works.* Vol. V. (London, 1878.)
TULLOCH, J. *Movements of Religious Thought in Britain.* (London, 1885.)
VESEY, G. *Individual Liberty.* (London, 1867.)
WHITTAKER, T. *Comte and Mill.* (London, 1908.)

Chapter XI.
KINGSLEY AND CHRISTIAN SOCIALISM

EVERY generation of ideas has begun or ended with some movement concerning Nature—an impulse towards, a reaction against, her. From the days of Greek philosophy and before them, from the times of the Fathers and St. Augustine and the conflict between Free Will and Predestination, the pivot has been the same. Mediaevalism, with its chivalrous device and monastic ideals—with its effort to order and feudalise men's appetites—made against Nature. She took her revenge at the Renaissance, the heyday of humanists and artists, her *preux chevaliers*, who vindicated her rights. So did Luther and the first reformers. The pendulum, however, oscillated, and the Puritans worked havoc in men's consciousness with a sterner asceticism than the world had ever known. Then came the seventeenth century, the period of the grand style and of the pre-eminence of the Roi Solei in Europe. Nature was drugged to sleep, was counterfeited by etiquette and Le Notre, by Lely and Kneller, in their false arcadias, with intricate side alleys for intrigue. Rousseau followed them—Nature's Peter the Hermit, who preached the Crusade without the Cross, proclaiming the return to Nature's bosom. The world took up his doctrine, and the French Revolution was the result, to be succeeded by natural movements everywhere —in the Lake School of English Poetry—in the landscape painters of England and France—in the educational systems of Maria Edgeworth and Pestalozzi—no less in the abolition of slavery, in land reforms and in repeals of corn laws. Upon these came the Second Renaissance, the reign of Science, the investigation of Nature's laws, the arrogance of discovery, the protest of the Oxford Movement, of Pre-Raphaelite visions in the world of art and of Socialism in the world of industry. The cause represented by Socialism is the cause of the poor and needy. Men, according to Spinoza, are so constituted that they pity those in evil case and envy those in good; adding that they are more prone to envy than to pity. The poor and the needy are an object of pity, which takes different forms. It may be contemptuous or impatient; it may be sympathetic and patient. Different influences, springing from many sources, bear upon society at different times, and determine the magnitude and the direction of particular currents of feeling. Concern for the poor has been subject to such influences from time to time, and has varied in strength and form accordingly. Christianity, being pre-eminently the religion of suffering, gave it an immense stimulus. The ethical element in Socialism is borrowed from Christianity. Nor has the Church ever given up the cause, though her practice has often been feeble and perverted. Some of her members, however, feel the truth of what King Oscar of Sweden said to Barrère, "A young man, my dear Minister, who has not been a Socialist before he is five and twenty shows that he has no heart. But if he continues to be one after five and twenty he shows that he has no head."

It has been the permanent misfortune of mankind that Watt invented the steam engine when he did. It came on the eve of the twenty-two years' struggle with Napoleon, with the result that the Government could bestow neither time nor thought upon it. The inventors in industry changed the face of England more in the course of a generation than it had changed in all the generations from the Norman Conquest to the accession of George III to the throne in 1760. The French Revolution had raised the question of liberty, emancipation from political oppression, and the Industrial Revolution was destined to raise the question of economic oppression. To the old ethical view of poverty as a misfortune, claiming pity and help from society, were added ideas of oppression and inequity, both claiming redress. The cause of the poor and needy not only received powerful reinforcement from the ideals of liberty and equity, which appeal to impulses not less deeply seated in human nature than pity, but under these influences it took a new direction. The aim was no longer the mitigation of an accepted evil, but its abolition by the removal of its social causes. Here we have the double basis of Socialism, which is reflected in the two main tendencies it has ever since exhibited. They are often divergent, and sometimes in direct antagonism; but this is due to the inability of men, especially those of an ardent temperament, to see more than one thing or one side at a time. The two tendencies are really complementary, and both spring from live roots which ensure their persistent vitality, through all vicissitudes of season and weather.

Karl Marx (1818–83) came into the movement when it had been in full swing for more than a generation, and had passed through several phases, in which all the leading ideas had been worked out to the surface and found expression. He was no pioneer; there is not a single idea in his entire system which can be said to be wholly his own or truly original. Godwin, Thompson, Hall, Gray, Hodgskin, and Bray had all anticipated him during the opening decades of the nineteenth century.

What is the explanation of the unique position of Marx in the movement, and the resounding authority of his name? In the first place he appeared as the reviver of a cause which had suffered a temporary eclipse, but was itself indestructible—a cause immemorially old, yet perennially young. The ground lay fallow, not worked out, but rather fertilised by the previous labours which men like Thompson spent upon it—though that seemed spent in vain—and ready to yield its increase to a skilful husbandman. In the second place the season was favourable as well as the ground. It was a time of general revolutionary ferment in Europe; the air was full of movement and men were expecting things to happen in the forties. This both stimulated Marx, who came to manhood with it and was caught in its spirit, and also gave him opportunity. At the same time it misled him. With the ardour of youth he expected immediate results and impossible ones, which have not yet occurred, and show no signs of occurring in the form he expected. But the miscalculation belongs to another part of the subject; it does not negative the fact that he entered the field under peculiar conditions, offering an exceptional opportunity for a man of capacity to make his mark. And he made it because he had the capacity. He was a skilful husbandman.

There were two men in Marx, curiously mingled; the philosopher or reflecting man, and the prophet or agitating man. The one appealed to the intellect, the other to the emotion; and his influence rests on this double basis. It is hard to say which of the two has contributed more to the reverence in which his name is held by the sect, which has canonised him in both capacities; but the combination is the secret of his fame. The one has impressed the few, who are given to study and theory; the other has attracted the many, who respond to a cry. It is worth while comparing him with Robert Owen, the only other Socialist whose name is equally famous. Two men could hardly be more different. Owen was a real pioneer, but he had little bent for theory or speculation, and never passed beyond the child-like determinism of the "New Moral Order." Nor had he any revolutionary leanings as Marx had, though all his life he laboured at practical schemes planning and urging to the last, undismayed by repeated failures and always confident of immediate success for the latest project. Marx, whose domineering arrogance was worthy of his native land, treated that sort of thing, as he treated his predecessors and most of his contemporaries, with supreme contempt. He and Engels, who played the Boswell to his Johnson, claimed for themselves the only true light, and ridiculed the previous labours of French and English socialists as Utopian. Yet their own dream of the immediate violent overthrow of all existing social conditions by the united proletariat of all countries, with abolition of classes and disappearance of the State, was more thoroughly Utopian than any project of Owen or the Owenites, from whom, by the way, they condescended to borrow all the economic groundwork of their own superior system. This forecast was set out in the Communist Manifesto, issued in 1848.

The Communist Manifesto reveals Marx the leader of the populace and the bearer of a cause. There is plenty of argument in it, and indeed it contains all the essential points of his system, but the argument is used to work up to a climax, which is a call to action. In it Marx raised a standard. He was a Mahdi preaching a holy war, a Peter the Hermit preaching a crusade for the recovery of the holy city from the infidels, who had impiously taken possession of it. Only the name of that holy city is Wealth, the infidels are the capitalists, and the motives appealed to are somewhat different. To this day the manifesto is more often quoted than part of the laboured disquisitions of *Das Kapital*. It is a call to arms, and there is more life in it than in the chilly and incompatible doctrine of Natur-notwendigkeit, or inevitable law of development, which is the working principle of "scientific" Socialism of to-day. It has the weight of the cause behind it, the cause not only of the poor, but of the disinherited and oppressed, which is far greater, more real and vital, than all the theories and schemes. He brought out strongly the weakness of capitalism *vis-à-vis* humanitarian demands. He brought out no less strongly the impossibility of individualism *à l'outrance*. As a prophet he is important because he gave the working class the sense of a great mission.

If Marx's reputation depended solely on his theories it would have been very different both in kind and degree, and would not have lasted as it has; for they have not stood the test of time and criticism. But in combination they have had a peculiar effect, out of all proportion to their intrinsic merits. The oracular style and air of profundity in which they are enveloped have thrown a halo around Marx, once established as the leader of a cause, and invested with an authority bordering on awe in the eyes of those who appreciate the cause and want a leader, but have no head for speculation. *Das Kapital* is little read and less understood. It would be interesting to set an examination paper on it to Socialists who profess familiarity with the text. Its very obscurity, however, has been a great asset. Those who do not like it can always fall back on the Manifesto, while others are positively impressed by it. Experience proves that obscurity and confusion are often taken for merits, and rather enhance than lessen a writer's reputation with readers who are not very well equipped for judging, and modestly ascribe unintelligibility to their own deficiency or find in it a sort of aesthetic satisfaction. Mesopotamia is not the only blessed word.

These qualities in Marx have had no small share in elevating him to a lofty eminence of aloofness. He has become a sort of Veiled Prophet, invested with a quasi-sacred character; and his word has acquired the authority of a revealed religion. This is not only apparent to outside observers, but admitted by Marxians, who accuse one another of adopting priestly attitude and apply the very word religion. It is true. Marxism is a religion, and bears the usual signs. It has a creed and a sacred text, which the faithful repeat. There are orthodox, unorthodox, and sub-divisions of them; the straitest sect of the Pharisees may be distinguished from the less strait. There are treatises on the articles of the faith, and there is a modernist criticism. This is not said in ridicule at all. The fact is interesting and perfectly natural. The Marxians have abjured other religions, especially Christianity. Mankind, however, is incurably religious, and when it parts with a creed in one form it speedily restores it in another. At one time the Marxians were openly and bitterly hostile to Christianity for several reasons. It crosses their purpose at several points. It accepts and even enjoins poverty and acquiescence in one's lot, whereas they want to abolish poverty and look to revolt as the means. It ordains duty and obedience, whereas they urge self-assertion. It looks to the moral law working in the individual to remove evil and elevate mankind, whereas they hold the existing system or social order wholly responsible and demand its abolition as the sole means of salvation.

The Marxians regard the Church as part of the existing order, and therefore doomed in their eyes. Wilhelm Liebknecht put it concisely at the German Socialist Congress at Halle in 1890: "The Church, whether Catholic or Protestant, is to-day nothing but a prop, an instrument of the class-State." He was, however, against any open attack, not out of any regard for religion, but because such action excited opposition in quarters where they could make converts. In short, it was inexpedient, and in spite of many attempts to induce the party to assume a more hostile attitude it has abided by the decision, adopted in 1875, to treat religion as a private matter. The German lead has been followed by Marxians generally with the outstanding exception of Russia. Religion is officially treated with a somewhat ostentatious indifference. Nevertheless, they need a faith of some kind themselves. In spite of the lofty superiority to the weaknesses of less enlightened minds which they affect, they are built of the same stuff as other devotees. They are not cynical worldlings or cold-blooded speculators, but enthusiasts. It is to their credit. They pursue an ideal, in the end a lofty ideal, though they pursue it by exploiting the most sordid motives, not in themselves, but in others, and they must have some guide to cling to, some authority to look up to, some faith to hold—in short, a religion. Liebknecht urged that very claim on the occasion just mentioned. He was arguing against a resolution declaring active opposition to all churches and religious dogmas, and pledging members to profess irreligion. He pointed out that this would be an infringement of personal liberty, and further reminded them that they had a religion of their own. "Have we not that which forms the strength of religion, faith in the highest ideals?" The parallelism was even closer than he knew. The same temperamental elements have produced similar effects. The apparatus of religion they needed was found in Marx, who took the place of the law and the prophets.

Now there must be something in a body of doctrine which obtains and keeps such a hold upon highly educated and intelligent men, as most Socialist leaders, and particularly Marxians, undoubtedly are. It is one of the curious facts about Socialism that though it stands for the struggle of one class (the proletariate in Marxian phraseology) against another (the bourgeoisie) all its greatest leaders have always belonged to the latter. Marx and Engels were of typical bourgeois origin. Both came of the well-to-do middle class families; the one was the son of a lawyer, the other of a cotton spinner. Both were highly educated. And as the founders of Marxism, so have been its prominent supporters in all countries. Bebel indeed began life as a wage-earner, but he soon started for himself, and before long became a manufacturing employer. After five-and-twenty years in business he retired and died in very comfortable circumstances. But it is significant that Bebel, who sprang from the proletariate, was never a real Marxian. He was essentially a politician and a Parliamentary leader of rare capacity, but he had little use for theory, and admits in his autobiography that he could not digest Marx's economics. The working classes in general at this moment are in the same plight; it is the other Marx, if any, who appeals to them, and there are many Socialists, especially here and in the United States, who are not Marxians at all. Even the "free" trade unions in Germany, which come nearest to the faith and have a working alliance with the Socialists, jealously guard their independence. So it comes about that the champion of the proletariate in the class war against the bourgeoisie are themselves bourgeois and in the strange position of preaching a class consciousness which they themselves cannot possess. This, however, is where their faith comes in. They are fighting for others, not for selfish ends, and the massive inertia or positive resistance of their clients is a more formidable obstacle than the opposition of the enemy. They cling to Marxism because they find encouragement in it. How far is their faith justified?

The cardinal virtues of the doctrine in their eyes is its "scientific" character, which lends it logical certainty. The root ideas are that the evolution of society is an orderly process, progressing by definite stages and governed by definite laws, and that the determining elements in this process are economic. The first idea is derived from Hegel, whose influence was still in full swing when Marx studied philosophy at the university; the second is a particular version, or inversion, of the Hegelian theory suggested by Feuerbach's materialism, to which the youthful Marx became a convert. All the rest is built on this purely philosophical basis. The Hegelian process—called "dialectic," because it resembles that of formal logic—postulates three stages of development, namely, affirmation, contradiction, and solution; or thesis, antithesis, and synthesis. That is to say, it consists of two opposites or contradictories, which dissolve into a single proposition; this in turn raises its own contradiction, and the process begins over again. In applying this formula to social evolution Marx found his two contradictories in two classes of society, differentiated by economic conditions and in a state of antagonism, which is dissolved and the process completed in their union. This constitutes the "economic interpretation of history," and consists in filling up these formulae with details derived from an examination of past economic relations and an analysis of the present stage of development, which is "capitalism," tracing its origin and nature and deducing from them its inevitable outcome, which is the resolution of the class war between bourgeoisie and proletariate by their union into one, brought about by the collapse of capitalism, on which Mr. and Mrs. Webb lay such stress, and the opening of a new era. A particular feature of the economic analysis is a minute study of the labour theory of value and surplus value to explain the origin and development of capitalism.

From this outline it is easy to understand the impression made by such a combination of first principles and historical facts, presenting an appearance of logical coherence and unassailable certainty. And the impression was deepened by the Darwinian theory of evolution through the struggle for existence. Science became the watchword, intellectual and popular of the day; and the superficial resemblance between Marx's class struggle and Darwin's biological struggle invested the former with the prestige belonging to the latter. But there was more than that. The Hegelian conception of history as a logical consecutive process is an illuminating idea, and Marx's insistence on the economic factor was valid up to a point and valuable. Further, his historical researches into the past development of commerce and industry were a real contribution to the subject. Finally, the labour theory of value and the theory of surplus value both have their recognised place in economics, though Marx did much more to confuse than to elucidate them. The former boasts a long pedigree, reaching back, through Ricardo, Adam Smith, Locke and Petty, to Hobbes; the latter was chiefly set out by William Thompson when Marx was in the nursery. There is, however, much solid material in the Marxian system, and he put it together with great industry and conspicuous ability.

Yet it has not withstood the elements; it has been falsified by the course of events and has crumbled away. The reason is the faulty method of building. Marx began at the wrong end with a ready-made formula. It is the weakness of the philosopher who seeks for a master-key to unlock all doors. In the realm of pure thought that does no harm; but when applied to real life and made the basis of a policy it leads to error and failure, because the master-key will not unlock all doors and its inventor is constrained to tamper with the locks in order to make them fit his key. In other words, he trims the facts to fit his formula; and that is precisely what Marx did. He selected his evidence, exaggerated some factors and ignored others, used the same terms now in one sense and now in another to suit the argument. Science begins with observation, and Marx never attempted it; he studied documents, not life at first hand. If he had studied workmen, for instance, he would have known better than to say that they have "no country" and have been "stripped of every trace of national character," and that their relations to wife and children have "no longer anything in common with the bourgeois family relations." If he had studied the factories of which he wrote so much he would have discovered the founder, in nine cases out of ten, not in a capitalist, but in an exceptionally capable workman, who had become a capitalist by his own exertions and thrift. If he had studied the business of production he would have discovered that what makes all the difference between failure and success is the conduct of the enterprise, which demands a special faculty, and that the man who possesses it is the real mainspring. If he had studied industry and trade and agriculture, he might have corrected the hasty generalisation that the small man was destined to disappear. He correctly noted the accumulation and concentration of capital, but failed to notice the opposite tendency which has produced a multitude of small capitalists and gone so far that the saying of Sir William Harcourt that "We are all Socialists now" may, with equal truth, be exchanged for "We are all Capitalists now."

If he had not been obsessed by his formulae he would have avoided many untenable propositions, such as the interpretation of history by the economic class warfare and the absurd dichotomy of the population into bourgeoisie and proletariate, terms, which in their proper meaning, present no true antithesis and which in their distorted Marxian meaning have no equivalent in other languages, because they correspond to no reality. Nevertheless, Marx's name will always remain a landmark. The tide of economic and social development has flowed away from his scientific system and left it derelict. The growth of human knowledge has wrought destruction to the Marxian system: *tempus edax rerum.*

In tidal rivers a curious phenomenon commonly occurs at the turn of the tide. There is a period during which the water runs in opposite directions at the sides and in the middle; the old motion persists in part after the new has begun. This natural phenomenon, familiar to those who occupy their business in such waters, is recalled by the present movement of thought in regard to Marxian Socialism; it is still running at the sides, but it is turning back in the middle. That is to say, while it is being spread by systematic propaganda among workmen, it is being rejected by a growing number of former intellectual adherents. This reaction is not confined to Marxian Socialists; the most vehement critics of Socialism to-day in general are disillusioned Socialists. In the Socialists themselves we also perceive another reaction. Men like Mr. Sidney Webb no longer entertain the old belief in the State as a highly centralised body, and they are increasingly coming to believe in its decentralisation under the Socialist *régime*. We are bidden to turn to the local, not to the central authorities as the boards destined to work out our social salvation. Mr. and Mrs. Webb insist that "the deliberate intensification of this searchlight of published knowledge we regard as the corner-stone of successful Democracy." Is any local body so likely to employ this published knowledge to the same extent as the central body? What they visualise is "a community so variously organised, and so highly differentiated in function as to be not only invigorated by a sense of personal freedom, but also constantly swept by the fresh air of experiment, observation and verification. We want to get rid of the 'stuffiness' of private interests which now infects our institutions, and to usher in a reign of 'Measurement and Publicity.'"

The day when Whitehall was to regulate everything has faded into the dim distance of the past. There is a reaction against the central as well as the sovereign State. Gierke and Maitland have taught us that all systems of law dealing in a practical way with the affairs of men have to recognise the existence of groups of men united, more or less permanently, for all kinds of purposes. There are ordinary trading or business partnerships, and there are, as Figgis delighted in pointing out, clubs of all sorts, cathedral and collegiate churches, churches themselves, numerous bodies administering local government from the parish vestry to the Corporation of the city of London, and so on almost indefinitely. The last half century has also witnessed the creation of a countless number of limited liability companies formed for all manner of objects. These associations obtain property, make contracts, and generally acquire legal rights and subject themselves to legal duties with the utmost freedom. Among these groups in the forties there are few more interesting than the co-operative companies formed by the Christian Socialists, and to them and their aims we turn our attention.

Charles Kingsley (1819–75) was the man among the Christian Socialists who caught the ear of the public. The scenery amid which his early boyhood was passed, alike the wildness of the Great Fen of North Huntingdonshire and the richness of North Devonshire, left its mark on all the writings of his mature years. Not only that, but living from his childhood in a country peculiarly rich in wild life, and brought up with a familiar knowledge of it, with a habit of observing it, which was cultivated by his father—himself an able naturalist and an accomplished scholar—the love of nature and of nature's works grew with him rather as an instinct than a science, and continued throughout life the passion and delight of his less busy hours. Fond as he was of studying all objects of the natural world, for botany and geology he had an absolute enthusiasm. In 1838 he entered Magdalene College, Cambridge, and his wife's biography enables us to glean something of the inward development of his mind, the growth of his character, the reception and adoption of his ideas, and the formation of tone and thought which is thenceforth to direct and constrain his words and actions. Coleridge and Carlyle were among the authors to whom he turned most readily. The Oxford Movement was then creating no little stir, but from it he kept himself aloof. It is significant that historians like Hallam and Grote, Macaulay and Carlyle, the great novelists from Dickens to George Eliot, poets like Tennyson and Browning, Clough and M. Arnold, and theologians like Hatch and Hort, Westcott and Lightfoot, Maurice and F. W. Robertson also stood aloof from it. In fact, the broad stream of English thought was flowing in other directions than that of the Oxford Movement.

In 1839 Kingsley met his future wife, one of the abiding influences in his life, though her biography of her husband has done him disservice. In 1842 he was ordained for the curacy of Eversley in Hampshire where he settled down to care for a neglected parish. In the spring of 1844 he married, and was appointed shortly after rector of Eversley where he spent his life. For thirty-three years he laboured among his people, and laboured successfully. He became personally intimate with every soul in the parish—with the men at their field-work, with the women at their wash-tubs, with the babies in their cradles. He started clubs and schools, a maternal society and a loan fund, a lending library and educational classes, and all the machinery of a well-worked parish. To-day it is usual, but in the forties it was unusual. A muscular Christian, Kingsley endeared himself to the men of his parish. Unamuno is another muscular Christian in our day, and bears a remarkable resemblance to Kingsley. There is the chance resemblance that both were university professors teaching subjects curiously alien to them. There is the real resemblance that both were Christian social reformers, never tired of protesting against the injustice, cruelty, and ignorance of the world around them.

Admiration for Maurice, one of the most outstanding of theologians, induced Kingsley to write in 1844 to him for advice and assistance with his theological reading. Henceforth he was a pupil of one of the foremost men of his day, a man who achieved in theology what Mazzini achieved in history through the unity of Italy, for both men were pre-eminently prophets. To Maurice's *Kingdom of God* Kingsley confessed that he owed more than to any other book he had ever read. From it Kingsley learnt that human society is a body consisting of many members, not a collection of warring atoms; that true workmen must be fellow-workers and not rivals; and that a principle of justice, not of selfishness, must govern exchanges. These were to be the animating principles of the Christian Socialists, and it was Maurice who taught them these principles. Maurice never held that all thine is mine, but he passionately held that all mine is thine. Coleridge had at last come into some of his own, for he was the master of the thought of Maurice and Kingsley alike. Matthew Arnold, Ruskin, and Gladstone might belittle Maurice, but to Tennyson he was "the greatest mind of them all." There is the solitude of genius, and Maurice well knew what it meant.

Maurice stood behind Kingsley, and behind them both stood Ludlow, the man who supplied motive power to the new government. His political creed was based on faith in the people, and with this faith he combined his sense of the value of association, "the great school of self-government for the people." Owen had held that a change in circumstance would work wonders. Ludlow saw more deeply, for he held to a change in the social order and he also held to a change of heart. Reform the members of society and at the same time reform the social order. Change the characters of the members and at the same time change the structure of society. Such was the message of Ludlow. Like Coleridge and like Disraeli, he believed in monarchy, aristocracy, and humanity as necessary elements of an organic Christian society. Ludlow was a leader who never impressed the public. Nevertheless, he was the man who could drive others. Maurice supplied him with the ideas which he was quick to transmute into action. The figure of Kingsley was the one that arrested the attention of people whom Maurice could never move. For he was able to do through his devoted follower what he could never do through himself. After all, the disciple is as necessary as the master.

The ideal of Kingsley in religion was not that of the hymn, "Change and decay in all around I see"; it was rather, "O all ye works of the Lord, bless ye the Lord; praise Him, and magnify Him for ever." He had read Coleridge's *Day Sermons*, which are the first authentic voice of Christian Socialism, and read it to some purpose. For his desire was to translate his reading into action. Coleridge might talk, Carlyle might talk, but he, for his part, was determined to act. He reveals his character and his wife's character in his writings. The big, strong, fearless, self-contained man, with a keen sense of duty, brought to a knowledge of his own utter weakness—whether he is called Lancelot Smith, or Raphael Aben-Ezra, Amyas Leigh, Thomas Thurnall, or even Hereward—constantly appears before us, decked out indeed in new clothes, with new surroundings, but the same ideal figure throughout. For his favourite women, the characters which he has delineated with the greatest care—Elizabeth of Hungary, Argemone, Hypatia, Mrs. Leigh, Grace Harvey—have much in common, and though under different names and disguises, are all shaped on one model. Like Mill, he upheld the necessity for a great improvement in the education of women.

The year 1848, the year of his contributions to the pamphlets, *Politics for the People*, was one in which Europe was in revolt. It witnessed the shaking of the foundations of nearly all the most powerful States on the Continent. France and Italy, Germany and Austria, all endured nothing short of political convulsion. Thomas Cooper's *Autobiography of a Chartist*, and Ebenezer Elliott's *Corn-law Rhymes* alike testify to what was happening in England. The Revolution here was beaten by the will of the nation, as it generally has been in England, in 1926 as in 1848.

On April 10th, 1848, when the great Chartist demonstration was threatened Kingsley mixed himself up with the agitation. In consultation with Maurice and other able, earnest men, he wrote and posted all over London a placard addressed to the "Workmen of England." Its tone is earnest, grave, but as anti-revolutionary as anything can possibly be. Will the Charter, it asks, make you, the Workmen of England, free? Will it free you from slavery to ten-pound bribes? Slavery to beer and gin? Slavery to every spouter who flatters your self-conceit? From such slavery neither Charter nor Act of Parliament can free you. There can be no true freedom without virtue, no true industry without the fear of God. He is neither ashamed nor afraid to denounce the vices of the labourer with the passion of Mill himself. Other papers like *The Voice of the People* and *The Christian Socialist* were to appear, and they lasted for a short time, influencing people. The first secured two thousand readers, the second three thousand, and both attracted writers as well as readers.

Kingsley's two outstanding novels from our angle are *Yeast*, published in 1848, and *Alton Locke*, published in 1850. These attracted an attention never bestowed on either Maurice or Ludlow. Now Disraeli had written *Coningsby* in 1844, *Sybil* in 1845, and *Tancred* in 1847, and in his trilogy he had sketched the condition of England with a master hand. The social evils of the day are diagnosed with the wealth of the glowing imagination of Disraeli and Kingsley. The weaknesses of the Manchester School are exposed at length and exposed with vehemence. There is, however, no desire to advocate the claims of Conservatism on the part of Kingsley as there is on the part of Disraeli. The former wrote *Yeast* with his heart's blood, and all his deep feeling for the agricultural labourer is poured into it. A novel it is in form: a pamphlet on the reform of the game-laws, the housing of the rural poor, the question of insanitary cottages, village morality, indiscriminate charity, and the like, it is in essence. In his parish he saw, in the working of the land system, the degradation of the women, the despair of the men, and the depopulation of the country side, leaving a residuum sunk to as low a depth as the submerged tenth of the towns. *Yeast* is also a powerful representation of the mental struggles of the time, and on this ground it at once found favour with young men, especially the undergraduates at the two ancient universities. "I think this will explain a good deal of Maurice," he observed to his pupil, John Martineau. The Cornish game-keeper Tregarva is powerfully drawn, yet the author was no more a novelist proper than he or Carlyle was an historian. Kingsley was a teacher first and a novelist last. He suggests no remedies, for he believed that it was his duty as a parson to call attention to what he saw all around him. Take Tregarva's fierce lyric on "The Bad Squire":

> There's blood on your new foreign shrubs, squire,
>   There's blood on your pointer's feet,
> There's blood on the game you sell, squire,
>   And there's blood on the game you eat.
>
> You have sold the labouring man, squire,
>   Body and soul to shame,
> To pay for your seat in the House, squire,
>   And to pay for the feed of your game.
>
> You make him a poacher yourself, squire,
>   When you'd give neither work nor meat,
> And your barley-fed hares robbed the garden
>   At our starving children's feet.
>
> When, packed in one reeking chamber,
>   Man, maid, mother, and little ones lay:
> When the rain pattered in on the rotting bride-bed,
>   And the walls let in the day.
>
> * * * * * *
>
> Our daughters with base-born babies
>   Have wandered away in their shame;
> If your misses had slept, squire, where they did,
>   Your misses might do the same.
>
> Can your lady patch hearts that are breaking,
>   With handfuls of coals and rice,
> Or dealing out flannel and sheeting
>   A little below cost price?

Yeast was a cry from the human heart, and it was a cry to which the public responded more quickly than they did to the contemporary message of Marx. Three editions of the novel appeared within little over a year. The national conscience had been challenged by the events of 1848, and a novel of 1848 came to remind its readers that a clergyman of the Church was not unmindful of the spectacle of a Continent in revolt and of the deep-seated causes of that revolt.

What *Yeast* did for the country *Alton Locke* did for the town. With that keen sympathy he had for suffering humanity, with that warm appreciation of the wrongs of the poor which had been forced upon him by his parochial work, he felt impelled to speak out, to give vent to the cry of anguish and pain that was well nigh choking him. If he said more, and spoke more strongly, than balanced judgment would allow, there is little cause for wonder when he contemplated the condition of the worker in the town. The book was written "for the sake of the rich who read, and the poor who suffer."

Carlyle thought the character of Saunders Mackaye nearly perfect in *Alton Locke*, and there is much reason for agreement with this verdict. Mackaye exhibits a sardonic humour which is otherwise absent from this book. There is a touching account of his despair at the inefficiency of the Chartist leaders on April 10th, 1848, and the account of his death is equally touching. The home of the seamstress is described with grim fascination, and indeed the whole novel forms one long terrible indictment of the merciless manufacturers. *Sybil* had analysed Chartism from 1838 to 1843, and Kingsley completed the analysis by carrying on the story of this movement from 1844 to 1848. There is a fire in the pages of Kingsley's novel which makes the blood in one's veins course as rapidly as when one reads Mrs. Gaskell's *Mary Barton*. Kingsley's book is too realistic; the careless world was compelled to receive the horrible pictures in it as a true representation of what the town worker was enduring in their midst. Nor did the world thrust it on one side. Its earnestness and its enthusiasm captivated its readers who read it with the utmost eagerness.

For Political Economy Kingsley manifested but scanty respect. The laboured abstractions of Ricardo failed to move him as the vital pages of Mill's book, published in 1848, might have moved him. *Laissez-faire* seemed to be one of its fundamental maxims, and his own eyes informed him of the fatal consequences of this policy in town and country. If there were men composed of steel and men composed of glass living in the same neighbourhood, any Government worthy of the name would ordain that the men of steel and the men of glass should not travel by the same road. Yet while there were men of steel able to compete, there were also men of glass quite unable. Was there no remedy for this state of affairs save *laissez-faire*? The heart of the novelist protested, while his head refused to note that the despised policy had achieved triumphs in its day, though now it might have outlived those triumphs. In 1857 he remarked, "As yet political economy has produced nothing. It has merely said *laissez-faire*." Mill had said much more, and indeed his exceptions to *laissez-faire* would have covered some of the schemes for which Kingsley pleaded. In 1852 he wrote: "Next you have the Manchester School, from whom Heaven defend us. . . . To pretend to be the workmen's friends, by keeping down the price of bread, when all they want thereby is to keep down wages, and increase profits, and in the meantime to widen the gulf between the working man and all that is time-honoured, refined and chivalrous in English society, that they may make the men their divided slaves, that is—perhaps half unconsciously, for there are excellent men among them—the game of the Manchester School."

In his pamphlet on *Cheap Clothes and Nasty* Kingsley assailed what he believed to be another maxim of the Manchester School. It was an indictment of competition and a plea for co-operation in keeping with the principles of Maurice. The iniquities of the sweating system are laid bare with a burning eloquence. The colonels of regiments in the forties and fifties received a fixed sum for the clothing of the soldiers, and they contracted privately for its supply. The contractors made the clothes, and in the making there is no doubt that the sweating system manifested itself in all its horrors. One of their number, William Shaw, protested to the War Office on the working of the system, and the answer was in exact keeping with *laissez-faire*: "I am commanded by their lordships to inform you that they have no control whatever over the wages paid for making up contract clothing. Their duty is to take care that the articles supplied are of good quality, and well made: the cost of the material and the workmanship are matters which rest with the contractor. . . . The men's wages depend upon the amount of competitors for employment amongst themselves." Such an answer was logical, but it did not endear the Manchester School to the Christian Socialists. Ludlow and Maurice were spending their best efforts in the encouragement of co-operation and all that co-operation meant in the improvement of the character of the men taking part in it.

Co-operation was beginning in 1850, and it is not a little remarkable that it began in the field of production, not in the field of distribution where on the whole it has achieved its outstanding success. Co-operative societies were formed for the manufacture of clothes, boots, houses, and the like. In time we find associations of silk-weavers at Bethnal Green, plush-weavers at Banbury, cloth-weavers at Galashiels, calico-weavers at Salford, saw-makers at Sheffield, and stonemasons in Sunderland. The success in London was meagre compared with the success in Manchester, a result that is distinctly ironical. The system of control in some of the societies anticipated the methods now proposed by the Guild Socialists. Nor were the leaders of the Christian Socialists unmindful of the part the trade unions were playing, and they manifested their desire to work together with the leaders of these unions, then but rising into power. Ludlow wrote in 1867: "I want Trade-Unionism to expand into humanity and finally lose itself in it." His idea was that these Unions should expand into self-governing Associations—the Guilds of our day,—taking over the whole business of production and exchange. It was a bold dream to dream in the sixties, and if it had been possible to turn it into reality, what a transformation of industry would have happened! The truth is that the workmen were not fitted either morally or educationally for the tasks the leaders of the Christian Socialists desired to commit to their hands. The verdict of Kingsley in 1856 was: "it will require two generations of training both in morality and in drill," and it certainly was the verdict of his colleagues. In our own day Marshall, in his *Industry and Trade*, sums up his view: "Experience has partly moderated and partly confirmed the bright hopes entertained about half a century ago, to the effect that co-operative production and co-partnership together would gradually develop a set of working class leaders with wide business experience. . . . In the last two generations much has been learnt as to what can be done even under present conditions, and what could be done under a nearer approach to ideal perfection of human nature."

The leaders plainly saw that for this approach to ideal perfection of human nature education was sorely required, and the outcome of this view was the establishment of the Working Men's College in London in 1854. Maurice maintained, characteristically enough that "the College was established first for the benefit of us the teachers, secondly for the benefit of those whom we taught. The statement sounds discreditable; but I maintain that it is true and should not be concealed." It was not in his nature to conceal anything, and out of this foundation issued the Settlement, the Mission, the Workers' Educational Association, and the like. Men like Ruskin and Rossetti, Litchfield and the two Lushingtons, have been on the staff of the Working Men's College with benefit to themselves as well as to their pupils.

Kingsley largely left the control of the Co-operative movement to Ludlow and Maurice. His was the work of the preacher and writer, and in these capacities he rendered untold service to the cause of Christian Socialism. He secured for it speedy recognition and he secured for it lasting influence. In his later writings he showed himself the apostle of cleanliness which he certainly ranked next to godliness. His views on this subject had been extreme from the first; and his early sermons on cholera are as outspoken as anything he afterwards uttered. The difference is that though he had in earlier years associated sanitary reform with political, and though he was, even in 1848, ready to urge on the workmen of London, then agitating for the Charter, the necessity of social improvements and cleanliness of mind and body, as leading to benefits far beyond those which any Charter or Act of Parliament could bestow, the world at large had paid more attention to his political teaching, and had been more inclined to consider him a would-be political reformer. In his later years he dropped the political side of the question altogether; his name was no longer mixed up with political disturbances, and his teaching of the requirements of sanitary science, whether by word of mouth or by pen, assumed greater importance. With Disraeli he said *sanitas sanitatum, omnia sanitas*. Violation of sanitary laws is injurious to health, and acts most of all injuriously on the young; sanitary laws ought therefore, in Kingsley's judgment, to be obeyed by the free will and enlightenment of the people. Nevertheless if they are not so obeyed, he was quite prepared to advocate their enforcement by legislation. "Do noble deeds, not dream them all day long," was an injunction of Kingsley's, and this injunction applied to sanitation as well as to everything else.

The characters of Lamennais and Kingsley—not their careers—are strikingly similar. To the superficial glance, what contrast could be more startling than between the Roman priest and the Anglican minister? So true it is that environment determines the differences between men; character, the resemblances. Both were impetuous in thought and equally impetuous in action. Both were sanguine of the success of all they undertook, and were never much daunted by failure. Both were nervously excitable, a quality which rendered association with them at all times difficult and sometimes impossible. Their energy and their enthusiasm produced exhaustion of mind and body which hampered the progress of the many tasks they undertook. They manifested the same astonishing gift of putting flame into their words and winning the recalcitrant, a zeal for God's house which eats them up, exhibiting the intensity and the noble rage of a prophet. Diverse as were the conditions of their lives and fortunes, each acted out his life with thorough sincerity, giving to the world his best, pure and unalloyed. A love of nature was common to both men, yet while it solaced Kingsley it saddened Lamennais. They passed through a season of scepticism before they saw their way to ordination.

The Zeitgeist was manifest in Lamennais and Kingsley.

In the view of Sainte-Beuve the mind of the former was "oxidised by the age," and it is equally true of the latter. They were the children of two Revolutions, Lamennais of the French Revolution and Kingsley of the Chartist one. When they reached the age of consciousness society was in a surging state of rebellion, and this left a permanent mark on them. It turned Lamennais against tyranny, and it turned Kingsley towards the cause of the people. Neither, it is true, propounded practical remedies for the distress they witnessed around them. That was not their rôle. Theirs was the mission of affirming and accentuating what had been affirmed and accentuated before, but to do so with a powerful enthusiasm and a religious fervour which proved contagious.

Lamennais and Kingsley insisted on the duties as well as the rights of property. "The Bible," according to the latter, "not only dwells on the rights of property and the duties of labour," but "for once that it does, it preaches ten times over, the duties of property and the rights of labour." It is a view that Marx ignored, but it is one that is pressed home by Lamennais quite as much as by Kingsley. Both alike scorned injustice and strove to ameliorate the lot of the lowly. They lived for their social reforms, and it was for others—not for them—to carry them into effect. If they spoke and wrote too intensely and too emphatically, they believed that this intensity and this emphasis were sorely required. Sainte-Beuve points out that it was the mission of Lamennais to awaken society out of its Epicurean dream of slothful indifference to social grievances, and it was also the mission of Kingsley. They both heartily believed that no mere extension of political freedom would improve the condition of the workman. If *laissez-faire* was wrong, the extension of the franchise was not the main mode of its correction. The spirit of brotherhood, the sense of the Divine, will unite employer and employed as nothing else can. In this association of these two a solution of the social problem is to be found. Christianity can still, in the days of the Industrial Revolution, regenerate mankind. This means self-sacrifice on the part of all, but in this self-sacrifice Lamennais and Kingsley see the salvation of society.

References

Beer, M. *The Life and Teaching of Karl Marx.* (London, 1921.)
Brentano, L. *Die christlich-soziale Bewegung in England.* (Leipzig, 1883.)
Cazamian, L. *Le roman social en Angleterre.* (Paris, 1904.)
Collins, W. E., Ed. *Typical English Churchmen.* (London, 1902.)
Dorner, I. A. *Die Mansel-Maurice' sche Controverse.* (Berlin, 1861.)
Dyboski, R. *Charles Kingsley.* (Wien, 1909.)
Greg, W. R. *Literary and Social Judgments.* (London, 1869.)
Harrison, F. *C. Kingsley's Place in Literature.* (London, 1895.
Huber, V. A. *Ueber die cooperativen Arbeiterassociationen.* (Berlin, 1852.)
Huber, V. A. *Reisebriefe aus Belgien, Frankreich, u. England im Sommer,* 1854. (Hamburg, 1855.)
Jacobson, A. *C. Kingsleys Beziehungen zu Deutschland.* (Heidelberg, 1917.)
Kaufmann, M. *Christian Socialism.* (London, 1888.)
Kaufmann, M. *Charles Kingsley, Socialist and Social Reformer.* (London, 1892.)
Keller, L. *C. Kingsley u. die religiöse-sozialen Kämpfe in England im* 19. *Jahrhundert.* (Jena, 1911.)
Kingsley, Mrs. *Charles Kingsley, his Letters and Memories of his Life.* (London, 1871.)
Kingsley, C. *Frederick Denison Maurice.* (London, 1872.)
Laski, H. J. *Karl Marx.* (London, 1921.)
Lindsay, A. D. *Karl Marx's Capital.* (Oxford, 1925.)
Marriott, Sir J. A. R. *Charles Kingsley, Novelist.* (London, 1892.)
Masterman, C. F. G. *Frederick Denison Maurice.* (London, 1907.)
Maurice, F. *Frederick Denison Maurice.* (London, 1884.)
Mehring, F. *Karl Marx.* (Leipzig, 1918.)
Nicholson, J. S. *The Revival of Marxism.* (London, 1921.)
Rait, R. S. *Memorials of A. V. Dicey.* (London, 1925.)
Raven, C. E. *Christian Socialism,* 1848–54. (London, 1920.)
Rigg, J. M. *Modern Anglican Theology.* (London, 1880.)
Salter, F. R. *Karl Marx and Modern Socialism.* (London, 1921.)
Scott, J. W. *Karl Marx on Values.* (London, 1920.)
Stanley, A. P. *Charles Kingsley.* (London, 1875.)
Stephen, Sir L. *Hours in a Library.* Vol. III. (London, 1892.)
Stubbs, C. W. *Charles Kingsley and the Christian Social Movement.* (London, 1897.)

Index

ABERDEEN, Countess of, her election, 241.
Acton, Lord, appreciates Bentham, 63; and Coleridge, 196; and Carlyle, 328.
Adams, John Quincy, Owen's pamphlets, 147.
Aeschines, 378.
Aesop, 377.
Agitation, three movements, 365.
Aikin, John, quoted, 131.
Akbar, 389.
Akenside, Mark, his feeling, 165.
Alexander I, thanks Bentham, 76; answer, 347.
Alexander, William, his poem, 270.
Alfonso the Wise, 298.
Alfred, 184.
Allen, William, the Quaker humanitarian, 99.
Allingham, William, Carlyle's confession, 318-9.
Alverstone, Lord, Free Church appeal, 288
Alypius, 399.
Amadeus III, 111.
Anacreon, 378.
Andrewes, Lancelot, 181.
Angelo, Michael (Buonarotti), 390; fascinates Carlyle, 313; loneliness, 399.
Animals, cruelty to, 83, 165.
Anson, George, Lord, voyages, 378.
Anthony, St., a flagellant, 15.
Aquinas, St. Thomas, 270.
Aranda, Pedro Pablo Abarca de Bolea, 111.
Arblay, Alexandre d', marries Fanny Burney, 53.
Argyle, Earl of, his moving letter, 8.
Aristotle, 387-8, 410, the topic of population, 11; care for the State, 64; the ideal State, 417; political combination, 418; *Rhetoric*, 378; *Organon*, 379; *Analytics*, 379; *Ethics*, 392.
Arkwright, Sir Richard, 58; his spinning mill, 158; his water frame, 131.
Arnold, Thomas, values Coleridge, 182, 193, 195; Oriel School, 252; the Church, 266; supports Hampden, 270; appreciates Carlyle, 328.
Arnold, Matthew, 392, sees Georges Sand, 54; a preacher, 163; verdict of Coleridge, 193-4, 197-8; exalts Wilson, 256; praises Hayward, 305; aloofness, 444; belittles Maurice, 445.
Asceticism, its place, 13, 14-5, 69-70.

Ashworth, Henry, Corn Laws, 359.
Augustine, St., 432, predestination, 99; Coleridge's respect, 181; the people consent, 203; loneliness, 399.
Aulard, Alphonse, the French Revolution 325.
Austen, Jane, 225; *Mansfield Park*, 53.
Austin, Charles, 254.
Austin, John, 254, 411; sovereign authority, 48; founder of Utilitarian jurisprudence, 98-9; sovereignty, 266-9, 277 281, 291; the two-kingdom theory, 293 *Province of Jurisprudence Determined* 266-8.
Austin, Sarah, *Goethe and his Contemporaries*, 305.
Austin, Sara, Disraeli's Egeria, 239; breac with Mill, 384.
Averroes, Ibn Roschid, 388.

BABEUF, François Noel, 8.
Bach, Johann Sebastian, his Passio music, 106.
Bacon, Francis, 66, 188, 388; his work 120.
Bagehot, Walter, verdict on Mill, 387 pre-Mill, 394; estimates Mill, 427-8.
Bain, Alexander, Mill's article, 107 Mill's infatuation, 406; consternation 420; estimates Mill, 427-8.
Baines, Edward, proprietor of the Leed *Mercury*, 141.
Balfour, Gerald, 138.
Balfour, Earl of, his Factory Act, 237.
Balzac, Honoré de, 222-3; novel o purpose, 226.
Baring, Lady Harriet, breach with Mil 384.
Barré, Isaac, meets Bentham, 51; Bent ham's book, 54.
Barrère, Camille, 433.
Barrès, Maurice, his message, 227.
Barrow, Sir John, the *Quarterly*, 103.
Baxter, Richard, estimates Cromwell, 339
Bayard, Pierre du Terrail, Chevalier d at Pavia, 335-6.
Beaconsfield, Lord. *See* Disraeli.
Beattie, James, common sense, 55-6.
Beaverbrook, Lord, lowers Parliament 368-9.

INDEX

Beccaria, Bonesana Cesare, 83; outlines law reform, 44; the greatest happiness, 63; against torture, 85.
Beethoven, Ludwig van, his *Fidelio*, 400.
Bell, Andrew, reforms schools, 15, 143.
Belleisle, Charles Louis Auguste Fouquet, Duc, 343.
Benbow, William, the General Strike, 155.
Bentham, Jeremy, 137, 204, 337, 381, 411, 412, 413; his influence, 35; a weakly child, 38; Chap. 2 *passim*; father of J. Mill, 96-7, 377; J. Mill with him, 98; learnt little from travel, 101; outside Parliament, 102; *Westminster Review*, 104-5; fond of music, 106; attitude to women, 108; sinister interests, 111; Thompson a pupil, 120; education, 144; partner with Owen, 147; his triumphal reception, 149, 161; Dumont's share, 176; Industrial Revolution, 177; J. S. Mill's appreciation, 194; his humanitarianism, 208; happiness of the people, 209; sovereignty, 266; influences J. S. Mill, 385, 394; race, 417; Mill's modification, 419; *Critical Elements of Jurisprudence*, 46; *Introduction to the Principles of Morals and Legislation*, 46, 54-5, 56-7, 82; *Fragment on Government*, 47-8, 50, 54; *Rationale of Punishments and Rewards*, 51; *Théorie des Peines et des Recompenses*, 51; *Defence of Usury*, 57; *Political Tactics*, 59; *Emancipate your Colonies*, 64, 77; *Traités des Legislation*, 65-6; *Introductory View*, 74; *Rationale of Evidence*, 74; *Constitutional Code*, 76; *Pannomion*, 78; *Theory of Legislation*, 78; *Catechism of Parliamentary Reform*, 86; *Radicalism not Dangerous*, 87; *Church-of-Englandism and its Catechism Examined*, 99.
Bentham, Samuel, Jeremy's visit, 57.
Bentinck, Lord William, admires Bentham, 78.
Bergson, Henri, his ironical utterance, 244.
Berkeley, George, his *Querist*, 29.
Bernstorff, Andreas, 111.
Birth-control, 36.
Bismarck-Schonhaüsen, Otto Eduard Leopold von, 38, 240, 392, 410; defends the throne, 216; greatness, 335; Carlyle's appreciation, 345-6; Cobden, 373, 403; a statesman, 376.
Black, John, edits the *Chronicle*, 118.
Blackstone, Sir William, 76; Bentham's attack, 47, 49-50; the protagonist of Bentham, 78; *Commentaries*, 43-4, 47, 48-9, 73, 78.
Blair, Hugh, spirituality, 279.
Blanc, Louis, the French Revolution, 325; influences Mill, 385.

Blanca, Florida, 111.
Blessington, Lady, knows Disraeli, 209, 239.
Boccaccio, Giovanni, 390.
Boehme, Jacob, mysticism, 179.
Boethius, 90.
Bohr, Niels, 391.
Bolingbroke, Viscount, 223, half a Frenchman, 52; Disraeli's sketch, 214; a true Tory, 216-7, 226.
Bolivar y Ponte, Simon, consults Bentham, 77.
Bonald, Louis Gabriel Ambroise, Comte, 251.
Bonnington, Richard Parkes, friend of Lawrence and Wilkie, 54.
Borgia, Cesare, 338.
Borrow, George Henry, 76; the Romantics, 250.
Bosquet, Pierre François Joseph, his *obiter dictum*, 70.
Boswell, James, 435; Macaulay's depreciation, 307; Carlyle's appreciation, 307-10.
Bourget, Paul, visits Oxford, 54.
Bowden, John William, 269.
Bowring, Sir John, edits Bentham, 78.
Bradford, Countess of, 239; Disraeli's confidant, 240.
Bray, John Francis, 128; the unearned increment, 119; *Labour's Wrongs*, 126-7.
Bremond, Henri, Newman's egoism, 263.
Brewster, Sir David, Mill's preaching, 97.
Bright, John, 206-7; 235, 401; the diplomatic service, 110; Corn Laws, 117; admires *Popanilla*, 208; influences Russell, 218; his fine leadership, 221-2; hostile to the Factory Acts, 235; meets Cobden, 359-60; partnership, 360-1, 364; Elliott's rhymes, 364; the manufacturer, 366; Peel's conversion, 366-7; declaration, 368; lowered Parliament, 368-9, 370-1; Burke's secret, 374; mistaken outlook, 402-4.
Brindley, James, canals, 118.
Brissot de Warville, Jacques Pierre, 62.
Brontë, Anne, 392.
Brontë, Charlotte, 392; *Shirley*, 225.
Brontë, Emily Jane, 392.
Brougham, Henry Peter, Baron Brougham and Vaux, a friend of Bentham, 66; Mill's circle, 98; letter from Mill, 118-9; knows Owen, 147; the doctrinaire, 235; Austinianism, 281.
Brown, Thomas, 105; the association philosophy, 300.
Browning, Elizabeth Barrett, 392.
Browning, Robert, 392; quoted, 309; creed, 318; represents S. John, 319; misunderstood, 400; aloofness, 444.

2 F

Bruckner, Johann, anticipates Malthus, 11–2.
Bryce, Lord, estimates, 327, 390; fatalism of the multitude, 408.
Brydges Willyams, Sarah, 239.
Buckle, Henry Thomas, his *History of Civilisation*, 210–1.
Buddha, voluntary renunciation, 69.
Bull, George, 181.
Buller, Charles, in the House, 102; Utilitarian influence, 254; Imperialism, 347–8.
Bulwer, William Henry Lytton Earle, knows Disraeli, 209; *obiter dictum*, 346.
Bunsen, Christian Carl Josias, 274.
Bunyan, John, 392; *Pilgrim's Progress*, 8, 129, 399.
Burdett, Sir Francis, Radical bluster, 82.
Bürger Gottfried, August, 386.
Burke, Edmund, 213, 367, 418, 433; a weakly child, 38; morality mysterious, 40; the place of conscience, 41; public spirit, 64–5; Bentham's verdict, 67; paramount position, 161; the French Revolution, 164, 167; his scorn, 177; parallel with Coleridge, 184, 189–90, 199–204; parallel with Disraeli, 214; Disraeli's appreciation, 226–7; the past, 246, 322–3; his thraldom, 328; impatience, 356–7; patience, 369; political relativity, 373–4; *Letter to a Noble Lord*, 168; *Reflections on the Revolution in France*, 173.
Burke, William, 64–5.
Burnet, Gilbert, 378.
Burnet, Thomas, *Theory of the Earth*, 43.
Burney, Fanny, a backward girl, 38; her marriage, 53.
Burns, Robert, 337, his compassion, 165; a poet of the people, 166; Carlyle's appreciation, 313; equality, 334.
Burr, Aaron, appeals to Bentham, 77.
Burrow, Harriet, marries Mill, 97.
Burt, Thomas, approval of Disraeli, 236.
Bute, Marquis of, the General Assembly, 283.
Butler, Joseph, the place of conscience, 41, 68, 71; love of our neighbour, 72; his question, 149; probability the guide, 257; *Analogy*, 99.
Butler, Samuel, satirises the Puritans, 15.
Butler, Samuel, 162, 392.
Buxton, Sir Thomas Fowell, 235.
Byng, John, unjustly shot, 368.
Byron, George Noel Gordon, Lord, 392, 400, a backward boy, 38; his weakness, 163; the past, 188; the art of poetry, 192; Landor's verdict, 193; his sister's love, 206; his fame, 207; his death, 249; parallel with Carlyle, 297; Carlyle's judgment, 311; perverse judgment, 312–3.

CAIRD, John 285.
Cairnes, John Elliot, influences Mill, 393; estimates Mill, 427.
Calas, Jean, broken on the wheel, 91.
Calvin, John, 410; his dogma, 99–100, 298-9; Coleridge's approval, 181.
Calvinism, of Mill, 99–100, 380–1; of Carlyle, 297–300, 317–9.
Cambridge Platonists, 181.
Cambridge University, 1–3, 64, 162, 237, 252, 254, 443–4.
Camden, Earl of, Bentham's book, 47, 54; meets Bentham, 51.
Campbell, John McCleod, Candlish's assault, 285.
Candlish, Robert Smith, influence, 279; his Convocation, 282; his victory, 285; his orthodoxy, 286, 291.
Canning, George, 107–8, 213, the *Quarterly*, 103; the great Foreign Secretary, 217; high aims, 219–20; *Anti-Jacobin*, 305.
Capet, Hugh, 325.
Carey, Henry Charles, attacks Malthusian ratios, 35.
Carlstadt, Andreas Rudolf Bodenstein, influences Luther, 255.
Carlyle, Janet, 302; her son's devotion, 299; his teacher, 300.
Carlyle, James, 303; a Scots Adam Bede, 297–8; influences Thomas, 300.
Carlyle, Thomas, equality, 80; exaggerates Chartism, 156; verdict on Coleridge, 180, 194–5, 197–8; Acton's depreciation, 196; against Liberalism, 223; seriousness 251–2; Chap. 8 *passim*; a northerner, 356; calico millennium, 373; attacks society, 383; breach with Mill, 384; Mill's verdict, 385–6; Imperialism, 394; imperious temper, 398; heroes, 401; prescience, 403; demand, 404; shakes Burke, 413; a good despot, 415; altered views, 421; influences Kingsley, 444, 446; appreciates him, 449; *Sartor Resartus*, 300, 303, 304, 314–5, 320, 329–32, 348; *Heroes and Hero Worship*, 300, 332, 333, 335, 348; *Recollections*, 303; *Wilhelm Meister*, 305, 315; *Life of Schiller*, 305, 315; *French Revolution*, 312, 325–9, 339, 342, 352–3; *Latter-day Pamphlets*, 317–8, 332, 333, 334–5, 348; *Historic Survey of German Poetry*, 322; *On History*, 322; *Chartism*, 323, 348; *History of Frederick the Great*, 326, 342–4, 346–7; *Past and Present*, 332,

338, 348, 349, 350, 404; *Miscellanies*, 332; *Life and Letters of O. Cromwell*, 338–42; *John Sterling*, 342; *Occasional Discourse*, 347; *Shooting Niagara*, 347; *New Downing Street*, 350.
Cartwright, Edmund, power loom, 118.
Cartwright, John, 186; childish remedies, 82.
Castlereagh, Viscount, Carlyle's sneer, 312.
Catherine II, 111, 343, 415; codification of law, 57; answers Diderot, 157.
Catherine of Siena, a mystic, 158.
Cato, 337.
Cave, William, his *Lives of the Apostles*, 43.
Cavour, Camillo Benso, Comte, 392, 403, 410.
Celibacy, considered, 36.
Cellini, Benvenuto, *Life*, 376.
Cervantes Saavedra, Miguel de, *Don Quixote*, 8, 399; quoted, 400.
Chalmers, Thomas, seriousness, 251–2; sovereignty, 277; parallel with Newman, 277–8; the leader, 279; the Church, 280–1; resolution, 282; Disruption, 284–5; meets Carlyle, 301–2; agitation, 365–6, 368–9; private affairs, 367.
Chamberlain, Houston Stewart, *Foundations of the Nineteenth Century*, 230–1.
Chambers, Robert, *Vestiges of the Natural History of Creation*, 5.
Charlemagne, 389, 412.
Charles I, 223, 274, 345.
Charles III, 111.
Charles the Bold, 246.
Charles, Frederick, 111.
Charles, Theodore, 111.
Chartists, the, their petition, 112; Co-operation, 128–9; Trade Unions, 156; attitude of Disraeli, 221, 225; effects of Free Trade, 222; attitude of Carlyle, 323; the French Revolution, 348; attitude of Mill, 415; of Kingsley, 446–7, 449.
Chateaubriand, François René, Vicomte, 251; an exile, 53; *Atala*, 245; *René*, 245.
Chatham, Earl of, 213, 343; Shakespeare's power, 190; high aims, 219–20; Byng, 368; inspiration, 392.
Chatterton, Thomas, 245; a backward boy, 38; Rossetti's estimate, 249.
Chaucer, Geoffrey, 245, 390; his nearness, 250.
Chesterfield, Countess of, 239.
Chesterfield, Earl of, 52.
Choiseul, Etienne François, 90.
Christian VII, 111.
Church, the, Chap. 7 *passim*; conception of Mill, 113–4; of Coleridge, 182–4, 185–6, 200–2, 266; of Burke, 200–2; of Disraeli, 223–4, 227–30; of Whately, 261; of Newman, 261–3, 269, 270, **276–7**, 279; of Arnold, 266; of Palmer, 268; of Keble, 268–9; of Gladstone, 270–2; of Ward, 275–6; of Chalmers, 278, 280–2; of Melville, 279, 284; of Pusey, 282.
Church, Richard William, 276; quoted, 255; Newman's sermons, 262; estimates Cromwell, 341–2.
Churchill, Lord Randolph, lowered Parliament, 368–9.
Cicero, Marcus Tullius, 337, 378; the State divine, 201.
Cincinnatus, 237.
Clarendon, Earl of, estimates Cromwell, 339.
Clarke, Edward Daniel, a friend of Malthus, 4.
Clarke, Samuel, the fitness of things, 55–6.
Clarkson, Thomas, 337; knows Owen, 147; a humanitarian, 252.
Claudian, imperial Rome, 417.
Clerk, Lord Justice, Free Church appeal, 288–90.
Clerk-Maxwell, James, 391; pixies, 389.
Clive, Robert, outlook, 401.
Clough, Arthur Hugh, 392; altered views, 420; aloofness, 444.
Cobbett, William, attacks Malthus, 34–5; viewy, 82; opposes Owen, 148.
Cobden, Richard, 206–7, 235, 401; Corn Laws, 117; influences Russell, 218; his fine leadership, 221–2; hostile to Factory Acts, 235; Chap. 9 *passim*; mistaken outlook, 402–4; *England, Ireland, and America*, 357; *Russia*, 357.
Colbert, Jean Baptiste, his colonial empire, 24.
Coleridge, Lord, Newman's sermons, 262.
Coleridge, Samuel Taylor, 206, 249, 445; his name taken off, 3; the desire of marriage, 13; attacks Malthus, 35; meets Owen, 134–5; a Pantisocracy, 150; Chap. 5 *passim*; a mystic, 208; system of estates, 209, 215; money considerations, 222; a Tory, 226–7; transforms poetry, 247; no renegade, 248; understanding and reason, 264; the Church, 266; Gladstone's appreciation, 271; a Romantic, 297; opium, 303–4; a forerunner, 305; Carlyle's verdict, 310–1; *obiter dictum*, 353; influences Mill, 385, 387, 388; lassitude, 399; good government, 414; Toryism, 416; altered views, 420; influences Kingsley, 444, 445, 446; *Table Talk*, 162, 176, 187, 203; *Conciones ad Populum*, 164; *The Plot Discovered*, 164; *France*, 167, 169, 170, 172; *Lyrical Ballads*, 168; *Ancient Mariner*, 168–9, 170, 198; *Christabel*, 168–9; *Kubla Khan*, 168–9; *Work*

without Hope, 170–1; *Biographia Literaria*, 172; *Statesman's Manual*, 175, 178; *Essays on his own Times*, 175; *Aids to Reflection*, 182; *Constitution of Church and State*, 182, 189; *The Friend*, 189; *Wallenstein*, 305; *Day Sermons*, 446.

Coligny, Gaspard de, a Huguenot State, 23.

Collins, David, *New South Wales*, 378.

Colonies, the, attitude of J. Mill, 110; of Coleridge, 177; of Disraeli, 208–9, 348; of Bright, 208–9, 402–4; of the Utilitarians, 347; of Carlyle, 346–51, 394; of Kipling, 348; of McCulloch, 349–50; of Lewis, 351; of J. S. Mill, 394–5; of Cobden, 402–4.

Colour Bar, the, 151.

Comte, Auguste, 383, 385, 428; love of humanity, 71; Law of the Three Stages, 387–8; good government, 414.

Condé, Louis, 2nd Duc, at Rocroi, 335–6.

Condorcet, Marie Jean Antoine Nicolas, Marquis, human perfectibility, 1, 7, 14–5, 35, 157–8; inequality, 7–8; attitude to women, 9; problem of population, 9–10; Malthus's analysis, 11–3, 35; influences Mill, 98; *Esquisse d'un tableau historique des Progrès*, 1, 8, 9.

Confucius, 388–9.

Conservatism, of Bentham, 61, 106; of Coleridge, 177–8, 200–4; of Burke, 200–4; a review of its history, 216–21; attitude of Walpole, 216–7; of Pitt, 217; of Canning, 217–8; of Peel, 218–9; of Palmerston, 218–9; of Disraeli, 224–5, 227; of Mill, 416.

Constable, John, a weakly child, 38; revolutionises French painting, 53–4.

onstant, Benjamin, 245.

Cooper, Thomas, *Autobiography of a Chartist*, 446.

Copeland, William John, 269, 276.

Co-operation, its progress, 451–3.

Copleston, Edward, a convert of Malthus, 34; meets Newman, 265.

Corn Laws, their continuance, 117; Disraeli's ridicule, 208–9; attitude of Peel, 218–9; Chap. 9 *passim*.

Cort, Henry, process of puddling, 118.

Covenanters, the Scots, 15.

Cowley, Abraham, his retirement, 164.

Cowper, William, 400; feeling, 164; a poet of the people, 166.

Cranmer, Thomas, 266, 273.

Cripps, John Marten, a friend of Malthus, 4.

Croce, Benedetto, criticises the Utilitarians, 68; his *obiter dictum*, 191.

Croker, John Wilson, the *Quarterly*, 103; invents the term Conservative, 200.

Croker, Thomas Crofton, meets Disraeli, 207.

Crome, John, 323; last words, 401.

Crompton, Samuel, spinning mule, 118, 131.

Cromwell, Oliver, 345; *obiter dictum*, 92; a mystic, 158; a hero, 332, 336; lying, 336–7; Carlyle's worship, 337, 338; attitudes assumed towards him, 339–42; 352; a great soldier, 376.

Cromwell, Richard, 341.

Cromwell, Thomas, 129.

Cross, Sir Richard, 236.

Cudworth, Ralph, 181.

Cuvier, George, Baron, travels with Owen, 149.

D'ALEMBERT, Jean le Rond, La Barre's execution, 91.

De Biran, Maine, quoted, 430.

De Coux, Comte, a social reformer, 215.

Du Deffand, Madame, contrasts French and English, 25.

De Feuillide (Eliza Hancock), Comtesse, her marriage, 53.

De Liancourt, Duc, 51.

De Lyra, Nicholas, 385.

De Maistre, Joseph, Comte, his steps, 251.

De Muralt, Béat, contrasts French and English, 24–5.

De Musset, Alfred, 222–3.

De Nemours, Dupont, Quesnay's influence, 393–4.

D'Orsay, Comte, knows Disraeli, 209.

De Quincey, Thomas, verdict on Coleridge, 193; opium, 303–4.

De la Rochefoucauld, Duc, parliamentary tactics, 59.

De la Rochejacquelin, Henri, *obiter dictum*, 334–5.

De Stael, Madame, 245, 251; Bentham's rudeness, 67; Napoleon's attack, 174; a forerunner, 305; Alexander I's reply, 347; *De l'Allemagne*, 305.

De Tocqueville, Alexis, the French Revolution, 325.

De la Tour du Pin, Marquis, a social reformer, 215.

De Vega, Lope, 76.

De Vigny, Alfred, 386.

Dale, Anne Caroline, marries Owen, 135.

Dale, David, his factory, 135; a humane employer, 140.

Dalgairns, John Dobree, the Oxford Movement, 254.

Dalton, John, meets Owen, 134; atomic theory, 391.

Dante, Alighieri, 390, 400; Carlyle's appreciation, 309–10, 313, 336; four-square, 399; loneliness, 400.

INDEX

Darwin, Erasmus, the idea of evolution, 44.
Darwin, Sir Francis, his *Life of C. Darwin*, 5–6.
Darwin, Charles, reads Malthus, 5–6; evolution, 7, 391; slow advance, 36; poor health, 38; his work, 44; Carlyle's attitude, 313–4; Mill's anticipation, 387, 408–9; Newman's anticipation, 387; Socialism, 440; *Origin of Species*, 314, 408.
Daudet, Alphonse, visits London, 54.
Davenant, Sir John, *Gondibert*, 313.
Davey, Lord, Free Church appeal, 288, 292.
David, his census, 26.
Davidson, Andrew Bruce, Biblical scholar, 286.
Davidson, Christopher, the Thirty-nine Articles, 274.
Davy, Sir Humphry, 313, 427.
Debrett, John, *The Crisis*, 3.
Delacroix, Ferdinand Victor Eugène, friend of Lawrence and Wilkie, 54.
Democracy, the attitude of J. Mill, 107–10; of Mackintosh, 110; of Macaulay, 110–3; of Coleridge, 184–8, 200–4, 209; of Burke, 200–4; of Disraeli, 209; of the Whigs, 209–10; of the Tories, 209–10; of O'Connell, 215; of Carlyle, 327.
Democritus, 304.
Demosthenes, *On the Crown*, 9.
Derby, Earl of, attacks Whig policy, 220; the Reform Bill, 253.
Dicey, Albert Venn, Bentham's dominance, 44; public opinion, 414.
Dickens, Charles, 356, 392; a weakly child, 38; knows Paris, 54; aloofness, 444; *Oliver Twist*, 225; *Nicholas Nickleby*, 225; *Hard Times*, 225, 404; *Tale of Two Cities*, 328.
Diderot, Denis, questions Catherine II, 157; Carlyle's appreciation, 313; his attitude, 321, 415.
Dilke, Sir Charles Wentworth, *Greater Britain*, 395.
Diminishing Returns, the law of, 17; Malthus's attitude, 28.
Diogenes, 377.
Disraeli, Benjamin, 392, 445; characterises Paris, 52; treaty of commerce, 53; Coleridge's influence, 182; Chap. 6 *passim*; the Reform Bill, 253; the place of emotion, 257; Carlyle's judgment, 312; Manchester School, 356; attacks Peel, 367; verdict on Mill, 383; sanitation, 453; *Coningsby*, 53, 197, 206, 224–5, 227, 233, 447; *Lord George Bentinck*, 206, 229–30; *Lothair*, 206, 233; *Vivian Grey*, 207, 209; *Venetia*, 207, 252; *Voyage of Captain Popanilla*, 208; *Tancred*, 209, 223–4, 227–31, 233, 447; *The Young Duke*, 209; *Contarini Fleming*, 210; *Wondrous Tale of Alroy*, 211; *What is he?* 211; *Vindication of the English Constitution*, 214–6; *Spirit of Whiggism*, 221; *Sybil*, 225–7, 233, 404, 447, 449; *Endymion*, 229–30, 237, 239, 240–1.
Disraeli, Isaac, *Curiosities of Literature*, 206.
Disraeli, Sarah, her brother's love, 206.
Disruption Movement, the, 277–94.
Döllinger, Johann Joseph Ignatius von, Coleridge's influence, 196.
Donne, John, 181.
Doubleday, Henry, high feeding, 35.
Dowden, Edward, on Coleridge, 170.
Drummond, Edward, shot, 365.
Drummond, Henry, *Natural Law in the Spiritual World*, 241; strange personality, 286.
Drummond, Thomas, the duties of property, 202.
Dumas, Alexandre (père), 222–3.
Dumas, Alexandre, the unclassed, 226.
Dumont, Etienne, 67; Bentham's method, 45–6; Bentham's editor, 51–2, 65, 176; parliamentary tactics, 59; makes his way, 66; worships Bentham, 76.
Duncan, William, his *Logick*, 2.
Dunning, John (Baron Ashburton), Bentham's book, 47, 54; meets Bentham, 51.
Dupleix, Joseph François, Marquis, his Indian empire, 24.
Durham, Earl of, Imperialism, 348.

Eckermann, Johann Peter, Goethe's remark, 319.
Edgeworth, Maria, 432; tales, 378.
Edinburgh Review, 301, 312; supports Malthus, 35; its growth, 102–5; Mill's article, 106; Mackintosh's article, 109; poetical criticism, 192; Carlyle's work, 315.
Education, the attitude of Bell, 15, 143; of Lancaster, 15, 143; of Owen, 143–5, 147.
Edward VII, l'oncle de l'Europe, 232.
Eichhorn, Johann Gottfried, teaches Pusey, 305.
Einstein, Albert, physical relativity, 373, 391.
Eldon, Lord (John Scott), 176; at Oxford, 43; abuses of equity, 74–5; law of trusts, 291–2; Toryism, 401–2.
Eliot, Sir John, 337.
Eliot, George, 392; her *obiter dictum*, 71, 403; aloofness, 444; *Adam Bede*, 252, 297, 312, 409.

Elizabeth, her royal progresses, 232.
Ellice, Lady Hannah, Bentham's letter, 46.
Elliott, Ebenezer, poetry, 361; *Corn Law Rhymes*, 361, 446.
Ellis, George, the *Quarterly*, 103.
Emerson, Ralph Waldo, Carlyle's German furore, 306; admires Carlyle, 328, 346.
Engels, Friedrich, 435; bourgeois, 438–9.
Equality, attitude of Condorcet, 8; of Bentham, 71, 79–81; of St. Just, 78; of Robespierre, 78; of Carlyle, 80, 334; of Godwin, 120; of Thompson, 121; of Hall, 122–3; of Bray, 126–7; of Owen, 151; of Coleridge, 175–6; of Disraeli, 223, 230; of Burns, 334; of Malthus, 419.
Erasmus, Desiderius, 262; Bentham's ideal, 42.
Erskine, Henry, denounces Eldon, 74–5; champion of freedom, 167.
Erskine, Thomas, appreciates Keble, 258; a pioneer, 420–1.
Eugenics, shortly considered, 36–8.
Evangelicalism, 195; its individualism, 82; its humanitarianism, 83–4; its deficiencies, 252; attitude of Newman, 261; the Scots variety, 280–1.
Evolution, Malthus its grandfather, 5; Chap. 1 *passim*; E. Darwin's idea, 44; attitude of Coleridge, 196–7; of Newman, 228; of Disraeli, 228; Socialism, 440.

FABER, Frederick William, the Oxford Movement, 223, 254.
Factory Acts, of 1802, 133; of 1818, 140, 176; of 1844, 225; of 1878, 236; of 1901, 237; attitude of Malthus, 31; of Shaftesbury, 235; of Peel, 235; of Graham, 235; of O'Connell, 235; of Brougham, 235; of Bright, 235; of Cobden, 235, 358; of Gladstone, 235; of Martineau, 236; of Mill, 394.
Fairbairn, Patrick, 285–6.
Faraday, Michael, 313, 391, 427; devotion to science, 69; Tyndall's appreciation, 314.
Fawcett, Henry, influences Mill, 393.
Fellenberg, Philip Emmanuel de, 150.
Fénelon, François Salignac de la Mothe, his *Télémaque*, 43, 129.
Feuerbach, Ludwig Andrew, materialism, 439.
Fichte, Johann Gottlieb, 383; Coleridge's attitude, 185; the State divine, 201; influences Carlyle, 320–1, 329; the hero, 332; influence, 429; *On the Nature of a Scholar*, 332.
Field, Richard, 181.
Fielding, Henry, 225.

Figgis, John Neville, groups of men, 443.
Firth, Sir Charles Harding, 340.
FitzGerald, Edward, criticises Carlyle, 328; translation, 409.
Flaubert, Gustave, the petite bourgeoisie, 226.
Fleury, André Hercules de, 90.
Foch, Ferdinand, 410.
Forster, John, 340.
Fortescue, Sir John, 176.
Fourier, Charles, 161; parallel with Owen, 157–9.
Fox, Caroline, Bentham's love, 51, 58.
Fox, Charles James, 97; appreciates Bentham, 66; Coleridge's work, 174; his impossibility, 217; the gambler, 237–8.
Fox, George, mysticism, 179.
Foy, Maximilien Sebastien, greets Bentham, 78.
Francis I, 345; his question, 23; colonial empire, 23–4.
Francis, St., of Assisi, 38; the Lady Poverty, 69.
Franklin, Benjamin, the topic of population, 11; the spread of fennel, 16.
Frauenlob, Heinrich, 423.
Frederick II (the Great), 111; victories, 326; real kingship, 326–7; a hero, 332, 338, 341; Carlyle's life, 342–4, 346; rise, 347; a great soldier, 376; position, 415.
Frederick Augustus, 111.
Frederick William I, buffoonery, 335; attracts Carlyle, 343.
Freeman, Edward Augustus, 250.
French Revolution, the, grievances, 1; the effects of population, 34; Fénelon's influence, 43; attitude of Bentham, 58–60, 61, 79; of Wordsworth, 131, 166–8, 171–2; of Coleridge, 131, 164, 166–70, 172–3; of Southey, 131, 164, 171; of Burke, 164, 167; effects in England, 217; attitude of the historians, 325; of Carlyle, 325–9, 353; of Michelet, 352–3; nature, 432; liberty, 433.
Frend, William, liberal views, 162.
Fricker, Sara, marries Coleridge, 164.
Frontenac et Pallua, Louis de Buade, Comte, ill supported, 23.
Froude, Hurrell, 269; good deed, 253; deep impression, 253–4; influences Newman, 261; *Remains*, 253, 273.
Froude, James Anthony, 376; Carlyle's biographer, 315; Carlyle's cry, 319; an interpreter, 322, 328; altered views, 420.

GAINSBOROUGH, Thomas, 401.
Gallienus, 164.

Galton, Sir Francis, eugenist, 36–8.
Gardiner, Samuel Rawson, estimates Cromwell, 340, 342.
Garibaldi, Guiseppe, 401.
Garrick, David, 106.
Gaskell, Elizabeth Cleghorn, 392; *Mary Barton*, 225, 404, 449.
Gaskell, James Milnes, 323.
Gautier, Theophile, characterises Scott, 245–6.
George I, 226.
George II, 226, 243.
George III, 433; shakes off the Whigs, 226.
George IV, 250; a great blackguard, 210, 232; his death, 238.
George, Henry, attacks Malthusian ratios, 35.
Ghiberti, Lorenzo, 390.
Gibbon, Edward, 300, 378; Malthus reads his book, 3; writes French, 43; knows Paris, 52; describes Boethius, 90; his triumph, 92; attitude to religion, 99; the past, 246; solitary pre-eminence, 250; *obiter dictum*, 301; Carlyle's attitude, 324; accuracy, 327; *Decline and Fall of the Roman Empire*, 3, 46, 301, 302; *Autobiography*, 376.
Gibson, James, 285–6.
Gierke, Otto von, groups of men, 443.
Gifford, William, edits the *Quarterly*, 103.
Gilbert, Sir William Schwenck, quoted, 180.
Giotto or Angiolotto, 390.
Gissing, George Robert, 392.
Gladstone, William Ewart, 213; insular, 208; parallel with Disraeli, 212–3; a Radical, 219–20; comprehensive reform, 220; the Queen's opposition, 322; hostile to the Factory Acts, 235; Midlothian campaign, 237; contrast with Disraeli, 239; a Tory, 256; case for Establishment, 270–3; sovereignty, 277; his letter, 323; characterises Mill, 285; belittles Maurice, 445; *The State in its relations with the Church*, 270–1; *A Chapter of Autobiography*, 271; *Gleanings*, 272.
Gobineau, Arthur, Comte, doctrine of race, 230.
Goderich, Lord, 239.
Godwin, William, 128, 147, 434; his assumptions, 3–4; believes in perfectibility, 1, 7–8, 9, 14–5, 35, 123; inequality, 7–8; inward development, 10-1, 13, 15; Malthus's analysis, 12–3; attacks Malthus, 34–5; his revolutionary creed, 82; the father of Socialism, 120, 135, 136; novel of purpose, 225; *The Inquirer*, 3; *Political Justice*, 3, 120.

Goethe, Johann Wolfgang von, 352, 383; comforts Carlyle, 304–5; Carlyle's appreciation, 306, 313; writes to Carlyle, 315; estimates Carlyle, 319, 329; quoted 329, 399; *Faust*, 240, 306; *The Tale*, 306; *Dichtung u. Wahrheit*, 376.
Goldsmith, Oliver, a backward boy, 38; feeling, 165; *The Deserted Village*, 67, 222; *The Traveller*, 72.
Gordon, Margaret, Blumine, 303.
Görres, Johann Joseph, 251.
Gosse, Sir Edmund, the clash of the generations, 42.
Graham, Cunningham, his intervention, 241.
Graham, Sir James, hostile to Shaftesbury, 235; Austinianism, 282–3.
Gray, John, 128, 434; the unearned increment, 119; *Human Happiness*, 123–4.
Gray, Thomas, 52, 245; feeling, 165.
Great Man, the Problem of, attitude of Carlyle, 324; of Mill, 388–93; general considerations, 390–3.
Gregory of Heimberg, 269.
Green, John Richard, accuracy, 327.
Green, Joseph Henry, Coleridge's interpreter, 176.
Green, Thomas Hill, verdict on Utilitarianism, 72–3; influence, 429.
Grey, Earl, 106–7; Reform Bill, 217–8.
Grote, Harriet, breach with Mill, 384.
Grote, George, a colleague of Malthus, 5; historian of Greece, 98–9; in the House, 102; accuracy, 327; Corn Laws, 359; Mill's infatuation, 407; aloofness, 444.
Guizot, François Pierre Guillaume, 385.
Gustavus III, 111.
Gustavus Adolphus, 342, 344.

HALÉVY, Elie, the authority on Bentham, 51–2; knows us intimately, 54; Bentham's Radicalism, 59, 61, 87; Bentham's triumphal reception, 78.
Hall, Charles, 128, 434; the unearned increment, 119; his patients, 122; a noble doctor, 132; *Effects of Civilisation*, 122–3.
Hallam, Arthur, 253.
Hallam, Henry, a convert of Malthus, 34; Reform Bill, 253; cold impartiality, 323; criticises Carlyle, 328; estimates Cromwell, 340; aloofness, 444.
Hamilton, Alexander, 77.
Hamilton, Sir William, his view, 285.
Hampden, John, 240, 337.
Hampden, Renn Dickson, opposed, 270.
Harcourt, Sir William, George Granville Venables Vernon, *obiter dictum*, 441.
Hardie, James Keir, his career, 241–2.

Hare, Julius Charles, appreciates Coleridge, 195.
Hare, Thomas, proportional representation, 415.
Hargreaves, James, spinning jenny, 118, 131.
Harley, Robert (Earl of Oxford), 214.
Hartley, David, 174–9; influences Mill, 105; and Wordsworth, 167.
Hatch, Edwin, aloofness, 444.
Hawkesworth, John, voyages, 378.
Hawkins, Edward, Provost of Oriel, 259–60.
Hayley, Williams, *Triumphs of Temper*, 313.
Hayward, Abraham, *Faust*, 305.
Hazlitt, William, attacks Malthus, 34–5; *obiter dictum*, 143, 170; verdict on Coleridge, 193.
Heber, Reginald, piety and literature, 252.
Hegel, Georg Wilhelm Friedrich, 383; Coleridge's attitude, 185; the State divine, 201; misunderstood, 400; influence, 429, 439.
Heine, Heinrich, his sister's love, 206; Romanticism, 251; mystical brotherhood, 400–1.
Helvetius, Claude Adrian, the importance of legislation, 45.
Hengst, 350.
Henry IV, colonial empire, 23–4; at Ivry, 335–6.
Henry V, at Agincourt, 335–6.
Henry VIII, 266.
Heraclitus, 304.
Herbert, Sidney, Lord, Peel's conversion, 366–7.
Herder, Johann Gottfried von, 188, 385; history and geography, 20.
Herodotus, 238, 337–8.
Herschel, Sir William, 427.
Hobbema, Meindert, 401.
Hobbes, Thomas, 107, 379, 440; a weakly child; 38; the obligation of right, 40; what is law, 48; the papacy, 49; Maine's verdict, 61; influences Mill, 105; perverse judgment, 312–3; Stephen's admiration, 411; the State, 412.
Hodgskin, Thomas, 128, 434; the labourer's rights, 118; the unearned increment, 119; studies Locke, 124; *Labour Defended*, 125–6; *Rights of Property*, 125–6.
Hogarth, William, *obiter dictum*, 83.
Holland, Lord, 66, 67.
Holstein, Duke of, stays with Owen, 147.
Holyoake, George Jacob, *History of Co-operation*, 128.
Homer, 313, 378.
Hook, Walter Farquhar, 276; favours No. 90, 274.

Hooke, Nathaniel, 378.
Hooker, Richard, 181; Church and State, 182; Keble's edition, 256; *Ecclesiastical Polity*, 256.
Hope, David, his Calvinism, 300.
Horace, 378.
Horsa, 350.
Hort, Fenton John Anthony, aloofness, 444.
Howard, John, 58, 337; love of humanity, 71.
Howley, William, 266.
Hugo, Victor Marie, Vicomte, 222–3; social injustice, 226; *Les Misérables*, 225; *L'Homme qui rît*, 306; *Légende des Siècles*, 409.
Humanitarianism, its growth, 83–6, 89, 99, 165, 208, 226–7, 252.
Humboldt, Friedrich Heinrich Alexander von, meets Owen, 149–50; test of greatness, 410; *Personal Narrative*, 5.
Hume, David, 250, 378, 428; Malthus reads him, 3, 11; a backward boy, 38; Utilitarianism, 40–2; knows Paris, 52; impresses Mill, 105; Coleridge's attitude, 173; influence, 279; Carlyle's attitude, 310–1, 324; estimates Cromwell, 340; Positivism, 388; *Essays*, 40; *On Morals*, 41.
Hume, Joseph, the relentless reformer, 66; school-fellow of Mill, 97, 98; befriends Mill, 102; repeal of Combination Laws, 124; Corn Laws, 359.
Hunt, Henry, blusterer, 82; opposes Owen, 148.
Hus, Johann, 269.
Hutcheson, Francis, the greatest happiness, 41, 63; moral sense, 55–6.
Hutton, Richard Holt, altered views, 421.
Huxley, Thomas Henry, the moral law independent, 36; materialism, 211; his friends, 367; consternation, 420.

Imperialism, attitude of Disraeli, 231–3; of Pitt, 312; of Carlyle, 312, 347–51, 394; of Cromwell, 340; of Mill, 394.
Industrial Revolution, 128, 138, 177; its progress, 15, 117, 131–3; attitude of Hall, 122–3; of Gray, 124; of Owen, 131; the masters victims, 131; shiftings of folk, 178; *Coningsby*, 224–5; the north, 358–9.
Inequality, attitude of Godwin, 7–8.
Inquisition, the, its effects, 36.
Irving, Edward, seriousness, 251–2; meets Carlyle, 302–3, 314; Carlyle's German furore, 306; penetrates into Carlyle's heart, 315–16.
Isocrates, 377.

INDEX

Ivernois, Sir Francis, his uncanny prescience, 22.

JACKSON, John, 181.
James I, Melville's attitude, 279; *obiter dictum*, 299.
James, Lord, Free Church appeal, 288.
Jeffrey, Francis, Lord, edits the *Edinburgh Review*, 103, 301; meets Carlyle, 315; praises him, 328.
Jeffreys, George, Lord, 74.
Jenner, Edward, 313.
Jerome, St., 385.
Jewel, John, 273.
Joan of Arc, love of country, 71.
John, Prince, visits Owen, 147.
John of Paris, 269.
Johnson, Samuel, 435; Bentham's book, 47; Bentham's verdict, 67; his poetry, 72; a forerunner, 82; disparages Garrick, 106; no Romantic, 245; metaphysical poets, 258; Boswell's attachment, 308-9; Carlyle's appreciation, 313; Carlyle's style, 322.
Joseph II, benevolent despot, 111, 415.
Joseph of Portugal, 111.
Joule, James Prescott, 391.
Joyce, Jeremiah, *Scientific Dialogues*, 378.
Julian, his apostasy, 265.
Julius Caesar, 337, 388-9.
Just, Baron, presents medal, 147.

KANT, Immanuel, influences Coleridge, 179-80, 185; a systematic speculator, 191; *Critique of Pure Reason*, 105.
Keats, John, 249, 392; a weakly child, 38; nature, 166; pure poetry, 169; the art of poetry, 192, 194; Carlyle's judgment, 311; quoted, 399.
Keble, John, 276; Romanticism, 195-6; prays for Scott, 246; Assize sermon, 253; his reputation, 255; his conviction, 255-6; his ideas, 256-7; his indifference, 257; his outlook, 258-60; Froude's infection, 261; the Church, 268-9; No. 90, 274; Carlyle's view, 312; *The Christian Year*, 256-9.
Keble, Thomas, 269, 276.
Kelvin, Lord, 390.
Kent, Duke of, supports Owen, 147; introduces Owen, 149; examines Owen's scheme, 150.
Kepler, Johann, 178-9.
Kettler, Baron von, a social reformer, 215.
Kingsley, Charles, 392; appreciates Carlyle, 328; Chap. 11 *passim*; *Alton Locke*, 225, 404, 447, 449; *Hypatia*, 225; *Yeast*, 225, 447-9; *Politics for the People*, 446; *Cheap Clothes and Nasty*, 450.

Kinnoull, Earl of, his presentation, 281.
Kneller, Sir Godfrey, 432.
Knox, John, 278, 285, 336, 378, 410.
Kosciusko, Tadeusz Andrzej Bonaventura, champion of freedom, 167.
Koser, Reinhold, 342.

LA BARRE, Chevalier de, his execution, 91.
Le Notre, André, 432.
Labour Theory of Value, of Ricardo, 117, 119, 121-2, 124, 126, 128, 148, 440; of A. Smith, 119, 440; of Thompson, 120-2; of Gray, 124; of Hodgskin, 125-6; of Bray, 126-7; its long pedigree, 440.
Lafayette, Gilbert Mottier, Marquis, friend of Bentham, 78.
Lagrange, Joseph Louis, 391.
Laissez-faire, the attitude of Malthus, 15, 33; of Bentham, 82; of Coleridge, 176, 178; of Carlyle, 338; of Cobden, 358; of Mill, 394, 405-8; its accomplishments, 404; attitude of Cairnes, 406; of Kingsley, 449-51, 454.
Lally-Tollendal, Trophime Gerard, Marquis, 92.
Lamartine, Alphonse Marie Louis de Prat de, the French Revolution, 325.
Lamb, Charles, Coleridge's friend, 161; his weakness, 162; verdict on Coleridge, 171, 192; Carlyle's attitude, 312.
Lamennais, Hugues Felicité Robert de, his steps, 251; parallel with Kingsley, 453-4.
Lancaster, Joseph, reforms schools, 15, 143, 145.
Landor, Walter Savage, his republicanism, 164; verdict on Coleridge, 193.
Langhorne, John, *Plutarch*, 378.
Lansdowne, Lord. See the Earl of Shelburne.
Laplace, Pierre Simon, Marquis, 391, 427; meets Owen, 149-50.
Larévellière-Lépeaux, Louis Marie de, his question, 115.
Larmor, Sir Joseph, 391.
Lassalle, Ferdinand, iron law of wages, 122, 125.
Laud, William, Coleridge's disapproval, 185-6.
Lauderdale, Earl of, 176.
Lawrence, Sir Thomas, 54.
League of Nations, 417-8.
Lecky, William Edward Hartpole, humanitarianism, 84; attacks Carlyle, 339.
Lee, George Augustus, 134.
Lee, Robert, 285.
Leighton, Robert, his commentary, 181.
Leipzig University, 3.
Lely, Sir Peter, 432.

INDEX

Lenin, Nicholas (U. L. Ulianov), 410.
Leopardi, Giacomo, Comte, *Dialogue between Nature and a Soul*, 399.
Leslie, Sir John, teaches Carlyle, 300.
Leslie, Thomas Edward Cliffe, influences Mill, 393.
Lessing, Gotthold Ephraim, 188; restless search, 163.
Lewis, Sir George Cornewall, Little Englander, 351; *Government of Dependencies*, 351.
Lewis, Matthew, Gregory, 305.
Liberty, the conception of Bentham, 62-3, 79; of Coleridge, 169; of Wordsworth, 248; of Milton, 248; of Mill, 385, 389, 397, 407-9, 410-3.
Liebknecht, Wilhelm, the Church, 437-8.
Lightfoot, Joseph Barber, aloofness, 444.
Lincoln, Abraham, 319, 390, 392, 412.
Lindley, Lord, Free Church appeal, 288, 290, 291.
Lippmann, Walter, public opinion, 414.
List, Friedrich, national protection, 222.
Liverpool, Countess of, Owen's pamphlets, 146-7.
Liverpool, Earl of, interviews Owen, 146-7.
Livy, 378.
Locke, John, 178-9, 300, 428, 440; pain v. pleasure, 12; impresses Mill, 105; the child mind, 149; Coleridge's attitude, 173; view of poetry, 191-2.
Lockhart, John Gibson, edits the *Quarterly*, 103-4; comforts Carlyle, 316-7.
Londonderry, Marchioness of, 239.
Loreburn, Lord, Free Church appeal, 288, 292.
Louis IX, 341.
Louis XI, 246, 345.
Louis XIV, 357, 432; immersed in home affairs, 23; his grasping policy, 24; *obiter dictum*, 29, 131-2; ruins France, 344, 345.
Louis XV, 345; his death, 327.
Louis XVI, his pathetic petition, 8; his death, 326.
Louis Philippe, adds Algiers, 24; interviews Owen, 149.
Lovell, Robert, marries, 163.
Lovett, William, Owen's failure, 154; a Chartist, 156.
Low, Lord, Free Church Appeal, 288-90.
Lowe, Robert, Viscount Sherbrooke, Cave of Adullam, 220.
Lowell, Abbott Lawrence, public opinion, 414.
Lowell, James Russell, verdict on Carlyle, 324, 346.
Loyola, Ignatius de (Inigo Lopez de Recalde), sincerity, 336.

Lucian, 377.
Ludendorff, Erich Friedrich Wilhelm, von, 410.
Ludlow, Edmund, 340; estimates Cromwell, 339.
Ludlow, John Malcolm, political creed, 445; influences Kingsley, 447; co-operation, 451-3.
Luther, Martin, 255, 336, 388-9, 410, 432; not Bentham's ideal, 42; Coleridge's praise 181; hymns, 258; his attitude, 298.
Lycurgus, 388-9.
Lyell, Sir Charles, 313; denies originality of Darwin, 7; catastrophic change, 20; *Principles of Geology*, 5, 20.
Lyndhurst, Lord, Disraeli's *Vindication of the English Constitution*, 214.
Lysias, 378.
Lytton, Lord, novel of purpose, 225.

McCulloch, John Ramsay, Carlyle's attitude, 349-50; influences Mill, 393; the stationary State, 397.
MacCleod, Norman, 285.
Mably, Gabriel Bonnot, Abbé de, 8.
Macaulay, Thomas Babington, Lord, 57, 206-7; attacks Sadler, 35; the literature of France, 52; attacks Mill, 107, 110-3; his sister's love, 206; his lines, 238; his question, 271; the 1712 Act, 280; depreciates Boswell, 307-8; accuracy, 327; appreciates Cromwell, 340; aloofness, 444; *History of England*, 312.
Macaulay, Zachary, knows Owen, 147; a humanitarian, 252.
Maccabaeus, Judas, 211; his death, 69.
Macdonald, Alexander, verdict on Disraeli, 237.
Machiavelli, Nicholas, 390; influences Cromwell, 337; *Il Principe*, 63.
Mackintosh, Sir James, 106-7; reads Malthus, 4; values him, 5; the philosophical historian, 66; knows Owen, 147.
Maclaurin, Colin, 2.
Maclure, William, breaks with Owen, 152.
Macnaghten, Lord, Free Church appeal, 288, 290-3.
Madison, James, 77.
Maine, Sir Henry Sumner, *obiter dictum*, 61; Bentham's influence, 63-4; Coleridge's influence, 196; accuses Bentham, 413; *Ancient Law*, 196.
Maitland, Frederick William, 250; Coleridge's power, 196; groups of men, 443.
Mallet, David, his compassion, 165.
Malthus, Daniel, believes in perfectibility, 1; his son's expenses, 2.

INDEX

Malthus, Thomas Robert, 137, 147, 162, 337, 392; Chap. 1 *passim*; confutes Godwin, 82; standard of comfort, 85; principle of population, 96; doubts perfectibility, 98; influences Ricardo, 116; influences Hall, 123; Coleridge's view, 176–7; influences Mill, 394; equality, 419; *The Crisis*, 3; *Essay on Population*, 4, 5–6, 7, 13, 18, 36; *High Price of Provisions*, 4.

Manchester School, the, 208–9, 221–2, 234, 235, 236, Chap. 9 *passim*, 396, 401–4, 406, 447, 450–1.

Manners, Lord John, his couplet, 223, 229, 364.

Manning, Henry Edward, 233.

Mansfield, Earl of, case-law, 45; Bentham's book, 47, 54.

Manu, 78.

Marcus Aurelius Antoninus, 341; lonely heart, 399.

Margaret of Anjou, 246.

Maria Theresa, 343.

Marlowe, Christopher, 386.

Marriot, Charles, 276.

Marshall, Alfred, 426–7; accords a high place to Malthus, 12; *Principles of Economics*, 69; *Economics of Industry*, 379; *Industry and Trade*, 451–2.

Marshall, James Garth, in the House, 102.

Marsiglio of Padua, 270.

Martineau, Harriet, hostile to Factory Acts, 236; breach with Mill, 384.

Martineau, James, altered views, 421.

Martineau, John, 447–8.

Marx, Karl, 448; the labourer's hopeless position, 35–6; anticipated, 120, 124–6; reviver of a cause, 434; two men, 435; air of profundity, 436; a religion, 437; bourgeois, 438; scientific, 439; class struggle, 440; ready-made formula, 441; a landmark, 442; ignores views, 454; *Das Kapital*, 122, 436.

Maurice, Frederick Denison, Coleridge's influence, 195; No. 90, 274; Ward's case, 275; his heresies, 285; a pioneer, 420–1; aloofness, 444; influences Kingsley, 444–8, 450; co-operation, 451–3; *Kingdom of God*, 445.

Mavrocordato, Alessandro, 76.

Maximilian Joseph, 111.

Maximilian, Prince, visits Owen, 147.

Mazarin, Jules (Giulio Mazzarino), alters French character, 24.

Mazzini, Guiseppe, 410; *obiter dictum*, 70; frets Carlyle, 312; criticises him, 327–8; a prophet, 445.

Melanchthon, Philip, Coleridge's approval, 181.

Melbourne, Lord, questions Disraeli, 212.

Melville, Andrew, the Church, 279, 284, 293.

Mendelssohn-Bartholdy, Jakob Ludwig Felix, his sister's love, 206.

Mercantile Theory, the, French attitude, 28–9.

Meredith, George, 392; the lesson of the flesh, 15; *Ordeal of Richard Feverel*, 409.

Michelet, Jules, 327, 385; *obiter dictum*, 131–2; the French Revolution, 325; parallel with Carlyle, 351–3.

Middleton, Thomas Fanshaw, protects Coleridge, 161.

Mignet, François Auguste Alexis, the French Revolution, 325.

Mill, James, 137, 204, 217, 392; a colleague of Malthus, 5; a convert of Malthus, 34; friend of Bentham, 66, 116; Chap. 3 *passim*; Ricardian doctrine, 128; education, 144; knows Owen, 147; Coleridge's view, 176; property, 184–5; the middle class, 209; his objects, 254; son of Bentham, 377; educates his son, 377–83, 386; race, 417; attitude to religion, 420; fame, 429; *Introductory View*, 74; *History of India*, 98, 101–2, 108, 378, 379; *Analysis of the Phenomena of the Human Mind*, 105; *Elements of Political Economy*, 116, 117.

Mill, John Stuart, 326; law of diminishing returns, 17; the stationary state, 20; range of reading, 42–3; the similarity of mankind, 60; defends Bentham, 67; edits the *Rationale of Evidence*, 74; his father's disciple, 96; his father's principles, 97; describes his father, 100–1; *Westminster Review*, 105; his father's article, 107; attitude to women, 108; Macaulay's influence, 110; the 18th century, 188; appreciates Coleridge, 194, 197; startles Morley, 197; the finishing governess, 239; his father's objects, 254; hails Puseyism, 275; admires Carlyle, 328; Chap. 10 *passim*; education of women, 446; *Principles of Political Economy*, 17, 20, 197, 384, 385, 393, 401, 405, 406, 408, 409, 417, 428, 449; *Autobiography*, 43, 100–1, 376–8, 381, 385–6, 396–7, 406, 416; *Letters*, 376, 396, 416; *Logic*, 384, 387, 406, 413, 428; *On Liberty*, 385, 389, 397, 407–9, 421, 428; *Unsettled Questions*, 393; *Laws of Interchange*, 393; *Profits and Interest*, 393; *Dissertations*, 394; *Representative Government*, 395, 413–5, 417, 429; *Subjection of Women*, 407–8, 422–6; *Utilitarianism*, 418–21; *Three Essays on Religion*, 420.

Millar, John, 378.

468 INDEX

Milman, Henry Hart, liberality, 252; accuracy, 327.
Milton, John, 193, 247, 300, 380, 390; passion for liberty, 248; *obiter dictum*, 279; lion at creation, 383; condition of genius, 400.
Mirabeau, Honoré Gabriel Riquetti, Vicomte, our procedure, 59; the hero, 326.
Miranda, Francesco, admires Bentham, 77; emancipates Venezuela, 99.
Mirandola, Giovanni Francesco Pico, Sig. della, paragon of precocity, 378.
Moberley, George, 276.
Mohammed, 78, 336, 338, 388, 390, 399.
Molesworth, Sir William, Imperialism, 347-8; Corn Laws, 359.
Moltke, Helmuth Carl Bernard von, Graf, 412.
Mommsen, Theodore, brazen image, 337, 340.
Montaigne, Michel de, a humanitarian, 85.
Montcalm, Gozon de St. Véran, Louis Joseph, Marquis, fights Wolfe, 24.
Montesquieu, Charles Louis de Secondat, Baron, 75, 413; the topic of population, 11; mixed government, 47; adaptation of law, 60; retaliation, 65; Bentham's verdict, 67; title-deeds of humanity, 89; abuse of power, 108.
Montrose, Marquis of, his proud verses, 8; on the battlefield, 335-6.
Monypenny, William Flavelle, party affiliations, 213.
Moody, Dwight Lyman, 286.
More, Henry, 181.
More, Sir Thomas, denounces severity, 85.
Morley, Lord, startled by Mill, 197; consternation, 420.
Morris, William, 249; kin with Chaucer, 250.
Morrison, James, Owen's quarrel, 155.
Moseley, Henry, 391.
Mosheim, Johann Lorenzo, 378.
Mozley, James Bowling, 276; estimates Cromwell, 341-2.
Murray, John, owns the *Quarterly*, 103; meets Disraeli, 207.

Napoleon, 178, 189, 336, 338, 345-6, 352, 357, 390, 433; a despot, 34; place of religion, 99; ideals, 144; Owen's pamphlet, 147; Wordsworth's view, 168, 247-8; Coleridge's view, 174; French admiration, 213; his sayings, 234; benefits landlords, 361-2.
Napoleon III, 240; personal impulse, 411.
Napier, Sir Charles, handles Chartism, 156-7.
Napier, John, his father, 37.

Napier, Macvey, 106-7; edits the *Encyclopædia Britannica*, 107.
Nature, the Natural Law, the attitude of Bentham, 68, 79-80.
Natural Rights, the attitude of Blackstone, 43-4; of Bentham, 43-4, 62, 78-9.
Nature, the attitude of Pope, 165; of Wordsworth, 166, 261; of Coleridge, 166; of Keats, 166; of Keble, 256-7, 258; of Newman, 256-7, 261; various attitudes, 432-3.
Nelson, Lord, last signal, 334-5.
Newman, John Henry, 250; the worth of dogma, 42; Mill's Church, 113-4; his Romanticism, 195-6; Coleridge's influence, 196; *obiter dictum*, 213; against Liberalism, 223, 253, 276; theory of evolution, 228; prays for Scott, 246; verdict on Scott, 252; verdict on Froude, 253; Ward's Pope, 254; Ward's influence, 255; Keble's influence, 256; votes against Keble, 259; no ritualist, 260; his success, 261; the *Tracts*, 262; dualism, 263; a born leader, 264-5, 269; disintegrating influence, 270; Gladstone's letter, 272; the Thirty-nine Articles, 273-4; the Prussian blow, 274-5; secession, 276; his tragedy, 276-7; parallel with Chalmers, 277-8; the Church, 279; Carlyle's attitude, 312; verdict on Carlyle, 328; agitation, 365-6, 368-9; private affairs, 367; anticipates Darwin, 387; altered views, 421; *Callista*, 225; *Loss and Gain*, 225; *Apologia*, 253, 276, 376.
Newton, Sir Isaac, 2, 42, 66, 178-9, 390, 427, 428; a weakly child, 38; philosophy, 388; problem, 389, 390; supreme triumph, 391.
Nicholas I, visits Owen, 147.
Nietzsche, Friedrich Wilhelm, parallel with Carlyle, 337-8.
Northcliffe, Lord, lowered Parliament, 368-9.
Novalis, or Friedrich von Hardenberg, Carlyle's insight, 313.
Novel of Purpose, 225-6, 404.

Oastler, Richard, a Tory, 226-7.
Oberlin, Jean Frederic, 150.
O'Brien, Bronterre, a revolutionist, 156.
O'Connell, Daniel, 216; the prince of agitators, 66; the people, 215; hostile to Factory Acts, 235; agitation, 365-6, 368-9; private affairs, 367.
O'Connor, Feargus, his dream, 157.
Odin, 336.
Oscar II, his *obiter dictum*, 433.
Otter, William, a friend of Malthus, 4.

Index

Owen, Robert, 161, 396; impresses Thompson, 120–1; influences Gray, 124; Chap. 4 *passim*; environment, 164; Industrial Revolution, 177; disdains parliamentary reform, 178; influences Mill, 385; parallel with Marx, 435; *A New View of Society*, 135, 137, 141, 144, 145, 150; *Observations on the Effect of the Manufacturing System*, 135; *Address delivered to the Inhabitants of New Lanark*, 135; *Peace on Earth*, 135; *Statement concerning the New Lanark Establishment*, 141; *Address delivered to the Inhabitants of New Lanark*, 141–2; *Address to the Superintendents of Manufacturers*, 146; *Report to the Committee*, 147; *New Existence*, 147; *Report to the County*, 148; *Villages of Co-operation*, 149, 150; *Discourses on a New System of Society*, 150.

Owen, Robert (son), his screaming, 142–3.

Oxford Movement, the, 173, 182, 186, 195, 213, 223–4; Chap. 7 *passim*, 365, 444.

Oxford University, 43, 64, 237, Chap. 7 *passim*, 301.

PALEY, William, a convert of Malthus, 34; a forerunner, 82; theological ideals, 173, 195; *Principles of Moral and Political Philosophy*, 82.

Palm, Johann Philip, victim of Napoleon, 174.

Palmer, William, 269, 276; his views, 268; favours No. 90, 274.

Palmerston, Lord, 213; his policy, 218–9.

Panmure, Lord, supports Chalmers, 282; his motion, 282–3.

Parr, Samuel, reads Malthus, 4; geometrical ratios, 18; appreciates Bentham, 66.

Pascal, Blaise, 38; *obiter dictum*, 11; quoted, 257.

Pattison, Mark, his verdict, 262.

Pearson, Charles Henry, *National Life and Character*, 391.

Peel, Sir Robert (the first), the factory children, 132–3.

Peel, Sir Robert, 213, 338; no original contribution, 11; Factory Act, 176, 235; insular, 208; his policy, 218–20, 222; the middle class, 223; hostile to Shaftesbury, 235; double first, 255; Austinianism, 282–3; Corn Laws, 362–3, 369–70; the manufacturer, 364; attacks Cobden, 365; Cobden's argument, 366–7; his comment, 368; belief, 371; commercial policy, 402.

Pentland, Lord, his election, 241.

Perceval, Arthur Philip, 269.

Perceval, Spencer, 239.

Percival, Thomas, a noble doctor, 132.

Percy, Thomas, 245.

Pestalozzi, John Henry, 145, 150, 432.

Petrarch, Francesco, 390; loneliness, 400.

Petty, Sir William, 440.

Phaedrus, 358.

Philip II, 357.

Philippe Egalité (Duke of Orleans), his vote, 327.

Pictet, Marc Auguste, travels with Owen, 149.

Pitt, William, 18, 97, 206–7, 213, 226; Malthus attacks him, 3; no original contribution, 11; a convert of Malthus, 34; meets Bentham, 51; the Panopticon, 58; Owen's letter, 30; Michelet's view, 132; Wordsworth's view, 167; Coleridge's view, 174; his policy, 217; reciprocity, 222; Imperialism, 312.

Place, Francis, 157; the agitator, 98–9, 125; influence on Mill, 105; letter from Mill, 118; dissuades Hodgskin, 124; knows Owen, 147; welcomes Lovett, 156.

Plato, 76, 97, 137, 263, 377, 379; the topic of population, 11; verdict of Bentham, 67; the deepest matter, 201.

Plotinus, 161; his retirement, 164.

Poincaré, Henri, laws of science, 389–90.

Pombal, Sebastian Joseph de Carvalho e Mello, 111.

Pompey, 340.

Pope, Alexander, 245; attitude to Nature, 165; studies men, 166; literary ideals, 173, 191.

Population, the principle and problem of, Chap. 1 *passim*, 40, 96.

Poor Law, the Elizabethan Poor Law, 32; Gilbert's Act, 117; Poor Law of 1834, 33, 117, 221; the attitude of Malthus, 31–3; of Bentham, 87; of Disraeli, 221.

Prescott, William Hickling, criticises Carlyle, 328.

Preuss, Otto Franz Bernard, 342.

Price, Richard, used by Malthus, 11; the understanding, 55–6.

Priestley, Joseph, his influence, 35; the greatest happiness, 44, 63; influences Wordsworth, 167.

Progress, attitude of Mill, 387, 388, 419.

Property, the conception of Bentham, 70–1, 78–80; of Proudhon, 71; of Godwin, 120, 122; of Hodgskin, 125–6; of Bray, 126–7; of Coleridge, 162, 184, 186–7, 203; of J. Mill, 184–5; of Drummond, 202.

Proudhon, Pierre Joseph, *obiter dictum*, 71; moulds Rodbertus, 120; a national bank, 153.

Pugin, Augustus Charles, a Romantic, 249–50.
Puritanism of Bentham, 42–3; of Mill, 101, 115, 381, 383; of Owen, 129; of Carlyle, 299–300, 302, 317–8, 328.
Puritans, the, 15.
Pusey, Edward Bouverie, 255, 273, 276; his Romanticism, 195–6; a triumvir, 253; a theologian, 259; German thought, 259–60; a Liberal, 261; favours No. 90, 274; sermon condemned, 275; parallel with Chalmers, 282; Maurice's heresies, 285; at Eichhorn's feet, 305.
Pym, John, 337.

QUARTERLY REVIEW, 392; supports Malthus, 35; its growth, 102–5; poetical criticism, 192.
Quesnay, François, power, 393–4.
Quinet, Edgar, Michelet's friend, 352.
Quintilian, 379.

RACE, attitude of Mill, 60, 417; of Disraeli, 211, 227, 229–30; of Gobineau, 230; of Chamberlain, 230–1.
Radcliffe, Ann, 245; her fustian, 305.
Radicalism of Bentham, 61, 86–7, 106.
Rainy, Robert, ecclesiastical statesman, 286.
Raleigh, Sir Walter, *History of the World*, 8; his toil, 97, 232.
Ranke, Leopold von, accuracy, 327, 342
Raphael de Rhegio (Raffaelino), his *Transfiguration*, 92.
Rapin, Paul de, Sieur de Thoyras, *History of England*, 43.
Rapp, George, his community, 150.
Reade, Charles, 283, 392; *It is Never too Late to Mend*, 225; *Hard Cash*, 225; *Put Yourself in his Place*, 225.
Renan, Joseph Ernest, Hibbert lecture, 54; parallel with Newman, 276; rationality, 417.
René of Provence, 246.
Rent, the theory of, 5; Malthus's analysis, 28.
Reuchlin (Capnio), Johann, his remark, 385.
Rhodes, Cecil John, 206–7.
Ricardo, David, 185, 396, 426–7, 440; the theory of rent, 5; favours invention, 15; a convert of Malthus, 34; his influence, 35; J. Mill's disciple, 66, 96, 98, 116; befriends Mill, 102; economic teaching, 116–9, 121–2; labour theory of value, 117, 119, 121–2, 124, 126, 128, 148; impresses Thompson, 120; knows Owen, 147; Coleridge's view, 176; *obiter dictum*, 178; influences J. S. Mill, 385, 392; laboured abstractions, 449.

Richard I, 246.
Richardson, Samuel, 129; novel of purpose, 225.
Richelieu, Armand Jean Duplessis, alters French character, 24.
Richter, Jean Paul Friedrich, Carlyle's insight, 312; language, 329.
Robertson, Frederick William, Coleridge's influence, 195; aloofness, 444.
Robertson, James, power, 279, 285.
Robertson, William, 250, 378; his attraction, 279, 285; *Charles V*, 301.
Robertson, Lord, Free Church appeal, 288, 292.
Robespierre, Maximilien François Marie Isidore de, 353; the Reign of Terror, 8; equality, 78; his Jacobinism, 156.
Robinson, Henry Crabb, Coleridge's letter, 176.
Rodbertus, Carl Johann, 120.
Roebuck, John, method of smelting, 118.
Roebuck, John Arthur, in the House, 102; Corn Laws, 359.
Rogers, Samuel, meets Disraeli, 207; Byron's appreciation, 313.
Roland, Marie Jean Philipon, her ejaculation, 277.
Romanticism, 244–51; the conception of Coleridge, 195–6; of Disraeli, 222–3; of Rousseau, 245, 246–7; of Scott, 245–7; of Newman, 246, 297; of Keble, 246; of Chalmers, 277; of Carlyle, 296, 306, 311, 356.
Romilly, Sir Samuel, Bentham's chief expounder, 51, 64, 65; our procedure, 59; friend of Bentham, 66; denounces Eldon, 74–5; approval of Pannomion, 77; a humanitarian, 83; supplanted, 96; Mill's circle, 98.
Rose, George, the *Quarterly*, 103.
Rose, Hugh James, 269; attacks German theology, 260.
Rossetti, Dante Gabriel, 249; lecturer, 452.
Rousseau, Jean Jacques, 8, 312, 336, 432; visits England, 54; the general will, 203; parent of Romanticism, 245, 246–7; his passion, 385; the despotic State, 428; *Emile*, 1; *Les Confessions*, 376; *Contrat Social*, 428.
Rufus, William, consultation, 334.
Ruskin, John, 249; the Romantics, 250; Scott's sorrow, 312; appreciates Carlyle, 346; calico millennium, 373; artist's position, 398; belittles Maurice, 445; lecturer, 452; *Unto this Last*, 404.
Russell, Lord John, 338; an opportunist, 218; Reform Bill, 220; the State, 269–70, 283, 392.
Rutherford, Sir Ernest, 211, **391**.

INDEX

St. Davids, Lord, his election, 241.
St. Just, Antoine Louis Léon de Richebourg de, equality, 78.
Sainte-Beuve, Charles Auguste, mind oxidised, 454.
Saint Simon, Claude Henri de Rouvroy, Comte de, 128–9, 383, 396.
Sadler, Michael Thomas, attacks Malthus, 35; a Tory, 227.
Saladin or Salah-eddyn, Malek Nasser Youssouf, 246.
Sallust, 378.
Sand, Georges (Armandine Lucile Aurore Dudevant), 54, 22–3, 312.
Sankey, Ira David, 286.
Santander, Francisco de Paula, admires Bentham, 77.
Savigny, Friedrich Carl von, law and national life, 75–6; his warning, 78; *On the Mission of our Time*, 75.
Say, Jean Baptiste Léon, favours invention, 15; power, 393–4.
Schelling, Friedrich Wilhelm Joseph von, spiritual perception, 195.
Schiller, Johann Christoph Friedrich von, 306; Carlyle's life, 305, 315; *obiter dictum*, 326.
Schleiermacher, Friedrich Daniel Ernst, 251.
Schopenhauer, Arthur, describes a genius, 398.
Scott, Thomas, Newman's verdict, 252.
Scott, Sir Walter, 161, 225, 249; satirises the Covenanters, 15; a backward boy, 38; the attraction of affairs, 64; his early love, 97; starts the *Quarterly*, 103–4; *obiter dictum*, 162; the past, 188; the art of poetry, 191–2; verdict on Coleridge, 192–3; Landor's verdict, 193; a great Romantic, 245–7, 250; seriousness, 251–2; father of the Oxford Movement, 252–3; a favourite with Newman, 261; a forerunner, 305; Carlyle's judgment, 311–2; *Redgauntlet*, 44; *Götz von Berlichingen*, 305.
Secret Societies, 233.
Sedgwick, Adam, 384.
Seeley, Sir John Robert, poor health, 38.
Senior, Nassau William, a convert of Malthus, 34; influences Mill, 393.
Shaftesbury, Earl of, social reformer, 215, 226; Melbourne's verdict, 227; Disraeli's support, 234–5, 236.
Shairp, John Campbell, verdict on Newman, 264.
Shakespeare, William, 80, 193, 245, 249, 380, 390; Mill's verdict, 106; Coleridge's interpretation, 190–1; Carlyle's appreciation, 313; an interpreter, 322, 328.
Shand, Lord, 288.
Sharpe, Granville, a humanitarian, 252.

Shaw, William, 450–1.
Shelburne, Earl of, befriends Bentham, 50; Bentham's request, 64; appreciates the *Traités*, 66; and Macaulay's articles, 110; struggles with the Whigs, 226.
Shelley, Percy Bysshe, 384, 392, 400; his powers, 169; enormous hopes, 172; the art of poetry, 192.
Shenstone, William, the negro, 165.
Sidgwick, Henry, Mill's powers, 396–7; estimates Mill, 427–8.
Sidmouth, Lord, Owen's pamphlets, 147.
Sidney, Algernon, 240.
Sidney, Sir Philip, at Zutphen, 335–6.
Sièyes, Emmanuel Joseph, Comte, 174.
Simon Stylites, St., a pillar saint, 15.
Simpson, Patrick Carnegie, 286.
Sismondi, Charles Simonde de, meets Owen, 150.
Smiles, Samuel, *Self Help*, 34, 356.
Smith, Adam, 66, 300, 337, 379, 393, 396, 440; Malthus reads him, 3; Mackintosh values him, 5; his inquiry into wealth, 7; his originality, 11; recommends schools, 15; import of food, 28; his influence, 35; low opinion of academic education, 43; doctrine of sympathy, 55–6; usury laws 57; labour theory of value, 119, 122, 124; inspires Hodgskin, 125–6; stationary state, 397; *The Wealth of Nations*, 46, 126.
Smith, Goldwin, 233.
Smith, John, 181.
Smith, William Robertson, his trial, 286.
Smith, Sydney, favours Malthus, 35.
Smyth, Ethel, *Impressions that Remained*, 376.
Smythe, George, *Historic Fancies*, 223.
Social Contract, the attitude of Blackstone, 47, 55; of Bentham, 47.
Socialism, 128; and inequality, 7–8; the attitude of Thompson, 120–2; of Hall, 123–4; of Gray, 123–4; of Hodgskin, 124–6; of Bray, 126–7; of Godwin, 120; of Owen, 136–7; of Kingsley, 225; of Mill, 385, 394, 396–7; its double basis, 433–4; Christian Socialism, Chap. 11 *passim.*
Socrates, 80; Bentham's verdict, 67.
Solitariness of genius, 398–401, 445.
Solon, 76.
Sophocles, 321.
Sorel, Albert, the French Revolution, 325.
Southey, Robert, attacks Malthus, 35; the *Quarterly*, 103; a Pantisocracy, 150; meets Coleridge, 163; Coleridge's lectures, 164; ardour of youth, 171; verdict of Coleridge, 192; a Tory, 226–7; transforms poetry, 247; praises Carlyle, 328; Toryism, 416.

Sovereignty, the conception of Bentham, 47–8, 266; of Hobbes, 48; of Austin, 48, 266–8.

Spencer, Herbert, intellectual development, 35; rising standard, 85; consternation, 420; estimates Mill, 427–8.

Spinoza, Benedict de (Baruch), the issue of right, 40; a systematic speculator, 191; *obiter dictum*, 432–3.

Standard of living, Malthus's attitude, 25, 85.

Stanley, Arthur Penrhyn, Disraeli's reminder, 224; *obiter dictum*, 259, 274; befriends Ward, 275.

Stephen, Sir James Fitzjames, appreciates Carlyle, 329–30; expression, 409; attacks Mill, 411–3; *Liberty, Equality, Fraternity*, 411–2.

Stephen, Sir Leslie, his view, 338–9; Mill's influence, 387; consternation, 420.

Sterling, John, Coleridge's influence, 195; Carlyle's German furore, 306; his art furore, 313; praises Carlyle, 328; Carlyle's biography, 342; altered views, 420; Mill's letter, 421–2.

Sterne, Laurence, knows Paris, 52.

Stewart, Dugald, his lectures, 97, 105.

Stewart, Sir James, the topic of population, 11.

Story, Robert, 285.

Strafford, Thomas Wentworth, Earl of, 345.

Strike, the General, 155.

Strutt, Edward, Baron Belper, in the House, 102.

Stuart, Daniel, Coleridge's letter, 186.

Stuart, Sir John, 97; his kindness, 105.

Stuart, Wilhelmina, Scott's early love, 97.

Stubbs, William, appreciates Carlyle, 346–7.

Sue, Eugène, social injustice, 225.

Süssmilch, Johann Peter, anticipates Malthus, 11; *Divine Plan*, 12.

Sutton, Charles Manners, reads Owen, 147.

Swedenborg, Emmanuel, *obiter dictum*, 305.

Swift, Jonathan, his satire, 208; wit, 316, 329; *Battle of the Books*, 21; *Tale of a Tub*, 329.

Swinburne, Algernon Charles, 249; wrongheadedness, 306.

Sybel, Heinrich von, the French Revolution, 325.

Synesius of Cyrene, 161.

TACITUS, Caius Cornelius, 379; *Life of Agricola*, 2.

Taine, Hippolyte Adolphe, visits us, 54; the French Revolution, 325; criticises Carlyle, 328; estimates Mill, 427–9.

Tait, Archibald Campbell, appreciates Disraeli, 237; opposes No. 90, 274, 275.

Talleyrand-Perigord, Charles Maurice, compliments Bentham, 78; his retort, 115.

Tanucci, Bernard, Marquis, 111.

Taylor, Harriet, Mill's friend, 326; his wife, 384; her influence, 385, 386, 406–7.

Taylor, Sir Henry, describes Carlyle, 317, 339; *Autobiography*, 339.

Taylor, Jeremy, 181.

Taylor, William, *Historic Survey of German Poetry*, 305.

Temple, Sir William, his *Essay*, 21.

Tennyson, Lord, 390, 392; aloofness, 444; appraises Maurice, 445.

Terence, 378.

Tertullian, Quintus Septimius Florens, *obiter dictum*, 69.

Thackeray, William Makepeace, 392; knows Paris, 54; quoted, 259; appreciates Carlyle, 328; Barry Lyndon, 424.

Themistocles, 388–9.

Theocritus, 378.

Thierry, Amédée Simon Dominic, 250.

Thiers, Louis Adolphe, the French Revolution, 325.

Thirlwall, Connop, accuracy, 327.

Thompson, William, 128, 434, 440; unearned increment, 119; moulds Marx, 120; a communist, 121; a Socialist, 135, 136; *Inquiry into the Distribution of Wealth*, 121–2.

Thompson, William Hepworth, his *obiter dictum*, 138.

Thomson, James, 392; his compassion, 165.

Thomson, Sir Joseph John, 211, 391.

Thornton, Henry, influences Mill, 393; Wages-fund, 394.

Thucydides, 378.

Toleration, the attitude of Bentham, 93; of Voltaire, 93; of J. Mill, 113; of Coleridge, 202–3; of Burke, 202–3; of the pre-Raphaelites, 249.

Tooke, Thomas, a colleague of Malthus, 5.

Torrens, Robert, Mill's attack, 393.

Toryism, its genius, 214, 223, 242–3.

Townshend, Joseph, the topic of population, 11; *Dissertation on the Poor Laws*, 11.

Trade Union, Combination Laws (1824), 124–5, 128; Chartism, 156; the 1875 Act, 236; attitude of Cobden, 403.

Trajan, 248.

Trayner, Lord, Free Church appeal, 288–90.

Treitschke, Heinrich Gotthard von, *obiter dictum*, 42; ideals, 144; lectures, 210–1.

Trevelyan, Sir George Otto, 241.

Trollope, Anthony, 392.

INDEX

Tulloch, John, 285.
Turgenieff, Ivan Sergievich, the clash of the generations, 42.
Turner, Joseph Mallard William, insight, 400.
Tyndall, John, materialism, 211; lecturers, 314.

UNAMUNO, Miguel de, parallel with Kingsley, 444.
Utilitarianism, 35; the conception of Bentham, 40, 44–5, 54–5, 56–7, 59–60, 68–9, 70–1, 82–3, 221–2; of Spinoza, 40; of Hume, 40–2; of Hutcheson, 41; of Croce, 69; of Maine, 72; of Green, 72–3; of J. Mill, 96, 98, 101, 105–6; of Paley, 179; of Disraeli, 208–9, 214–5; of Austin, 266–8; of Stephen, 411–2; of J. S. Mill, 418, 21.
Utilitarians, the, attitude to the law of diminishing returns, 17; banned history, 200; the Colonies, 347.
Uzzah, 265.

VANDYKE, Sir Anthony, 401.
Vane, Sir Henry, 340.
Vauvenargues, Luke de Clapiers, Marquis, *obiter dictum*, 104–5, 353.
Vedel-Petersen, K. O., *Losses of Life*, 22.
Victor Emmanuel, 410.
Victoria, Queen, 147, 227; Coleridge's prophecy, 187–8; Disraeli's realisation, 210, 232; Empress of India, 231; the "Great White Mother," 232–3; gracious to Disraeli, 239.
Villeneuve-Bargemont, Vicomte, a social reformer, 215.
Villiers, Charles Pelham, in the House, 102; Corn Laws, 358.
Villiers, Hyde, in the House, 102.
Virgil, 313, 378.
Völkerwanderung, the, 20.
Voltaire, François Marie Arouet de, 161, 245, 250, 343; visits England, 54; attitude to history, 60; public service, 69; parallel with Bentham, 86–94; the past, 246; Carlyle's attitude, 310–1, 313, 328; *Essai sur les Moeurs*, 98.
Vortigern, 245.

WAGES, the conception of Malthus, 31–3; of J. Mill, 116–7; of Lassale, 122; of Thompson, 120–2.
Wages Fund, the attitude of Malthus, 30.
Wakefield, Gilbert, teaches Malthus, 1; Imperialism, 347–8.
Wallace, Alfred Russel, reads Malthus, 5–6; evolution theory, 7; *My Life*, 5–6.
Wallace, Robert, used by Malthus, 11; anticipates him, 11–2; *Various Prospects of Mankind*, 12.

Wallace, Robert, 285.
Walpole, Horace, Earl of Orford, 25, 245; Macaulay's essay, 72.
Walpole, Sir Robert, policy, 216–7.
Warburton, William, Church and State, 182.
Ward, Wilfrid George, 249–50, 253, 261; a Utilitarian, 254; influences Newman, 255; letter to Pusey, 273; condemnation, 275–6; *Ideal of a Christian Church*, 275.
Warton, Thomas, 245.
Washington, George, Citizen of France, 60, 64.
Watson, Robert, 378.
Watt, James, 58; his steam engine, 117, 131, 433.
Webb, Beatrice, collapse of capitalism, 440; successful democracy, 442–3.
Webb, Sidney, Lord Passfield, collapse of capitalism, 440; decentralisation, 442–3.
Weber, Carl Maria Friedrich Ernst von, his despair, 400.
Webster, Alexander, 279.
Wedderburn, Alexander, Baron Loughborough, attacks Bentham, 54.
Wellington, Duke of, verdict on Peel, 222, 367; Corn Laws, 362; Toryism, 401–2.
Welsh, David, his document, 283–4.
Welsh, Jane, meets Carlyle, 315; his devotion, 316.
Wesley, John, encourages Wilberforce, 82–3; a humanitarian, 93; the French Revolution, 131.
Westcott, Brooke Foss, aloofness, 444.
Westminster Review, 104–5; J. Mill's article, 113; attacks Disraeli, 209; Sterling's article, 328.
Whately, Richard, acute, 252; influences Newman, 261.
Whewell, William, 384.
Whichcote, Benjamin, *obiter dictum*, 113.
Wilberforce, Samuel, 206–7, 233.
Wilberforce, William, 337; the Panopticon, 58; Citizen of France, 60; Wesley's encouragement, 82–3; a humanitarian, 93, 252; the Factory Act, 133; knows Owen, 147; slavery, 178; *Practical Christianity*, 251.
Wilhelmina, Margravine of Bayreuth, 343.
Wilkie, Sir David, 54.
William I, 410.
William II, 347.
William III, 226, 342.
William IV, 210, 410; unattractive character, 232; his death, 233.
William the Silent, 342.
Williams, Isaac, 269, 276; on reserve, 256.
Wilmington, Lord, 239.

Wilson, George, Corn Laws, 359.
Wilson, Sir Henry, 410.
Wilson, Thomas, Keble's edition of his *Maxims*, 256.
Wilson, Woodrow, self-determination, 417.
Wolfe, James, fights Montcalm, 24, 335.
Wollstonecraft, Mary, position of women, 424; *Vindication of the Rights of Women*, 422.
Women, the attitude of Condorcet, 8–9; of Bentham, 80, 86, 108; of J. Mill, 108; of J. S. Mill, 108, 239, 407–8, 422–6; of Thompson, 121; of Disraeli, 239–40; of Stephen, 413; of Rousseau, 422; of Wollstonecraft, 422, 424; of Kingsley, 446.
Wordsworth, Dorothy, 247.
Wordsworth, William, 161, 390, 392; a Pantisocracy, 150; Nature, 166; the French Revolution, 166–8, 171–2; kind of stupidity, 169; philosophy, 170; ardour of youth, 171; Coleridge's reference, 188; new attitude to poetry, 171–2; verdict on Coleridge, 192; Landor's verdict, 193; transforms poetry 247; patriotism, 248–9; teaches Keble, 258; Platonism, 264; criticises Carlyle, 328; phrase, 378; quoted, 398; Toryism, 416; *Peter Bell*, 165; *Religious Musings*, 167; *France*, 167; *Lyrical Ballads*, 168.
Wotton, William, *Reflections*, 21.
Wyclif, John, 269.

YOUNG, Arthur, the topic of population, 11; *Scarcity and its Remedies*, 26.
Young, Edward, *Night Thoughts*, 129.
Young, Thomas, 391.
Young, Lord, Free Church appeal, 288–90.
Young England Movement, 223–5, 229, 235–6, 247, 364.

ZOLA, Emile Edouard Charles Antoine, the novel of purpose, 226.

Printed by
W. Heffer & Sons Ltd.
Cambridge.